The Political Thought of American Statesmen

The Political Thought of American Statesmen

SELECTED WRITINGS and SPEECHES

Edited by

Morton J. Frisch

Northern Illinois University

and

Richard G. Stevens

Rockford College

F. E. PEACOCK PUBLISHERS, INC. • ITASCA, ILLINOIS 60143

ACKNOWLEDGMENTS

WE THANK PROFESSORS HARVEY C. MANSFIELD, JR. of Harvard University, Martin Diamond of Northern Illinois University, Robert K. Faulkner of Boston College, Ralph Lerner of the University of Chicago, Harry V. Jaffa of Claremont Men's College, Herbert J. Storing of the University of Chicago, Walter Berns of the University of Toronto, and Harry Clor of Kenyon College for their assistance in bringing together this compilation, and Robert Evans of Northern Illinois University for his editorial assistance.

CONTENTS

The House Divided

The Test of Liberal Democracy

INTRODUCTION

THIS COMPILATION OF SELECTED WRITINGS and speeches of American statesmen is intended to introduce the literature of American political thought. These sources reflect the penetrating and intensive thought that leading American statesmen have given to the serious problems they have faced.

The aim has generally been to include complete writings and speeches, although this necessarily involves some repetition. We do not think that this is undesirable, for it is useful to see the continuing themes and the reaffirmation of certain principles over an extended period of time. Of course, the complete speeches include some discussion of particular problems and situations that may seem dated. It would be difficult to edit out all such material, however, and we have endeavored to select writings and speeches that contain a minimum of passing problems and a maximum of lasting principles, doctrines, and purposes.

The task of studying American political thought is very different from studying political philosophy. American political thought, insofar as it is peculiarly American, does not rise to the rank of disinterested philosophic inquiry as does the thought of, say, Aristotle. It does not even match the philosophic rank of Locke. In fact, there is an unphilosophic alloy to *all* political philosophy. Thus, even in the case of Aristotle, the apparently disinterested discussion of tyranny in Book V of the *Politics* cannot help but have implicit in it an effort to ameliorate tyranny. Contrary to what some men now say, the very impetus to study politics precludes neutrality as between better and worse. Those who say the contrary and who profess simply to "play with the data" are politically irrelevant triflers. What distinguishes American political thought from the more truly philosophic thought of Aristotle is that the highest and best thought about politics in America has been the product of America's *statesmen*. Therefore it presents itself always imbedded in the context of an active contest between contrary political claims raised within the particular confines of the here and now.

To understand American political thought and its approximation to political philosophy in the highest and fullest sense, it is necessary to put observations on the relationship between political philosophy and statesmanship together with the facts about statesmanship as it has been practiced in America. In order to do so, we must identify the great political crises in American history and the statesmen who predominated in them, and subject the political thought of these statesmen to careful inquiry. The first was the crisis of the nation's founding. The Constitutional Convention was the critical moment in American history. It was the end of the Articles of Confederation, the threshold of the new Constitution, and the moment of actualization for the principles asserted in the Declaration of Independence. *The Federalist Papers*, rightly considered the most authoritative commentary on the Constitution, represented the first appearance of political philosophy on the American scene. To appreciate the alternatives one would have to examine the political thought of Thomas Jefferson and the anti-Federalists, and for the completion of the founding one must turn to the views of John Marshall.

The second crisis was that of the house divided, which resulted from the nation's being tempted to repudiate its ancient faith, its fundamental beliefs, and the principles of political freedom contained in the Declaration of Independence. Lincoln saw that a house divided could not stand, that a nation half free and half slave would willy-nilly become all one or all the other, and, lest it become all slave, he set himself to putting it back on the footing on which it had first stood—that of a free nation. He contributed mightily to that transformation of public opinion in America which made possible the awareness that no man can rightfully retain his freedom if he would deny that right to any other man. Lincoln understood, moreover, the tensions inherent in a free society between its substantive and procedural principles (that is, between freedom and equality on the one hand and consent on the other) and sought the highest degree of freedom and equality for which general consent could be obtained. In so doing, he was attacked both by the abolitionists and by those who held that slavery was a positive good. But while Lincoln's statesmanship surely dominated the period, the arguments of John C. Calhoun and Frederick Douglass (as well as Henry Clay, Daniel Webster, Stephen A. Douglas and others) must be taken into account.

The third crisis was the crisis of the confrontation of liberal democracy with the extremist ideologies of the left and right, which showed itself dramatically in the Great Depression. The towering figure in this struggle was Franklin D. Roosevelt, who effected a fundamental change in the orientation of government in its relation to economic life. He convincingly demonstrated that laws could be passed limiting the accumulation of property, rules could be established for the use of property, and rigorous governmental action could be taken to redistribute property or to benefit the propertyless, and we could still have a free society. The third crisis continues to show itself in the struggles the country has experienced in attempts to formulate and reconcile internal and external policy. Though first starkly presented in the form of the Great Depression, the slogans of "Making the world safe for democracy" and "Clear and present dangers of evils Congress has a right to prevent" which preceded the Depression and of "Black Power" which followed it by a quarter of a century are all a part of this crisis. Therefore the thought of such men as Oliver Wendell Holmes, Jr., Felix Frankfurter, and Woodrow Wilson (and others) is relevant. When viewed from the perspective of the great crises in American history, the American experiment in self-government was faced in the 1930s with what was perhaps its greatest test. While in the crises of the 18th and 19th centuries America was to be regarded as a test case for liberal democracy, in the 20th century it has become not the mere example but the very citadel of that concept.

We have, of course, not included writings and speeches of all the more notable figures in American political thought. Within the limits of a sensibly sized book, and true to our intention to include as nearly as possible only *complete* things so that we do not introduce sweeping and facile misconceptions, we have compiled selections here only from Jefferson, the *Federalist,* Marshall, Calhoun, Lincoln, Frederick Douglass, Holmes, Wilson, Franklin D. Roosevelt, and Frankfurter. These are the statesmen whose thought is analyzed in commentaries in our earlier book, *American Political Thought: The Philosophic Dimension of American Statesmanship* (New York: Charles Scribner's Sons, 1971). We believe that we have been able to retain a sweep which is broad enough to encompass the major questions, yet selective enough to avoid shallowness.

THE FOUNDING

It has been frequently remarked that it seems to have been reserved to the people of this country, by their conduct and example, to decide the important question, whether societies of men are really capable or not of establishing good government from reflection and choice, or whether they are forever destined to depend for their political constitutions on accident and force. If there be any truth in the remark, the crisis at which we are arrived may with propriety be regarded as the era in which that decision is to be made; and a wrong election of the part we shall act may, in this view, deserve to be considered as the general misfortune of mankind.

Federalist number 1

I

THOMAS JEFFERSON
(1743–1826)

THOMAS JEFFERSON is not the only spring of American political thought, but he is the primary one. All the principles of American political life, and all the tensions among those principles, show themselves in his works and words. He served in the Virginia House of Burgesses and House of Delegates and as governor of Virginia and was a delegate to the Continental Congress from 1775 to 1776 and again from 1783 to 1785. Appointed a member of a committee to which Congress assigned the task of drafting a statement declaring and justifying the separation of the American colonies from England, he was deferred to by his fellow committee members and thus emerged as the principal author of the Declaration of Independence. That Declaration, appealing before the opinions and judgment of all of mankind to principles of right embodied in nature, manifested the fundamentals upon which the United States rests and to which all modern liberal democracies look.

As Washington's Secretary of State from 1790 to 1793, Jefferson engaged in a great struggle with Secretary of the Treasury Alexander Hamilton over the future course of the country. Under the electoral system established in the original Constitution (which had to be corrected by the Twelfth Amendment), Jefferson was elected Vice-President when John Adams was elected President in 1797, and in 1801 he was tied for first place with Aaron Burr, each receiving 73 electoral votes. The election therefore went to the House of Representatives, which elected Jefferson President on the 36th ballot, partly as a result of Alexander Hamilton's influence on some of the Federalist members of the House. Hamilton disagreed with Jefferson, but he mistrusted Burr. (Hamilton used his influence again, by the way, to secure Burr's defeat in the New York gubernatorial election in 1804, and Burr subsequently killed him in a duel.)

Jefferson served two terms as President. One of the most notable acts of his Presidency was the purchase of the Louisiana Territory from Napoleon in 1803, which nearly doubled the size of the United States. After his Presidency, he influenced national politics through James Madison and James Monroe. Back in Virginia, he established the University of Virginia; as a man of enormous accomplishments, his interests ranged from the Greek and Latin classics to the latest developments in science and technology. He died at Monticello on the 50th anniversary of the Declaration of Independence, July 4, 1826.

The Declaration of Independence, as well as letters from Jefferson to Henry Lee in 1825 and Roger C. Weightman in 1826, show some of Jefferson's views as to the character and place of the Declaration. Also given here are Jefferson's resolutions, adopted with some modification in 1798 by the Kentucky legislature, in opposition to the Alien and Sedition Laws.

Relations between the United States and France were greatly strained in the last few years of the 18th century, and it looked to many as though war would result. In 1798 Congress passed, and President Adams signed, laws relating to naturalization, the treatment of aliens, and the punishment of sedition. These Alien and Sedition Laws became a rallying point for the partisans of the Federalists, who had passed them, and the Republicans, who had opposed them. They also were the occasion for the pronouncement of doctrines interpreting the Constitution. Jefferson's resolutions opposing the Alien and Sedition Laws declared that it was beyond the Constitutional power of Congress to have enacted them and asserted that the states were free to nullify such unconstitutional enactments. This power to nullify was based on the argument that the Constitution was a "compact" among the states *as states* and, that "as in all other cases of compact among powers having no common judge, each party has an equal right to judge for itself, as well of infractions as of the mode and measure of redress."

In reading these resolutions, it must not be forgotten that the language used is the language of John Locke's second *Treatise of Govern-*

ment and that to have "no common judge" meant to be "in a state of nature" *vis-à-vis* one another. Although Locke pokerfacedly denied that "a state of nature" and "a state of war" were the same, he showed by the character of his argument that he believed otherwise. It is, of course, precisely to guard against such a state of dormant warfare that *The Federalist Papers* claim the Constitution is established and the central government is endowed with energy. The Civil War had to be fought to give the Constitution an interpretation which seemed to settle the question raised by the doctrine of nullification.

Letters to James Madison in January 1787, December 1787, and March 1789 show Jefferson's willingness to tolerate a certain amount of disorder to keep governments fresh, his approval of and reservations regarding the proposed Constitution, and his views on the necessity of a bill of rights. Letters to John Adams in 1813 and to Pierre Samuel Dupont de Nemours, John Taylor, and Isaac Tiffany in 1816 give further indications of Jefferson's view of the true character of republican government. A letter to Samuel Kercheval in 1816, returning to the matter of governmental viability, gives Jefferson's view of the need for regular revision of the frame of government.

1
THE DECLARATION OF INDEPENDENCE
July 4, 1776

W HEN IN THE COURSE OF HUMAN EVENTS it becomes necessary for one people to dissolve the political bands which have connected them with another, and to assume among the powers of the earth, the separate and equal station to which the Laws of Nature and of Nature's God entitle them, a decent respect to the opinions of mankind requires that they should declare the causes which impel them to the separation.

We hold these truths to be self-evident, that all men are created equal, that they are endowed by their Creator with certain unalienable Rights, that among these are Life, Liberty and the pursuit of Happiness.—That to secure these rights, Governments are instituted among Men, deriving their just powers from the consent of the governed.—That whenever any Form of Government becomes destructive of these ends, it is the Right of the People to alter or to abolish it, and to institute new Government, laying its foundation on such principles, and organizing its powers in such form, as to them shall seem most likely to effect their Safety and Happiness. Prudence, indeed, will dictate that Governments long established should not be changed for light and transient causes; and accordingly all experience hath shewn, that mankind are more disposed to suffer, while evils are sufferable, than to right themselves by abolishing the forms to which they are accustomed. But when a long train of abuses and usurpations, pursuing invariably the same Object, evinces a design to reduce them under absolute Despotism, it is their right, it is their duty, to throw off such Government, and to provide new Guards for their future security.—Such has been the patient sufferance of these Colonies; and such is now the necessity which constrains them to alter their former Systems of Government. The history of the present King of Great Britain is a history of repeated injuries and usurpations, all having in direct object the establishment of an absolute Tyranny over these States. To prove this, let Facts be submitted to a candid world.

He has refused his Assent to Laws, the most wholesome and necessary for the public good.

He has forbidden his Governors to pass Laws of immediate and pressing importance, unless suspended in their operation till his Assent should be obtained; and when so suspended, he has utterly neglected to attend to them.

He has refused to pass other Laws for the accommodation of large districts of people, unless those people would relinquish the right of Representation in the Legislature, a right inestimable to them and formidable to tyrants only.

He has called together legislative bodies at places unusual, uncomfortable, and distant from the depository of their public Records, for the sole purpose of fatiguing them into compliance with his measures.

He has dissolved Representative Houses repeatedly, for opposing with manly firmness his invasions on the rights of the people.

He has refused for a long time, after such dissolutions, to cause others to be elected; whereby the Legislative powers, incapable of Annihilation, have returned to the People at large for their exercise; the State remaining in the mean time exposed to all the dangers of invasion from without, and convulsions within.

He has endeavoured to prevent the population of these States; for that purpose obstructing the Laws for Naturalization of Foreigners; refusing to pass others to encourage their migrations hither, and raising the conditions of new Appropriations of Lands.

He has obstructed the Administration of Justice, by refusing his Assent to Laws for establishing Judiciary powers.

He has made Judges dependent on his Will alone, for the tenure of their offices, and the amount and payment of their salaries.

He has erected a multitude of New Offices, and sent hither swarms of Officers to harrass our people, and eat out their substance.

He has kept among us, in times of peace, Standing Armies without the Consent of our legislatures.

He has affected to render the Military independent of and superior to the Civil power.

He has combined with others to subject us to a jurisdiction foreign to our constitution, and unacknowledged by our laws; giving his Assent to their Acts of pretended Legislation:

For quartering large bodies of armed troops among us:

For protecting them, by a mock Trial, from punishment for any Murders which they should commit on the Inhabitants of these States:

For cutting off our Trade with all parts of the world:

For imposing Taxes on us without our Consent:

For depriving us in many cases, of the benefits of Trial by Jury:

For transporting us beyond Seas to be tried for pretended offences:

For abolishing the free System of English Laws in a neighbouring Province, establishing therein an Arbitrary government, and enlarging its Boundaries so as to render it at once an example and fit instrument for introducing the same absolute rule into these Colonies:

For taking away our Charters, abolishing our most valuable Laws, and altering fundamentally the Forms of our Governments:

For suspending our own Legislatures, and declaring themselves invested with power to legislate for us in all cases whatsoever.

He has abdicated Government here, by declaring us out of his Protection and waging War against us.

He has plundered our seas, ravaged our Coasts, burnt our towns, and destroyed the lives of our people.

He is at this time transporting large Armies of foreign Mercenaries to compleat the works of death, desolation and tyranny, already begun with circumstances of Cruelty & perfidy scarcely paralleled in the most barbarous ages, and totally unworthy the Head of a civilized nation.

He has constrained our fellow Citizens taken Captive on the high Seas to bear Arms against their Country, to become the executioners of their friends and Brethren, or to fall themselves by their Hands.

He has excited domestic insurrections amongst us, and has endeavoured to bring on the inhabitants of our frontiers; the merciless Indian Savages, whose known rule of warfare, is an undistinguished destruction of all ages, sexes and conditions.

In every stage of these Oppressions We have Petitioned for Redress in the most humble terms: Our repeated Petitions have been answered only by repeated injury. A Prince, whose character is thus marked by every act which may define a Tyrant, is unfit to be the ruler of a free people.

Nor have We been wanting in attentions to our British brethren. We have warned them from time to time of attempts by their legislature to extend an unwarrantable jurisdiction over us. We have reminded them of the circumstances of our emigration and settlement here. We have appealed to their native justice and magnanimity, and we have conjured them by the ties of our common kindred to disavow these usurpations, which would inevitably interrupt our connections and correspondence. They too have been deaf to the voice of justice and of consanguinity. We must, therefore, acquiesce in the necessity, which denounces our Separation, and hold them, as we hold the rest of mankind, Enemies in War, in Peace Friends.

We, therefore, the Representatives of the united States of America, in General Congress, Assembled, appealing to the Supreme Judge of the world for the rectitude of our intentions, do, in the Name, and by Authority of the good People of these Colonies solemnly publish and declare, That these United Colonies are, and of Right ought to be Free and Independent States; that they are Absolved from all Allegiance to the British Crown, and that all political connection between them and the State of Great Britain, is and ought to be totally dissolved; and that as Free and Independent States, they have full Power to levy War, conclude Peace, contract Alliances, establish Commerce, and to do all other Acts and Things which Independent States may of right do.

And for the support of this Declaration, with a firm reliance on the protection of divine Providence, we mutually pledge to each other our Lives, our Fortunes and our sacred Honor.

Bᴜᴛ ᴡɪᴛʜ ʀᴇsᴘᴇᴄᴛ ᴛᴏ ᴏᴜʀ ʀɪɢʜᴛs, and the acts of the British government contravening those rights, there was but one opinion on this side of the water. All American Whigs thought alike on these subjects. When forced, therefore, to resort to arms for redress, an appeal to the tribunal of the world was deemed proper for our justification. This was the object of the Declaration of Independence. Not to find out new principles, or new arguments, never before thought of, not merely to say things which had never been said before; but to place before mankind the common sense of the subject, in terms so plain and firm as to command their assent, and to justify ourselves in the independent stand we are compelled to take. Neither aiming at originality of principle or sentiment, nor yet copied from any particular and previous writing, it was intended to be an expression of the American mind, and to give to that expression the proper tone and spirit called for by the occasion. All its authority rests then on the harmonizing sentiments of the day, whether expressed in conversation, in letters, printed essays, or in the elementary books of public right, as Aristotle, Cicero, Locke, Sidney, etc. The historical documents which you mention as in your possession, ought all to be found, and I am persuaded you will find, to be corroborative of the facts and principles advanced in that Declaration. . . .

3
JEFFERSON TO
ROGER C. WEIGHTMAN
June 24, 1826

THE KIND INVITATION I RECEIVE from you, on the part of the citizens of the city of Washington, to be present with them at their celebration on the fiftieth anniversary of American Independence, as one of the surviving signers of an instrument pregnant with our own, and the fate of the world, is most flattering to myself, and heightened by the honorable accompaniment proposed for the comfort of such a journey. It adds sensibly to the sufferings of sickness, to be deprived by it of a personal participation in the rejoicings of that day. But acquiescence is a duty, under circumstances not placed among those we are permitted to control. I should, indeed, with peculiar delight, have met and exchanged there congratulations personally with the small band, the remnant of that host of worthies, who joined with us on that day, in the bold and doubtful election we were to make for our country, between submission or the sword; and to have enjoyed with them the consolatory fact, that our fellow citizens, after half a century of experience and prosperity, continue to approve the choice we made. May it be to the world, what I believe it will be (to some parts sooner, to others later, but finally to all), the signal of arousing men to burst the chains under which monkish ignorance and superstition had persuaded them to bind themselves, and to assume the blessings and security of self-government. That form which we have substituted, restores the free right to the unbounded exercise of reason and freedom of opinion. All eyes are opened, or opening, to the rights of man. The general spread of the light of science has already laid open to every view the palpable truth, that the mass of mankind has not been born with saddles on their backs, nor a favored few booted and spurred, ready to ride them legitimately, by the grace of God. These are grounds of hope for others. For ourselves, let the annual return of this day forever refresh our recollections of these rights, and an undiminished devotion to them. . . .

JEFFERSON'S DRAFT OF
THE KENTUCKY RESOLUTIONS
November 1798

1. *Resolved,* That the several States composing the United States of America, are not united on the principle of unlimited submission to their general government; but that, by a compact under the style and title of a Constitution for the United States, and of amendments thereto, they constituted a general government for special purposes—delegated to that government certain definite powers, reserving, each State to itself, the residuary mass of right to their own self-government; and that whensoever the general government assumes undelegated powers, its acts are unauthoritative, void, and of no force: that to this compact each State acceded as a State, and is an integral party, its co-States forming, as to itself, the other party: that the government created by this compact was not made the exclusive or final judge of the extent of the powers delegated to itself; since that would have made its discretion, and not the Constitution, the measure of its powers; but that, as in all other cases of compact among powers having no common judge, each party has an equal right to judge for itself, as well of infractions as of the mode and measure of redress.

2. *Resolved,* That the Constitution of the United States, having delegated to Congress a power to punish treason, counterfeiting the securities and current coin of the United States, piracies, and felonies committed on the high seas, and offences against the law of nations, and no other crimes whatsoever; and it being true as a general principle, and one of the amendments to the Constitution having also declared, that "the powers not delegated to the United States by the Constitution, nor prohibited by it to the States, are reserved to the States respectively, or to the people," therefore the act of Congress, passed on the 14th day of July, 1798, and intituled "An Act in addition to the act intituled An Act for the punishment of certain crimes against the United States," as also the act passed by them on the ____ day of June, 1798, intituled "An Act to punish frauds committed on the bank of the United States," (and all their other acts which assume to create, define, or punish crimes, other than those so enumerated in the Constitution,) are

altogether void, and of no force; and that the power to create, define, and punish such other crimes is reserved, and, of right, appertains solely and exclusively to the respective States, each within its own territory.

3. *Resolved,* That it is true as a general principle, and is also expressly declared by one of the amendments to the Constitution, that "the powers not delegated to the United States by the Constitution, nor prohibited by it to the States, are reserved to the States respectively, or to the people"; and that no power over the freedom of religion, freedom of speech, or freedom of the press being delegated to the United States by the Constitution, nor prohibited by it to the States, all lawful powers respecting the same did of right remain, and were reserved to the States or the people: that thus was manifested their determination to retain to themselves the right of judging how far the licentiousness of speech and of the press may be abridged without lessening their useful freedom, and how far those abuses which cannot be separated from their use should be tolerated, rather than the use be destroyed. And thus also they guarded against all abridgment by the United States of the freedom of religious opinions and exercises, and retained to themselves the right of protecting the same, as this State, by a law passed on the general demand of its citizens, had already protected them from all human restraint or interference. And that in addition to this general principle and express declaration, another and more special provision has been made by one of the amendments to the Constitution, which expressly declares, that "Congress shall make no law respecting an establishment of religion, or prohibiting the free exercise thereof, or abridging the freedom of speech or of the press": thereby guarding in the same sentence, and under the same words, the freedom of religion, of speech, and of the press: insomuch, that whatever violated either, throws down the sanctuary which covers the others, and that libels, falsehood, and defamation, equally with heresy and false religion, are withheld from the cognizance of federal tribunals. That, therefore, the act of Congress of the United States, passed on the 14th day of July, 1798, intituled "An Act in addition to the act intituled An Act for the punishment of certain crimes against the United States," which does abridge the freedom of the press, is not law, but is altogether void, and of no force.

4. *Resolved,* That alien friends are under the jurisdiction and protection of the laws of the State wherein they are: that no power over them has been delegated to the United States, nor prohibited to the individual States, distinct from their power over citizens. And it being true as a general principle, and one of the amendments to the Constitution having also declared, that "the powers not delegated to the United States by the Constitution, nor prohibited by it to the States, are reserved to the States respectively, or to the people," the act of the Congress of the United States, passed on the ____ day of July, 1798, intituled "An Act concerning aliens," which assumes

power over alien friends, not delegated by the Constitution, is not law, but is altogether void, and of no force.

5. *Resolved,* That in addition to the general principle, as well as the express declaration, that powers not delegated are reserved, another and more special provision, inserted in the Constitution from abundant caution, has declared that "the migration or importation of such persons as any of the States now existing shall think proper to admit, shall not be prohibited by the Congress prior to the year 1808": that this commonwealth does admit the migration of alien friends, described as the subject of the said act concerning aliens: that a provision against prohibiting their migration, is a provision against all acts equivalent thereto, or it would be nugatory: that to remove them when migrated, is equivalent to a prohibition of their migration, and is, therefore, contrary to the said provision of the Constitution, and void.

6. *Resolved,* That the imprisonment of a person under the protection of the laws of this commonwealth, on his failure to obey the simple *order* of the President to depart out of the United States, as is undertaken by said act intituled "An Act concerning aliens," is contrary to the Constitution, one amendment to which has provided that "no person shall be deprived of liberty without due process of law"; and that another having provided that "in all criminal prosecutions the accused shall enjoy the right to public trial by an impartial jury, to be informed of the nature and cause of the accusation, to be confronted with the witnesses against him, to have compulsory process for obtaining witnesses in his favor, and to have the assistance of counsel for his defence," the same act, undertaking to authorize the President to remove a person out of the United States, who is under the protection of the law, on his own suspicion, without accusation, without jury, without public trial, without confrontation of the witnesses against him, without hearing witnesses in his favor, without defence, without counsel, is contrary to the provision also of the Constitution, is therefore not law, but utterly void, and of no force: that transferring the power of judging any person, who is under the protection of the laws, from the courts to the President of the United States, as is undertaken by the same act concerning aliens, is against the article of the Constitution which provides that "the judicial power of the United States shall be vested in courts, the judges of which shall hold their offices during good behavior"; and that the said act is void for that reason also. And it is further to be noted, that this transfer of judiciary power is to that magistrate of the general government who already possesses all the Executive, and a negative on all Legislative powers.

7. *Resolved,* That the construction applied by the General Government (as is evidenced by sundry of their proceedings) to those parts of the Constitution of the United States which delegate to Congress a power "to lay and collect taxes, duties, imports, and excises, to pay the debts, and provide

for the common defence and general welfare of the United States," and "to make all laws which shall be necessary and proper for carrying into execution the powers vested by the Constitution in the government of the United States, or in any department or officer thereof," goes to the destruction of all limits prescribed to their power by the Constitution: that words meant by the instrument to be subsidiary only to the execution of limited powers, ought not to be so construed as themselves to give unlimited powers, nor a part to be so taken as to destroy the whole residue of that instrument: that the proceedings of the General Government under color of these articles, will be a fit and necessary subject of revisal and correction, at a time of greater tranquillity, while those specified in the preceding resolutions call for immediate redress.

8th. *Resolved,* That a committee of conference and correspondence be appointed, who shall have in charge to communicate the preceding resolutions to the Legislatures of the several States; to assure them that this commonwealth continues in the same esteem of their friendship and union which it has manifested from that moment at which a common danger first suggested a common union: that it considers union, for specified national purposes, and particularly to those specified in their late federal compacts, to be friendly to the peace, happiness and prosperity of all the States: that faithful to that compact, according to the plain intent and meaning in which it was understood and acceded to by the several parties, it is sincerely anxious for its preservation: that it does also believe, that to take from the States all the powers of self-government and transfer them to a general and consolidated government, without regard to the special delegations and reservations solemnly agreed to in that compact, is not for the peace, happiness or prosperity of these States; and that therefore this commonwealth is determined, as it doubts not its co-States are, to submit to undelegated, and consequently unlimited powers in no man, or body of men on earth: that in cases of an abuse of the delegated powers, the members of the general government, being chosen by the people, a change by the people would be the constitutional remedy; but, where powers are assumed which have not been delegated, a nullification of the act is the rightful remedy: that every State has a natural right in cases not within the compact, (*casus non fœderis,*) to nullify of their own authority all assumptions of power by others within their limits: that without this right, they would be under the dominion, absolute and unlimited, of whosoever might exercise this right of judgment for them: that nevertheless, this commonwealth, from motives of regard and respect for its co-States, has wished to communicate with them on the subject: that with them alone it is proper to communicate, they alone being parties to the compact, and solely authorized to judge in the last resort of the powers exercised under it, Congress being not a party, but merely the creature of the compact, and subject as to its assumptions of power to the final judgment of those by whom, and for whose use itself and its powers were all created and modified: that if the acts before specified should stand, these conclusions would flow from them; that the general government may place any act they think proper on the list of crimes, and punish it themselves whether enumerated or not enumerated by the constitution as cognizable by them: that they may transfer its cognizance to the President, or any other person, who may himself be the accuser, counsel, judge and jury, whose *suspicions* may be the evidence, his *order* the sentence, his *officer* the executioner, and his breast the sole record of the transaction: that a very numerous and valuable description of the inhabitants of these States being, by this precedent, reduced, as outlaws, to the absolute dominion of one man, and the barrier of the Constitution thus swept away from us all, no rampart now remains against the passions and the powers of a majority in Congress to protect from a like exportation, or other more grievous punishment, the minority of the same body, the legislatures, judges, governors and counsellors of the States, nor their other peaceable inhabitants, who may venture to reclaim the constitutional rights and liberties of the States and people, or who for other causes, good or bad, may be obnoxious to the views, or marked by the suspicions of the President, or be thought dangerous to his or their election, or other interests, public or personal: that the friendless alien has indeed been selected as the safest subject of a first experiment; but the citizen will soon follow, or rather, has already followed, for already has a sedition act marked him as its prey: that these and successive acts of the same character, unless arrested at the threshold, necessarily drive these States into revolution and blood, and will furnish new calumnies against republican government, and new pretexts for those who wish it to be believed that man cannot be governed but by a rod of iron: that it would be a dangerous delusion were a confidence in the men of our choice to silence our fears for the safety of our rights: that confidence is everywhere the parent of despotism—free government is founded in jealousy, and not in confidence; it is jealousy and not confidence which prescribes limited constitutions, to bind down those whom we are obliged to trust with power: that our Constitution has accordingly fixed the limits to which, and no further, our confidence may go; and let the honest advocate of confidence read the Alien and Sedition acts, and say if the Constitution has not been wise in fixing limits to the government it created, and whether we should be wise in destroying those limits. Let him say what the government is, if it be not a tyranny, which the men of our choice have conferred on our President, and the President of our choice has assented to, and accepted over the friendly strangers to whom the mild spirit of our country and its laws have pledged hospitality and protection: that the men of our choice have more respected the bare *suspicions* of the President, than the solid right of innocence, the claims of justification, the sacred force of truth, and the forms and substance of law and justice. In questions of power, then, let no more be heard of confidence in man, but bind him down from mischief by the chains of the Constitution. That this commonwealth does therefore call on its co-States for an expression of their sentiments on the acts concerning aliens, and for the punishment of certain crimes herein before specified, plainly declaring whether these acts are or are not authorized by the federal compact, And it doubts not that their sense will be so announced as to prove their attachment unaltered to limited government, whether general or particular. And that the rights and liberties of their co-States will be exposed to no dangers by remaining embarked in a common bottom with their own. That they will concur with this commonwealth in considering the said acts as so palpably against the Constitution as to amount to an undisguised declaration that that compact is not meant to be the measure of the powers of the General Government, but that it will proceed in the exercise over these States, of all powers whatsoever: that they will view this as seizing the rights of the States, and consolidating them in the hands of the General Government, with a power assumed to bind the States (not merely as the cases made federal, *casus fœderis* but), in all cases whatsoever, by laws made, not with their consent, but by others against their consent: that this would be to surrender the form of government we have chosen, and live under one deriving its powers from its own will, and not from our authority; and that the co-States, recurring to their natural right in cases not made federal, will concur in declaring these acts void, and of no force, and will each take measures of its own for providing that neither these acts, nor any others of the General Government not plainly and intentionally authorized by the Constitution, shall be exercised within their respective territories.

9th. *Resolved,* That the said committee be authorized to communicate by writing or personal conferences, at any times or places whatever, with any person or persons who may be appointed by any one or more co-States to correspond or confer with them; and that they lay their proceedings before the next session of Assembly.

5
JEFFERSON TO
JAMES MADISON
January 30, 1787

I AM IMPATIENT TO LEARN your sentiments on the late troubles in the eastern States. So far as I have yet seen they do not appear to threaten serious consequences. Those States have suffered by the stoppage of the channels of their commerce, which have not yet found other issues. This must render money scarce and make the people uneasy. This uneasiness has produced acts absolutely unjustifiable, but I hope they will provoke no severities from their governments. A consciousness of those in power that their administration of the public affairs has been honest may, perhaps, produce too great a degree of indignation, and those characters wherein fear predominates over hope may apprehend too much from these instances of irregularity. They may conclude too hastily that nature has formed man insusceptible of any other government than that of force, a conclusion not founded in truth nor experience. Societies exist under three forms, sufficiently distinguishable: (1) without government, as among our Indians; (2) under governments wherein the will of everyone has a just influence, as is the case in England in a slight degree and in our States in a great one; (3) under governments of force, as is the case in all other monarchies and in most of the other republics. To have an idea of the curse of existence under these last, they must be seen. It is a government of wolves over sheep. It is a problem, not clear in my mind, that the first condition is not the best. But I believe it to be inconsistent with any great degree of population. The second state has a great deal of good in it. The mass of mankind under that enjoys a precious degree of liberty and happiness. It has its evils, too, the principal of which is the turbulence to which it is subject. But weigh this against the oppressions of monarchy and it becomes nothing. *Malo periculosam libertatem quam quietam servitutem.* Even this evil is productive of good. It prevents the degeneracy of government and nourishes a general attention to the public affairs. I hold it that a little rebellion now and then is a good thing, and as necessary in the political world as storms

20

in the physical. Unsuccessful rebellions, indeed, generally establish the encroachments on the rights of the people which have produced them. An observation of this truth should render honest republican governors so mild in their punishment of rebellions as not to discourage them too much. It is a medicine necessary for the sound health of government.

6
JEFFERSON TO
JAMES MADISON
December 20, 1787

I LIKE MUCH THE GENERAL IDEA of framing a government, which should go on of itself, peaceably, without needing continual recurrence to the State legislatures. I like the organization of the government into legislative, judiciary and executive. I like the power given the legislature to lexy taxes, and for that reason solely, I approve of the greater House being chosen by the people directly. For though I think a House so chosen, will be very far inferior to the present Congress, will be very illy qualified to legislate for the Union, for foreign nations, &c., yet this evil does not weigh against the good, of preserving inviolate the fundamental principle, that the people are not to be taxed but by representatives chosen immediately by themselves. I am captivated by the compromise of the opposite claims of the great and little States, of the latter to equal, and the former to proportional influence. I am much pleased too, with the substitution of the method of voting by person, instead of that of voting by States; and I like the negative given to the Executive, conjointly with a third of either House; though I should have liked it better, had the judiciary been associated for that purpose, or invested separately with a similar power. There are other good things of less moment. I will now tell you what I do not like. First, the omission of a bill of rights, providing clearly, and without the aid of sophism, for freedom of religion, freedom of the press, protection against standing armies, restriction of monopolies, the eternal and unremitting force of the habeas corpus laws, and trials by jury in all matters of fact triable by the laws of the land, and not by the laws of nations. To say, as Mr. Wilson does, that a bill of rights was not necessary, because all is reserved in the case of the general government which is not given, while in the particular ones, all is given which is not reserved, might do for the audience to which it was addressed; but it is surely a *gratis dictum,* the reverse of which might just as well be said; and it is opposed by strong inferences from the body of the instrument, as well as from the omission of the cause of our present Confederation, which had made the reservation in express terms. It was hard to conclude, because there has been a want of uniformity among the States as to the cases triable by jury, because some have been so incautious as to dispense with this mode of trial in certain cases, therefore, the more prudent States shall be reduced to the same level of calamity. It would have been much more just and wise to have concluded the other way, that as most of the States had preserved with jealousy this sacred palladium of liberty, those who had wandered, should be brought back to it; and to have established general right rather than general wrong. For I consider all the ill as established, which may be established. I have a right to nothing, which another has a right to take away; and Congress will have a right to take away trials by jury in all civil cases. Let me add, that a bill of rights is what the people are entitled to against every government on earth, general or particular; and what no just government should refuse, or rest on inference.

The second feature I dislike, and strongly dislike, is the abandonment, in every instance, of the principle of rotation in office, and most particularly in the case of the President. Reason and experience tell us, that the first magistrate will always be re-elected if he may be re-elected. He is then an officer for life. This once observed, it becomes of so much consequence to certain nations, to have a friend or a foe at the head of our affairs, that they will interfere with money and with arms. A Galloman, or an Anglo-man, will be supported by the nation he befriends. If once elected, and at a second or third election outvoted by one or two votes, he will pretend false votes, foul play, hold possession of the reigns of government, be supported by the States voting for him, especially if they be the central ones, lying in a compact body themselves, and separating their opponents; and they will be aided by one nation in Europe, while the majority are aided by another. The election of a President of America, some years hence, will be much more interesting to certain nations of Europe, than ever the election of a King of Poland was. Reflect on all the instances in history, ancient and modern, of elective monarchies, and say if they do not give foundation for my fears; the Roman Emperors, the Popes while they were of any importance, the German Emperors till they became hereditary in practice, the Kings of Poland, the Deys of the Ottoman dependencies. It may be said, that if elections are to be attended with these disorders, the less frequently they are repeated the better. But experience says, that to free them from disorder, they must be rendered less interesting by a necessity of change. No foreign power, nor domestic party, will waste their blood and money to elect a person, who must go out at the end of a short period. The power of removing every fourth year by the vote of the people, is a power which they will not exercise, and if they were disposed to exercise it, they would not be permitted. The King of Poland is removable every day by the diet. But they never remove him. Nor would Russia, the Emperor, &c., permit them to do it. Smaller objections are, the appeals on matters of fact as well as laws; and the binding all persons, legislative, executive and judiciary by oath, to maintain that constitution. I do not pretend to decide, what would be the best method of procuring the establishment of the manifold good things in this constitution, and of getting rid of the bad. Whether by adopting it, in hopes of future amendment; or after it shall have been duly weighed and canvassed by the people, after seeing the parts they generally dislike, and those they generally approve, to say to them, "We see now what you wish. You are willing to give to your federal government such and such powers; but you wish, at the same time, to have such and such fundamental rights secured to you, and certain sources of convulsion taken away. Be it so. Send together deputies again. Let them establish your fundamental rights by a sacrosanct declaration, and let them pass the parts of the constitution you have approved. These will give powers to your federal government sufficient for your happiness."

This is what might be said, and would probably produce a speedy, more perfect and more permanent form of government. At all events, I hope you will not be discouraged from making other trials, if the present one should fail. We are never permitted to despair of the commonwealth. I have thus told you freely what I like, and what I dislike, merely as a matter of curiosity; for I know it is not in my power to offer matter of information to your judgment, which has been formed after hearing and weighing everything which the wisdom of man could offer on these subjects. I own, I am not a friend to a very energetic government. It is always oppressive. It places the governors indeed more at their ease, at the expense of the people. The late rebellion in Massachusetts has given more alarm, than I think it should have done. Calculate that one rebellion in thirteen States in the course of eleven years, is but one for each State in a century and a half. No country should be so long without one. Nor will any degree of power in the hands of government, prevent insurrections. In England, where the hand of power is heavier than with us, there are seldom half a dozen years without an insurrection. In France, where it is still heavier, but less despotic, as Montesquieu supposes, than in some other countries, and where there are always two or three hundred thousand men ready to crush insurrections, there have been three in the course of the three years I have been here, in every one of which greater numbers were engaged than in Massachusetts, and a great deal more blood was spilt. In Turkey, where the sole nod of the despot is death, insurrections are the events of every day. Compare again the ferocious depredations of their insurgents, with the order, the moderation and the almost self-extinguishment of ours. And say, finally, whether peace is best preserved by giving energy to the government, or information to the people. This last is the most certain, and the most legitimate engine of government. Educate and inform the whole mass of the people. Enable them to see that it is their interest to preserve peace and order, and they will preserve them. And it requires no very high degree of education to convince them of this. They are the only sure reliance for the preservation of our liberty. After all, it is my principle that the will of the majority should prevail. If they approve the proposed constitution in all its parts, I shall concur in it cheerfully, in hopes they will amend it, whenever they shall find it works wrong. This reliance cannot deceive us, as long as we remain virtuous; and I think we shall be so, as long as agriculture is our principal object, which will be the case, while there remains vacant lands in any part of America. When we get piled upon one another in large cities, as in Europe, we shall become corrupt as in Europe, and go to eating one another as they do there. I have tired you by this time with disquisitions which you have already heard repeated by others, a thousand and a thousand times; and therefore, shall only add assurances of the esteem and attachment with which I have the honor to be, dear Sir, your affectionate friend and servant.

7
JEFFERSON TO
JAMES MADISON
March 15, 1789

IN THE ARGUMENTS in favor of a declaration of rights, you omit one which has great weight with me; the legal check which it puts into the hands of the judiciary. This is a body, which, if rendered independent and kept strictly to their own department, merits great confidence for their learning and integrity. In fact, what degree of confidence would be too much, for a body composed of such men as Wythe, Blair and Pendleton? On characters like these, the *"civium ardor prava jubentium"* would make no impression. I am happy to find that, on the whole, you are a friend to this amendment.

The declaration of rights is, like all other human blessings, alloyed with some inconveniences, and not accomplishing fully its object. But the good in this instance, vastly overweighs the evil. I cannot refrain from making short answers to the objections which your letter states to have been raised. 1. That the rights in question are reserved, by the manner in which the federal powers are granted. Answer. A constitutive act may, certainly, be so formed, as to need no declaration of rights. The act itself has the force of a declaration, as far as it goes; and if it goes to all material points, nothing more is wanting. In the draught of a constitution which I had once a thought of proposing in Virginia, and printed afterwards, I endeavored to reach all the great objects of public liberty, and did not mean to add a declaration of rights. Probably the object was imperfectly executed; but the deficiencies would have been supplied by others, in the course of discussion. But in a constitutive act which leaves some precious articles unnoticed, and raises implications against others, a declaration of rights becomes necessary, by way of supplement. This is the case of our new federal constitution. This instrument forms us into one State, as to certain objects, and gives us a legislative and executive body for these objects. It should, therefore, guard us against their abuses of power, within the field submitted to them. 2. A positive declaration of some essential rights could not be obtained in the requisite latitude. Answer. Half a loaf is better than no bread. If we cannot secure all our rights, let us secure what we can. 3. The limited powers of the federal government, and jealousy of the subordinate governments, afford a security which exists in no other instance. Answer. The first member of this seems resolvable into the first objection before stated. The jealousy of the subordinate governments is a precious reliance. But observe that those governments are only agents. They must have principles furnished them, whereon to found their opposition. The declaration of rights will be the text, whereby they will try all the acts of the federal government. In this view, it is necessary to the federal government also; as by the same text, they may try the opposition of the subordinate governments. 4. Experience proves the inefficacy of a bill of rights. True. But though it is not absolutely effica-cious under all circumstances, it is of great potency always, and rarely inefficacious. A brace the more will often keep up the building which would have fallen, with that brace the less. There is a remarkable difference between the characters of the inconveniences which attend a declaration of rights, and those which attend the want of it. The inconveniences of the declaration are, that it may cramp government in its useful exertions. But the evil of this is short-lived, moderate and reparable. The inconveniences of the want of a declaration are permanent, afflicting and irreparable. They

are in constant progression from bad to worse. The executive, in our governments, is not the sole, it is scarcely the principal object of my jealousy. The
tyranny of the legislatures is the most formidable dread at present, and will
be for many years. That of the executive will come in its turn; but it will
be at a remote period. I know there are some among us, who would now
establish a monarchy. But they are inconsiderable in number and weight
of character. The rising race are all republicans. We were educated in
royalism; no wonder, if some of us retain that idolatry still. Our young
people are educated in republicanism; an apostasy from that to royalism,
is unprecedented and impossible. I am much pleased with the prospect that
a declaration of rights will be added; and I hope it will be done in that way,
which will not endanger the whole frame of government, or any essential
part of it.

8
JEFFERSON TO
JOHN ADAMS
October 28, 1813

For I AGREE WITH YOU that there is a natural aristocracy among men.
The grounds of this are virtue and talents. Formerly bodily powers gave
place among the aristoi. But since the invention of gunpowder has armed
the weak as well as the strong with missile death, bodily strength, like
beauty, good humor, politeness and other accomplishments, has become
but an auxiliary ground of distinction. There is also an artificial aristocracy
founded on wealth and birth, without either virtue or talents; for with these
it would belong to the first class. The natural aristocracy I consider as the
most precious gift of nature for the instruction, the trusts, and government
of society. And indeed it would have been inconsistent in creation to have
formed man for the social state, and not to have provided virtue and wisdom
enough to manage the concerns of the society. May we not even say that
that form of government is the best which provides the most effectually for
a pure selection of these natural aristoi into the offices of government? The

artificial aristocracy is a mischievous ingredient in government, and provision should be made to prevent it's ascendancy. On the question, What is the best provision, you and I differ; but we differ as rational friends, using the free exercise of our own reason, and mutually indulging it's errors. *You* think it best to put the Pseudo-aristoi into a separate chamber of legislation where they may be hindered from doing mischief by their coordinate branches, and where also they may be a protection to wealth against the Agrarian and plundering enterprises of the Majority of the people. I think that to give them power in order to prevent them from doing mischief, is arming them for it, and increasing instead of remedying the evil. For if the coordinate branches can arrest their action, so may they that of the coordinates. Mischief may be done negatively as well as positively. Of this a cabal in the Senate of the U. S. has furnished many proofs. Nor do I believe them necessary to protect the wealthy; because enough of these will find their way into every branch of the legislation to protect themselves. From 15. to 20. legislatures of our own, in action for 30. years past, have proved that no fears of an equalisation of property are to be apprehended from them.

I think the best remedy is exactly that provided by all our constitutions, to leave to the citizens the free election and separation of the aristoi from the pseudo-aristoi, of the wheat from the chaff. In general they will elect the real good and wise. In some instances, wealth may corrupt, and birth blind them; but not in sufficient degree to endanger the society.

It is probable that our difference of opinion may in some measure be produced by a difference of character in those among whom we live. From what I have seen of Massachusets and Connecticut myself, and still more from what I have heard, and the character given of the former by yourself, who know them so much better, there seems to be in those two states a traditionary reverence for certain families, which has rendered the offices of the government nearly hereditary in those families. I presume that from an early period of your history, members of these families happening to possess virtue and talents, have honestly exercised them for the good of the people, and by their services have endeared their names to them.

In coupling Connecticut with you, I mean it politically only, not morally. For having made the Bible the Common law of their land they seem to have modelled their morality on the story of Jacob and Laban. But altho' this hereditary succession to office with you may in some degree be founded in real family merit, yet in a much higher degree it has proceeded from your strict alliance of church and state. These families are canonised in the eyes of the people on the common principle 'you tickle me, and I will tickle you.' In Virginia we have nothing of this. Our clergy, before the revolution, having been secured against rivalship by fixed salaries, did not give themselves the trouble of acquiring influence over the people. Of wealth, there were great accumulations in particular families, handed down from generation to generation under the English law of entails. But the only object of ambition for the wealthy was a seat in the king's council. All their court then was paid to the crown and it's creatures; and they Philipised in all collisions between the king and people. Hence they were unpopular; and that unpopularity continues attached to their names. A Randolph, a Carter, or a Burwell must have great personal superiority over a common competitor to be elected by the people, even at this day.

At the first session of our legislature after the Declaration of Independance, we passed a law abolishing entails. And this was followed by one abolishing the privilege of Primogeniture, and dividing the lands of intestates equally among all their children, or other representatives. These laws, drawn by myself, laid the axe to the root of Pseudo-aristocracy. And had another which I prepared been adopted by the legislature, our work would have been compleat. It was a Bill for the more general diffusion of learning. This proposed to divide every county into wards of 5. or 6. miles square, like your townships; to establish in each ward a free school for reading, writing and common arithmetic; to provide for the annual selection of the best subjects from these schools who might receive at the public expence a higher degree of education at a district school; and from these district schools to select a certain number of the most promising subjects to be compleated at an University, where all the useful sciences should be taught. Worth and genius would thus have been sought out from every condition of life, and compleatly prepared by education for defeating the competition of wealth and birth for public trusts.

My proposition had for a further object to impart to these wards those portions of self-government for which they are best qualified, by confiding to them the care of their poor, their roads, police, elections, the nomination of jurors, administration of justice in small cases, elementary exercises of militia, in short, to have made them little republics, with a Warden at the head of each, for all those concerns which, being under their eye, they would better manage than the larger republics of the county or state. A general call of ward-meetings by their Wardens on the same day thro' the state would at any time produce the genuine sense of the people on any required point, and would enable the state to act in mass, as your people have so often done, and with so much effect, by their town meetings. The law for religious freedom, which made a part of this system, having put down the aristocracy of the clergy, and restored to the citizen the freedom of the mind, and those of entails and descents nurturing an equality of condition among them, this on Education would have raised the mass of the people to the high ground of moral respectability necessary to their own safety, and to orderly government; and would have compleated the great object of qualifying them to select the veritable aristoi, for the trusts of government, to the exclusion of the Pseudalists: and the same Theognis who has furnished the epigraphs of your two letters assures us that ["Curnis, good men have never harmed any city."] Altho' this law has not yet been acted on but in a small and inefficient degree, it is still considered as before the legislature, with other bills of the revised code, not yet taken up, and I have great hope that some patriotic spirit will, at a favorable moment, call it up, and make it the key-stone of the arch of our government.

With respect to Aristocracy, we should further consider that, before the establishment of the American states, nothing was known to History but the Man of the old World, crouded within limits either small or over-charged, and steeped in the vices which that situation generates. A govern-ment adapted to such men would be one thing; but a very different one than for the Man of these states. Here every one may have land to labor for himself if he chuses; or, preferring the exercise of any other industry, may exact for it such compensation as not only to afford a comfortable subsistence, but wherewith to provide for a cessation from labor in old age. Every one, by his property, or by his satisfactory situation, is inter-ested in the support of law and order. And such men may safely and advan-tageously reserve to themselves a wholsome controul over their public affairs, and a degree of freedom, which in the hands of the Canaille of the cities of Europe, would be instantly perverted to the demolition and destruc-tion of every thing public and private. The history of the last 25. years of France, and of the last 40. years in America, nay of it's last 200. years, proves the truth of both parts of this observation.

But even in Europe a change has sensibly taken place in the mind of Man. Science had liberated the ideas of those who read and reflect, and the American example had kindled feelings of right in the people. An insurrec-tion has consequently begun, of science, talents and courage against rank and birth, which have fallen into contempt. It has failed in it's first effort, because the mobs of the cities, the instrument used for it's accomplishment, debased by ignorance, poverty and vice, could not be restrained to rational action. But the world will recover from the panic of this first catastrophe. Science is progressive, and talents and enterprize on the alert. Resort may be had to the people of the country, a more governable power from their principles and subordination; and rank, and birth, and tinsel-aristocracy will finally shrink into insignificance, even there. This however we have no right to meddle with. It suffices for us, if the moral and physical condition of our own citizens qualifies them to select the able and good for the direc-tion of their government, with a recurrence of elections at such short periods as will enable them to displace an unfaithful servant before the mischief he meditates may be irremediable. . . .

JEFFERSON TO
PIERRE SAMUEL DUPONT
DE NEMOURS
April 24, 1816

I RECEIVED, MY DEAR FRIEND, your letter covering the constitution for your Equinoctial republics. . . . I suppose it well-formed for those for whom it was intended, and the excellence of every government is its adaptation to the state of those to be governed by it. For us it would not do. Distinguishing between the structure of the government and the moral principles on which you prescribe its administration, with the latter we concur cordially, with the former we should not. We of the United States, you know, are constitutionally and conscientiously democrats. We consider society as one of the natural wants with which man has been created; that he has been endowed with faculties and qualities to effect its satisfaction by concurrence of others having the same want; that when, by the exercise of these faculties, he has procured a state of society, it is one of his acquisitions which he has a right to regulate and control, jointly indeed with all those who have concurred in the procurement, whom he cannot exclude from its use or direction more than they him. We think experience has proved it safer, for the mass of individuals composing the society, to reserve to themselves personally the exercise of all rightful powers to which they are competent, and to delegate those to which they are not competent to deputies named, and removable for unfaithful conduct by themselves immediately. Hence, with us, the people (by which is meant the mass of individuals composing the society) being competent to judge of the facts occurring in ordinary life, they have retained the functions of judges of facts under the name of jurors; but being unqualified for the management of affairs requiring intelligence above the common level, yet competent judges of human character, they chose, for their management, representatives, some by themselves immediately, others by electors chosen by themselves. . . .

But when we come to the moral principles on which the government is to be administered, we come to what is proper for all conditions of society.

I meet you there in all the benevolence and rectitude of your native character, and I love myself always most where I concur most with you. Liberty, truth, probity, honor are declared to be the four cardinal principles of your society. I believe with you that morality, compassion, generosity are innate elements of the human constitution; that there exists a right independent of force; that a right to property is founded in our natural wants, in the means with which we are endowed to satisfy these wants, and the right to what we acquire by those means without violating the similar rights of other sensible beings; that no one has a right to obstruct another exercising his faculties innocently for the relief of sensibilities made a part of his nature; that justice is the fundamental law of society; that the majority, oppressing an individual, is guilty of a crime, abuses its strength, and by acting on the law of the strongest breaks up the foundations of society; that action by the citizens in person, in affairs within their reach and competence, and in all others by representatives, chosen immediately and removable by themselves, constitutes the essence of a republic; that all governments are more or less republican in proportion as this principle enters more or less into their composition; and that a government by representation is capable of extension over a greater surface of country than one of any other form. These, my friend, are the essentials in which you and I agree; however, in our zeal for their maintenance we may be perplexed and divaricate as to the structure of society most likely to secure them.

In the constitution of Spain, as proposed by the late Cortes, there was a principle entirely new to me and not noticed in yours, that no person born after that day should ever acquire the rights of citizenship until he could read and write. It is impossible sufficiently to estimate the wisdom of this provision. Of all those which have been thought of for securing fidelity in the administration of the government, constant ralliance to the principles of the constitution, and progressive amendments with the progressive advances of the human mind or changes in human affairs, it is the most effectual. Enlighten the people generally, and tyranny and oppressions of body and mind will vanish like evil spirits at the dawn of day. Although I do not with some enthusiasts believe that the human condition will ever advance to such a state of perfection as that there shall no longer be pain or vice in the world, yet I believe it susceptible of much improvement, and most of all in matters of government and religion, and that the diffusion of knowledge among the people is to be the instrument by which it is to be effected.

On MY RETURN FROM A LONG JOURNEY and considerable absence from home, I found here the copy of your "Enquiry into the Principles of our Government," which you had been so kind as to send me; and for which I pray you to accept my thanks. The difficulties of getting new works in our situation, inland and without a single bookstore, are such as had prevented my obtaining a copy before; and letters which had accumulated during my absence, and were calling for answers, have not yet permitted me to give to the whole a thorough reading; yet certain that you and I could not think differently on the fundamentals of rightful government, I was impatient, and availed myself of the intervals of repose from the writing-table, to obtain a cursory idea of the body of the work.

I see in it much matter for profound reflection; much which should confirm our adhesion, in practice, to the good principles of our Constitution, and fix our attention on what is yet to be made good. The sixth section on the good moral principles of our government, I found so interesting and replete with sound principles, as to postpone my letter-writing to its thorough perusal and consideration. Besides much other good matter, it settles unanswerably the right of instructing representatives, and their duty to obey. The system of banking we have both equally and ever reprobated. I contemplate it as a blot left in all our Constitutions, which, if not covered, will end in their destruction, which is already hit by the gamblers in corruption, and is sweeping away in its progress the fortunes and morals of our citizens. Funding I consider as limited, rightfully, to a redemption of the debt within the lives of a majority of the generation contracting it; every generation coming equally, by the laws of the Creator of the world to the free possession of the earth He made for their subsistence, unincumbered by their predecessors, who, like them, were but tenants for life. You have successfully and completely pulverized Mr. Adams' system of orders, and his opening the mantle of republicanism to every government of laws, whether consistent or not with natural right. Indeed, it must be acknowledged, that the term *republic* is of very vague application in every language. Witness the self-styled republics of Holland, Switzerland, Genoa, Venice, Poland. Were I to assign to this term a precise and definite idea, I would say, purely and simply, it means a government by its citizens in mass, acting directly and personally, according to rules established by the majority; and that every other government is more or less republican, in proportion as it has in its composition more or less of this ingredient of the direct action of the citizens. Such a government is evidently restrained to very narrow limits of space and population. I doubt if it would be practicable beyond the extent of a New England township. The first shade from this pure element, which, like that of pure vital air, cannot sustain life of itself, would be where the powers of the government, being divided, should be exercised each by representatives chosen either *pro hac vice,* or for such short terms as should render secure the duty of expressing the will of their constituents. This I should consider as the nearest approach to a pure republic, which is practicable on a large scale of country or population. And we have examples of it in some of our State Constitutions, which, if not poisoned by priest-craft, would prove its excellence over all mixtures with other elements; and, with only equal doses of poison, would still be the best. Other shades of republicanism may be found in other forms of government, where the executive, judiciary and legislative functions, and the different branches of the latter, are chosen by the people more or less directly, for longer terms of years, or for life, or made hereditary; or where there are mixtures of authorities, some dependent on, and others independent of the people. The further the departure from direct and constant control by the citizens, the less has the government of the ingredient of republicanism; evidently none where the authorities are hereditary, as in France, Venice, etc., or self-chosen, as in Holland; and little, where for life, in proportion as the life continues in being after the act of election.

The purest republican feature in the government of our own State, is the House of Representatives. The Senate is equally so the first year, less the second, and so on. The Executive still less, because not chosen by the people directly. The Judiciary seriously anti-republican, because for life; and the national arm wielded, as you observe, by military leaders, irresponsible but to themselves. Add to this the vicious constitution of our county courts (to whom the justice, the executive administration, the taxation, police, the military appointments of the county, and nearly all our daily concerns are confided), self-appointed, self-continued, holding their authorities for life, and with an impossibility of breaking in on the perpetual succession of any faction once possessed of the bench. They are in truth, the executive, the judiciary, and the military of their respective counties, and the sum of the counties makes the State. And add, also, that one-half of our brethren who

fight and pay taxes, are excluded, like Helots, from the rights of representation, as if society were instituted for the soil, and not for the men inhabit-
ing it; or one-half of these could dispose of the rights and the will of the
other half, without their consent.

What constitutes a State?
Not high-raised battlements, or labor'd mound,
Thick wall, or moated gate;
Not cities proud, with spires and turrets crown'd;
No: men, high-minded men;
Men, who their duties know;
But know their rights; and knowing, dare maintain.
These constitute a State.

In the General Government, the House of Representatives is mainly
republican; the Senate scarcely so at all, as not elected by the people
directly, and so long secured even against those who do elect them; the
Executive more republican than the Senate, from its shorter term, its election by the people, in *practice,* (for they vote for A only on an assurance
that he will vote for B,) and because, *in practice also,* a principle of rotation seems to be in a course of establishment; the judiciary independent of
the nation, their coercion by impeachment being found nugatory.

If, then, the control of the people over the organs of their government
be the measure of its republicanism, and I confess I know no other measure,
it must be agreed that our governments have much less of republicanism
than ought to have been expected; in other words, that the people have less
regular control over their agents, than their rights and their interests require.
And this I ascribe, not to any want of republican dispositions in those who
formed these Constitutions, but to a submission of true principle to European authorities, to speculators on government, whose fears of the people
have been inspired by the populace of their own great cities, and were
unjustly entertained against the independent, the happy, and therefore
orderly citizens of the United States. Much I apprehend that the golden
moment is past for reforming these heresies. The functionaries of public
power rarely strengthen in their dispositions to abridge it, and an unorganized call for timely amendment is not likely to prevail against an organized opposition to it. We are always told that things are going on well; why
change them? *"Chista bene, non si muove,"* said the Italian, "let him who
stands well, stand still." This is true; and I verily believe they would go
on well with us under an absolute monarch, while our present character
remains, of order, industry and love of peace, and restrained, as he would
be, by the proper spirit of the people. But it is while it remains such, we
should provide against the consequences of its deterioration. And let us rest

in the hope that it will yet be done, and spare ourselves the pain of evils which may never happen.

On this view of the import of the term *republic,* instead of saying, as has been said, "that it may mean anything or nothing," we may say with truth and meaning, that governments are more or less republican, as they have more or less of the element of popular election and control in their composition; and believing, as I do, that the mass of the citizens is the safest depository of their own rights and especially, that the evils flowing from the duperies of the people, are less injurious than those from the egoism of their agents, I am a friend to that composition of government which has in it the most of this ingredient. And I sincerely believe, with you, that banking establishments are more dangerous than standing armies; and that the principle of spending money to be paid by posterity, under the name of funding, is but swindling futurity on a large scale. . . .

11

JEFFERSON TO
ISAAC H. TIFFANY
August 26, 1816

Bᴜᴛ ꜱᴏ ᴅɪꜰꜰᴇʀᴇɴᴛ ᴡᴀꜱ ᴛʜᴇ ꜱᴛʏʟᴇ ᴏꜰ ꜱᴏᴄɪᴇᴛʏ then and with those people from what it is now and with us that I think little edification can be obtained from their writings on the subject of government. They had just ideas of the value of personal liberty, but none at all of the structure of government best calculated to preserve it. They knew no medium between a democracy (the only pure republic, but impracticable beyond the limits of a town) and an abandonment of themselves to an aristocracy or a tyranny independent of the people. It seems not to have occurred that where the citizens cannot meet to transact their business in person, they alone have the right to choose the agents who shall transact it; and that in this way a republican or popular government of the second grade of purity may be exercised over any extent of country. The full experiment of a government democratical but representative was and is still reserved for us. The idea (taken, indeed, from the little specimen formerly existing in the English constitution but now lost) has been carried by us more or less into all our legislative and executive departments; but it has not yet by any of us been pushed into all the ramifications of the system, so far as to leave no authority existing not responsible to the people, whose rights, however, to the exercise and fruits of their own industry can never be protected against the selfishness of rulers not subject to their control at short periods. The introduction of this new principle of representative democracy has rendered useless almost everything written before on the structure of government, and in a great measure relieves our regret if the political writings of Aristotle or of any other ancient have been lost or are unfaithfully rendered or explained to us. My most earnest wish is to see the republican element of popular control pushed to the maximum of its practicable exercise. I shall then believe that our government may be pure and perpetual.

12
JEFFERSON TO
SAMUEL KERCHEVAL
July 12, 1816

I AM NOT AMONG THOSE WHO FEAR the people. They, and not the rich, are our dependence for continued freedom. And to preserve their independence, we must not let our rulers load us with perpetual debt. We must make our election between *economy and liberty,* or *profusion and servitude.* If we run into such debts, as that we must be taxed in our meat and in our drink, in our necessaries and our comforts, in our labors and our amusements, for our callings and our creeds, as the people of England are, our people, like them, must come to labor sixteen hours in the twenty-four, give the earnings of fifteen of these to the government for their debts and daily expenses; and the sixteenth being insufficient to afford us bread, we must live, as they now do, on oatmeal and potatoes; have no time to think, no means of calling the mismanagers to account; but be glad to obtain subsistence by hiring ourselves to rivet their chains on the necks of our fellow sufferers. Our landholders, too, like theirs, retaining indeed the title and stewardship of estates called theirs, but held really in trust for the treasury, must wander, like theirs, in foreign countries, and be contented with penury, obscurity, exile, and the glory of the nation. This example reads to us the salutary lesson, that private fortunes are destroyed by public as well as by private extravagance. And this is the tendency of all human governments. A departure from principle in one instance becomes a precedent for a second; that second for a third; and so on, till the bulk of the society is reduced to be mere automatons of misery, to have no sensibilities left but for sinning and suffering. Then begins, indeed, the *bellum omnium in omnia,* which some philosophers observing to be so general in this world, have mistaken it for the natural, instead of the abusive state of man. And the fore horse of this frightful team is public debt. Taxation follows that, and in its train wretchedness and oppression.

Some men look at constitutions with sanctimonious reverence, and deem them like the ark of the covenant, too sacred to be touched. They ascribe to the men of the preceding age a wisdom more than human, and suppose what they did to be beyond amendment. I knew that age well; I belonged to it, and labored with it. It deserved well of its country. It was very like the present, but without the experience of the present; and forty years of experience in government is worth a century of bookreading; and this they would say themselves, were they to rise from the dead. I am certainly not an advocate for frequent and untried changes in laws and constitutions. I think moderate imperfections had better be borne with; because, when once known, we accommodate ourselves to them, and find practical means of correcting their ill effects. But I know also, that laws and institutions must go hand in hand with the progress of the human mind. As that becomes more developed, more enlightened, as new discoveries are made, new truths disclosed, and manners and opinions change with the change of circumstances, institutions must advance also, and keep pace with the times. We might as well require a man to wear still the coat which fitted him when a boy, as civilized society to remain ever under the regimen of their barbarous ancestors. It is this preposterous idea which has lately deluged Europe in blood. Their monarchs, instead of wisely yielding to the gradual change of circumstances, of favoring progressive accommodation to progressive improvement, have clung to old abuses, entrenched themselves behind steady habits, and obliged their subjects to seek through blood and violence rash and ruinous innovations, which, had they been referred to the peaceful deliberations and collected wisdom of the nation, would have been put into acceptable and salutary forms. Let us follow no such examples, nor weakly believe that one generation is not as capable as another of taking care of itself, and of ordering its own affairs. Let us, as our sister States have done, avail ourselves of our reason and experience, to correct the crude essays of our first and unexperienced, although wise, virtuous, and well-meaning councils. And lastly, let us provide in our Constitution for its revision at stated periods. What these periods should be, nature herself indicates. By the European tables of mortality, of the adults living at any one moment of time, a majority will be dead in about nineteen years. At the end of that period then, a new majority is come into place; or, in other words, a new generation. Each generation is as independent of the one preceding, as that was of all which had gone before. It has then, like them, a right to choose for itself the form of government it believes most promotive of its own happiness; consequently, to accommodate to the circumstances in which it finds itself, that received from its predecessors; and it is for the peace and good of mankind, that a solemn opportunity of doing this every nineteen or twenty years, should be provided by the Constitution; so that it may be handed on, with periodical repairs, from generation to generation, to the end of time, if anything human can so long endure. It is now forty years since the constitution of Virginia was formed. The same tables inform us, that, within that period, two-thirds of the adults then living are now dead. Have then the remaining third, even if they had the wish, the right to hold in obedience to their will and to laws theretofore made by them, the other two-thirds, who, with themselves, compose the present mass of adults? If they have not, who has? The dead? But the dead have no rights. They are nothing; and nothing cannot own something. Where there is no substance, there can be no accident. This corporeal globe, and everything upon it, belong to its present corporeal inhabitants, during their generation. They alone have a right to direct what is the concern of themselves alone, and to declare the law of that direction; and this declaration can only be made by their majority. That majority, then, has a right to depute representatives to a convention, and to make the Constitution what they think will be the best for themselves. But how collect their voice? This is the real difficulty. If invited by private authority, or county or district meetings, these divisions are so large that few will attend; and their voice will be imperfectly, or falsely, pronounced. Here, then, would be one of the advantages of the ward divisions I have proposed. The mayor of every ward, on a question like the present, would call his ward together, take the simple yea or nay of its members, convey these to the county court, who would hand on those of all its wards to be the proper general authority; and the voice of the whole people would be thus fairly, fully, and peaceably expressed, discussed, and decided by the common reason of the society. If this avenue be shut to the call of sufferance, it will make itself heard through that of force, and we shall go on, as other nations are doing, in the endless circle of oppression, rebellion, reformation; and oppression, rebellion, reformation, again; and so on forever. . . .

II

THE *FEDERALIST PAPERS*
1787–88

THE FEDERALIST PAPERS were originally written as a series of short essays in the newspapers of New York, between October 27, 1787, and April 4, 1788, for the purpose of influencing that state's ratification of the proposed Constitution, not as a systematic treatise on political philosophy. Shortly before the last few of the 85 essays appeared in the newspapers, they were published as a book and circulated among the leading supporters of the proposed Constitution in other states. Their chief authors were Alexander Hamilton (1755–1804) and James Madison (1751–1836), and five were contributed by John Jay (1745–1829). All the essays, however, were signed with the same name, Publius, after Publius Valerius Poplicola, described in Plutarch's *Lives* as the man who saved the Roman Republic.

In the first of these essays, Publius (Hamilton) outlines the general plan for the entire work. The papers are divided among six branches of inquiry:

1. The utility of the Union—papers 1–14.
2. The insufficiency of the present Confederation—papers 15–22.
3. The necessity of energetic government—papers 23–36.
4. The republicanism of the proposed Constitution—papers 37–84.
5. The analogy of the proposed Constitution to the constitution of New York. This topic appears throughout the papers.

6. The additional security the adoption of the proposed Constitution could afford. This topic also appears throughout.

The first three headings, however, have a single theme—the immediate political question of what is to be done about the proposed Union, showing why it is good, what is inadequate about the Articles of Confederation, and what kind of government is needed to secure a stronger union. Then all that needs to be shown is the republicanism of the proposed Constitution—the work of the fourth branch of the inquiry, which includes the largest group of essays, 48 papers. Therefore the organization of the essays in their simplest form is: Union and republicanism. While it would be seriously misleading to present *The Federalist* as a systematic treatise on political philosophy, it did propose a republicanism involving a new view of the problem of Union. Prior to the proposed Constitution, Americans were already living under republican governments and a confederal union of these republics. The assumption of *The Federalist* was that the principle behind these individual republics and their union was false.

In the Constitutional Convention, the forces proposing a more perfect union encountered the argument that preserving republican freedom in a large country is impossible. There had been small republics in the past, but all large countries had been without that sense of oneness, or community, which made freedom, the mutual respect of citizens, and so, self-government, possible. They had required the strength of monarchy that disallows freedom; in place of citizens, there were only subjects. The proponents of great union met that argument by asserting that only in a country which was large enough (given a certain commercial character, along with the establishment of proper republican institutions) could you have a republic that lasted and retained its virtues. The proponents of such a union won in the Convention, and as their proposed Constitution went out to conventions in the several states for ratification, it was necessary to carry the argument to the people.

Carefully choosing among several adjectives that could have expressed the factor of smallness, Publius (Hamilton) argued in *Federalist* No. 9 that "the petty Republics of Greece and Italy . . . were kept in a state of perpetual vibration, between the extremes of tyranny and anarchy." Freedom and order could *now* be had at the same time because of great improvements in the science of politics. One could have a great increase in external force and security, as well as suppress factions and guard internal tranquillity, without suppressing freedom. The great virtue of the large republic, provided it was fashioned according to true republican principles and possessed of that economic diversity fostered by commerce, is, as Publius (Madison) argued in *Federalist* 10, that it is composed of such a great number and diversity of factions as well as of sects that no single faction could become a majority and so, under the mask of majoritarian legitimacy, oppress the minority and deprive it of its rights. Various smaller groups would have to bargain with each other, and publicly at that, in order to form a majority on any issue. The public character of the bargaining would insure that the argument would be made in the name of the public good. Thus, the public good—including public order—would be approximated even though each of the smaller parties was pursuing its own private good.

Publius (Madison) took the commercial character of the truly republican country for granted in his argument in *Federalist* 10. But it is surely necessary if there is to be a *diversity,* and therefore a multiplicity of factions; otherwise the two factions existing in *any* country, the few rich and the many poor, would both simply get larger in a larger country. He did explicitly and emphatically assert the necessity of proper republican institutions, directed ultimately by the "deliberate sense of the community," a combination of sound feelings and prudent calculations about what constitutes the common interest or public good.

13
FEDERALIST NO. 1 (HAMILTON)
October 27, 1787

AFTER AN UNEQUIVOCAL EXPERIENCE of the inefficacy of the subsisting F ederal Government, you are called upon to deliberate on a new Constitution for the United States of America. The subject speaks its own importance; comprehending in its consequences, nothing less than the existence of the UNION, the safety and welfare of the parts of which it is composed, the fate of an empire, in many respects, the most interesting in the world. It has been frequently remarked, that it seems to have been reserved to the people of this country, by their conduct and example, to decide the important question, whether societies of men are really capable or not, of establishing good government from reflection and choice, or whether they are forever destined to depend, for their political constitutions, on accident and force. If there be any truth in the remark, the crisis, at which we are arrived, may with propriety be regarded as the æra in which that decision is to be made; and a wrong election of the part we shall act, may, in this view, deserve to be considered as the general misfortune of mankind.

This idea will add the inducements of philanthropy to those of patriotism to heighten the solicitude, which all considerate and good men must feel for the event. Happy will it be if our choice should be directed by a judicious estimate of our true interests, unperplexed and unbiassed by considerations not connected with the public good. But this is a thing more ardently to be wished, than seriously to be expected. The plan offered to our deliberations, affects too many particular interests, innovates upon too many local institutions, not to involve in its discussion a variety of objects foreign to its merits, and of views, passions and prejudices little favourable to the discovery of truth. . . .

It is not, however, my design to dwell upon observations of this nature. I am well aware that it would be disingenuous to resolve indiscriminately the opposition of any set of men (merely because their situations might subject them to suspicion) into interested or ambitious views: Candour will oblige us to admit, that even such men may be actuated by upright intentions; and it cannot be doubted that much of the opposition which has made its appearance, or may hereafter make its appearance, will spring from sources, blameless at least, if not respectable, the honest errors of minds led astray by preconceived jealousies and fears. So numerous indeed and so powerful are the causes, which serve to give a false bias to the judgment, that we upon many occasions, see wise and good men on the wrong as well as on the right side of questions, of the first magnitude to society. This circumstance, if duly attended to, would furnish a lesson of moderation to those, who are ever so much persuaded of their being in the right, in any controversy. And a further reason for caution, in this respect, might be drawn from the reflection, that we are not always sure, that those who advocate the truth are influenced by purer principles than their antagonists. Ambition, avarice, personal animosity, party opposition, and many other motives, not more laudable than these, are apt to operate as well upon those who support as upon those who oppose the right side of a question. Were there not even these inducements to moderation, nothing could be more illjudged than that intolerant spirit, which has, at all times, characterised political parties. For, in politics as in religion, it is equally absurd to aim at making proselytes by fire and sword. Heresies in either can rarely be cured by persecution.

And yet however just these sentiments will be allowed to be, we have already sufficient indications, that it will happen in this as in all former cases of great national discussion. A torrent of angry and malignant passions will be let loose. To judge from the conduct of the opposite parties, we shall be led to conclude, that they will mutually hope to evince the justness of their opinions, and to increase the number of their converts by the loudness of their declamations, and by the bitterness of their invectives. An enlightened zeal for the energy and efficiency of government will be stigmatized, as the off-spring of a temper fond of despotic power and hostile to the principles of liberty. An overscrupulous jealousy of danger to the rights of the people, which is more commonly the fault of the head than of the heart, will be represented as mere pretence and artifice; the bait for popularity at the expence of public good. It will be forgotten, on the one hand, that jealousy is the usual concomitant of violent love, and that the noble enthusiasm of liberty is too apt to be infected with a spirit of narrow and illiberal distrust. On the other hand, it will be equally forgotten, that the vigour of government is essential to the security of liberty; that, in the contemplation of a sound and well informed judgment, their interest can never be separated; and that a dangerous ambition more often lurks behind the specious mask of zeal for the rights of the people, than under the forbidding appearance of zeal for the firmness and efficiency of government. History will teach us, that the former has been found a much more certain road to the introduction of despotism, than the latter, and that of those men who have overturned the liberties of republics the greatest number have begun their carreer, by paying an obsequious court to the people, commencing Demagogues and ending Tyrants.

In the course of the preceeding observations I have had an eye, my Fellow Citizens, to putting you upon your guard against all attempts, from whatever quarter, to influence your decision in a matter of the utmost moment to your welfare by any impressions other than those which may result from the evidence of truth. You will, no doubt, at the same time, have collected from the general scope of them that they proceed from a source not unfriendly to the new Constitution. Yes, my Countrymen, I own to you, that, after having given it an attentive consideration, I am clearly of opinion, it is your interest to adopt it. I am convinced, that this is the safest course for your liberty, your dignity, and your happiness. I effect not reserves, which I do not feel. I will not amuse you with an appearance of deliberation, when I have decided. I frankly acknowledge to you my convictions, and I will freely lay before you the reasons on which they are founded. The consciousness of good intentions disdains ambiguity. I shall not however multiply professions on this head. My motives must remain in the depository of my own breast: My arguments will be open to all, and may be judged of by all. They shall at least be offered in a spirit, which will not disgrace the cause of truth.

I propose in a series of papers to discuss the following interesting particulars—*The utility of the* UNION *to your political prosperity*—*The insufficiency of the present Confederation to preserve that Union*—*The necessity of a government at least equally energetic with the one proposed to the attainment of this object*— *The conformity of the proposed constitution to the true principles of republican government*—*Its analogy to your own state constitution*—and lastly, *The additional security, which its adoption will afford to the preservation of that species of government, to liberty and to property.*

In the progress of this discussion I shall endeavour to give a satisfactory answer to all the objections which shall have made their appearance that may seem to have any claim to your attention. . . .

As noted above, *Federalists* 1 through 14 deal with the "utility of the Union." The second through the eighth papers explore that utility with regard to foreign dangers and conflicts between the states. These were the traditional objects of confederal unions and had been familiarly discussed during the preceding decade. *Federalists* 9, 10, and 14 deal with the subject of "domestic faction," raising novel and important theoretical considerations regarding republicanism and federalism.

14

FEDERALIST NO. 9 (HAMILTON)
November 21, 1787

A FIRM UNION WILL BE of the utmost moment to the peace and liberty of the States as a barrier against domestic faction and insurrection. It is impossible to read the history of the petty Republics of Greece and Italy, without feeling sensations of horror and disgust at the distractions with which they were continually agitated, and at the rapid succession of revolutions, by which they were kept in a state of perpetual vibration, between the extremes of tyranny and anarchy. If they exhibit occasional calms, these only serve as short-lived contrasts to the furious storms that are to succeed. If now and then intervals of felicity open themselves to view, we behold them with a mixture of regret arising from the reflection that the pleasing scenes before us are soon to be overwhelmed by the tempestuous waves of sedition and party-rage. If momentary rays of glory break forth from the gloom, while they dazzle us with a transient and fleeting brilliancy, they at the same time admonish us to lament that the vices of government should pervert the direction and tarnish the lustre of those bright talents and exalted indowments, for which the favoured soils, that produced them, have been so justly celebrated.

From the disorders that disfigure the annals of those republics, the advocates of despotism have drawn arguments, not only against the forms of republican government, but against the very principles of civil liberty. They have decried all free government, as inconsistent with the order of society, and have indulged themselves in malicious exultation over its friends and partizans. Happily for mankind, stupendous fabrics reared on the basis of liberty, which have flourished for ages, have in a few glorious instances refuted their gloomy sophisms. And, I trust, America will be the broad and solid foundation of other edifices not less magnificent, which will be equally permanent monuments of their errors.

But it is not to be denied that the portraits, they have sketched of republican government, were too just copies of the originals from which they were taken. If it had been found impracticable, to have devised models of a more perfect structure, the enlightened friends to liberty would have been obliged to abandon the cause of that species of government as indefensible. The science of politics, however, like most other sciences has received great improvement. The efficacy of various principles is now well understood, which were either not known at all, or imperfectly known to the ancients. The regular distribution of power into distinct departments—the introduction of legislative ballances and checks—the institution of courts composed of judges, holding their offices during good behaviour—the representation of the people in the legislature by deputies of their own election—these are either wholly new discoveries or have made their principal progress towards perfection in modern times. They are means, and powerful means, by which the excellencies of republican government may be retained and its imperfections lessened or avoided. To this catalogue of circumstances, that tend to the amelioration of popular systems of civil government, I shall venture, however novel it may appear to some, to add one more on a principle, which has been made the foundation of an objection to the New Constitution, I mean the ENLARGEMENT of the ORBIT within which such systems are to revolve either in respect to the dimensions of a single State, or to the consolidation of several smaller States into one great confederacy. The latter is that which immediately concerns the object under consideration. It will however be of use to examine the principle in its application to a single State which shall be attended to in another place. . . .

The balance of this paper deals with the way in which *confederal* enlargement helps solve the problem of domestic faction. Montesquieu is quoted extensively to show that, contrary to antifederal usage, his great authority supports the idea of a strong confederal union.

15

FEDERALIST NO. 10 (MADISON)
November 22, 1787

AMONG THE NUMEROUS ADVANTAGES promised by a well constructed Union, none deserves to be more accurately developed than its tendency to break and control the violence of faction. The friend of popular governments, never finds himself so much alarmed for their character and fate, as when he contemplates their propensity to this dangerous vice. He will not fail therefore to set a due value on any plan which, without violating the principles to which he is attached, provides a proper cure for it. The instability, injustice and confusion introduced into the public councils, have in truth been the mortal diseases under which popular governments have every where perished; as they continue to be the favorite and fruitful topics from which the adversaries to liberty derive their most specious declamations. The valuable improvements made by the American Constitutions on the popular models, both ancient and modern, cannot certainly be too much admired; but it would be an unwarrantable partiality, to contend that they have as effectually obviated the danger on this side as was wished and expected. Complaints are every where heard from our most considerate and virtuous citizens, equally the friends of public and private faith, and of public and personal liberty; that our governments are too unstable; that the public good is disregarded in the conflicts of rival parties; and that measures are too often decided, not according to the rules of justice, and the rights of the minor party; but by the superior force of an interested and over-bearing majority. However anxiously we may wish that these complaints had no foundation, the evidence of known facts will not permit us to deny that they are in some degree true. It will be found indeed, on a candid review of our situation, that some of the distresses under which we labor, have been erroneously charged on the operation of our governments; but it will be found, at the same time, that other causes will not alone account for many of our heaviest misfortunes; and particularly, for that prevailing and increasing distrust of public engagements, and alarm for private rights, which are echoed from one end of the continent to the other. These must be chiefly, if not wholly, effects of the unsteadiness and injustice, with which a factious spirit has tainted our public administrations.

By a faction I understand a number of citizens, whether amounting to a majority or minority of the whole, who are united and actuated by some common impulse of passion, or of interest, adverse to the rights of other citizens, or to the permanent and aggregate interests of the community.

There are two methods of curing the mischiefs of faction: the one, by removing its causes; the other, by controling its effects.

There are again two methods of removing the causes of faction: the one by destroying the liberty which is essential to its existence; the other, by giving to every citizen the same opinions, the same passions, and the same interests.

It could never be more truly said than of the first remedy, that it is worse than the disease. Liberty is to faction, what air is to fire, an aliment without which it instantly expires. But it could not be a less folly to abolish liberty, which is essential to political life, because it nourishes faction, than it would be to wish the annihilation of air, which is essential to animal life, because it imparts to fire its destructive agency.

The second expedient is as impracticable, as the first would be unwise. As long as the reason of man continues fallible, and he is at liberty to exercise it, different opinions will be formed. As long as the connection subsists between his reason and his self-love, his opinions and his passions will have a reciprocal influence on each other; and the former will be objects to which the latter will attach themselves. The diversity in the faculties of men from which the rights of property originate, is not less an insuperable obstacle to a uniformity of interests. The protection of these faculties is the first object of Government. From the protection of different and unequal faculties of acquiring property, the possession of different degrees and kinds of property immediately results: and from the influence of these on the sentiments and views of the respective proprietors, ensues a division of the society into different interests and parties.

The latent causes of faction are thus sown in the nature of man; and we see them every where brought into different degrees of activity, according to the different circumstances of civil society. A zeal for different opinions concerning religion, concerning Government and many other points, as well of speculation as of practice; an attachment to different leaders ambitiously contending for pre-eminence and power; or to persons of other descriptions whose fortunes have been interesting to the human passions, have in turn divided mankind into parties, inflamed them with mutual animosity, and rendered them much more disposed to vex and oppress each other, than to co-operate for their common good. So strong is this propensity of mankind to fall into mutual animosities, that where no substantial occasion presents itself, the most frivolous and fanciful distinctions have been sufficient to kindle their unfriendly passions, and excite their most violent conflicts. But the most common and durable source of factions, has been the various and unequal distribution of property. Those who hold, and those who are without property, have ever formed distinct interests in society. Those who are creditors, and those who are debtors, fall under a like discrimination. A landed interest, a manufacturing interest, a mercantile interest, a monied interest, with many lesser interests, grow up of necessity in civilized nations, and divide them into different classes, actuated by different sentiments and views. The regulation of these various and interfering interests forms the principal task of modern Legislation, and involves the spirit of party and faction in the necessary and ordinary operations of Government.

No man is allowed to be a judge in his own cause; because his interest would certainly bias his judgment, and, not improbably, corrupt his integrity. With equal, nay with greater reason, a body of men, are unfit to be both judges and parties, at the same time; yet, what are many of the most important acts of legislation, but so many judicial determinations, not indeed concerning the rights of single persons, but concerning the rights of large bodies of citizens; and what are the different classes of legislators, but advocates and parties to the causes which they determine? Is a law proposed concerning private debts? It is a question to which the creditors are parties on one side, and the debtors on the other. Justice ought to hold the balance between them. Yet the parties are and must be themselves the judges; and the most numerous party, or, in other words, the most powerful faction must be expected to prevail. Shall domestic manufactures be encouraged, and in what degree, by restrictions on foreign manufactures? are questions which would be differently decided by the landed and the manufacturing classes; and probably by neither, with a sole regard to justice and the public good. The apportionment of taxes on the various descriptions of property, is an act which seems to require the most exact impartiality; yet, there is perhaps no legislative act in which greater opportunity and temptation are given to a predominant party, to trample on the rules of justice. Every shilling with which they over-burden the inferior number, is a shilling saved to their own pockets.

It is in vain to say, that enlightened statesmen will be able to adjust these clashing interests, and render them all subservient to the public good. Enlightened statesmen will not always be at the helm: Nor, in many cases, can such an adjustment be made at all, without taking into view indirect and remote considerations, which will rarely prevail over the immediate interest which one party may find in disregarding the rights of another, or the good of the whole.

The inference to which we are brought, is, that the *causes* of faction cannot be removed; and that relief is only to be sought in the means of controling its *effects*.

If a faction consists of less than a majority, relief is supplied by the republican principle, which enables the majority to defeat its sinister views by regular vote: It may clog the administration, it may convulse the society; but it will be unable to execute and mask its violence under the forms of the Constitution. When a majority is included in a faction, the form of popular government on the other hand enables it to sacrifice to its ruling passion or interest, both the public good and the rights of other citizens. To secure the public good, and private rights, against the danger of such a faction, and at the same time to preserve the spirit and the form of popular government, is then the great object to which our enquiries are directed: Let me add that it is the great desideratum, by which alone this form of government can be rescued from the opprobrium under which it has so long labored, and be recommended to the esteem and adoption of mankind.

By what means is this object attainable? Evidently by one of two only. Either the existence of the same passion or interest in a majority at the same time, must be prevented; or the majority, having such co-existent passion or interest, must be rendered, by their number and local situation, unable to concert and carry into effect schemes of oppression. If the impulse and the opportunity be suffered to coincide, we well know that neither moral nor religious motives can be relied on as an adequate control. They are not found to be such on the injustice and violence of individuals, and lose their efficacy in proportion to the number combined together; that is, in proportion as their efficacy becomes needful.

From this view of the subject, it may be concluded, that a pure Democracy, by which I mean, a Society, consisting of a small number of citizens, who assemble and administer the Government in person, can admit of no cure for the mischiefs of faction. A common passion or interest will, in almost every case, be felt by a majority of the whole; a communication and concert results from the form of Government itself; and there is nothing to check the inducements to sacrifice the weaker party, or an obnoxious individual. Hence it is, that such Democracies have ever been spectacles of turbulence and contention; have ever been found incompatible with personal security, or the rights of property; and have in general been as short in their lives, as they have been violent in their deaths. Theoretic politicians, who have patronized this species of Government, have erroneously supposed, that by reducing mankind to a perfect equality in their political rights, they would, at the same time, be perfectly equalized and assimilated in their possessions, their opinions, and their passions.

A Republic, by which I mean a Government in which the scheme of representation takes place, opens a different prospect, and promises the cure for which we are seeking. Let us examine the points in which it varies from pure Democracy, and we shall comprehend both the nature of the cure, and the efficacy which it must derive from the Union.

The two great points of difference between a Democracy and a Republic are, first, the delegation of the Government, in the latter, to a small number of citizens elected by the rest: secondly, the greater number of citizens, and greater sphere of country, over which the latter may be extended.

The effect of the first difference is, on the one hand to refine and enlarge the public views, by passing them through the medium of a chosen body of citizens, whose wisdom may best discern the true interest of their country, and whose patriotism and love of justice, will be least likely to sacrifice it to temporary or partial considerations. Under such a regulation, it may well happen that the public voice pronounced by the representatives of the people, will be more consonant to the public good, than if pronounced by the people themselves convened for the purpose. On the other hand, the effect may be inverted. Men of factious tempers, of local prejudices, or of sinister designs, may by intrigue, by corruption or by other means, first obtain the suffrages, and then betray the interests of the people. The question resulting is, whether small or extensive Republics are most favorable to the election of proper guardians of the public weal: and it is clearly decided in favor of the latter by two obvious considerations.

In the first place it is to be remarked that however small the Republic may be, the Representatives must be raised to a certain number, in order to guard against the cabals of a few; and that however large it may be, they must be limited to a certain number, in order to guard against the confusion of a multitude. Hence the number of Representatives in the two cases, not being in proportion to that of the Constituents, and being proportionally greatest in the small Republic, it follows, that if the proportion of fit characters, be not less, in the large than in the small Republic, the former will present a greater option, and consequently a greater probability of a fit choice.

In the next place, as each Representative will be chosen by a greater number of citizens in the large than in the small Republic, it will be more difficult for unworthy candidates to practise with success the vicious arts, by which elections are too often carried; and the suffrages of the people being more free, will be more likely to centre on men who possess the most attractive merit, and the most diffusive and established characters.

It must be confessed, that in this, as in most other cases, there is a mean, on both sides of which inconveniencies will be found to lie. By enlarging too much the number of electors, you render the representative too little acquainted with all their local circumstances and lesser interests; as by reducing it too much, you render him unduly attached to these, and too little fit to comprehend and pursue great and national objects. The Federal Constitution forms a happy combination in this respect; the great and aggregate interests being referred to the national, the local and particular, to the state legislatures.

The other point of difference is, the greater number of citizens and extent of territory which may be brought within the compass of Republican, than of Democratic Government; and it is this circumstance principally which renders factious combinations less to be dreaded in the former, than in the latter. The smaller the society, the fewer probably will be the distinct parties and interests composing it; the fewer the distinct parties and interests, the more frequently will a majority be found of the same party; and the smaller the number of individuals composing a majority, and the smaller the compass within which they are placed, the more easily will they concert and execute their plans of oppression. Extend the sphere, and you take in a greater variety of parties and interests; you make it less probable that a majority of the whole will have a common motive to invade the rights of other citizens; or if such a common motive exists, it will be more difficult for all who feel it to discover their own strength, and to act in unison with each other. Besides other impediments, it may be remarked, that where there is a consciousness of unjust or dishonorable purposes, communication is always checked by distrust, in proportion to the number whose concurrence is necessary.

Hence it clearly appears, that the same advantage, which a Republic has over a Democracy, in controling the effects of faction, is enjoyed by a large over a small Republic—is enjoyed by the Union over the States composing it. Does this advantage consist in the substitution of Representatives, whose enlightened views and virtuous sentiments render them superior to local prejudices, and to schemes of injustice? It will not be denied, that the Representation of the Union will be most likely to possess these requisite endowments. Does it consist in the greater security afforded by a greater variety of parties, against the event of any one party being able to outnumber and oppress the rest? In an equal degree does the encreased variety of parties, comprised within the Union, encrease this security. Does it, in fine, consist in the greater obstacles opposed to the concert and accomplishment of the secret wishes of an unjust and interested majority? Here, again, the extent of the Union gives it the most palpable advantage.

The influence of factious leaders may kindle a flame within their particular States, but will be unable to spread a general conflagration through the other States: a religious sect, may degenerate into a political faction in a part of the Confederacy; but the variety of sects dispersed over the entire face of it, must secure the national Councils against any danger from that source: a rage for paper money, for an abolition of debts, for an equal division of property, or for any other improper or wicked project, will be less apt to pervade the whole body of the Union, than a particular member of it; in the same proportion as such a malady is more likely to taint a particular county or district, than an entire State.

In the extent and proper structure of the Union, therefore, we behold a

Republican remedy for the diseases most incident to Republican Government. And according to the degree of pleasure and pride, we feel in being Republicans, ought to be our zeal in cherishing the spirit, and supporting the character of Federalists.

16
FEDERALIST NO. 14 (MADISON)
November 30, 1787

W<small>E HAVE SEEN THE NECESSITY</small> of the union as our bulwark against foreign danger, as the conservator of peace among ourselves, as the guardian of our commerce and other common interests, as the only substitute for those military establishments which have subverted the liberties of the old world; and as the proper antidote for the diseases of faction, which have proved fatal to other popular governments, and of which alarming symptoms have been betrayed by our own. All that remains, within this branch of our enquiries, is to take notice of an objection, that may be drawn from the great extent of country which the union embraces. A few observations on this subject will be the more proper, as it is perceived that the adversaries of the new constitution are availing themselves of a prevailing prejudice, with regard to the practicable sphere of republican administration, in order to supply by imaginary difficulties, the want of those solid objections, which they endeavor in vain to find.

The error which limits Republican Government to a narrow district, has been unfolded and refuted in preceding papers. I remark here only, that it seems to owe its rise and prevalence, chiefly to the confounding of a republic with a democracy: And applying to the former reasonings drawn from the nature of the latter. The true distinction between these forms was also adverted to on a former occasion. It is, that in a democracy, the people meet and exercise the government in person; in a republic they assemble and administer it by their representatives and agents. A democracy consequently will be confined to a small spot. A republic may be extended over a large region.

To this accidental source of the error may be added the artifice of some celebrated authors, whose writings have had a great share in forming the modern standard of political opinions. Being subjects either of an absolute, or limited monarchy, they have endeavored to heighten the advantages or palliate the evils of those forms; by placing in comparison with them, the vices and defects of the republican, and by citing as specimens of the latter, the turbulent democracies of ancient Greece, and modern Italy. Under the confusion of names, it has been an easy task to transfer to a republic, observations applicable to a democracy only, and among others, the observation that it can never be established but among a small number of people, living within a small compass of territory.

Such a fallacy may have been the less perceived as most of the governments of antiquity were of the democratic species; and even in modern Europe, to which we owe the great principle of representation, no example is seen of a government wholly popular, and founded at the same time wholly on that principle. If Europe has the merit of discovering this great mechanical power in government, by the simple agency of which, the will of the largest political body may be concentred, and its force directed to any object, which the public good requires; America can claim the merit of making the discovery the basis of unmixed and extensive republics. It is only to be lamented, that any of her citizens should wish to deprive her of the additional merit of displaying its full efficacy on the establishment of the comprehensive system now under her consideration.

As the natural limit of a democracy is that distance from the central point, which will just permit the most remote citizens to assemble as often as their public functions demand; and will include no greater number than can join in those functions; so the natural limit of a republic is that distance from the center, which will barely allow the representatives of the people to meet as often as may be necessary for the administration of public affairs. Can it be said, that the limits of the United States exceed this distance? It will not be said by those who recollect that the Atlantic coast is the longest side of the union; that during the term of thirteen years, the representatives of the States have been almost continually assembled; and that the members from the most distant States are not chargeable with greater intermissions of attendance, than those from the States in the neighbourhood of Congress. . . .

Publius continues here, and in several later paragraphs, with some detailed geographical considerations that support his argument.

Favorable as this view of the subject may be, some observations remain which will place it in a light still more satisfactory.

In the first place it is to be remembered, that the general government is not to be charged with the whole power of making and administering laws. Its jurisdiction is limited to certain enumerated objects, which concern all the members of the republic, but which are not to be attained by the separate provisions of any. The subordinate governments which can extend their care to all those other objects, which can be separately provided for, will retain their due authority and activity. Were it proposed by the plan of the Convention to abolish the governments of the particular States, its adversaries would have some ground for their objection, though it would not be difficult to shew that if they were abolished, the general government would be compelled by the principle of self-preservation, to reinstate them in their proper jurisdiction. . . .

Let it be remarked in the third place, that the intercourse throughout the union will be daily facilitated by new improvements. Roads will every where be shortened, and kept in better order; accommodations for travellers will be multiplied and meliorated; and interior navigation on our eastern side will be opened throughout, or nearly throughout the whole extent of the Thirteen States. The communication between the western and Atlantic districts, and between different parts of each, will be rendered more and more easy by those numerous canals with which the beneficence of nature has intersected our country, and which art finds it so little difficult to connect and complete. . . .

I submit to you my fellow citizens, these considerations, in full confidence that the good sense which has so often marked your decisions, will allow them their due weight and effect; and that you will never suffer difficulties, however formidable in appearance or however fashionable the error on which they may be founded, to drive you into the gloomy and perilous scene into which the advocates for disunion would conduct you. Hearken not to the unnatural voice which tells you that the people of America, knit together as they are by so many chords of affection, can no longer live together as members of the same family; can no longer continue the mutual guardians of their mutual happiness; can no longer be fellow citizens of one great respectable and flourishing empire. Hearken not to the voice which petulantly tells you that the form of government recommended for your adoption is a novelty in the political world; that it has never yet had a place in the theories of the wildest projectors; that it rashly attempts what it is impossible to accomplish. No my countrymen, shut your ears against this unhallowed language. Shut your hearts against the poison which it conveys; the kindred blood which flows in the veins of American citizens, the mingled blood which they have shed in defence of their sacred rights, consecrate their union, and excite horror at the idea of their becoming aliens, rivals, enemies. And if novelties are to be shunned, believe me the most alarming of all novelties, the most wild of all projects, the most rash of all attempts, is that of rending us in pieces, in order to preserve our liberties and promote our happiness. But why is the experiment of an extended republic to be rejected merely because it may comprise what is new? Is it not the glory of the people of America, that whilst they have paid a decent regard to the opinions of former times and other nations, they have not suffered a blind veneration for antiquity, for custom, or for names, to overrule the suggestions of their own good sense, the knowledge of their own situation, and the lessons of their own experience? To this manly spirit, posterity will be indebted for the possession, and the world for the example of the numerous innovations displayed on the American theatre, in favor of private rights and public happiness. Had no important step been taken by the leaders of the revolution for which a precedent could not be discovered, no government established of which an exact model did not present itself, the people of the United States might, at this moment, have been numbered among the melancholy victims of misguided councils, must at best have been labouring under the weight of some of those forms which have crushed the liberties of the rest of mankind. Happily for America, happily we trust for the whole human race, they pursued a new and more noble course. They accomplished a revolution which has no parallel in the annals of human society: They reared the fabrics of governments which have no model on the face of the globe. They formed the design of a great confederacy, which it is incumbent on their successors to improve and perpetuate. If their works betray imperfections, we wonder at the fewness of them. If they erred most in the structure of the union; this was the work most difficult to be executed; this is the work which has been new modelled by the act of your Convention, and it is that act on which you are now to deliberate and to decide.

17

FEDERALIST NO. 15 (HAMILTON)
December 1, 1787

WE MAY INDEED WITH PROPRIETY be said to have reached almost the last stage of national humiliation. There is scarcely any thing that can wound the pride, or degrade the character of an independent nation, which we do not experience. Are there engagements to the performance of which we are held by every tie respectable among men? These are the subjects of constant and unblushing violation. Do we owe debts to foreigners and to our own citizens contracted in a time of imminent peril, for the preservation of our political existence? These remain without any proper or satisfactory provision for their discharge. Have we valuable territories and important posts in the possession of a foreign power, which by express stipulations ought long since to have been surrendered? These are still retained, to the prejudice of our interests not less than of our rights. Are we in a condition to resent, or to repel the aggression? We have neither troops nor treasury nor government. Are we even in a condition to remonstrate with dignity? The just imputations on our own faith, in respect to the same treaty, ought first to be removed. Are we entitled by nature and compact to a free participation in the navigation of the Mississippi? Spain excludes us from it. Is public credit an indispensable resource in time of public danger? We seem to have abandoned its cause as desperate and irretrievable. Is commerce of importance to national wealth? Ours is at the lowest point of declension. Is respectability in the eyes of foreign powers a safeguard against foreign encroachments? The imbecility of our Government even forbids them to treat with us: Our ambassadors abroad are the mere pageants of mimic sovereignty. Is a violent and unnatural decrease in the value of land a symptom of national distress? The price of improved land in most parts of the country is much lower than can be accounted for by the quantity of waste land at market, and can only be fully explained by that want of private and public confidence, which are so alarmingly prevalent among all ranks and which have a direct tendency to depreciate property of every kind. Is private credit the friend and patron of industry? That most useful kind which relates to borrowing and lending is reduced within the narrowest limits, and this still more from an opinion of insecurity than from the scarcity of money. To shorten an enumeration of particulars which can afford neither pleasure nor instruction it may in general be demanded, what indication is there of national disorder, poverty and insignificance that could befal a community so peculiarly blessed with natural advantages as we are, which does not form a part of the dark catalogue of our public misfortunes?

This is the melancholy situation, to which we have been brought by those very maxims and councils, which would now deter us from adopting the proposed constitution; and which not content with having conducted us to the brink of a precipice, seem resolved to plunge us into the abyss, that awaits us below. Here, my Countrymen, impelled by every motive that ought to influence an enlightened people, let us make a firm stand for our safety, our tranquillity, our dignity, our reputation. Let us at last break the fatal charm which has too long seduced us from the paths of felicity and prosperity.

It is true, as has been before observed, that facts too stubborn to be resisted have produced a species of general assent to the abstract proposition that there exist material defects in our national system; but the usefulness of the concession, on the part of the old adversaries of fœderal measures, is destroyed by a strenuous opposition to a remedy, upon the only principles, that can give it a chance of success. While they admit that the Government of the United States is destitute of energy; they contend against conferring upon it those powers which are requisite to supply that energy: They seem still to aim at things repugnant and irreconcilable—at an augmentation of Fœderal authority without a diminution of State authority—at sovereignty in the Union and complete independence in the members. They still in fine seem to cherish with blind devotion the political monster of an *imperium in imperio*. This renders a full display of the principal defects of the confederation necessary, in order to shew, that the evils we experience do not proceed from minute or partial imperfections, but from fundamental errors in the structure of the building which cannot be amended otherwise than by an alteration in the first principles and main pillars of the fabric.

The great and radical vice in the construction of the existing Confederation is in the principle of LEGISLATION for STATES or GOVERNMENTS, in their CORPORATE or COLLECTIVE CAPACITIES and as contradistinguished from the INDIVIDUALS of whom they consist. Though this principle does not run through all the powers delegated to the Union; yet it pervades and governs those, on which the efficacy of the rest depends. Except as to the rule of apportionment, the United States have an indefinite discretion to make requisitions for men and money; but they have no authority to raise either by regulations extending to the individual citizens of America. The consequence of this is, that though in theory their resolutions concerning those objects are laws, constitutionally binding on the members of the Union, yet in practice they are mere recommendations, which the States observe or disregard at their option.

It is a singular instance of the capriciousness of the human mind, that after all the admonitions we have had from experience on this head, there should still be found men, who object to the New Constitution for deviating from a principle which has been found the bane of the old; and which is in itself evidently incompatible with the idea of GOVERNMENT; a principle in short which if it is to be executed at all must substitute the violent and sanguinary agency of the sword to the mild influence of the Magistracy.

There is nothing absurd or impracticable in the idea of a league or alliance between independent nations, for certain defined purposes precisely stated in a treaty; regulating all the details of time, place, circumstance and quantity; leaving nothing to future discretion; and depending for its execution on the good faith of the parties. Compacts of this kind exist among all civilized nations subject to the usual vicissitudes of peace and war, of observance and non observance, as the interests or passions of the contracting powers dictate. In the early part of the present century, there was an epidemical rage in Europe for this species of compacts; from which the politicians of the times fondly hoped for benefits which were never realised. With a view to establishing the equilibrium of power and the peace of that part of the world, all the resources of negotiation were exhausted, and triple and quadruple alliances were formed; but they were scarcely formed before they were broken, giving an instructive but afflicting lesson to mankind how little dependence is to be placed on treaties which have no other sanction than the obligations of good faith; and which oppose general considerations of peace and justice to the impulse of any immediate interest and passion.

If the particular States in this country are disposed to stand in a similar relation to each other, and to drop the project of a general DISCRETIONARY SUPERINTENDENCE, the scheme would indeed be pernicious, and would entail upon us all the mischiefs that have been enumerated under the first head; but it would have the merit of being at least consistent and practicable. Abandoning all views towards a confederate Government, this would bring us to a simple alliance offensive and defensive; and would place us in a situation to be alternately friends and enemies of each other as our mutual jealousies and rivalships nourished by the intrigues of foreign nations should prescribe to us.

But if we are unwilling to be placed in this perilous situation; if we will still adhere to the design of a national government, or which is the same thing of a superintending power under the direction of a common Council, we must resolve to incorporate into our plan those ingredients which may be considered as forming the characteristic difference between a league and a government; we must extend the authority of the union to the persons of the citizens,—the only proper objects of government.

Government implies the power of making laws. It is essential to the idea of a law, that it be attended with a sanction; or, in other words, a penalty or punishment for disobedience. If there be no penalty annexed to disobedience, the resolutions or commands which pretend to be laws will in fact amount to nothing more than advice or recommendation. This penalty, whatever it may be, can only be inflicted in two ways; by the agency of the Courts and Ministers of Justice, or by military force by the COERTION of the magistracy, or by the COERTION of arms. The first kind can evidently apply only to men—the last kind must of necessity be employed against bodies politic, or communities or States. It is evident, that there is no process of a court by which their observance of the laws can in the last resort be enforced. Sentences may be denounced against them for violation of their duty; but these sentences can only be carried into execution by the sword. In an association where the general authority is confined to the collective bodies of the communities that compose it, every breach of the laws must involve a state of war, and military execution must become the only instrument of civil obedience. Such a state of things can certainly not deserve the name of government, nor would any prudent man choose to commit his happiness to it.

There was a time when we were told that breaches, by the States, of the regulations of the fœderal authority were not to be expected—that a sense of common interest would preside over the conduct of the respective members, and would beget a full compliance with all the constitutional requisitions of the Union. This language at the present day would appear as wild as a great part of what we now hear from the same quarter will be thought, when we shall have received further lessons from that best oracle of wisdom, experience. It at all times betrayed an ignorance of the true springs by which human conduct is actuated, and belied the original inducements to the establishment of civil power. Why has government been instituted at all? Because the passions of men will not conform to the dictates of reason and justice, without constraint. Has it been found that bodies of men act with more rectitude or greater disinterestedness than individuals? The contrary of this has been inferred by all accurate observers of the conduct of mankind; and the inference is founded upon obvious reasons. Regard to reputation has a less active influence, when the infamy of a bad action is to be divided among a number, than when it is to fall singly upon one. A spirit of faction which is apt to mingle its poison in the deliberations of all bodies of men, will often hurry the persons of whom they are composed into improprieties and excesses, for which they would blush in a private capacity. . . .

18

FEDERALIST NO. 23 (HAMILTON)
December 18, 1787

T HE NECESSITY OF a Constitution, at least equally energetic with the one proposed, to the preservation of the Union, is the point, at the examination of which we are now arrived.

This enquiry will naturally divide itself into three branches—the objects to be provided for by a Fœderal Government—the quantity of power necessary to the accomplishment of those objects—the persons upon whom that power ought to operate. Its distribution and organization will more properly claim our attention under the succeeding head.

The principal purposes to be answered by Union are these—The common defence of the members—the preservation of the public peace as well against internal convulsions as external attacks—the regulation of commerce with other nations and between the States—the superintendence of our intercourse, political and commercial, with foreign countries.

The authorities essential to the care of the common defence are these—to raise armies—to build and equip fleets—to prescribe rules for the government of both—to direct their operations—to provide for their support. These powers ought to exist without limitation: *Because it is impossible to foresee or define the extent and variety of national exigencies, or the correspondent extent & variety of the means which may be necessary to satisfy them.* The circumstances that endanger the safety of nations are infinite; and for this reason no constitutional shackles can wisely be imposed on the power to which the care of it is committed. This power ought to be co-extensive with all the possible combinations of such circumstances; and ought to be under the direction of the same councils, which are appointed to preside over the common defence.

This is one of those truths, which to a correct and unprejudiced mind, carries its own evidence along with it; and may be obscured, but cannot be made plainer by argument or reasoning. It rests upon axioms as simple as they are universal. The *means* ought to be proportioned to the *end;* the persons, from whose agency the attainment of any *end* is expected, ought to possess *the means* by which it is to be attained.

Whether there ought to be a Fœderal Government intrusted with the care of the common defence, is a question in the first instance open to discussion; but the moment it is decided in the affirmative, it will follow, that that government ought to be cloathed with all the powers requisite to the complete execution of its trust. And unless it can be shewn, that the circumstances which may affect the public safety are reducible within certain determinate limits; unless the contrary of this position can be fairly and rationally disputed, it must be admitted, as a necessary consequence, that there can be no limitation of that authority, which is to provide for the defence and protection of the community, in any matter essential to its efficacy; that is, in any matter essential to the *formation, direction* or *support* of the NATIONAL FORCES. . . .

The omitted paragraphs deal in detail with some of the powers necessary to the "common defense."

Every view we may take of the subject, as candid enquirers after truth, will serve to convince us, that it is both unwise and dangerous to deny the Fœderal Government an unconfined authority, as to all those objects which are intrusted to its management. It will indeed deserve the most vigilant and careful attention of the people, to see that it be modelled in such a manner, as to admit of its being safely vested with the requisite powers. If any plan which has been, or may be offered to our consideration, should not, upon a dispassionate inspection, be found to answer this description, it ought to be rejected. A government, the Constitution of which renders it unfit to be trusted with all the powers, which a free people *ought to delegate to any government,* would be an unsafe and improper depository of the NATIONAL INTERESTS, wherever THESE can with propriety be confided, the co-incident powers may safely accompany them. This is the true result of all just reasoning upon the subject. And the adversaries of the plan, promulgated by the Convention, ought to have confined themselves to showing that the internal structure of the proposed government, was such as to render it unworthy of the confidence of the people. They ought not to have wandered into inflammatory declamations, and unmeaning cavils about the extent of the powers. The POWERS are not too extensive for the OBJECTS of Fœderal administration, or in other words, for the management of our NATIONAL INTERESTS; nor can any satisfactory argument be framed to shew that they are chargeable with such an excess. If it be true, as has been insinuated by some of the writers on the other side, that the difficulty arises from the nature of the thing, and that the extent of the country will not permit us to form a government, in which such ample powers can safely be reposed, it would prove that we ought to contract our views, and resort to the expedient of separate Confederacies, which will move within more practicable spheres. For the absurdity must continually stare us in the face of confiding to a government, the direction of the most essential national interests, without daring to trust it with the authorities which are indispensable to their proper and efficient management. Let us not attempt to reconcile contradictions, but firmly embrace a rational alternative.

I trust, however, that the impracticability of one general system cannot be shewn. I am greatly mistaken, if any thing of weight, has yet been advanced of this tendency; and I flatter myself, that the observations which have been made in the course of these papers, have sufficed to place the reverse of that position in as clear a light as any matter still in the womb of time and experience can be susceptible of. This at all events must be evident, that the very difficulty itself drawn from the extent of the country, is the strongest argument in favor of an energetic government; for any other can certainly never preserve the Union of so large an empire. If we embrace the tenets of those, who oppose the adoption of the proposed Constitution, as the standard of our political creed, we cannot fail to verify the gloomy doctrines, which predict the impracticability of a national system, pervading the entire limits of the present Confederacy.

Federalist 37 is a kind of preface to the examination of republican government. Rhetorically, it has a somewhat apologetic character; it appeals to the reader to be sympathetic with the profound difficulties the Constitutional Convention faced. The entire paper is important, but two specific paragraphs only are presented here.

19

FEDERALIST NO. 37 (MADISON)
January 11, 1788

THE NOVELTY OF THE UNDERTAKING immediately strikes us. It has been shewn in the course of these papers, that the existing Confederation is founded on principles which are fallacious; that we must consequently change this first foundation, and with it, the superstructure resting upon it. It has been shewn, that the other confederacies which could be consulted as precedents, have been viciated by the same erroneous principles, and can therefore furnish no other light than that of beacons, which give warning of the course to be shunned, without pointing out that which ought to be pursued. The most that the Convention could do in such a situation, was to avoid the errors suggested by the past experience of other countries, as well as of our own; and to provide a convenient mode of rectifying their own errors, as future experience may unfold them.

Among the difficulties encountered by the Convention, a very important one must have lain, in combining the requisite stability and energy in Government, with the inviolable attention due to liberty, and to the Republican form. Without substantially accomplishing this part of their undertaking, they would have very imperfectly fulfilled the object of their appointment, or the expectation of the public: Yet, that it could not be easily accomplished, will be denied by no one, who is unwilling to betray his ignorance of the subject. Energy in Government is essential to that security against external and internal danger, and to that prompt and salutary execution of the laws, which enter into the very definition of good Government. Stability in Government, is essential to national character, and to the advantages annexed to it, as well as to that repose and confidence in the minds of the people, which are among the chief blessings of civil society. An irregular and mutable legislation, is not more an evil in itself, than it is odious to the people; and it may be pronounced with assurance, that the people of this country, enlightened as they are, with regard to the nature, and interested, as the great body of them are, in the effects of good Government, will never be satisfied, till some remedy be applied to the vicissitudes and uncertainties, which characterize the State administrations. On comparing, however, these valuable ingredients with the vital principles of liberty, we must perceive at once, the difficulty of mingling them together in their due proportions. The genius of Republican liberty, seems to demand on one side, not only that all power should be derived from the people; but, that those entrusted with it should be kept in dependence on the people, by a short duration of their appointments; and, that, even during this short period, the trust should be placed not in a few, but in a number of hands. Stability, on the contrary, requires, that the hands, in which power is lodged, should continue for a length of time, the same. A frequent change of men will result from a frequent return of electors, and a frequent change of measures, from a frequent change of men: whilst energy in Government requires not only a certain duration of power, but the execution of it by a single hand. How far the Convention may have succeeded in this part of their work, will better appear on a more accurate view of it. From the cursory view, here taken, it must clearly appear to have been an arduous part. . . .

20
FEDERALIST NO. 39 (MADISON)
January 16, 1788

THE FIRST QUESTION that offers itself is, whether the general form and aspect of the government be strictly republican? It is evident that no other form would be reconcileable with the genius of the people of America; with the fundamental principles of the revolution; or with that honorable determination, which animates every votary of freedom, to rest all our political experiments on the capacity of mankind for self-government. If the plan of the Convention therefore be found to depart from the republican character, its advocates must abandon it as no longer defensible.

What then are the distinctive characters of the republican form? Were an answer to this question to be sought, not by recurring to principles, but in the application of the term by political writers, to the constitutions of different States, no satisfactory one would ever be found. Holland, in which no particle of the supreme authority is derived from the people, has passed almost universally under the denomination of a republic. The same title has been bestowed on Venice, where absolute power over the great body of the people, is exercised in the most absolute manner, by a small body of hereditary nobles. Poland, which is a mixture of aristocracy and of monarchy in their worst forms, has been dignified with the same appellation. The government of England, which has one republican branch only, combined with a hereditary aristocracy and monarchy, has with equal impropriety been frequently placed on the list of republics. These examples, which are nearly as dissimilar to each other as to a genuine republic, shew the extreme inaccuracy with which the term has been used in political disquisitions.

If we resort for a criterion, to the different principles on which different forms of government are established, we may define a republic to be, or at least may bestow that name on, a government which derives all its powers directly or indirectly from the great body of the people; and is administered by persons holding their offices during pleasure, for a limited period, or during good behaviour. It is *essential* to such a government, that it be derived from the great body of the society, not from an inconsiderable proportion, or a favored class of it; otherwise a handful of tyrannical nobles, exercising their oppressions by a delegation of their powers, might aspire to the rank of republicans, and claim for their government the honorable title of republic. It is *sufficient* for such a government, that the persons administering it be appointed, either directly or indirectly, by the people; and that they hold their appointments by either of the tenures just specified; otherwise every government in the United States, as well as every other popular government that has been or can be well organized or well executed, would be degraded from the republican character. According to the Constitution of every State in the Union, some or other of the officers of government are appointed indirectly only by the people. According to most of them the chief magistrate himself is so appointed. And according to one, this mode of appointment is extended to one of the coordinate branches of the legislature. According to all the Constitutions also, the tenure of the highest offices is extended to a definite period, and in many instances, both within the legislative and executive departments, to a period of years. According to the provisions of most of the constitutions, again, as well as according to the most respectable and received opinions on the subject, the members of the judiciary department are to retain their offices by the firm tenure of good behaviour.

On comparing the Constitution planned by the Convention, with the standard here fixed, we perceive at once that it is in the most rigid sense conformable to it. The House of Representatives, like that of one branch at least of all the State Legislatures, is elected immediately by the great body of the people. The Senate, like the present Congress, and the Senate of

Maryland, derives its appointment indirectly from the people. The President is indirectly derived from the choice of the people, according to the example in most of the States. Even the judges, with all other officers of the Union, will, as in the several States, be the choice, though a remote choice, of the people themselves. The duration of the appointments is equally conformable to the republican standard, and to the model of the State Constitutions. The House of Representatives is periodically elective as in all the States: and for the period of two years as in the State of South-Carolina. The Senate is elective for the period of six years; which is but one year more than the period of the Senate of Maryland; and but two more than that of the Senates of New-York and Virginia. The President is to continue in office for the period of four years; as in New-York and Delaware, the chief magistrate is elected for three years, and in South-Carolina for two years. In the other States the election is annual. In several of the States however, no constitutional provision is made for the impeachment of the Chief Magistrate. And in Delaware and Virginia, he is not impeachable till out of office. The President of the United States is impeachable at any time during his continuance in office. The tenure by which the Judges are to hold their places, is, as it unquestionably ought to be, that of good behaviour. The tenure of the ministerial offices generally will be a subject of legal regulation, conformably to the reason of the case, and the example of the State Constitutions.

Could any further proof be required of the republican complextion of this system, the most decisive one might be found in its absolute prohibition of titles of nobility, both under the Federal and the State Governments; and in its express guarantee of the republican form to each of the latter.

But it was not sufficient, say the adversaries of the proposed Constitution, for the Convention to adhere to the republican form. They ought, with equal care, to have preserved the *federal* form, which regards the union as a *confederacy* of sovereign States; instead of which, they have framed a *national* government, which regards the union as a *consolidation* of the States. And it is asked by what authority this bold and radical innovation was undertaken. The handle which has been made of this objection requires, that it should be examined with some precision.

Without enquiring into the accuracy of the distinction on which the objection is founded, it will be necessary to a just estimate of its force, first to ascertain the real character of the government in question; secondly, to enquire how far the Convention were authorised to propose such a government; and thirdly, how far the duty they owed to their country, could supply any defect of regular authority.

In order to ascertain the real character of the government it may be considered in relation to the foundation on which it is to be established; to the sources from which its ordinary powers are to be drawn; to the operation of those powers; to the extent of them; and to the authority by which future changes in the government are to be introduced. . . .

The omitted paragraphs deal in detail with the topics stated immediately above; Publius distinguishes the characteristics of the proposed government as federal in some respects and as national in others. The conclusion of *Federalist* 39 regarding this somewhat complicated and perplexing question follows.

The proposed Constitution therefore is in strictness neither a national nor a federal Constitution; but a composition of both. In its foundation, it is federal, not national; in the sources from which the ordinary powers of the Government are drawn, it is partly federal, and partly national: in the operation of these powers, it is national, not federal: In the extent of them again, it is federal, not national: And finally, in the authoritative mode of introducing amendments, it is neither wholly federal, nor wholly national.

Federalists 47 through 51 deal specifically with the question of the separation of powers. *Federalist* 51 is Publius's famous summary on this important theoretical issue.

21
FEDERALIST NO. 51 (MADISON)
February 6, 1788

To what expedient then shall we finally resort for maintaining in practice the necessary partition of power among the several departments, as laid down in the constitution? The only answer that can be given is, that as all these exterior provisions are found to be inadequate, the defect must be supplied, by so contriving the interior structure of the government, as that its several constituent parts may, by their mutual relations, be the means of keeping each other in their proper places. Without presuming to undertake a full developement of this important idea, I will hazard a few general observations, which may perhaps place it in a clearer light, and enable us to form a more correct judgment of the principles and structure of the government planned by the convention.

In order to lay a due foundation for that separate and distinct exercise of the different powers of government, which to a certain extent, is admitted on all hands to be essential to the preservation of liberty, it is evident that each department should have a will of its own; and consequently should be so constituted, that the members of each should have as little agency as possible in the appointment of the members of the others. Were this principle rigorously adhered to, it would require that all the appointments for the supreme executive, legislative, and judiciary magistracies, should be drawn from the same fountain of authority, the people, through channels, having no communication whatever with one another. Perhaps such a plan of constructing the several departments would be less difficult in practice than it may in contemplation appear. Some difficulties however, and some additional expence, would attend the execution of it. Some deviations therefore from the principle must be admitted. In the constitution of the judiciary department in particular, it might be inexpedient to insist rigorously on the principle; first, because peculiar qualifications being essential in the members, the primary consideration ought to be to select that mode of choice, which best secures these qualifications; secondly, because the permanent tenure by which the appointments are held in that department, must soon destroy all sense of dependence on the authority conferring them.

It is equally evident that the members of each department should be as little dependent as possible on those of the others, for the emoluments annexed to their offices. Were the executive magistrate, or the judges, not independent of the legislature in this particular, their independence in every other would be merely nominal.

But the great security against a gradual concentration of the several powers in the same department, consists in giving to those who administer each department, the necessary constitutional means, and personal motives, to resist encroachments of the others. The provision for defence must in this, as in all other cases, be made commensurate to the danger of attack. Ambition must be made to counteract ambition. The interest of the man must be connected with the constitutional rights of the place. It may be a reflection on human nature, that such devices should be necessary to controul the abuses of government. But what is government itself but the greatest of all reflections on human nature? If men were angels, no government would be necessary. If angels were to govern men, neither external nor internal controuls on government would be necessary. In framing a government which is to be administered by men over men, the great difficulty lies in this: You must first enable the government to controul the governed; and in the next place, oblige it to controul itself. A dependence on the people is no doubt the primary controul on the government; but experience has taught mankind the necessity of auxiliary precautions.

This policy of supplying by opposite and rival interests, the defect of better motives, might be traced through the whole system of human affairs, private as well as public. We see it particularly displayed in all the subordinate distributions of power; where the constant aim is to divide and arrange the several offices in such a manner as that each may be a check on the other; that the private interest of every individual, may be a centinel over the public rights. These inventions of prudence cannot be less requisite in the distribution of the supreme powers of the state.

But it is not possible to give to each department an equal power of self defence. In republican government the legislative authority, necessarily, predominates. The remedy for this inconveniency is, to divide the legislature into different branches; and to render them by different modes of election, and different principles of action, as little connected with each other, as the nature of their common functions, and their common dependence on the society, will admit. It may even be necessary to guard against dangerous encroachments by still further precautions. As the weight of the legislative authority requires that it should be thus divided, the weakness of the executive may require, on the other hand, that it should be fortified. An absolute negative, on the legislature, appears at first view to be the natural defence with which the executive magistrate should be armed. But perhaps it would be neither altogether safe, nor alone sufficient. On ordinary occasions, it might not be exerted with the requisite firmness; and on extraordinary occasions, it might be perfidiously abused. May not this defect of an absolute negative be supplied, by some qualified connection between this weaker department, and the weaker branch of the stronger department, by which the latter may be led to support the constitutional rights of the former, without being too much detached from the rights of its own department?

If the principles on which these observations are founded be just, as I persuade myself they are, and they be applied as a criterion, to the several state constitutions, and to the federal constitution, it will be found, that if the latter does not perfectly correspond with them, the former are infinitely less able to bear such a test.

There are moreover two considerations particularly applicable to the federal system of America, which place that system in a very interesting point of view.

First. In a single republic, all the power surrendered by the people, is submitted to the administration of a single government; and usurpations are guarded against by a division of the government into distinct and separate departments. In the compound republic of America, the power surrendered by the people, is first divided between two distinct governments, and then the portion allotted to each, subdivided among distinct and separate departments. Hence a double security arises to the rights of the people. The different governments will controul each other; at the same time that each will be controuled by itself.

Second. It is of great importance in a republic, not only to guard the society against the oppression of its rulers; but to guard one part of the society against the injustice of the other part. Different interests necessarily exist in different classes of citizens. If a majority be united by a common interest, the rights of the minority will be insecure. There are but two methods of providing against this evil: The one by creating a will in the community independent of the majority, that is, of the society itself; the other by comprehending in the society so many separate descriptions of citizens, as will render an unjust combination of a majority of the whole, very improbable, if not impracticable. The first method prevails in all governments possessing an hereditary or self appointed authority. This at best is but a precarious security; because a power independent of the society may as well espouse the unjust views of the major, as the rightful interests, of the minor party, and may possibly be turned against both parties. The second method will be exemplified in the federal republic of the United States. Whilst all authority in it will be derived from and dependent on the society, the society itself will be broken into so many parts, interests and classes of citizens, that the rights of individuals or of the minority, will be in little danger from interested combinations of the majority. In a free government, the security for civil rights must be the same as for religious rights. It consists in the one case in the multiplicity of interests, and in the other, in the multiplicity of sects. The degree of security in both cases will depend on the number of interests and sects; and this may be presumed to depend on the extent of country and number of people comprehended under the same government. This view of the subject must particularly recommend a proper federal system to all the sincere and considerate friends of republican government: Since it shews that in exact proportion as the territory of the union may be formed into more circumscribed confederacies or states, oppressive combinations of a majority will be facilitated, the best security under the republican form, for the rights of every class of citizens, will be diminished; and consequently, the stability and independence of some member of the government, the only other security, must be proportionally increased. Justice is the end of government. It is the end of civil society. It ever has been, and ever will be pursued, until it be obtained, or until liberty be lost in the pursuit. In a society under the forms of which the stronger faction can readily unite and oppress the weaker, anarchy may as truly be said to reign, as in a state of nature where the weaker individual is not secured against the violence of the stronger: And as in the latter state even the stronger individuals are prompted by the uncertainty of their condition, to submit to a government which may protect the weak as well as themselves: So in the former state, will the more powerful factions or parties be gradually induced by a like motive, to wish for a government which will protect all parties, the weaker as well as the more powerful. It can be little doubted, that if the state of Rhode Island was separated from the confederacy, and left to itself, the insecurity of rights under the popular form of government within such narrow limits, would be displayed by such reiterated oppressions of factious majorities, that some power altogether independent of the people would soon be called for by the voice of the very factions whose misrule had proved the necessity of it. In the extended republic of the United States, and among the great variety of interests, parties and sects which it embraces, a coalition of a majority of the whole society could seldom take place on any other principles than those of justice and the general good; and there being thus less danger to a minor from the will of the major party, there must be less pretext also, to provide for the security of the former, by introducing into the government a will not independent on the latter; or in other words, a will independent of the society itself. It is no less certain than it is important, notwithstanding the contrary opinions which have been entertained, that the larger the society, provided it lie within a practicable sphere, the more duly capable it will be of self government. And happily for the *republican cause,* the practicable sphere may be carried to a very great extent, by a judicious modification and mixture of the *federal principle.*

III

JOHN MARSHALL
(1755–1835)

JOHN MARSHALL, serving as a member of the Virginia convention called in 1788 to consider ratification of the proposed new Constitution of the United States, allied himself with James Madison, Edmund Randolph, and others who supported ratification. Marshall went to Paris in 1797–98 as a member of a three-man commission appointed by President John Adams to try to improve relations with France. He was elected to the U.S. House of Representatives as a Federalist in 1799 and the following year accepted President Adams's appointment as Secretary of State, although he had declined various appointments previously offered by Presidents Washington and Adams. He also accepted appointment as the Chief Justice of the United States in 1801 and served in that capacity until his death in 1835.

Marshall has no rival as a figure in the American judiciary. While the U.S. Supreme Court has become a more powerful political force than any other court in the English-speaking world, it has somehow managed to continue in high esteem as a *court*. It has, that is, been politically powerful in the highest sense without becoming politicized in the lowest. Marshall made a greater contribution to the character and rank of the Court than any other man. When late medieval commentators refer to "the Philosopher" with a capital P, there is no doubt in anyone's mind that they mean Aristotle. Similarly, when judges, lawyers, historians, and scholars speak of "the Great Chief Justice," there is no doubt but that it is Marshall of whom they speak.

Of all the cases in American Constitutional law, the most influential has been *Marbury* v. *Madison,* which involved questions that excited great partisan enmity between the Federalists and the Republicans (the party whose heirs are *now* known as the Democrats). The whole case could perhaps have been disposed of easily by the Court on narrow, technical grounds, but Marshall's opinion for the Court seemed to welcome the opportunity of facing the questions it found there. The chief question transcended the Federalist-Republican disputes of the day and provided the occasion for the assertion by the Court of its duty to *ignore* acts of Congress which it found to be contrary to provisions of the Constitution.

The question whether an act, repugnant to the constitution, can become the law of the land, is a question deeply interesting to the United States; but, happily, not of an intricacy proportioned to its interest. . . . The powers of the legislature are defined and limited; and that those limits may not be mistaken or forgotten, the constitution is written. . . . The distinction between a government with limited and unlimited powers is abolished . . . if acts prohibited and acts allowed, are of equal obligation. . . . The constitution is either a superior, paramount law, unchangeable by ordinary means, or it is on a level with ordinary legislative acts, and like other acts, is alterable when the legislature shall so please to alter it. If the former part of the alternative be true, then a legislative act, contrary to the constitution, is not law: if the latter part be true, then written constitutions are absurd attempts, on the part of the people, to limit a power, in its own nature illimitable.— *Marbury* v. *Madison,* 1 Cr. 137 (1803).

While the power of the national legislature is surely limited by the Constitution, however, Marshall elsewhere contended that there was no reason to construe the limitations in such a way as to negate the effect of those clauses that are affirmative grants of power. In another great case, he made these declarations for the Court:

This government is acknowledged by all, to be one of enumerated powers. . . . But the question respecting the extent of the powers actually granted, is perpetually arising, and will probably continue to arise, so long as our system shall exist. . . . [T]here is no phrase in the [Constitution] which, like the articles of confederation, excludes incidental or implied powers; and which requires that everything granted shall be expressly and minutely described. Even the 10th amendment . . . omits the word "expressly," . . . thus leaving the question, whether the particular power . . . has been delegated . . . to depend on a fair construction of the whole instrument. . . . In considering this question, then, we must never forget that it is a *constitution* we are expounding.—*McCulloch* v. *Maryland,* 4 Wheat. 316 (1819).

Because he owned property involved in another case, Marshall disqualified himself from taking part in the decision that held that decisions in civil cases by state courts were, if the right questions were raised, subject to review by the U.S. Supreme Court (*Martin* v. *Hunter's Lessee,* 1 Wheat. 304 [1816]). He did give the opinion for the Court in a later case that asserted the power of that court to review decisions by state courts in criminal cases (*Cohens* v. *Virginia,* 6 Wheat. 264 [1821]), as he did in the case that established that the first eight amendments were limitations on the actions of the United States only, not on the several states (*Barron* v. *Baltimore,* 7 Pet. 243 [1833]). In a series of cases, he expounded that clause in Article 1, §10 of the Constitution that declares, "No State shall . . . pass any . . . Law impairing the Obligation of Contracts." In one of those cases he held the states *themselves* to be bound by contractual obligations despite claims of sovereign power which purported to rise above such obligations.

The principle asserted is that one legislature is competent to repeal any Act which a former legislature was competent to pass; and that one legislature cannot abridge the powers of a succeeding legislature. The correctness of this principle, so far as respects general legislation can never be controverted. But if an act be done under a law, a succeeding legislature cannot undo it. The past cannot be recalled by the most absolute power. *Fletcher* v. *Peck,* 6 Cr. 87 (1810).

At the Virginia ratifying convention on the adoption of the Constitution, Patrick Henry made a speech attacking the proposed Constitution. Marshall, among others, appeared before the convention to respond to Henry, noting that "The object of our inquiry is, *Is the power necessary, and is it guarded?*" Marshall's answer was that since the powers given by the Constitution to the national government *were* both necessary and guarded, it ought to be ratified by Virginia. Included here are his speech on the 10th, the report of his remarks on the 14th indicating his belief that the Constitution did not deprive the states of the power to employ their militia, and his speech on June 20th, in which he defended and explained at length Article III, which establishes and empowers a national judiciary.

Marshall's views on the Alien and Sedition Acts, which he presented in the form of a minority address to the Virginia legislature in December 1798, are also given here. The Sedition Act of 1798 imposed fines and imprisonment on persons who were convicted of trying to arouse discontent with the government, through writing, speaking, or in other ways. The Jeffersonian argument against the law was that the states were the only proper authorities for suppressing sedition. Marshall countered that the states must attend to local subjects and the nation to national affairs. He affirmed that the power to protect the nation against the intrigues and conspiracies of dangerous citizens falls under the general power of the nation to preserve itself. He maintained, moreover, that the law did not violate the First Amendment guarantee of freedom of speech and press when properly construed.

22

SPEECH IN VIRGINIA
CONVENTION ON RATIFICATION
OF THE CONSTITUTION
June 10, 1788

M r. Chairman, I conceive that the object of the discussion now before us is, whether democracy or despotism be most eligible. I am sure that those who framed the system submitted to our investigation, and those who now support it, intend the establishment and security of the former. The supporters of the Constitution claim the title of being firm friends of the liberty and the rights of mankind. They say that they consider it as the best means of protecting liberty. We, sir, idolize democracy. Those who oppose it have bestowed eulogiums on monarchy. We prefer this system to any monarchy, because we are convinced that it has a greater tendency to secure our liberty and promote our happiness. We admire it, because we think it a well-regulated democracy. It is recommended to the good people of this country: they are, through us, to declare whether it be such a plan of government as will establish and secure their freedom.

Permit me to attend to what the honorable gentleman [Mr. Henry] has said. He has expatiated on the necessity of a due attention to certain maxims—to certain fundamental principles, from which a free people ought never to depart. I concur with him in the propriety of the observance of such maxims. They are necessary in any government, but more essential to a democracy than to any other. What are the favorite maxims of democracy? A strict observance of justice and public faith, and a steady adherence to virtue. These, sir, are the principles of a good government. No mischief, no misfortune, ought to deter us from a strict observance of justice and public faith. Would to Heaven that these principles had been observed under the present government! Had this been the case, the friends of liberty would not be so willing now to part with it. Can we boast that our government is founded on these maxims? Can we pretend to the enjoyment of political freedom or security, when we are told that a man has been, by an act of Assembly, struck out of existence without a trial by jury, without examination, without being confronted with his accusers and witnesses, without the benefits of the law of the land? Where is our safety, when we are told that this act was justifiable because the person was not a Socrates? What has become of the worthy member's maxims? Is this one of them? Shall it be a maxim that a man shall be deprived of his life without the benefit of law? Shall such a deprivation of life be justified by answering, that the man's life was not taken *secundum artem* because he was a bad man? Shall it be a maxim that government ought not to be empowered to protect virtue?

The honorable member, after attempting to vindicate that tyrannical legislative act to which I have been alluding, proceeded to take a view of the dangers to which this country is exposed. He told us that the principal danger arose from a government which, if adopted, would give away the Mississippi. I intended to proceed regularly, by attending to the clause under debate; but I must reply to some observations which were dwelt upon to make impressions on our minds unfavorable to the plan upon the table. Have we no navigation in, or do we derive no benefit from, the Mississippi? How shall we retain it? By retaining that weak government which has hitherto kept it from us? Is it thus that we shall secure that navigation? Give the government the power of retaining it, and then we may hope to derive actual advantages from it. Till we do this, we cannot expect that a government which hitherto has not been able to protect it, will have the power to do it hereafter. Have we attended too long to consider whether this government would be able to protect us? Shall we wait for further proofs of its inefficacy? If, on mature consideration, the Constitution will be found to be perfectly right on the subject of treaties, and containing no danger of losing that navigation, will he still object? Will he object because eight states are unwilling to part with it? This is no good ground of objection.

He then stated the necessity and probability of obtaining amendments. This we ought to postpone until we come to that clause, and make up our minds whether there be any thing unsafe in this system. He conceived it impossible to obtain amendments after adopting it. If he was right, does not his own argument prove that, in his own conception, previous amendments cannot be had? for, sir, if subsequent amendments cannot be obtained, shall we get amendments before we ratify? The reasons against the latter do not apply against the former. There are in this state, and in every state in the Union, many who are decided enemies of the Union. Reflect on the probable conduct of such men. What will they do? They will bring amendments which are local in their nature, and which they know will not be accepted. What security have we that other states will not do the same? We are told that many in the states were violently opposed to it. They are more mindful of local interests. They will never propose such amendments as they think would be obtained. Disunion will be their object. This will be attained by the proposal of unreasonable amendments. This, sir, though a strong cause, is not the only one that will militate against previous amendments. Look at the comparative temper of this country now, and when the late federal Convention met. We had no idea then of any particular system. The formation of the most perfect plan was our object and wish. It was imagined that the states would accede to, and be pleased with, the proposition that would be made them. Consider the violence of opinions, the prejudices and animosities which have been since imbibed. Will not these operate greatly against mutual concessions, or a friendly concurrence? This will, however, be taken up more properly at another time. He says, we wish to have a strong, energetic, powerful government. We contend for a well-regulated democracy. He insinuates that the power of the government has been enlarged by the Convention, and that we may apprehend it will be enlarged by others. The Convention did not, in fact, assume any power.

They have proposed to our consideration a scheme of government which they thought advisable. We are not bound to adopt it, if we disapprove of it. Had not every individual in this community a right to tender that scheme which he thought most conducive to the welfare of his country? Have not several gentlemen already demonstrated that the Convention did not exceed their powers? But the Congress have the power of making bad laws, it seems. The Senate, with the President, he informs us, may make a treaty which shall be disadvantageous to us; and that, if they be not good men, it will not be a good Constitution. I shall ask the worthy member only, if the people at large, and they alone, ought to make laws and treaties? Has any man this in contemplation? You cannot exercise the powers of government personally yourselves. You must trust to agents. If so, will you dispute giving them the power of acting for you, from an existing possibility that they may abuse it? As long as it is impossible for you to transact your business in person, if you repose no confidence in delegates, because there is a possibility of their abusing it, you can have no government; for the power of doing good is inseparable from that of doing some evil.

We may derive from Holland lessons very beneficial to ourselves. Happy that country which can avail itself of the misfortunes of others—which can

gain knowledge from that source without fatal experience! What has produced the late disturbances in that country? The want of such a government
as is on your table, and having, in some measure, such a one as you are
about to part with. The want of proper powers in the government, the consequent deranged and relaxed administration, the violence of contending
parties, and inviting foreign powers to interpose in their disputes, have subjected them to all the mischiefs which have interrupted their harmony. I
cannot express my astonishment at his high-colored eulogium on such a
government. Can any thing be more dissimilar than the relation between
the British government and the colonies, and the relation between Congress
and the states? We *were not* represented in Parliament. Here we are represented. Arguments which prove the impropriety of being taxed by Britain,
do not hold against the exercise of taxation by Congress.

Let me pay attention to the observation of the gentleman who was last
up, that the power of taxation ought not to be given to Congress. This
subject requires the undivided attention of this house. This power I think
essentially necessary; for without it there will be no efficiency in the government. We have had a sufficient demonstration of the vanity of depending on
requisitions. How, then, can the general government exist without this
power? The possibility of its being abused is urged as an argument against
its expediency. To very little purpose did Virginia discover the defects in
the old system; to little purpose, indeed, did she propose improvements;
and to no purpose is this plan constructed for the promotion of our happiness, if we refuse it now, because it is possible that it may be abused. The
Confederation has nominal powers, but no means to carry them into effect.
If a system of government were devised by more than human intelligence,
it would not be effectual if the means were not adequate to the power. All
delegated powers are liable to be abused. Arguments drawn from this
source go in direct opposition to the government, and in recommendation
of anarchy. The friends of the Constitution are as tenacious of liberty as
its enemies. They wish to give no power that will endanger it. They wish
to give the government powers to secure and protect it. Our inquiry here
must be, whether the power of taxation be necessary to perform the objects
of the Constitution, and whether it be safe, and as well guarded as human
wisdom can do it. What are the objects of the national government? To protect the United States, and to promote the general welfare. Protection, in
time of war, is one of its principal objects. Until mankind shall cease to have
ambition and avarice, wars will arise.

The prosperity and happiness of the people depend on the performance of
these great and important duties of the general government. Can these
duties be performed by one state? Can one state protect us, and promote our
happiness? The honorable gentleman who has gone before me (Governor
Randolph) has shown that Virginia cannot do these things. How, then, can

they be done? By the national government only. Shall we refuse to give it power to do them? We are answered, that the powers may be abused; that, though the Congress may promote our happiness, yet they may prostitute their powers to destroy our liberties. This goes to the destruction of all confidence in agents. Would you believe that men who had merited your highest confidence would deceive you? Would you trust them again after one deception? Why then hesitate to trust the general government? The object of our inquiry is, *Is the power necessary, and is it guarded?* There must be men and money to protect us. How are armies to be raised? Must we not have money for that purpose? But the honorable gentleman says that we need not be afraid of war. Look at history, which has been so often quoted. Look at the great volume of human nature. They will foretell you that a defenceless country cannot be secure. The nature of man forbids us to conclude that we are in no danger from war. The passions of men stimulate them to avail themselves of the weakness of others. The powers of Europe are jealous of us. It is our interest to watch their conduct, and guard against them. They must be pleased with our disunion. If we invite them by our weakness to attack us, will they not do it? If we add debility to our present situation, a partition of America may take place.

It is, then, necessary to give the government that power, in time of peace, which the necessity of war will render indispensable, or else we shall be attacked unprepared. The experience of the world, a knowledge of human nature, and our own particular experience, will confirm this truth. When danger shall come upon us, may we not do what we were on the point of doing once already—that is, appoint a dictator? Were those who are now friends to this Constitution less active in the defence of liberty, on that trying occasion, than those who oppose it? When foreign dangers come, may not the fear of immediate destruction, by foreign enemies, impel us to take a most dangerous step? Where, then, will be our safety? We may now regulate and frame a plan that will enable us to repel attacks, and render a recurrence to dangerous expedients unnecessary. If we be prepared to defend ourselves, there will be little inducement to attack us. But if we defer giving the necessary power to the general government till the moment of danger arrives, we shall give it then, and with an *unsparing hand.* America, like other nations, may be exposed to war. The propriety of giving this power will be proved by the history of the world, and particularly of modern republics. I defy you to produce a single instance where requisitions on several individual states, composing a confederacy, have been honestly complied with. Did gentlemen expect to see such punctuality complied with in America? If they did, our own experience shows the contrary.

We are told that the Confederation carried us through the war. Had not the enthusiasm of liberty inspired us with unanimity, that system would never have carried us through it. It would have been much sooner terminated had that government been possessed of due energy. The inability of Congress, and the failure of states to comply with the constitutional requisitions, rendered our resistance less efficient than it might have been. The weakness of that government caused troops to be against us which ought to have been on our side, and prevented all resources of the community from being called at once into action. The extreme readiness of the people to make their utmost exertions to ward off solely the pressing danger, supplied the place of requisitions. When they came solely to be depended on, their inutility was fully discovered. A bare sense of duty, or a regard to propriety, is too feeble to induce men to comply with obligations. We deceive ourselves if we expect any efficacy from these. If requisitions will not avail, the government must have the sinews of war some other way. Requisitions cannot be effectual. They will be productive of delay, and will ultimately be inefficient. By direct taxation, the necessities of the government will be supplied in a peaceable manner, without irritating the minds of the people. But requisitions cannot be rendered efficient without a civil war—without great expense of money, and the blood of our citizens. Are there any other means? Yes, that Congress shall apportion the respective quotas previously, and if not complied with by the states, that then this dreaded power shall be exercised. The operation of this has been described by the gentleman who opened the debate. He cannot be answered. This great objection to that system remains unanswered. Is there no other argument which ought to have weight with us on this subject? Delay is a strong and pointed objection to it.

We are told by the gentleman who spoke last, that direct taxation is unnecessary, because we are not involved in war. This admits the propriety of recurring to direct taxation if we were engaged in war. It has not been proved that we have no dangers to apprehend on this point. What will be the consequence of the system proposed by the worthy gentleman? Suppose the states should refuse!

The worthy gentleman who is so pointedly opposed to the Constitution, proposes remonstrances. It is a time for Congress to remonstrate, or compel a compliance with requisitions, when the whole wisdom of the Union, and the power of Congress, are opposed to a foreign enemy? Another alternative is, that, if the states shall appropriate certain funds for the use of Congress, Congress shall not lay direct taxes. Suppose the funds appropriated by the states for the use of Congress should be inadequate; it will not be determined whether they be insufficient till after the time at which the quota ought to have been paid; and then, after so long a delay, the means of procuring money, which ought to have been employed in the first instance, must be recurred to. May they not be amused by such ineffectual and temporizing alternatives from year to year, until America shall be enslaved? The failure in one state will authorize a failure in another. The calculation in some states that others will fail, will produce general failures. This will also be attended with all the expenses which we are anxious to avoid. What are the advantages to induce us to embrace this system? If they mean that requisitions should be complied with, it will be the same as if Congress had the power of direct taxation. The same amount will be paid by the people.

It is objected, that Congress will not know how to lay taxes so as to be easy and convenient for the people at large. Let us pay strict attention to this objection. If it appears to be totally without foundation, the necessity of levying direct taxes will obviate what the gentleman says; nor will there be any color for refusing to grant the power.

The objects of direct taxes are well understood: they are but few: what are they? Lands, slaves, stock of all kinds, and a few other articles of domestic property. Can you believe that ten men selected from all parts of the state, chosen because they know the situation of the people, will be unable to determine so as to make the tax equal on, and convenient for, the people at large? Does any man believe that they would lay the tax without the aid of other information besides their own knowledge, when they know that the very object for which they are elected is to lay the taxes in a judicious and convenient manner? If they wish to retain the affections of the people at large, will they not inform themselves of every circumstance that can throw light on the subject? Have they but one source of information? Besides their own experience—their knowledge of what will suit their constituents—they will have the benefit of the knowledge and experience of the state legislature. They will see in what manner the legislature of Virginia collects its taxes. Will they be unable to follow their example? The gentlemen who shall be delegated to Congress will have every source of information that the legislatures of the states can have, and can lay the taxes as equally on the people, and with as little oppression, as they can. If, then, it be admitted that they can understand how to lay them equally and conveniently, are we to admit that they will not do it, but that, in violation of every principle that ought to govern men, they will lay them so as to oppress us? What benefit will they have by it? Will it be promotive of their reëlection? Will it be by wantonly imposing hardships and difficulties on the people at large, that they will promote their own interest, and secure their reëlection? To me it appears incontrovertible that they will settle them in such a manner as to be easy for the people. Is the system so organized as to make taxation dangerous? I shall not go to the various checks of the government, but examine whether the immediate representation of the people be well constructed. I conceive its organization to be sufficiently satisfactory to the warmest friend of freedom. No tax can be laid without the consent of the House of Representatives. If there be no impropriety in the mode of electing the representatives, can any danger be apprehended? They are elected by those who can elect representatives in the state legislature. How can the votes of the electors be influenced? By nothing but the character and conduct of the man they vote for. What object can influence them when about choosing him? They have nothing to direct them in the choice but their own good. Have you not as pointed and strong a security as you can possibly have? It is a mode that secures an impossibility of being corrupted. If they are to be chosen for their wisdom, virtue, and integrity, what inducement have they to infringe on our freedom? We are told that they may abuse their power. Are there strong motives to prompt them to abuse it? Will not such abuse militate against their own interest? Will not they and their friends feel the effects of iniquitous measures? Does the representative remain in office for life? Does he transmit his title of representative to his son? Is he secured from the burden imposed on the community? To procure their reëlection, it will be necessary for them to confer with the people at large, and convince them that the taxes laid are for their good. If I am able to judge on the subject, the power of taxation now before us is wisely conceded, and the representatives are wisely elected.

The honorable gentleman said that a government should ever depend on the affections of the people. It must be so. It is the best support it can have. This government merits the confidence of the people, and, I make no doubt, will have it. Then he informed us again of the disposition of Spain with respect to the Mississippi, and the conduct of the government with regard to it. To the debility of the Confederation alone may justly be imputed every cause of complaint on this subject. Whenever gentlemen will bring forward their objections, I trust we can prove that no danger to the navigation of that river can arise from the adoption of this Constitution. I beg those gentlemen who may be affected by it, to suspend their judgment till they hear it discussed. Will, says he, the adoption of this Constitution pay our debts? It will compel the states to pay their quotas. Without this, Virginia will be unable to pay. Unless all the states pay, she cannot. Though the states will not coin money, (as we are told,) yet this government will bring forth and proportion all the strength of the Union. That economy and industry are essential to our happiness, will be denied by no man. But the present government will not add to our industry. It takes away the incitements to industry, by rendering property insecure and unprotected. It is the paper on your table that will promote and encourage industry. New Hampshire and Rhode Island have rejected it, he tells us. New Hampshire, if my information be right, will certainly adopt it. The report spread in this country, of which I have heard, is, that the representatives of that state having, on meeting, found they were instructed to vote against it, returned to their constituents without determining the question, to convince them of their being mistaken, and of the propriety of adopting it.

The extent of the country is urged as another objection, as being too great for a republican government. This objection has been handed from author to author, and has been certainly misunderstood and misapplied.

To what does it owe its source? To observations and criticisms on governments, where representation did not exist. As to the legislative power, was
it ever supposed inadequate to any extent? Extent of country may render
it difficult to execute the laws, but not to legislate. Extent of country does
not extend the power. What will be sufficiently energetic and operative in
a small territory, will be feeble when extended over a wide-extended country. The gentleman tells us there are no checks in this plan. What has become
of his enthusiastic eulogium on the American spirit? We should find a check
and control, when oppressed, from that source. In this country, there is no
exclusive personal stock of interest. The interest of the community is blended
and inseparably connected with that of the individual. When he promotes
his own, he promotes that of the community. When we consult the common
good, we consult our own. When he desires such checks as these, he will
find them abundantly here. They are the best checks. What has become of
his eulogium on the Virginia Constitution? Do the checks in this plan appear
less excellent than those of the Constitution of Virginia? If the checks in the
Constitution be compared to the checks in the Virginia Constitution, he
will find the best security in the former.

The temple of liberty was complete, said he, when the people of England
said to their king, that he was their servant. What are we to learn from this?
Shall we embrace such a system as that? Is not liberty secure with us, where
the people hold all powers in their own hands, and delegate them cautiously,
for short periods, to their servants, who are accountable for the smallest
mal-administration? Where is the nation that can boast greater security than
we do? We want only a system like the paper before you, to strengthen and
perpetuate this security.

The honorable gentleman has asked if there be any safety or freedom,
when we give away the sword and the purse. Shall the people at large hold
the sword and the purse without the interposition of their representatives?
Can the whole aggregate community act personally? I apprehend that every
gentleman will see the impossibility of this. Must they, then, not trust them
to others? To whom are they to trust them but to their representatives, who
are accountable for their conduct? He represents secrecy as unnecessary,
and produces the British government as a proof of its inutility. Is there no
secrecy there? When deliberating on the propriety of declaring war, or on
military arrangements, do they deliberate in the open fields? No, sir. The
British government affords secrecy when necessary, and so ought every government. In this plan, secrecy is only used when it would be fatal and pernicious to publish the schemes of government. We are threatened with the
loss of our liberties by the possible abuse of power, notwithstanding the
maxim, that those who give may take away. It is the people that give power,
and can take it back. What shall restrain them? They are the masters who
give it, and of whom their servants hold it.

He then argues against the system, because it does not resemble the British government in this—that the same power that declares war has not the means of carrying it on. Are the people of England more secure, if the Commons have no voice in declaring war? or are we less secure by having the Senate joined with the President? It is an absurdity, says the worthy member, that the same man should obey two masters—that the same collector should gather taxes for the general government and the state legislature. Are they not both the servants of the people? Are not Congress and the state legislatures the agents of the people, and are they not to consult the good of the people? May not this be effected by giving the same officer the collection of both taxes? He tells you that it is an absurdity to adopt before you amend. Is the object of your adoption to mend solely? The objects of your adoption are union, safety against foreign enemies, and protection against faction—against what has been the destruction of all republics. These impel you to its adoption. If you adopt it, what shall restrain you from amending it, if, in trying it, amendments shall be found necessary? The government is not supported by force, but depending on our free will. When experience shall show us any inconveniences, we can then correct it. But until we have experience on the subject, amendments, as well as the Constitution itself, are to try. Let us try it, and keep our hands free to change it when necessary. If it be necessary to change government, let us change that government which has been found to be defective. The difficulty we find in amending the Confederation will not be found in amending this Constitution. Any amendments, in the system before you, will not go to a radical change; a plain way is pointed out for the purpose. All will be interested to change it, and therefore all exert themselves in getting the change. There is such a diversity of sentiment in human minds, that it is impossible we shall ever concur in one system till we try it. The power given to the general government over the time, place, and manner of election, is also strongly objected to. When we come to that clause, we can prove it is highly necessary, and not dangerous.

The worthy member has concluded his observations by many eulogiums on the British constitution. It matters not to us whether it be a wise one or not. I think that, for America at least, the government on your table is very much superior to it. I ask you if your House of Representatives would be better than it is, if a hundredth part of the people were to elect a majority of them. If your senators were for life, would they be more agreeable to you? If your President were not accountable to you for his conduct,—if it were a constitutional maxim, that he could do no wrong,—would you be safer than you are now? If you can answer, Yes, to these questions, then adopt the British constitution. If not, then, good as that government may be, this is better. The worthy gentleman who was last up, said the confederacies of ancient and modern times were not similar to ours, and that consequently reasons which applied against them could not be urged against it. Do they not hold out one lesson very useful to us? However unlike in other respects, they resemble it in its total inefficacy. They warn us to shun their calamities, and place in our government those necessary powers, the want of which destroyed them. I hope we shall avail ourselves of their misfortunes, without experiencing them. There was something peculiar in one observation he made. He said that those who governed the cantons of Switzerland were purchased by foreign powers, which was the cause of their uneasiness and trouble.

How does this apply to us? If we adopt such a government as theirs, will it not be subject to the same inconvenience? Will not the same cause produce the same effect? What shall protect us from it? What is our security? He then proceeded to say, the causes of war are removed from us; that we are separated by the sea from the powers of Europe, and need not be alarmed. Sir, the sea makes them neighbors to us. Though an immense ocean divides us, we may speedily see them with us. What dangers may we not apprehend to our commerce! Does not our naval weakness invite an attack on our commerce? May not the Algerines seize our vessels? Cannot they, and every other predatory or maritime nation, pillage our ships and destroy our commerce, without subjecting themselves to any inconvenience? He would, he said, give the general government all necessary powers. If any thing be necessary, it must be so to call forth the strength of the Union when we may be attacked, or when the general purposes of America require it. The worthy gentleman then proceeded to show, that our present exigencies are greater than they will ever be again.

Who can penetrate into futurity? How can any man pretend to say that our future exigencies will be less than our present? The exigencies of nations have been generally commensurate to their resources. It would be the utmost impolicy to trust to a mere possibility of not being attacked, or obliged to exert the strength of the community. He then spoke of a selection of particular objects by Congress, which he says must necessarily be oppressive; that Congress, for instance, might select taxes, and that all but landholders would escape. Cannot Congress regulate the taxes so as to be equal on all parts of the community? Where is the absurdity of having thirteen revenues? Will they clash with, or injure, each other? If not, why cannot Congress make thirteen distinct laws, and impose the taxes on the general objects of taxation in each state, so as that all persons of the society shall pay equally, as they ought?

He then told you that your Continental government will call forth the virtue and talents of America. This being the case, will they encroach on the power of the state governments? Will our most virtuous and able citizens wantonly attempt to destroy the liberty of the people? Will the most virtuous act the most wickedly? I differ in opinion from the worthy gentleman. I think the virtue and talents of the members of the general government will tend to the security, instead of the destruction, of our liberty. I think that the power of direct taxation is essential to the existence of the general government, and that it is safe to grant it. If this power be not necessary, and as safe from abuse as any delegated power can possibly be, then I say that the plan before you is unnecessary; for it imports not what system we have, unless it have the power of protecting us in time of peace and war.

23

REMARKS IN VIRGINIA CONVENTION ON RATIFICATION OF THE CONSTITUTION
June 14, 1788

M R. JOHN MARSHALL asked if gentlemen were serious when they asserted that, if the state governments had power to interfere with the militia, it was by implication. If they were, he asked the committee whether the least attention would not show that they were mistaken. The state governments did not derive their powers from the general government; but each government derived its powers from the people, and each was to act according to the powers given it. Would any gentleman deny this? He demanded if powers not given were retained by implication. Could any man say so? Could any man say that this power was not retained by the states, as they had not given it away? For, says he, does not a power remain till it is given away? The state legislatures had power to command and govern their militia before, and have it still, undeniably, unless there be something in this Constitution that takes it away.

For Continental purposes Congress may call forth the militia,—as to suppress insurrections and repel invasions. But the power given to the states by the people is not taken away; for the Constitution does not say so. In the Confederation Congress had this power; but the state legislatures had it also. The power of legislating given them within the ten miles square is exclusive of the states, because it is expressed to be exclusive. The truth is, that when power is given to the general legislature, if it was in the state legislature before, both shall exercise it; unless there be an incompatibility in the exercise by one to that by the other, or negative words precluding the state governments from it. But there are no negative words here. It rests, therefore, with the states. To me it appears, then, unquestionable that the state governments can call forth the militia, in case the Constitution should be adopted, in the same manner as they could have done before its adoption. Gentlemen have said that the states cannot defend themselves without an application to Congress, because Congress can interpose! Does not every man feel a refutation of the argument in his own breast? I will show that there could not be a combination, between those who formed the Constitution, to take away this power. All the restraints intended to be laid on the state governments (besides where an exclusive power is expressly given to Congress) are contained in the 10th section of the 1st article. This power is not included in the restrictions in that section. But what excludes every possibility of doubt, is the last part of it—that "no state shall engage in war, unless actually invaded, or in such imminent danger as will not admit of delay." When invaded, they can engage in war, as also when in imminent danger. This clearly proves that the states can use the militia when they find it necessary. The worthy member last up objects to the Continental government's possessing the power of disciplining the militia, because, though all its branches be derived from the people, he says they will form an aristocratic government, unsafe and unfit to be trusted.

MR. GRAYSON answered, that he only said it was so constructed as to form a great aristocratic body.

MR. MARSHALL replied, that he was not certain whether he understood him; but he thought he had said so. He conceived that, as the government was drawn from the people, the feelings and interests of the people would be attended to, and that we should be safe in granting them power to regulate the militia. When the government is drawn from the people, continued Mr. Marshall, and depending on the people for its continuance, oppressive measures will not be attempted, as they will certainly draw on their authors the resentment of those on whom they depend. On this government, thus depending on ourselves for its existence, I will rest my safety, notwithstanding the danger depicted by the honorable gentleman. I cannot help being surprised that the worthy member thought this power so dangerous. What government is able to protect you in time of war? Will any state depend on its own exertions? The consequence of such dependence, and withholding this power from Congress, will be, that state will fall after state, and be a sacrifice to the want of power in the general government. *United we are strong, divided we fall.* Will you prevent the general government from drawing the militia of one state to another, when the consequence would be, that every state must depend on itself? The enemy, possessing the water, can quickly go from one state to another. No state will spare to another its militia, which it conceives necessary for itself. It requires a superintending power, in order to call forth the resources of all to protect all. If this be not done, each state will fall a sacrifice. This system merits the highest applause in this respect. The honorable gentleman said that a general regulation may be made to inflict punishments. Does he imagine that a militia law is to be ingrafted on the scheme of government, so as to render it incapable of being changed? The idea of the worthy member supposes that men renounce their own interests. This would produce general inconveniences throughout the Union, and would be equally opposed by all the states. But the worthy member fears, that in one part of the Union they will be regulated and disciplined, and in another neglected. This danger is enhanced by leaving this power to each state; for some states may attend to their militia, and others may neglect them. If Congress neglect our militia we can arm them ourselves. Cannot Virginia import arms? Cannot she put them into the hands of her militia-men?

He then concluded by observing, that the power of governing the militia was not vested in the states by implication, because, being possessed of it antecedent to the adoption of the government, and not being divested of it by any grant or restriction in the Constitution, they must necessarily be as fully possessed of it as ever they had been. And it could not be said that the states derived any powers from that system, but retained them, though not acknowledged in any part of it.

24

SPEECH IN VIRGINIA
CONVENTION ON RATIFICATION
OF THE CONSTITUTION
June 20, 1788

M<small>R.</small> C<small>HAIRMAN</small>, this part of the plan before us is a great improvement on that system from which we are now departing. Here are tribunals appointed for *the decision of controversies* which were before either not at all, or improperly, provided for. That many benefits will result from this to the members of the collective society, every one confesses. Unless its organization be defective, and so constructed as to injure, instead of accommodating, the convenience of the people, it merits our approbation. After such a candid and fair discussion by those gentlemen who support it,—after the very able manner in which they have investigated and examined it,—I conceived it would be no longer considered as so very defective, and that those who opposed it would be convinced of the impropriety of some of their objections. But I perceive they still continue the same opposition. Gentlemen have gone on an idea that the federal courts will not determine the causes which may come before them with the same fairness and impartiality with which other courts decide. What are the reasons of this supposition? Do they draw them from the manner in which the judges are chosen, or the tenure of their office? What is it that makes us trust our judges? Their independence in office, and manner of appointment. Are not the judges of the federal court chosen with as much wisdom as the judges of the state governments? Are they not equally, if not more independent? If so, shall we not conclude that they will decide with equal impartiality and candor? If there be as much wisdom and knowledge in the United States as in a particular state, shall we conclude that the wisdom and knowledge will not be equally exercised in the selection of judges?

The principle on which they object to the federal jurisdiction seems, to me, to be founded on a belief that there will not be a fair trial had in those courts. If this committee will consider it fully, they will find it has no foundation, and that we are as secure there as any where else. What mischief results from some causes being tried there? Is there not the utmost reason to conclude that judges, wisely appointed, and independent in their office, will never countenance any unfair trial? What are the subjects of its jurisdiction? Let us examine them with an expectation that causes will be as candidly tried there as elsewhere, and then determine. The objection which was made by the honorable member who was first up yesterday [Mr. Mason] has been so fully refuted that it is not worth while to notice it. He objected to Congress having power to create a number of inferior courts, according to the necessity of public circumstances. I had an apprehension that those gentlemen who placed no confidence in Congress would object that there might be no inferior courts. I own that I thought those gentlemen would think there would be no inferior courts, as it depended on the will of Congress, but that we should be dragged to the centre of the Union. But I did not conceive that the power of increasing the number of courts could be objected to by any gentleman, as it would remove the inconvenience of being dragged to the centre of the United States. I own that the power of creating a number of courts is, in my estimation, so far from being a defect, that it seems necessary to the perfection of this system. After having objected to the number and mode, he objected to the subject matter of their cognizance. [Here Mr. Marshall read the 2d section.]

These, sir, are the points of *federal jurisdiction* to which he objects, with a few exceptions. Let us examine each of them with a supposition that the same impartiality will be observed there as in other courts, and then see if any mischief will result from them. With respect to its cognizance in all cases arising under the Constitution and the laws of the United States, he says that, the laws of the United States being paramount to the laws of the particular states, there is no case but what this will extend to. Has the government of the United States power to make laws on every subject? Does he understand it so? Can they make laws affecting the mode of transferring property, or contracts, or claims, between citizens of the same state? Can they go beyond the delegated powers? If they were to make a law not warranted by any of the powers enumerated, it would be considered by the judges as an infringement of the Constitution which they are to guard. They would not consider such a law as coming under their jurisdiction. They would declare it void. It will annihilate the state courts, says the honorable gentleman. Does not every gentleman here know that the causes in our courts are more numerous than they can decide, according to their present construction? Look at the dockets. You will find them crowded with suits, which the life of man will not see determined. If some of these suits be carried to other courts, will it be wrong? They will still have business enough.

Then there is no danger that particular subjects, small in proportion, being taken out of the jurisdiction of the state judiciaries, will render them

useless and of no effect. Does the gentleman think that the state courts will
have no cognizance of cases not mentioned here? Are there any words in
this Constitution which exclude the courts of the states from those cases
which they now possess? Does the gentleman imagine this to be the case?
Will any gentleman believe it? Are not controversies respecting lands
claimed under the grants of different states the only controversies between
citizens of the same state which the federal judiciary can take cognizance
of? The case is so clear, that to prove it would be a useless waste of time.
The state courts will not lose the jurisdiction of the causes they now decide.
They have a concurrence of jurisdiction with the federal courts in those
cases in which the latter have cognizance.

How disgraceful is it that the state courts cannot be trusted! says the
honorable gentleman. What is the language of the Constitution? Does it
take away their jurisdiction? Is it not necessary that the federal courts
should have cognizance of cases arising under the Constitution, and the
laws, of the United States? What is the service or purpose of a judiciary,
but to execute the laws in a peaceable, orderly manner, without shedding
blood, or creating a contest, or availing yourselves of force? If this be the
case, where can its jurisdiction be more necessary than here?

To what quarter will you look for protection from an infringement on the
Constitution, if you will not give the power to the judiciary? There is no
other body that can afford such a protection. But the honorable member
objects to it, because he says that the officers of the government will be
screened from merited punishment by the federal judiciary. The federal
sheriff, says he, will go into a poor man's house and beat him, or abuse his
family, and the federal court will protect him. Does any gentleman believe
this? Is it necessary that the officers will commit a trespass on the property
or persons of those with whom they are to transact business? Will such
great insults on the people of this country be allowable? Were a law made
to authorize them, it would be void. The injured man would trust to a tribunal in his neighborhood. To such a tribunal he would apply for redress,
and get it. There is no reason to fear that he would not meet that justice
there which his country will be ever willing to maintain. But, *on appeal,* says
the honorable gentleman, what chance is there to obtain justice? This is
founded on an idea that they will not be impartial. There is no clause in
the Constitution which bars the individual member injured from applying
to the state courts to give him redress. He says that there is no instance of
appeals as to fact in common-law cases. The contrary is well known to you,
Mr. Chairman, to be the case in this commonwealth. With respect to mills,
roads, and other cases, appeals lie from the inferior to the superior court,
as to fact as well as law. Is it a clear case, that there can be no case in common law in which an appeal as to fact might be proper and necessary? Can
you not conceive a case where it would be productive of advantages to the

people at large to submit to that tribunal the final determination, involving facts as well as law? Suppose it should be deemed for the convenience of the citizens that those things which concerned foreign ministers should be tried in the inferior courts, if justice could be done, the decision would satisfy all. But if an appeal in matters of facts could not be carried to the superior court, then it would result that such cases could not be tried before the inferior courts, for fear of injurious and partial decisions.

But, sir, where is the necessity of discriminating between the three cases of chancery, admiralty, and common law? Why not leave it to Congress? Will it enlarge their powers? Is it necessary for them wantonly to infringe your rights? Have you any thing to apprehend, when they can in no case abuse their power without rendering themselves hateful to the people at large? When this is the case, something may be left to the legislature freely chosen by ourselves, from among ourselves, who are to share the burdens imposed upon the community, and who can be changed at our pleasure. Where power may be trusted, and there is no motive to abuse it, it seems to me to be as well to leave it undetermined as to fix it in the Constitution.

With respect to disputes between *a state and the citizens of another state,* its jurisdiction has been decried with unusual vehemence. I hope that no gentleman will think that a state will be called at the bar of the federal court. Is there no such case at present? Are there not many cases in which the legislature of Virginia is a party, and yet the state is not sued? It is not rational to suppose that the sovereign power should be dragged before a court. The intent is, to enable states to recover claims of individuals residing in other states. I contend this construction is warranted by the words. But, say they, there will be partiality in it if a state cannot be defendant—if an individual cannot proceed to obtain judgment against a state, though he may be sued by a state. It is necessary to be so, and cannot be avoided. I see a difficulty in making a state defendant, which does not prevent its being plaintiff. If this be only what cannot be avoided, why object to the system on that account? If an individual has a just claim against any particular state, is it to be presumed that, on application to its legislature, he will not obtain satisfaction? But how could a state recover any claim from a citizen of another state, without the establishment of these tribunals?

The honorable member objects to suits being instituted in the federal courts, by the citizens of one state, against the citizens of another state. Were I to contend that this was necessary in all cases, and that the government without it would be defective, I should not use my own judgment. But are not the objections to it carried too far? Though it may not in general be absolutely necessary, a case may happen, as has been observed, in which a citizen of one state ought to be able to recur to this tribunal, to recover a claim from the citizen of another state. What is the evil which this can produce? Will he get more than justice there? The independence of the judges forbids it. What has he to get? Justice. Shall we object to this, because the citizen of another state can obtain justice without applying to our state courts? It may be necessary with respect to the laws and regulations of commerce, which Congress may make. It may be necessary in cases of debt, and some other controversies. In claims for land, it is not necessary, but it is not dangerous. In the court of which state will it be instituted? said the honorable gentleman. It will be instituted in the court of the state where the defendant resides, where the law can come at him, and nowhere else. By the laws of which state will it be determined? said he. By the laws of the state where the contract was made. According to those laws, and those only, can it be decided. Is this a novelty? No; it is a principle in the jurisprudence of this commonwealth. If a man contracted a debt in the East Indies, and it was sued for here, the decision must be consonant to the laws of that country. Suppose a contract made in Maryland, where the annual interest is at six per centum, and a suit instituted for it in Virginia; what interest would be given now, without any federal aid? The interest of Maryland most certainly; and if the contract had been made in Virginia, and suit brought in Maryland, the interest of Virginia must be given, without doubt. It is now to be governed by the laws of that state where the contract was made. The laws which governed the contract at its formation govern it in its decision. To preserve the peace of the Union only, its jurisdiction in this case ought to be recurred to. Let us consider that, when citizens of one state carry on trade in another state, much must be due to the one from the other, as is the case between North Carolina and Virginia. Would not the refusal of justice to our citizens, from the courts of North Carolina, produce disputes between the states? Would the federal judiciary swerve from their duty in order to give partial and unjust decisions?

The objection respecting the assignment of a bond to a citizen of another state has been fully answered. But suppose it were to be tried, as he says; what would be given more than was actually due in the case he mentioned? It is *possible* in our courts, as they now stand, to obtain a judgment for more than justice. But the court of chancery grants relief. Would it not be so in the federal court? Would not depositions be taken to prove the payments, and if proved, would not the decision of the court be accordingly?

He objects, in the next place, to its jurisdiction in controversies between a state and a foreign state. Suppose, says he, in such a suit, a foreign state is cast; will she be bound by the decision? If a foreign state brought a suit against the commonwealth of Virginia, would she not be barred from the claim if the federal judiciary thought it unjust? The previous consent of the parties is necessary; and, as the federal judiciary will decide, each party will acquiesce. It will be the means of preventing disputes with foreign nations. On an attentive consideration of these points, I trust every part will appear satisfactory to the committee.

The exclusion of trial by jury, in this case, he urged to prostrate our rights. Does the word *court* only mean the judges? Does not the determination of a jury necessarily lead to the judgment of the court? Is there any thing here which gives the judges exclusive jurisdiction of matters of fact? What is the object of a jury trial? To inform the court of the facts. When a court has cognizance of facts does it not follow that they can make inquiry by a jury? It is impossible to be otherwise. I hope that in this country, where impartiality is so much admired, the laws will direct facts to be ascertained by a jury. But, says the honorable gentleman, the juries in the ten miles square will be mere tools of parties, with which he would not trust his person or property; which, he says, he would rather leave to the court. Because the government may have a district of ten miles square, will no man stay there but the tools and officers of the government? Will nobody else be found there? Is it so in any other part of the world, where a government has legislative power? Are there none but officers, and tools of the government of Virginia, in Richmond? Will there not be independent merchants, and respectable gentlemen of fortune, within the ten miles square? Will there not be worthy farmers and mechanics? Will not a good jury be found there, as well as any where else? Will the officers of the government become improper to be on a jury? What is it to the government whether this man or that man succeeds? It is all one thing. Does the Constitution say that juries shall consist of officers, or that the Supreme Court shall be held in the ten miles square? It was acknowledged, by the honorable member, that it was secure in England. What makes it secure there? Is it their constitution? What part of their constitution is there that the Parliament cannot change? As the preservation of this right is in the hands of Parliament, and it has ever been held sacred by them, will the government of America be less honest than that of Great Britain? Here a restriction is to be found. The jury is not to be brought out of the state. There is no such restriction in that government; for the laws of Parliament decide every thing respecting it. Yet gentlemen tell us that there is safety there, and nothing here but danger. It seems to me that the laws of the United Sates will generally secure trials by a jury of the vicinage, or in such manner as will be most safe and convenient for the people.

But it seems that the right of challenging the jurors is not secured in this Constitution. Is this done by our own Constitution, or by any provision of the English government? Is it done by their Magna Charta, or bill of rights? The privilege is founded on their laws. If so, why should it be objected to the American Constitution, that it is not inserted in it? If we are secure in Virginia without mentioning it in our Constitution, why should not this security be found in the federal court?

The honorable gentleman said much about the quitrents in the Northern Neck. I will refer it to the honorable gentleman himself. Has he not acknowledged that there was no complete title? Was he not satisfied that the right of the legal representatives of the proprietor did not exist at the time he mentioned? If so, it cannot exist now. I will leave it to those gentlemen who come from that quarter. I trust they will not be intimidated, on this account, in voting on this question. A law passed in 1782, which secures this. He says that many poor men may be harassed and injured by the representatives of Lord Fairfax. If he has no right, this cannot be done. If he has this right, and comes to Virginia, what laws will his claims be determined by? By those of this state. By what tribunals will they be determined? By our state courts. Would not the poor man, who was oppressed by an unjust prosecution, be abundantly protected and satisfied by the temper of his neighbors, and would he not find ample justice? What reason has the honorable member to apprehend partiality or injustice? He supposes that, if the judges be judges of both the federal and state courts, they will incline in favor of one government. If such contests should arise, who could more properly decide them than those who are to swear to do justice? If we can expect a fair decision any where, may we not expect justice to be done by the judges of both the federal and state governments? But, says the honorable member, laws may be executed tyrannically. Where is the independency of your judges? If a law be exercised tyrannically in Virginia, to what can you trust? To your judiciary. What security have you for justice? Their independence. Will it not be so in the federal court?

Gentlemen ask, What is meant by law cases, and if they be not distinct from facts? Is there no law arising on cases of equity and admiralty? Look at the acts of Assembly. Have you not many cases where law and fact are blended? Does not the jurisdiction in point of law as well as fact, find itself completely satisfied in law and fact? The honorable gentleman says that no law of Congress can make any exception to the federal appellate jurisdiction of facts as well as law. He has frequently spoken of technical terms, and the meaning of them. What is the meaning of the term *exception?* Does it not mean an alteration and diminution? Congress is empowered to make exceptions to the appellate jurisdiction, as to law and fact, of the Supreme Court. These exceptions certainly go as far as the legislature may think proper for the interest and liberty of the people. Who can understand this word, *exception,* to extend to one case as well as the other? I am persuaded that a reconsideration of this case will convince the gentleman that he was mistaken. This may go to the cure of the mischief apprehended. Gentlemen must be satisfied that this power will not be so much abused as they have said.

The honorable member says that he derives no consolation from the wisdom and integrity of the legislature, because we call them to rectify defects which it is our duty to remove. We ought well to weigh the good and evil before we determine. We ought to be well convinced that the evil will be really produced before we decide against it. If we be convinced that the good greatly preponderates, though there be small defects in it, shall we give up that which is really good, when we can remove the little mischief it may contain, in the plain, easy method pointed out in the system itself?

I was astonished when I heard the honorable gentleman say that he wished the trial by jury to be struck out entirely. Is there no justice to be expected by a jury of our fellow-citizens? Will any man prefer to be tried by a court, when the jury is to be of his countrymen, and probably of his vicinage? We have reason to believe the regulations with respect to juries will be such as shall be satisfactory. Because it does not contain all, does it contain nothing? But I conceive that this committee will see there is safety in the case, and that there is no mischief to be apprehended.

He states a case, that a man may be carried from a federal to an antifederal corner, (and *vice versa*) where men are ready to destroy him. Is this probable? Is it presumable that they will make a law to punish men who are of different opinions in politics from themselves? Is it presumable that they will do it in one single case, unless it be such a case as must satisfy the people at large? The good opinion of the people at large must be consulted by their representatives; otherwise, mischiefs would be produced which would shake the government to its foundation. As it is late, I shall not mention all the gentleman's argument, but some parts of it are so glaring that I cannot pass them over in silence. He says that the establishment of these tribunals, and more particularly in their jurisdiction of controversies between citizens of these states and foreign citizens and subjects, is like a retrospective law. Is there no difference between a tribunal which shall give justice and effect to an existing right, and creating a right that did not exist before? The debt or claim is created by the individual. He has bound himself to comply with it. Does the creation of a new court amount to a retrospective law?

We are satisfied with the provision made in this country on the subject of trial by jury. Does our Constitution direct trials to be by jury? It is required in our bill of rights, which is not a part of the Constitution. Does any security arise from hence? Have you a jury when a judgment is obtained on a replevin bond, or by default? Have you a jury when a motion is made for the commonwealth against an individual; or when a motion is made by one joint obligor against another, to recover sums paid as security? Our courts decide in all these cases, without the intervention of a jury; yet they are all civil cases. The bill of rights is merely recommendatory. Were it otherwise, the consequence would be that many laws which are found convenient would be unconstitutional. What does the government before you say? Does it exclude the legislature from giving a trial by jury in civil cases? If it does not forbid its exclusion, it is on the same footing on which your state government stands now. The legislature of Virginia does not give a trial by jury where it is not necessary, but gives it wherever it is thought expedient. The federal legislature will do so too, as it is formed on the same principles.

The honorable gentleman says that unjust claims will be made, and the defendant had better pay them than go to the Supreme Court. Can you suppose such a disposition in one of your citizens, as that, to oppress another man, he will incur great expenses? What will he gain by an unjust demand? Does a claim establish a right? He must bring his witnesses to prove his claim. If he does not bring his witnesses, the expenses must fall upon him. Will he go on a calculation that the defendant will not defend it, or cannot produce a witness? Will he incur a great deal of expense, from a dependence on such a chance? Those who know human nature, black as it is, must know that mankind are too well attached to their interest to run such a risk. I conceive that this power is absolutely necessary, and not dangerous; that, should it be attended by little inconveniences, they will be altered, and that they can have no interest in not altering them. Is there any real danger? When I compare it to the exercise of the same power in the government of Virginia, I am persuaded there is not. The federal government has no other motive, and has every reason for doing right which the members of our state legislature have. Will a man on the eastern shore be sent to be tried in Kentucky, or a man from Kentucky be brought to the eastern shore to have his trial? A government, by doing this, would destroy itself. I am convinced the trial by jury will be regulated in the manner most advantageous to the community.

25
ADDRESS ON
CONSTITUTIONALITY OF
ALIEN AND SEDITION LAWS
December 1798

THE AWFUL CRISIS which has arrived must be felt by us all, however we may differ as to the causes which have produced it, or the measures which may avert its calamity. That our fellow-citizens may be fully informed of the part taken by their public functionaries, in all the measures touching this subject, it is deemed fair and proper, to submit the following resolutions offered in the House of Delegates, by the Member from Prince George, as a substitute for those adopted, which are subjoined. Nor can it be deemed improper to notice the prevailing distinction between the resolutions. In the latter, declarations of uniting in the common defence are mingled with insinuations of distrust in the Government of the United States, the only political mean by which efficacy can be given to resistance against an invading foe.

Having passed the resolutions, it would seem that the General Assembly had finished their deliberations on the subject, but a novel course was pursued, alike outraging the rules of the Legislature, and derogating from the discernment of their constituents, by a laboured detail of the reasons which induced the legislative adoption of the resolutions. It became necessary, therefore, to meet this second paper, by counter arguments, but this was done with reluctance, and after every attempt to arrest the proposition had failed. Our sharing in the impropriety of departure from usage, must be attributed to the imperious necessity of the case.

The counter arguments are displayed in the following address submitted to the committee of the whole by the Member from Westmoreland. An effort was made in the House, to obtain the circulation of the counter address among the people, by subjoining it to a compilation of papers, in which is inserted the address adopted, directed to be published at the public expence; this request was as will appear by reference to the Journals. To the liberality of individuals, who have subscribed a sufficient fund for the purpose, is the minority indebted for the publication of their opinions on the very interesting subject which has engaged the attention of the General Assembly, and cannot fail to engage the fullest deliberation of their constituents, who alone can apply a radical remedy to the political disease.

FELLOW-CITIZENS

OPPOSING, as we did, resolutions of the General Assembly, passed on the 24th day of December, we cannot remain silent under the unprecedented example exhibited in support of them, by a detailed display of those reasons which influenced their adoption. We lament their existence; and we deprecate the deviation from our legislative usage, which their adoption has produced. If this was the only evil resulting from the system of which they form a conspicuous feature, we should in silence wait your application of the constitutional corrective, which you annually dispense: but considering the happiness united America enjoys, and foreseeing the evils which disunited America must inevitably suffer, we cannot shrink from the discharge of the momentous duty to which we are unexpectedly called, and on which we reluctantly enter.

To place the present crisis plainly before you, it is necessary to recur to past transactions.

For the purpose of perpetuating the blessings of our national independence, the people of united America were induced to exchange their first political association for that now existing. The will of the majority produced, ratified, and conducts it. This first principle in our federal pact cannot be impaired without proportionate injury to the body politic.

The fallibility of man, prohibits the hope of perfection in his works; and the best rule for freemen to adopt, in the opinion of our ancestors, was that which inculcates obedience to laws, enacted by a majority of functionaries appointed by the people. Foreseeing the terrible effects which ensue from differences of opinion on national subjects, they added to this first principle two others, which promised immortality to the work of their hands; they declared the compact amendable, and plainly pointed out the ways: they limited power to fixed periods; recurring to the choice of the people for the delegation of authority. Under a constitution thus formed, the prosperity of America was great and unexampled. War broke out in another quarter of the globe, the government and the people of the United States bemoaned alike the distresses incident to a vast portion of the human race; distresses not within their controul, and in the termination of which they did not possess even a remote influence. Avoiding the existing carnage, the continuance of our existing happiness, became, as was proper, the primary object of the attention of government. The President of the United States, a citizen the most tried, and the most beloved, weighing all the difficulties to which our relation to the belligerent powers exposed us, promulgated by proclamation the existing state of things, and warned his fellow-citizens of the pernicious consequences which would follow the dereliction of their neutral condition. An adherence to this situation was enjoined by law, and approved by the general plaudit of our country. Yet, unfortunately for America, and for republican government, a few openly, and more secretly, lifted their voice against their country's will. A foreign minister's contumelious appeal from the acts of government to the people, whose honor and comfort, alike commanded their support of that government, was maintained with affection to the foreign agent, and with acrimony against the constituted authorities of the nation. The subject became familiar to the whole people; and their voice spontaneously uttered, sunk into temporary and contemptuous oblivion, the abettors of this wicked effort. Smothered for a while only, the unextinguished fire rekindled as occasion afforded fuel.

The treaty which terminated our revolutionary war, although followed by the immediate possession of the main good, yet held some secondary objects unsettled. The consequence of war is a state of mental ire, which yields only to acts of mutual beneficence, and to time. The state of mental warfare had not ceased, when the unjustifiable conduct of our late foe, especially on the ocean, rekindled our ardor for hostility and revenge. The Executive of the United States, uninfluenced by the passions of hatred or affection, continuing to view peace, so long as it was to be preserved without dishonor, as his highest duty, in a moment menacing war, made his last effort to avert its miseries from our land. He sent a minister to Great-Britain, for the purpose of settling the existing discord. Peace was preserved, with honor. This event, instead of confirming our internal tranquillity, was turned with much dexterity to the renewal of past animosities; the views of Genet were re-acted in a different dress, and the Executive of the Union was branded with every epithet of opprobrium, because in preventing war, every good wished for by one of the parties to the contract of peace had not been obtained. Here the indignation of the American mind was addressed with considerable effect. At length the people, roused by self-attention, spoke—all was tranquil; and error, whether resulting from mistaken confidence, or vicious intention, sunk again into oblivion. France, our ally, to whom our government had, from the beginning of their war, presented repeated proofs of sincere friendship, taught by the bickerings among ourselves, on the subject of the British treaty, re-echoed American reproaches with French views and French objects. Similitude of sentiment, too often begets union in design—our commerce became a prey to French cruisers; our citizens were captured, and all the injuries heretofore received from the British nation, were repeated on our defenceless country, with this striking difference. A former foe, claiming unexecuted stipulations, inflicted the first; while the latter proceeded from the hand of a former friend, bound to us by the ties of a solemn treaty, and receiving from us every good in our power to bestow, without violating our neutrality, and thereby committing suicide on our national and individual happiness.

Influenced by the same pacific principle, the President, (the same tried and beloved Washington) attempted, as before, by a timely interference to avert the impending war. He sent a minister to France, with full powers to remove by candid explanations mistaken opinions, to renew ancient friendships, and to perpetuate the blessings of mutual peace. This minister was not even received, but was ordered to depart with marks of contumely and threats of imprisonment.

The successor of Washington, actuated by the same principles, and anxious for the same beneficent end, made a second effort to restore peace and paid an unusual compliment to the French government, by sending three envoys extraordinary, with ample powers to hear, to explain, to redress, and to bury every complaint in a fair, honorable and friendly adjustment. This renewed testimony of our desire for peace, was returned by increase of insolence and affront.

Thus situated, we had but to choose between submission to the will of a foreign nation, and the maintenance of our independence. What American could hesitate in the opinion? The choice being made, self-preservation commanded preparations for self-defence. With this view, and to this end, various defensive measures were adopted by the last Congress, the most effectual of which were, the equipment of a fleet, the raising of an army, a provision for the removal of dangerous aliens, and for the punishment of seditious citizens. The two first are charged with the atrocious design of creating a monarchy on the ruins of our free government, and the two last are declared to be usurpations of power, in violation of the constitution; while all of them are viewed as parts of a fixed system, tending to the establishment of despotism. This serious accusation, if true, commands your effectual interposition; if untrue, it ought to guard you against the warnings of those who from error, or with the most pernicious design, invite you to the adoption of measures baneful to American happiness and fatal to American liberty.

When the most powerful nation in Europe, by whose insidious policy and numerous armies, populous, warlike and wealthy states have been overturned; whose lust of dominion is insatiable, and whose only rule of conduct is her will; has demanded tribute at our hands, and menaced us with the fate of nations conquered and debased, what means could have been adopted more convenient or more likely to secure our defence? The equipment of a fleet guards the remains of our commerce from their privateers, enables us to incommode any offensive attempts which their enmity might dictate, and to facilitate our exertions for self-defence, by facilitating the conveyance of the requisite supplies for military operations in our extensive country.

Important already have been the beneficial consequences to our commerce, flowing from this wise measure, and every benefit to trade in an increased ratio, enlivens and invigorates agriculture: more important will be its effects in securing our protection, should we be forced to the last appeal in defence of our liberty and property.

Upon so solemn an occasion, what curses would be adequate to the supineness of our government, if militia were the only resort for safety, against the invasion of a veteran army, flushed with repeated victories, strong in the skill of its officers, and led by distinguished commanders? Should not the American citizen be prepared to meet the eventual combat, by those acquirements which place him on an equal footing on the day of battle? Or, is he so little esteemed as to be designedly submitted to an unequal conflict? What more than placing him on an equality with his foe is proposed by raising an army? Thus our ancestors acted in the revolutionary war; and suspicions perverting their intention, like those now disseminated, would have been treated with contempt, or punished as the schemes of men devoted to the enemy. Where is the change in our situation which authorizes condemnation of a measure now, then admitted to be wise and indispensable? Does it argue a love of country, to paralize means adopted for its defence? Does it demonstrate affection to our fellow citizens, to reprobate endeavours which bestow upon them equality of skill with their antagonists? Does it evince a wish to disregard and distrust our militia, when an army is formed of citizen soldiers, for that very militia to rally around, and hand in hand to march to attack the foe? Can that army be called mercenary, which is composed of our brothers and our sons, levied by law, paid by law, and embodied to defend their and our common rights? Would your Washington lead a mercenary army? Is he not again your General? Why, then, these unfounded suspicions, and this opprobrious, unwarrented epithet, but to inflame your passions, and to mislead your judgments? Pause, reflect, and say, whether counsel thus administered, can have your good for its object? And whether, under the pretence of promoting your happiness, it does not lead to an issue disastrous to America, and calamitous to Virginia?

Alike erroneous, and alike destructive of the common weal, is the distorted construction of the Alien and Sedition Laws.

Nevertheless, these acts are confidently pronounced unconstitutional, so much so, that to many of our fellow citizens the question may appear to have been completely decided.

In the opinion of some, to deliberate on this subject is criminal, and to pause before we declare that the constituted authorities have knowingly and intentionally violated that sacred charter by which they hold their political existence, is to be inimical to that republican liberty, which constitutes the pride and happiness of our country, and which can only be preserved by preserving that government which is now so boldly arraigned. Had the measures which profess their origin from these laws, been confined to ordinary peaceable and constitutional efforts to effect their repeal; had a decent respect for the real majority of the American people been maintained, no opposition would have been made by those who now address you. —But when a partial irritation, in some degree produced by misconception, is sought to be excited into general hostility against the government of our country, is seized as affording a fair occasion for proceedings which may sap the foundation of our union, we must in obedience to that duty which gave birth to this reply, submit to our fellow citizens, some reflections on these laws.

The act concerning aliens, makes it lawful for the President of the United States, to order all such aliens as he shall judge dangerous to the peace and safety of the United States, or shall have reasonable grounds to suspect are concerned in any treasonable or secret machinations against the government thereof, to depart out of the territory of the United States within such time as shall be expressed in such order.

This law has been declared to be unconstitutional, because—first, it transcends the powers of Congress; 2nd, it violates that article which restrains the prohibition of migration till 1808; 3d, it unites legislative, executive and judicial powers in the chief magistrate; 4th, it deprives aliens of the constitutional right of the trial by jury.

Time will not allow a minute investigation of this subject, the several objections will be but briefly reviewed.

1st, It is alledged to be an exercise of a power not delegated. The constitution of the United States, is in its organization dissimilar to any scheme of government which has been heretofore devised.

It presents to us for many purposes an entire nation, and for other purposes several distinct and perfect sovereignties—Perpetual peace among ourselves; a complete participation of privileges through all the states, and above all safety from abroad, were perhaps the strong motives which induced America to unite under one government. All objects which are general in their nature, which interest all America, which are connected with the general safety; all external objects can only be obtained by the co-operation of the whole, and therefore the powers necessary for their attainment would be naturally vested in the government of the whole. The vast mass of local and interior regulation can be most beneficially attended to by the state sovereignties, and therefore the government of the union is, and ought to be excluded from participating in their formation.

When we examine the situation of the United States, and the objects for which its government must necessarily have been formed, the mind is irresistably led to the demarcation of a plain line of partition between the general and particular sovereignties. Since the general and state governments equally represent the people, and are alike dependent on them for their origin and their continuance, and are alike accountable to them for their misconduct, those powers which are essential to our happiness and protection, may, with equal safety, as to their abuse, be trusted to the one or to the other. It is therefore rational to suppose, that they are placed where they can be exercised most beneficially, and that they are given to that government which is destined to effect the particular object for which those powers are calculated. This obvious principle seems to have actuated those who framed our constitutions; the powers of peace, war and commerce, of external intercourse in all its variety of forms, of calling out and directing the force and wealth of the nation, are placed in the general government: they are rightly placed, because to that government we look for protection from enemies of every denomination.

With respect to these objects, America is one nation, and therefore the state governments are restrained from interfering with these great acts of sovereignty: The power of protecting the nation from the intrigues and conspiracies of dangerous aliens who may have introduced themselves into the bosom of our country, seems to be of the class with those necessarily delegated to the general government: security to the union from their wicked machinations, cannot otherwise be ensured, and this security is essential to the common good. The means of obtaining intelligence of their plots are in possession only of the general government, nor can any one state do more than expel them from its territory; their right of residence is not unfrequently provided for in treaties, and treaties can only be formed or dissolved by the general government. If in the act of removing them unjustifiable injuries be committed, reparation is demandable by the sovereign of their nation.

This reparation is demandable not from the state, but from the United States government. All America is therefore interested in the manner in which this power shall be exercised, and would consequently choose to place it in hands which all America controls.

In conformity then with the general theory of our government, the power of protecting us from the conspiracies of aliens should be associated in the same hands with the force of the nation and the general power of protection from hostility of every kind. Yet it is admitted, that if in the formation of our constitution a different arrangement is made, that arrangement, however inconvenient, must be sacredly obeyed till constitutionally changed.

It behoves us, however, to satisfy ourselves completely on this interesting point.

The government of the United States is indubitably limited as to its objects, however it may be as to the means of obtaining those objects. It possesses only delegated powers, and it is proper to enquire whether the power now under consideration be delegated or not. It is necessary, in pursuing this enquiry, to bear in mind that we are investigating a constitution which must unavoidably be restricted in various points to general expressions, making the great outlines of a subject, and not a law which is capable of descending to every minute detail.

If we construe the former by rules strictly applicable to the latter, the power of fortifying our ports and harbours might well be questioned; nor could the utility of the clause authorising Congress to make all laws necessary and proper for carrying into execution all powers vested by the constitution in the government of the United States, or in any department or officer thereof, be readily pointed out. It would be difficult too to assign a reason for omitting, in the 12th amendment of our constitution which is evidently copied from the 2nd article of the ancient confederation, the very material word *expressly*. That article of the ancient confederation, and the amendment of our constitution, were designed as a plain and explicit admission of the principle, that the powers not delegated are retained. In the confederation all powers not *expressly* delegated, are retained, but in the amendment this very operative word is wisely omitted.

In reviewing then our constitution, to decide on the powers vested for general purposes, in our general government, we must examine the whole paper, we must examine it fairly, but liberally.

Congress has power "to declare war, grant letters of marque and reprisal, and make rules concerning captures on land and water." To make reprisals is a power distinct from, and which not unfrequently precedes war; as a branch of this power, those members of Congress who are decided in their declarations against the alien law, united in 1794 in support of the bill for sequestering British *property*. But reprisals may be made on the *persons* as well as the *property* of aliens; and as sequestration is the exercise, in an inferior degree, of the general power of reprisal on property, so may the removal of aliens be power of reprisal on persons. If the whole power of reprisal be delegated, the particular degree or manner in which it shall be exercised, is a question of particular discretion, and not of constitutional authority.

Congress has power "to define and punish piracies and felonies, committed on the high seas, *and offences against the law of nations.*"

By the law of nations, or by particular treaty, an alien acquires a right of residence in a country at peace with his own, and it is an offence against that law to become dangerous to the peace and safety or to be concerned in any treasonable or secret machinations against the government of the country in which he resides. These offences congress may both *define* and *punish*.

Congress may call forth the militia, "to suppress insurrections and repel invasions;" and further, "the United States shall guarantee to every state in the union, a republican form of government, and *shall protect each of them against invasions.*"

By this latter clause, something further was intended than merely to *repel* invasion. Invasion actually made is to be *repelled,* and for that purpose the militia may be called out. But congress is to do more than merely to repel the actual invasion. This power having been granted by the 8th section of the first article, the constitution in the 4th section of the fourth article, gives the additional power, and makes it the duty of Congress to *protect* each state against invasion. To *protect* against an evil, includes the right of taking proper and necessary steps for its prevention. Of these proper and necessary steps, the government possessed of the power must judge. To cause to depart from our territory the individuals of a nation from whom invasion was apprehended, is most obviously a measure of precaution dictated by prudence and warranted by justice. It appears then to be fairly deducible, from the theory of the constitution, and from a correct view of its particular parts, that the power of protecting the American commonwealth against dangerous aliens, whether dispersed through the interior of our country, or embodied in arms against us, is an existing efficient power placed like all others necessary for the common safety, in the only hands which can bring it into complete and beneficial operation.

2d. The exercise of this power is supposed to have been suspended until the year 1808, by the 9th section of the 1st article of the constitution.

The words are "the migration or importation of such persons as any of the states now existing shall think proper to admit, shall not be prohibited by the Congress prior to the year 1808, but a tax or duty may be imposed on such importation, not exceeding ten dollars for each person."

This is obviously designed as an exception to some given power. It would be extravagantly absurd to restrain until the year 1808, the exercise of a power which could not be exercised after that year. Whatever then is suspended by the article just recited, was considered as an existing thing on which the suspended clause could operate. It is the importation and migration of such persons as any of the states then existing should think proper to admit. But for this cause then, it would be in the power of congress to prohibit the migration of aliens into the United States. It will not be easy to find in the constitution a grant of power competent to forbid their entry, which is not equally competent to forbid their continuance in our country. But while this clause furnishes a strong argument in favor of the general power of Congress over the subject, it is necessary to show that the exception to that general power which it specifies, does not so modify it as to expose us to the machinations of aliens, who, in our bosom, may be conspiring our destruction.

To forbid indiscriminately the admission of certain classes of persons, and to order individuals of those classes to depart when they become dangerous, are certainly two distinct acts, which may be performed separately, and which do not necessarily interfere with each other. This cannot be questioned—but it is said that the power of ordering suspected aliens to leave our country may be so used as to destroy substantially the power of tolerating their migration; and it is granted that it may be so used, but the possibility of abusing a principle is never supposed to be a correct argument against its use. That the militia may be kept in the field throughout the year is no argument against the power of training them, nor can it be admitted that the possibility of extracting the last shilling from the purse of every individual, is a sufficient objection to the existence of the power of taxation. The right of ordering aliens to depart from the United States is confined to those who are deemed dangerous; and such a construction of the law as would substantially deprive the states of the benefits resulting from the migration of such persons as they might think proper to admit, would be a perversion, and not an execution of it.

It may also be said with respect to Virginia, that she has not chosen to admit the migration of such persons as the alien law enjoins to depart. No law of this state authorises the migration into it of persons of the description comprehended in the act of the United States: on the contrary, our laws expressly authorise the executive to apprehend and secure, or compel to depart this commonwealth, all suspicious persons, being the subjects of any foreign power or state, from whom the president of the United States shall apprehend hostile designs against the said states. If then the power of ordering certain persons to depart is to be connected with that of admitting their migration, the state of Virginia does not admit, but excludes from her territory all those who are contemplated by the alien law.

3dly. This law is also objected to, because it unites legislative, executive and judiciary powers in the President of the United States.

Legislation is the act of making or giving laws, Congress therefore in making this law, performed the part of the legislature, nor is there any thing legislative in the execution of it. If indeed Congress by itself, or perhaps by commissioners appointed by itself, had executed the law, the charge would have worn some semblance of truth; but the commission of the execution of this law to the person charged by the constitution with the execution of all the laws of the union, is certainly in itself unexceptionable. Nor does this act transfer to the President powers belonging properly to the judiciary. It does not involve a decision that its object has committed a crime. It is a measure of general safety, in its nature political and not forensic, the execution of which is properly trusted to the department which represents the nation in all its interior relations—Every law, in its execution, requires some judgment, but the execution of the law is not on that account judicial.

4th. This act deprives the alien of his right of trial by jury. To this extraordinary allegation, it has again and again been answered, that this is a measure of preventive and not of punishing justice. Who would require that a jury should be impannelled, in order to decide whether a nation had or had not cause to suspect a particular alien of dangerous designs against its peace? who would require that the President should unfold to juries throughout the United States all the intelligence he may have received, perhaps from persons within the reach of those employing the aliens, and which establishes in his mind the reality of the danger to be apprehended. Certainly a vested right is to be taken from no individual without a solemn trial, but the right of remaining in our country is vested in no alien; he enters and remains by the courtesy of the sovereign power, and that courtesy may at pleasure be withdrawn. That Virginia considers the two last objections groundless, is demonstrated by her own act on the same subject. By the 2d section of the sixty-second chapter of our laws, it is enacted, that "it shall and may be lawful for the Governor, with the advice of the council of state, to apprehend and secure, or cause to be apprehended and secured, or compelled to depart this commonwealth, all suspicious persons, being the subjects of any foreign power or state who shall have made a declaration of war, or actually commenced hostilities against the said states, or from whom the President of the United States shall apprehend hostile designs against the said states; provided information thereof shall have been previously received by the executive from him. And in all such cases the Governor, with the advice of the council of state, shall, and he is hereby empowered to send for the person and papers of any foreigner within this state, in order to obtain such information as he may judge necessary."

If the alien law of the United States be an union of legislative, executive and judiciary powers, so is that of Virginia: if one is unconstitutional by depriving an alien of trial by jury, so is the other. This is a question entirely separated from the powers of the different governments; because the provisions of the one constitution, are in these respects as explicit as those of the other. This act of our legislature was not passed hastily or inconsiderately—It was originally enacted in 1785 under the auspices of some of the most zealous opposers of powers of the act of Congress—It was revised, corrected, and reported by the judges and others appointed to collate and digest all the laws of the state. It was then re-enacted in 1792.

Never, during this investigation and re-investigation, did it occur to a single individual, that to order an alien to depart the commonwealth, first under the suggestion of Congress under the old confederation, and afterwards on the suggestion of the President under our improved constitution, united legislative, executive and judicial powers, or deprived an alien of a trial to which he was entitled, viz. trial by jury.

That this measure should originally have been suggested as necessary for national safety, that it should have been preserved through a long course of reflection, that it should be deemed free from the objection of uniting the powers of different departments in the executive, as also of depriving an alien from his residence without a trial by jury, and yet that it should for the same causes produce a ferment in some states, as soon as the principle was adopted by Congress, might warrant reflections which we will not permit ourselves to express.

The act entitled "An act in addition to the act entitled an act for the punishment of certain crimes against the United States," and which is commonly called the Sedition Law, subjects to a fine not exceeding two thousand dollars, and to imprisonment not exceeding two years, any person who shall write, print, utter or publish, or cause or procure to be written, printed, uttered or published, any false, scandalous, malicious writing or writings against the government of the United States, or either house of Congress of the United States, or the President of the United States, with intent to defame the said government, or either house of Congress, or the said President, or to bring them, or either of them, into contempt or disrepute, or to excite against them, or either or any of them, the hatred of the good people of the United States, or to stir up sedition within the United States, or to excite any unlawful combinations therein for opposing or resisting any law of the United States, or any act of the President of the United States, done in pursuance of such a law, or of the powers in him vested by the constitution of the United States, or to resist, oppose or defeat any such law or act; or to aid, encourage or abet any hostile design of any foreign nation, against the United States, their people or government; the person accused is to be tried by jury, and may give in evidence the proof of the matter contained in the libel.

To constitute the crime, the writing must be false, scandalous and malicious, and the intent must be to effect some one of the ill purposes described in the act.

To contend that there does not exist a power to punish writings coming within the description of this law, would be to assert the inability of our nation to preserve its own peace, and to protect themselves from the attempt of wicked citizens, who incapable of quiet themselves, are incessantly employed in devising means to disturb the public repose.

Government is instituted and preserved for the general happiness and safety; the people therefore are interested in its preservation, and have a right to adopt measures for its security, as well against secret plots as open hostility. But government cannot be thus secured, if, by falsehood and malicious slander, it is to be deprived of the confidence and affection of the people. It is in vain to urge that truth will prevail, and that slander, when detected, recoils on the calumniator. The experience of the world, and our own experience, prove that a continued course of defamation will at length sully the fairest reputation, and will throw suspicion on the purest conduct. Although the calumnies of the factious and discontented may not poison the minds of a majority of the citizens, yet they will infect a very considerable number, and prompt them to deeds destructive of the public peace, and dangerous to the general safety. This the people have a right to prevent: and therefore, in all the nations of the earth, where presses are known, some corrective of the licentiousness has been indispensable. But it is contended, that though this may be theoretically true, such is the peculiar structure of our government, that this power has either never been confided to, or has been withdrawn from the legislature of the union. We will examine these positions. The power of making all laws which shall be necessary and proper for carrying into execution all powers vested by the constitution in the government of the United States, or in any department or officer thereof, is by the concluding clause of the eighth section of the first article, expressly delegated to Congress. This clause is admitted to authorise Congress to pass any act for the punishment of those who would resist the execution of the law, because such an act would be incontestably necessary and proper for carrying into execution the power vested in the government. If it authorises the punishment of actual resistance, does it not also authorise punishment of those acts which are criminal in themselves, and which obviously lead to and prepare resistance? Would it not be strange, if, for the purpose of executing the legitimate powers of the government, a clause like that which has been cited should be so construed as to permit the passage of laws punishing acts which constitute the germ from which resistance springs? That the government must look on, and see preparation for resistance which it shall be unable to control, until they shall break out in open force? This would be an unreasonable and improvident construction of the article under consideration. That continued calumnies against the government have this tendency, is demonstrated by uninterrupted experience. They will, if unrestrained, produce in any society, convulsions which, if not totally destructive of, will yet be very injurious to its prosperity and welfare. It is not to be believed that the people of the western parts in Pennsylvania could have been deluded into that unprovoked and wanton insurrection, which called forth the militia of the neighbouring states, if they had not been at the same time irritated and seduced, by calumnies with which certain presses incessantly teemed, into the opinion that the people of America, instead of supporting their government and their laws, would join in their subversion. Those calumnies then, tended to prevent the execution of the laws of the union, and such seems to be their obvious and necessary tendency.

To publish malicious calumnies against an individual, with an intent to defame him, is a wrong on the part of the calumniator, and an injury to the individual, for which the laws afford redress. To write or print these calumnies is such an aggravation of the crime, as to constitute an offence against the government, and the author of the libel is subject to the additional punishment which may be inflicted under an indictment. To publish malicious calumnies against government itself, is a wrong on the part of the calumniator, and an injury to all those who have an interest in the government.

Those who have this interest and have sustained the injury, have, the natural right to an adequate remedy. The people of the United States have a common interest in their government, and sustain in common the injury which affects that government. The people of the United States therefore have a right to the remedy for that injury, and are substantially the party seeking redress. By the 2d section of the third article of the constitution, the judicial power of the United States is extended to controversies to which the United States shall be a party; and by the same article it is extended to all cases of law and equity arising under the constitution, the laws of the United States and treaties made or which shall be made under their authority. What are cases arising under the constitution, as contradistinguished from those which arise under the laws made pursuant thereof? They must be cases triable by a rule which exists independent of any act of the legislature of the union. That rule is the common or unwritten law which pervades all America, and which declaring libels against government to be a punishable offence, applies itself to, and protects any government which the will of the people may establish. The judicial power of the United States, then, being extended to the punishment of libels against the government, as a common law offence, arising under the constitution which creates the government, the general clause gives to the legislature of the union the right to make such laws as shall give that power effect.

That such was the contemporaneous construction of the constitution, is obvious from one of the amendments which have been made to it. The 3d amendment, which declares that Congress shall make no law abridging the property of the press, is a general construction made by all America on the original instrument, admitting its application to the subject: It would have been certainly unnecessary thus to have modified the legislative powers of Congress concerning the press, if the power itself does not exist.

But although the original constitution may be supposed to have enabled the government to defend itself against false and malicious libels, endangering the peace, and threatening the tranquility of the American people, yet it is contended the 3d amendment to that instrument, has deprived it of this power. The amendment is in these words. "Congress shall make no law respecting an establishment of religion, or prohibiting the free exercise thereof, or abridging the freedom of speech, or of the press."

In a solemn instrument, as is a constitution, words are well weighed and considered, before they are adopted. A remarkable diversity of expression is not used, unless it be designed to manifest a difference of intention. Congress is prohibited from making any law respecting a religious establishment, but not from making any law respecting the press. When the power of Congress relative to the press is to be limited, the word *respecting* is dropped, and Congress is only restrained from passing any law abridging its liberty. This difference of expression with respect to religion and the press, manifests a difference of intention with respect to the power of the national legislature over those subjects, both in the person who drew, and in those who adopted the amendment.

All abridgment of the freedom of the press is forbidden, but it is only an abridgment of that freedom which is forbidden. It becomes then necessary in order to determine whether the act in question be unconstitutional or not to inquire whether it does in fact *abridge* the freedom of the press.

The act is believed not to have that operation, for two reasons.

1st. A punishment of the licentiousness is not considered as a restriction of the freedom of the press.

2. The act complained of does not punish any writing not before punishable, nor does it inflict a more severe penalty than that to which the same writing was before liable.

1st. If by freedom of the press is meant a perfect exemption from all punishment for whatever may be published, that freedom never has, and most probably never will exist. It is known to all, that the person who writes or publishes a libel, may be both sued and indicted, and must bear the penalty which the judgment of his country inflicts upon him. It is also known to all that the person who shall libel the government of the state, is for that offence punishable in the like manner. Yet this liability to punishment for slanderous and malicious publications, has never been considered as detracting from the liberty of the press. In fact the liberty of the press is a term which has a definite and appropriate signification, completely understood. It signifies a liberty to publish, free from previous restraint, any thing and every thing at the discretion of the printer only, but not the liberty of spreading with impunity false and scandalous slanders, which may destroy the peace, and mangle the reputation, of an individual or of a community.

If this definition of the term be correct, and it is presumed that its correctness is not to be questioned, then a law punishing the authors and publishers of false, malicious and scandalous libels can be no attack on the liberty of the press.

But the act complained of is no abridgment of the liberty of the press, for another reason.

2d. It does not punish any writing not before punishable, nor does it inflict a heavier penalty than the same writing was before liable to.

No man will deny, that at common law, the author and publisher of a false, scandalous and malicious libel, against the government or an individual, were subject to fine and imprisonment, at the discretion of the judge. Nor will it be denied, that previous to our revolution, the common law was the law of the land throughout the United States.

We believe it to be a principle incontestibly true, that a change of government does not dissolve obligations previously created, does not annihilate existing laws, and dissolve the bonds of society; but that a people passing

from one form of government to another, retain in full force all their munici-
pal institutions, not necessarily changed by the change of government. If
this be true, then the common law continued to be the law of the land after
the revolution, and was of complete obligation even before the act of our
assembly for its adoption. Whether similar acts have been passed by the
legislatures of other states or not, it is certain that in every state the common
law is admitted to be in full force, except as it may have been altered by
the statute law. The only question is, whether the doctrines of the common
law are applicable to libels against the government of the United States,
as well as to libel against the governments of the particular states. For such
a distinction there seems to be no sufficient reason. It is not to a magistrate
of this or that description that the rules of the common law apply. That he
is a magistrate, that he is cloathed with the authority of the laws, that he
is invested with power chosen by the people, is a sufficient title to the protection of the common law. The government of the United States is for
certain purposes as entirely the government of each state, chosen by the
people thereof, and cloathed with their authority, as the government of each
particular state is the government of every subdivision of that state; and
no satisfactory reason has been heretofore assigned why a general rule common to all, and punishing generally the malicious calumniators of magistrates, should not be as applicable to magistrates chosen for the whole, as
those chosen for its different parts.

If then it were even true that the punishment of the printer of malicious
falsehoods affected the liberty of the press, yet the act does not *abridge* the
liberty, since it does not substitute a harsher or severer rule of punishment
than that which before existed.

On points so extremely interesting, a difference of opinion will be entertained. On such occasions all parties must be expected to maintain their
real opinions, but to maintain them with moderation and with decency. The
will of the majority must prevail, or the republican principle is abandoned,
and the nation is destroyed. If upon every constitutional question which
presents itself, or on every question we choose to term constitutional, the
constructions of the majority shall be forcibly opposed, and hostility to the
government excited throughout the nation, there is an end of our domestic
peace, and we may for ever bid adieu to our representative government.

The legislature of Virginia has itself passed more than one unconstitutional law, but they have not been passed with an intention to violate the
constitution. On being decided to be unconstitutional by the legitimate
authority, they have been permitted to fall. Had the judges deemed them
constitutional, they would have been maintained. The same check, nor is it
a less efficient one, exists in the government of the Union. The judges of
the United States are as independent as the judges of the state of Virginia,
nor is there any reason to believe them less wise and less virtuous. It is

their province and their duty to construe the constitution and the laws, and it cannot be doubted, but that they will perform this duty faithfully and truly. They will perform it unwarped by political debate, uninfluenced by party zeal. Let us in the mean time seek a repeal of any acts we may disapprove, by means authorized by our happy constitution; but let us not endeavor to disseminate among our fellow citizens the most deadly hating against the government of their own creation, against the government, on the preservation of which we firmly believe the peace and liberty of America to depend, because in some respects its judgments has differed from our own.

Various other points are noticed in the address alike calculated to excite your resentment, and provoke your resistance. Seriously do we regret the expression of such sentiments by a body so respectable.

At a time when all ought to unite in repelling every evidence of the existence of division in the United States, on which division our enemy calculates, and with her knowledge of which has had the presumption to upbraid us, it cannot but inflict a deep wound in the American mind to find the commonwealth of Virginia, exhibiting through her legislature, irresistable testimony of the degrading charge; nor will the embittering reflection be softened by the declaration of a determination to repel a foreign invasion, which is occasionally interspersed in those proceedings. Hatred to government is unapt to beget a disposition to unite in its defence, and more probably would project other schemes, coupling defence from invasion, with change of political system. The result of which might be union with the invader, for the purpose of accomplishing a *delectable* reform. Unfortunately for the human race, such coalitions have happened, and unfortunately for the American people, another influence of like conduct may be afforded. Exhortations to disregard foreign danger under pretence of opposing domestic usurpation, is an artifice which has often been used to divide and ruin republican governments. Switzerland has lately afforded a fatal proof of this melancholy truth, and may Heaven avert the like fate from us.

One other fertile topic of complaint against the general government, we must notice; its fiscal arrangements, and increasing expences.

In considering this subject, always recollect that our revolutionary war left the nation with a heavy debt, (the price of its independence), and bereft of the means of discharging it.

When an individual, or nation, cannot pay the principal of an honest debt and can pay the interest, every fair motive commands the principal to be secured, and the interest to be punctually paid. Obedience to this honest injunction produced the funded debt of the United States; and although we pretend not to say that some mode more consonant to the American character might not have been adopted, producing the same end, yet we do assert that the mode adopted was the result of much labor, and much investigation; and that it received the constitutional sanction. From this we infer that acquiescence in, and support of the system, is the proper conduct of every good citizen.

Added to this original debt, has been the vast expence of defending Kentucky and the western frontiers from the Indian enemy, and the establishment of government in the north and south-western territory.

At present, the defence of the United States claims money, and their defence cannot but swell considerably the public demands:—The stake is our all—and to save his all, who would begrudge a part?

But we derive great consolation in reminding ourselves of the following facts: That our resources are vast, are annually increasing, are managed with ability, and disbursed with integrity; that they are applied to promote the people's good, and the people's good only, consonant to their intention, and by their chosen servants: That the choice of our functionaries recurs as usual when the faithful servant will receive his reward, and the unfaithful be ordered to depart: That we are a great, powerful and independent nation—and that the safety and happiness of such a people cannot be promoted without proportionate supplies of their money: That the weight of taxation in the congressional system falls almost entirely on the rich: That the capacity to pay rises in proportion to our security from abroad, and our tranquility at home; that the preservation of peace is, as it has been, our constant desire, to prevent the interruption of which, our government has ably and perseveringly struggled that war, in defiance of all our endeavors, impends over our heads; and that to avert its calamity, we must be prepared to meet it like men.

Continuing to confide in our government; continuing to regard union as the rock of our political salvation, and the constitution as the mean of its preservation; continuing to prefer a state of peace without dishonor, we will not turn from the perils of war, with a degraded name; but, like our fathers, will be ready to risque life and fortune; expecting from the timely exertions of our government, to be enabled to meet any, and every enemy, on equal terms.

THE HOUSE DIVIDED

If we could first know *where* we are, and *whither* we are tending, we could then better judge *what* to do, and *how* to do it. We are now far into the *fifth* year, since a policy was initiated, with the avowed object, and *confident* promise, of putting an end to slavery agitation. Under the operation of that policy, that agitation has not only, not ceased but has *constantly augmented*. In *my* opinion, it *will* not cease, until a *crisis* shall have been reached, and passed. "A house divided against itself cannot stand." I believe that this government cannot endure, permanently half *slave* and half *free*. I do not expect the Union to be *dissolved*—I do not expect the house to *fall*—but I *do* expect it will cease to be divided. It will become *all* one thing, or *all* the other.

Abraham Lincoln, "A House Divided"
Speech at Springfield, Illinois,
June 16, 1858

IV

JOHN C. CALHOUN
(1782–1850)

JOHN C. CALHOUN's public service began when he was elected to the U.S. House of Representatives in 1810. He served there until 1817, when he was appointed Secretary of War. Eight years later he began two terms as Vice-President, first under John Quincy Adams and then under Andrew Jackson. He resigned the Vice-Presidency in 1832 in order to represent South Carolina in the Senate, remaining in that office until his death in 1850, with the exception of a brief term (1844–45) as Secretary of State under President Tyler.

Calhoun is known as the great advocate of the "positive good" doctrine of slavery. His "fixed principles" are elaborated in the "South Carolina Exposition and Protest" (1828) and the "Fort Hill Address" (1831).

An economic conflict between the North and the South emerged in the late 1820s over the issue of protectionist policies versus lower duties on imports. As an exporting section, the South's economy depended on foreign markets. She was also an importer, and it was in her interest to buy abroad as cheaply as possible. The manufacturing North, fearing competition from abroad, successfully pressed for governmental protection, and high duties were specified in the "Tariff of Abominations" of 1828. The original draft of Calhoun's first great document on the sectional question, the "Exposition and Protest," written in opposition to the passage of this tariff, was prepared as a report for a special committee of the South Carolina legislature.

118

Though the report was not officially adopted, the lower house ordered a printing of 5,000 copies, and therefore it has generally been considered an official document.

The "Exposition" states Calhoun's view of the effects of such tariff acts on the South. The Constitution gives the Congress the power to impose duties on imports for revenue, but this power was being used by the majority not only for revenue, but for "rearing up the industry of one section of the country on the ruins of another." The Constitution was thus violated by use of a power intended for a legitimate object to accomplish an illegitimate one. Moreover, through the tariff the South was contributing more than its fair share to the support of the national government and receiving an ever-less adequate return in benefits.

The doctrine of nullification, as presented in the "Exposition," was based on historical arguments for state sovereignty. From Calhoun's reading of the records of the Constitutional Convention, the Constitution emerged as an agreement made by sovereign states. As parties to the constitutional compact, the states retained the right, unrestricted in all areas not surrendered to the national government, to judge the extent of their obligations imposed by the compact, or constitution. More specifically, that reserved right meant the right to judge and, if necessary, to nullify national laws. Whenever a state convention, called for that purpose, decided that the state's constitutional rights were violated by a national law, the state had the right to declare that law null and void within its boundaries and to refuse to permit its enforcement there. By this exercise of its veto power, the state would force the federal government to submit the controversial federal law for adjudication to the several states through the amendment process. In the event of passage of the amendment by the necessary three-fourths majority, the state retained the right of secession.

By 1831, Calhoun defined his problem as one of reestablishing an equilibrium of powers, a balance of majority and minority interests within the American community. His "Fort Hill Address," on July 26 of that year, considered the relation between the states and "general government." For the protection of minority interests, Calhoun reasoned, separation of powers within the government and simple majority rule were not enough, for majorities within a major political party could gain control of the three branches of the federal government and violate the rights of minorities. What was needed was a principle calculated to prevent any one interest or combination of interests from using the powers of the government to aggrandize itself at the expense of other interests. This principle, based on interests as well as numbers, came to be called the theory of the concurrent majority; Calhoun first used the term in August 1832.

According to this theory, each sectional major-interest majority would have the constitutional power to veto acts of the national government (which merely represent the numerical majority) when they were considered by a majority of people comprising a section or interest to be contrary to their own welfare. The will of the sectional majority would thus act concurrently with the numerical majority, with the former applied by aggrieved minorities to guard against the encroachment of the latter. Calhoun believed that this device would unite the most opposite and conflicting sectional interests and blend the nation's populace into support of common goals.

Calhoun's theory of the concurrent majority, it should be noted, rested on the assumption of the positive goodness of slavery, and nullification was the device for ensuring it. When Calhoun asserted in the Senate in 1837 that slavery was a positive good, he was the first southern politician of major rank to do so. In 1842, moreover, he rejected the "created equal" proposition in the Declaration of Independence—the credo of the American regime. Think of the significance of a nation saying that the "created equal" proposition in the Declaration was not meant to include the black American! Calhoun developed the principle of an alternative regime, to be made possible by nullification. So, while the doctrine of nullification was the constitutional issue over which the North and South argued, the underlying issue in the sectional controversy was the clash of two contrary regimes, two opposing principles.

26

SOUTH CAROLINA EXPOSITION
AND PROTEST
December 1828

THE COMMITTEE HAVE BESTOWED on the subjects referred to them the deliberate attention which their importance demands; and the result, on full investigation, is a unanimous opinion that the act of Congress of the last session, with the whole system of legislation imposing duties on imports,— not for revenue, but the protection of one branch of industry at the expense of others,—is unconstitutional, unequal, and oppressive, and calculated to corrupt the public virtue and destroy the liberty of the country; which propositions they propose to consider in the order stated, and then to conclude their report with the consideration of the important question of the remedy.

The committee do not propose to enter into an elaborate or refined argument on the question of the constitutionality of the Tariff system. The General Government is one of specific powers, and it can rightfully exercise only the powers expressly granted, and those that may be necessary and proper to carry them into effect, all others being reserved expressly to the States or the people. It results, necessarily, that those who claim to exercise power under the Constitution, are bound to show that it is expressly granted, or that it is necessary and proper as a means to some of the granted powers. The advocates of the Tariff have offered no such proof. It is true that the third section of the first article of the Constitution authorizes Congress to lay and collect an impost duty, but it is granted as a tax power for the sole purpose of revenue,—a power in its nature essentially different from that of imposing protective or prohibitory duties. Their objects are incompatible. The prohibitory system must end in destroying the revenue from imports. It has been said that the system is a violation of the spirit, and not the letter of the Constitution. The distinction is not material. The Constitution may be as grossly violated by acting against its meaning as against its letter; but it may be proper to dwell a moment on the point in order to understand more fully the real character of the acts under which the interest of this, and other States similarly situated, has been sacrificed. The facts are few and simple. The Constitution grants to Congress the power of imposing a duty on imports for revenue, which power is abused by being converted into an instrument of rearing up the industry of one section of the country on the ruins of another. The violation, then, consists in using a power granted for one object to advance another, and that by the sacrifice of the original object. It is, in a word, a violation by perversion,—the most dangerous of all because the most insidious and difficult to resist. Others cannot be perpetrated without the aid of the judiciary;—this may be by the Executive and Legislative departments alone. The courts cannot look into the motives of legislators. They are obliged to take acts by their titles and professed objects, and if these be constitutional, they cannot interpose their power, however grossly the acts may, in reality, violate the Constitution. The proceedings of the last session sufficiently prove that the House of Representatives are aware of the distinction, and determined to avail themselves of its advantage.

In the absence of arguments, drawn from the Constitution itself, the advocates of the power have attempted to call in the aid of precedent. The committee will not waste their time in examining the instances quoted. If they were strictly in point, they would be entitled to little weight. Ours is not a Government of precedents, nor can they be admitted, except to a very limited extent, and with great caution, in the interpretation of the Constitution, without changing, in time, the entire character of the instrument. The only safe rule is the Constitution itself,—or, if that be doubtful, the history of the times. In this case, if doubts existed, the journals of the Convention itself would remove them. It was moved in that body to confer on Congress the very power in question to encourage manufactures, but it was deliberately withheld, except to the extent of granting patent rights for new and useful inventions. Instead of granting the power, permission was given to the States to impose duties, with the consent of Congress, to encourage their own manufactures; and thus, in the true spirit of justice, imposing the burden on those who were to be benefited. But, giving the precedents every weight that may be claimed for them, the committee feel confident that, in this case, there are none in point previous to the adoption of the present Tariff system. Every instance which has been quoted, may fairly be referred to the legitimate power of Congress, to impose duties on imports for revenue. It is a necessary incident of such duties to act as an encouragement to manufactures, whenever imposed on articles which may be manufactured in our country. In this incidental manner, Congress has the power of encouraging manufactures; and the committee readily concede that, in the passage of an impost bill, that body may, in modifying the details, so arrange the provisions of the bill, as far as it may be done consistently with its proper object, as to aid manufactures. To this extent Congress may constitutionally go, and has gone from the commencement of the Government, which will fully explain the precedents cited from the early stages of its operation. Beyond this they never proceeded till the commencement of the present system, the inequality and oppression of which they will next proceed to consider.

On entering on this branch of the subject, the committee feel the painful character of the duty which they must perform. They would desire never to speak of our country, as far as the action of the General Government is concerned, but as one great whole, having a common interest, which all the parts ought zealously to promote. Previously to the adoption of the Tariff system, such was the unanimous feeling of this State; but in speaking of its operation, it will be impossible to avoid the discussion of sectional interest, and the use of sectional language. On its authors, and not on us, who are compelled to adopt this course in self-defence, by injustice and oppression, be the censure.

So partial are the effects of the system, that its burdens are exclusively on one side and its benefits on the other. It imposes on the agricultural interest of the South, including the South-west, and that portion of the country particularly engaged in commerce and navigation, the burden not only of sustaining the system itself, but that also of the Government. In stating the case thus strongly, it is not the intention of the committee to exaggerate. If exaggeration were not unworthy of the gravity of the subject, the reality is such as to make it unnecessary. . . .

The question, in what manner the loss and gain of the system distribute themselves among the several classes of society, is intimately connected with that of their distribution among the several sections. Few subjects present more important points for consideration; but as it is not possible for the committee to enter fully into the discussion of them, without swelling their report beyond all reasonable bounds, they will pass them over with a few brief and general remarks.

The system has not been sufficiently long in operation with us, to display its real character in reference to the point now under discussion. To understand its ultimate tendency, in distributing the wealth of society among the several classes, we must turn our eyes to Europe, where it has been in action for centuries,—and operated as one among the efficient causes of that great inequality of property which prevails in most European countries. No system can be more efficient to rear up a moneyed aristocracy. Its tendency is, to make the poor poorer, and the rich richer. Heretofore, in our country, this tendency has displayed itself principally in its effects, as regards the different sections,—but the time will come when it will produce the same results between the several classes in the manufacturing States. After we are exhausted, the contest will be between the capitalists and operatives; for into these two classes it must, ultimately, divide society. The issue of the struggle here must be the same as it has been in Europe. Under the operation of the system, wages must sink more rapidly than the prices of the necessaries of life, till the operatives will be reduced to the lowest point,—when the portion of the products of their labor left to them, will be barely sufficient to preserve existence. For the present, the pressure of the system is on our section. Its effects on the staple States produce almost universal suffering. In the mean time, an opposite state of things exists in the manufacturing States. For the present, every interest among them,—except that of foreign trade and navigation, flourishes. Such must be the effect of a monopoly of so rich and extensive a market as that of the Southern States, till it is impoverished,—as ours rapidly must be, by the operation of the system, when its natural tendencies, and effects on the several classes of the community, will unfold themselves, as has been described by the committee.

It remains to be considered, in tracing the effects of the system, whether the gain of one section of the country be equal to the loss of the other. If such were the fact,—if all we lose be gained by the citizens of the other sections, we would, at least, have the satisfaction of thinking that, however unjust and oppressive, it was but a transfer of property, without diminishing the wealth of the community. Such, however, is not the fact; and to its other mischievous consequences we must add, that it destroys much more than it transfers. Industry cannot be forced out of its natural channel without loss; and this, with the injustice, constitutes the objection to the improper intermeddling of the Government with the private pursuits of individuals, who must understand their own interests better than the Government. The exact loss from such intermeddling, it may be difficult to ascertain, but it is not, therefore, the less certain. The committee will not undertake to estimate the millions, which are annually lost to our country, under the existing system; but some idea may be formed of its magnitude, by stating, that it is, at least, equal to the difference between the profits of our manufacturers, and the duties imposed for their protection, where these are not prohibitory. The lower the profit, and the higher the duty (if not, as stated, prohibitory),—the greater the loss. If, with these certain data, the evidence reported by the Committee on Manufactures at the last session of Congress, be examined, a pretty correct opinion may be formed of the extent of the loss of the country,—provided the manufacturers have fairly stated their case. With a duty of about forty per cent. on the leading articles of consumption (if we are to credit the testimony reported), the manufacturers did not realize, generally, a profit equal to the legal rate of interest; which would give a loss of largely upwards of thirty per cent. to the country on its products. It is different with the foreign articles of the same description. On them, the country, at least, loses nothing. There, the duty passes into the Treasury,—lost, indeed, to the Southern States, out of whose labor, directly or indirectly, it must, for the most part, be paid,—but transferred, through appropriations in a hundred forms, to the pockets of others. It is thus the system is cherished by appropriations; and well may its advocates affirm, that *they* constitute an essential portion of the American System. Let this conduit, through which it is so profusely supplied, be closed, and we feel confident that scarcely a State, except a real manufacturing one, would tolerate its burden. A total prohibition of importations, by cutting off the revenue, and thereby the means of making appropriations, would, in a short period, destroy it. But the excess of its loss over its gains leads to the consoling reflection, that its abolition would relieve us much more than it would embarrass the manufacturing States. We have suffered too much to desire to see others afflicted, even for our relief, when it can be possibly avoided. We would rejoice to see our manufactures flourish on any constitutional principle, consistent with justice and the public liberty. It is not against them, but the means by which they have been forced, to our ruin, that we object. As far as a moderate system, founded on imposts for revenue, goes, we are willing to afford protection, though we clearly see that, even under such a system, the national revenue would be based on our labor, and be paid by our industry. With such constitutional and moderate protection, the manufacturer ought to be satisfied. His loss would not be so great as might be supposed. If low duties would be followed by low prices, they would also diminish the costs of manufacturing; and thus the reduction of profit would be less in proportion than the reduction of the prices of the manufactured article. Be this, however, as it may, the General Government cannot proceed beyond this point of protection, consistently with its powers, and justice to the whole. If the manufacturing States deem further protection necessary, it is in their power to afford it to their citizens, within their own limits, against foreign competition, to any extent they may judge expedient. The Constitution authorizes them to lay an impost duty, with the assent of Congress, which, doubtless, would be given; and if that be not sufficient, they have the additional and efficient power of giving a direct bounty for their encouragement,—which the ablest writers on the subject concede to be the least burdensome and most effectual mode of encouragement. Thus, they who are to be benefited, will bear the burden, as they ought; and those who believe it is wise and just to protect manufactures, may have the satisfaction of doing it at their expense, and not at that of their fellow-citizens of the other States, who entertain precisely the opposite opinion.

The committee having presented its views on the partial and oppressive operation of the system, will proceed to discuss the next position which they proposed,—its tendency to corrupt the Government, and to destroy the liberty of the country.

If there be a political proposition universally true,—one which springs directly from the nature of man, and is independent of circumstances,—it is, that irresponsible power is inconsistent with liberty, and must corrupt those who exercise it. On this great principle our political system rests. We consider all powers as delegated by the people, and to be controlled by them, who are interested in their just and proper exercise; and our Governments, both State and General, are but a system of judicious contrivances to bring this fundamental principle into fair, practical operation. Among the most prominent of these is, the responsibility of representatives to their constituents, through frequent periodical elections, in order to enforce a faithful performance of their delegated trust. Without such a check on their powers, however clearly they may be defined and distinctly prescribed, our liberty would be but a mockery. The Government, instead of being directed to the general good, would speedily become but the instrument to aggrandize those who might be intrusted with its administration. On the other hand, if laws were uniform in their operation,—if that which imposed a burden on one, imposed it likewise on all—or that which acted beneficially for one, acted also, in the same manner, for all—the responsibility of representatives to their constituents would alone be sufficient to guard against abuse and tyranny—provided the people be sufficiently intelligent to understand their interest, and the motives and conduct of their public agents. But, if it be supposed that, from diversity of interests in the several classes and sections of the country, the laws act differently, so that the same law, though couched in general terms and apparently fair, shall, in reality, transfer the power and property of one class or section to another,—in such case, responsibility to constituents, which is but the means of enforcing fidelity of representatives to them, must prove wholly insufficient to preserve the purity of public agents, or the liberty of the country. It would, in fact, fall short of the evil. The disease would be in the community itself,—in the constituents, and not their representatives. The opposing interests of the community would engender, necessarily, opposing, hostile parties,—organized on this very diversity of interests,—the stronger of which, if the Government provided no efficient check, would exercise unlimited and unrestrained power over the weaker. The relation of equality between the parts of the community, established by the Constitution, would be destroyed, and in its place there would be substituted the relation of sovereign and subject, between the stronger and weaker interests, in its most odious and oppressive form. That this is a possible state of society, even where the representative system prevails, we have high authority. Mr. Hamilton, in the 51st number of the Federalist, says,—"It is of the greatest importance in a republic, not only to guard society against the oppression of its rulers, but to guard one part of society against the injustice of the other part. Different interests necessarily exist in different classes of citizens. If a majority be united by a common interest, the rights of the minority will be insecure." Again— "In a society, under the forms of which the stronger faction can readily unite and oppress the weaker, anarchy may be said as truly to reign, as in a state of nature, where the weaker individual is not secured against the violence of the stronger." We have still higher authority,—the unhappy existing example, of which we are the victims. The committee has labored to little purpose, if they have not demonstrated that the very case, which Mr. Hamilton so forcibly describes, does not now exist in our country, under the name of the AMERICAN SYSTEM,—and which, if not timely arrested, must be followed by all the consequences which never fail to spring from the exercise of irresponsible power. On the great and vital point—the industry of the country—which comprehends almost every interest—the interest of the two great sections is opposed. We want free trade,—they restrictions; we want moderate taxes, frugality in the Government, economy, accountability, and a rigid application of the public money to the payment of the debt, and to the objects authorized by the Constitution. In all these particulars, if we may judge by experience, their views of their interest are precisely the opposite. They feel and act, on all questions connected with the American System, as sovereigns,—as men invariably do who impose burdens on others for their own benefit; and we, on the other hand, like those on whom such burdens are imposed. In a word, to the extent stated, the country is divided and organized into two great parties—the one sovereign and the other subject—bearing towards each other all the attributes which must ever accompany that relation, under whatever form it may exist. That our industry is controlled by many, instead of one,—by a majority in Congress, *elected* by a majority in the community having an opposing interest, instead of by *hereditary* rulers,— forms not the slightest mitigation of the evil. In fact, instead of mitigating, it aggravates. In our case, one opposing branch of industry cannot prevail without associating others; and thus, instead of a single act of oppression, we must bear many. The history of the Woollen's Bill will illustrate the truth of this position. The woollen manufacturers found they were too feeble to enforce their exactions alone, and, of necessity, resorted to the expedient, which will ever be adopted in such cases, of associating other interests, till a majority be formed,—and the result of which, in this case, was, that instead of increased duties on woollens alone—which would have been the fact if that interest alone governed, we have to bear equally increased duties on more than a dozen other of the leading articles of consumption. It would be weakness to attempt to disguise the fact,—on a full knowledge of which, and of the danger it threatens, the hope of devising some means of security depends,—that different and opposing interests do, and must ever exist in all societies, against the evils of which representation opposes not the slightest resistance. Laws, so far from being uniform in their operation, are scarcely ever so. It requires the greatest wisdom and moderation to extend over any country a system of equal laws; and it is this very diversity of interests, which is found in all associations of men for a common purpose, be they private or public, that constitutes the main difficulty in forming and administering free and just governments. It is the door through which despotic power has, heretofore, ever entered, and must ever continue to enter, till some effectual barrier be provided. Without some such, it would be folly to hope for the duration of liberty;—as much so as to expect it without representation itself,—and for the same reason. The essence of liberty comprehends the idea of responsible power,—that those who make and execute the laws should be controlled by those on whom they operate,—that the *governed* should *govern*. To prevent rulers from abusing their trusts, constituents must control them through elections; and to prevent the major from oppressing the minor interests of society, the Constitution must provide (as the committee hope to prove it does) a check, founded on the same principle and equally efficacious. In fact, the abuse of delegated power, and the tyranny of the stronger over the weaker interests, are the two dangers, and the only two to be guarded against; and if this be done effectually, liberty must be eternal. Of the two, the latter is the greater and most difficult to resist. It is less perceptible. Every circumstance of life teaches us the liability of delegated power to abuse. We cannot appoint an agent without being admonished of the fact; and, therefore, it has become well understood, and is effectually guarded against in our political institutions. Not so as to the latter. Though it in fact exists in all associations, yet the law, the courts, and the Government itself, act as a check to its extreme abuse in most cases of private and subordinate companies, which prevents the full display of its real tendency. But let it be supposed that there was no paramount authority,—no court, no government to control, what sober individual, who expected himself to act honestly, would place his property in joint-stock with any number of individuals, however respectable, to be disposed of by the unchecked will of the majority, whether acting in a body as stockholders, or through representation, by a direction? Who does not see that a major and a minor interest would, sooner or later, spring up, and that the result would be that, after the stronger had divested the feebler of all interest in the concern, they would, in turn, divide until the whole would centre in a single interest? It is the principle which must ever govern such associations; and what is government itself, but a great joint-stock company, which comprehends every interest, and which, as there can be no higher power to restrain its natural operation, must, if not checked within itself, follow the same law? The actual condition of our race in every country, at this and all preceding periods, attests the truth of the remark. No government, based on the naked principle that the majority ought to govern, however true the maxim in its proper sense, and under proper restrictions, can preserve its liberty even for a single generation. The history of all has been the same;—violence, injustice, and anarchy,—succeeded by the government of one, or a few, under which the people seek refuge from the more oppressive despotism of the many. Those governments only which provide checks,—which limit and restrain within proper bounds the power of the majority, have had a prolonged existence, and been distinguished for virtue, patriotism, power, and happiness; and, what is strikingly true, they have been thus distinguished almost in exact proportion to the number and efficacy of their checks. If arranged in relation to these, we would place them in the order of the Roman, English, Spartan, the United Provinces, the Athenian, and several of the small confederacies of antiquity; and if arranged according to the higher attributes which have been enumerated, they would stand almost precisely in the same order. That this coincidence is not accidental, we may be fully assured. The latest and most profound investigator of the Roman History and Constitution (Niebuhr), has conclusively shown that, after the expulsion of the kings, this great commonwealth continued to decline in power, and was the victim of the most violent domestic struggles, which tainted both public and private morals, till the passage of the Licinian law, which gave to the people an efficient veto through their tribunes, as a check on the predominant power of the Patricians. From that period she began to rise superior to all other States in virtue, patriotism, and power. May we profit by the example, and restore the almost lost virtue and patriotism of the Republic, by giving due efficiency, in practice, to the check which our Constitution has provided against a danger so threatening,—and which constitutes the only efficient remedy against that unconstitutional and dangerous system which the committee have been considering,—as they will now proceed to show.

The committee has demonstrated that the present disordered state of our political system originated in the diversity of interests which exists in the country;—a diversity recognized by the Constitution itself, and to which it owes one of its most distinguished and peculiar features,—the division of the delegated powers between the State and General Governments. Our short experience, before the formation of the present Government, had conclusively shown that, while there were powers which in their nature were local and peculiar, and which could not be exercised by all, without oppression to some of the parts,—so, also, there were those which, in their operation, necessarily affected the whole, and could not, therefore, be exercised by any of the parts, without affecting injuriously the others. On this different character, by which powers are distinguished in their geographical operation, our political system was constructed. Viewed in relation to them, to a certain extent we have a community of interests, which can only be justly and fairly supervised by concentrating the will and authority of the several States in the General Government; while, at the same time, the States have distinct and separate interests, over which no supervision can be exercised by the general power without injustice and oppression. Hence the division in the exercise of sovereign powers. In drawing the line between the powers of the two—the General and State Governments—the great difficulty consisted in determining correctly to which of the two the various political powers ought to belong. This difficult task was, however, performed with so much success that, to this day, there is an almost entire acquiescence in the correctness with which the line was drawn. It would be extraordinary if a system, thus resting with such profound wisdom on the diversity of geographical interests among the States, should make no provision against the dangers to which its very basis might be exposed. The framers of our Constitution have not exposed themselves to the imputation of such weakness. When their work is fairly examined, it will be found that they have provided, with admirable skill, the most effective remedy; and that, if it has not prevented the danger with which the system is now threatened, the fault is not theirs, but ours, in neglecting to make its proper application. In the primary division of the sovereign powers, and in their exact and just classification, as stated, are to be found the first provisions or checks against the abuse of authority on the part of the absolute majority. The powers of the General Government are particularly enumerated and specifically delegated; and all powers not expressly delegated, or which are not necessary and proper to carry into effect those that are so granted, are reserved expressly to the States or the people. The Government is thus positively restricted to the exercise of those general powers that were supposed to act uniformly on all the parts,—leaving the residue to the people of the States, by whom alone, from the very nature of these powers, they can be justly and fairly exercised, as has been stated.

Our system, then, consists of two distinct and independent Governments. The general powers, expressly delegated to the General Government, are subject to its sole and separate control; and the States cannot, without violating the constitutional compact, interpose their authority to check, or in any manner to counteract its movements, so long as they are confined to the proper sphere. So, also, the peculiar and local powers reserved to the States are subject to their exclusive control; nor can the General Government interfere, in any manner, with them, without violating the Constitution.

In order to have a full and clear conception of our institutions, it will be proper to remark that there is, in our system, a striking distinction between *Government* and *Sovereignty*. The separate governments of the several States are vested in their Legislative, Executive, and Judicial Departments; while the sovereignty resides in the people of the States respectively. The powers of the General Government are also vested in its Legislative, Executive, and Judicial Departments, while the sovereignty resides in the people of the several States who created it. But, by an express provision of the Constitution, it may be amended or changed by three fourths of the States; and thus each State, by assenting to the Constitution with this provision, has modified its original right as a sovereign, of making its individual consent necessary to any change in its political condition; and, by becoming a member of the Union, has placed this important power in the hands of three fourths of the States,—in whom the highest power known to the Constitution actually resides. Not the least portion of this high sovereign authority resides in Congress, or any of the departments of the General Government. They are but the creatures of the Constitution, and are appointed but to execute its provisions; and, therefore, any attempt by all, or any of these departments, to exercise any power which, in its consequences, may alter the nature of the instrument, or change the condition of the parties to it, would be an act of usurpation.

It is thus that our political system, resting on the great principle involved in the recognized diversity of geographical interests in the community, has, in theory, with admirable sagacity, provided the most efficient check against their dangers. Looking to facts, the Constitution has formed the States into a community only to the extent of their common interests; leaving them distinct and independent communities as to all other interests, and drawing the line of separation with consummate skill, as before stated. It is manifest that, so long as this beautiful theory is adhered to in practice, the system, like the atmosphere, will press equally on all the parts. But reason and experience teach us that theory of itself, however excellent, is nugatory, unless there be means of efficiently enforcing it in practice;—which brings under consideration the highly important question,—What means are provided by the system for enforcing this fundamental provision?

If we look to the history and practical operation of the system, we shall find, on the side of the States, no means resorted to in order to protect their reserved rights against the encroachments of the General Government; while the latter has, from the beginning, adopted the most efficient to prevent the States from encroaching on those delegated to them. The 25th section of the Judiciary Act, passed in 1789,—immediately after the Constitution went into operation,—provides for an appeal from the State courts to the Supreme Court of the United States in all cases, in the decision of which, the construction of the Constitution,—the laws of Congress, or treaties of the United States may be involved; thus giving to that high tribunal the right of final interpretation, and the power, in reality, of nullifying the acts of the State Legislatures whenever, in their opinion, they may conflict with the powers delegated to the General Government. A more ample and complete protection against the encroachments of the governments of the several States cannot be imagined; and to this extent the power may be considered as indispensable and constitutional. But, by a strange misconception of the nature of our system,—and, in fact, of the nature of government,—it has been regarded as the ultimate power, not only of protecting the General Government against the encroachments of the governments of the States, but also of the encroachments of the former on the latter;—and as being, in fact, the only means provided by the Constitution of confining all the powers of the system to their proper constitutional spheres; and, consequently, of determining the limits assigned to each. Such a construction of its powers would, in fact, raise one of the departments of the General Government above the parties who created the constitutional compact, and virtually invest it with the authority to alter, at its pleasure, the relative powers of the General and State Governments, on the distribution of which, as established by the Constitution, our whole system rests;—and which, by an express provision of the instrument, can only be altered by three fourths of the States, as has already been shown. It would go farther. Fairly considered, it would, in effect, divest the people of the States of the sovereign authority, and clothe that department with the robe of supreme power. A position more false and fatal cannot be conceived. Fortunately, it has been so ably refuted by Mr. Madison, in his Report to the Virginia Legislature in 1800, on the Alien and Sedition Acts, as to supersede the necessity of further comments on the part of the committee. Speaking of the right of the State to interpret the Constitution for itself, in the last resort, he remarks:—"It has been objected that the Judicial Authority is to be regarded as the sole expositor of the Constitution. On this objection, it might be observed,—*first*—that there may be instances of usurped power" (the case of the Tariff is a striking illustration of the truth), "which the forms of the Constitution could never draw within the control of the Judicial Department;—*secondly*,—that if the decision of the Judiciary be raised above the authority of the sovereign parties to the Constitution, the decision of the other departments, not carried by the forms of the Constitution before the Judiciary, must be equally authoritative and final with the decision of that department. But the proper answer to the objection is, that the resolution of the General Assembly relates to those great and extraordinary cases in which the forms of the Constitution may prove ineffectual against infractions dangerous to the essential rights of the parties to it. The resolution supposes that dangerous powers not delegated, may not only be usurped and exercised by the other departments, but that the Judicial Department also may exercise or sanction dangerous powers beyond the grant of the Constitution; and consequently, that the ultimate right of the parties to the Constitution to judge whether the compact has been dangerously violated, must extend to violations by one delegated authority as well as by another; by the Judiciary as well as by the Executive or the Legislative. However true, therefore, it may be that the Judicial Department is, in all questions submitted to it by the forms of the Constitution, to decide in the last resort, this resort must necessarily be considered the last in relation to the authorities of the other departments of the Government; not in relation to the rights of the parties to the constitutional compact, from which the Judicial and all other departments hold their delegated trusts. On any other hypothesis the delegation of judicial power would annul the authority delegating it; and the concurrence of this department with others in usurped powers might subvert for ever, and beyond the possible reach of any rightful remedy, the very Constitution which all were instituted to preserve."

As a substitute for the rightful remedy, in the last resort, against the encroachments of the General Government on the reserved powers, resort has been had to a rigid construction of the Constitution. A system like ours, of divided powers, must necessarily give great importance to a proper system of construction; but it is perfectly clear that no rule of construction, however perfect, can, in fact, prescribe bounds to the operation of power. All such rules constitute, in fact, but an appeal from the minority to the justice and reason of the majority; and if such appeals were sufficient of themselves to restrain the avarice or ambition of those vested with power, then may a system of technical construction be sufficient to protect against the encroachment of power; but, on such supposition, reason and justice might alone be relied on, without the aid of any constitutional or artificial restraint whatever. Universal experience, in all ages and countries, however, teaches that power can only be restrained by power, and not by reason and justice; and that all restrictions on authority, unsustained by an equal antagonist power, must for ever prove wholly inefficient in practice. Such, also, has been the decisive proof of our own short experience. From the beginning, a great and powerful minority gave every force of which it was susceptible to construction, as a means of restraining the majority of Congress to the exercise of its proper powers; and though that original minority, through the force of circumstances, has had the advantage of becoming a majority, and to possess, in consequence, the administration of the General Government during the greater portion of its existence, yet we this day witness, under these most favorable circumstances, such an extension of its powers as to leave to the States scarcely a right worth the possessing. In fact, the power of construction, on which its advocates relied to preserve the rights of the States, has been wielded, as it ever must be, if not checked, to destroy those rights. If the minority has a right to prescribe its rule of construction, a majority, on its part, will exercise a similar right; but with this striking difference,—that the right of the former will be a mere nullity against that of the latter. But that protection, which the minor interests must ever fail to find in any technical system of construction, may be found in the reserved rights of the States themselves, if they be properly called into action; and there only will they ever be found of sufficient efficacy. The right of protecting their powers results, necessarily, by the most simple and demonstrative arguments, from the very nature of the relation subsisting between the States and General Government.

If it be conceded, as it must be by every one who is the least conversant with our institutions, that the sovereign powers delegated are divided between the General and State Governments, and that the latter hold their portion by the same tenure as the former, it would seem impossible to deny to the States the right of deciding on the infractions of their powers, and the proper remedy to be applied for their correction. The right of judging, in such cases, is an essential attribute of sovereignty,— of which the States cannot be divested without losing their sovereignty itself,—and being reduced to a subordinate corporate condition. In fact, to divide power, and to give to one of the parties the exclusive right of judging of the portion allotted to each, is, in reality, not to divide it at all; and to reserve such exclusive right to the General Government (it matters not by what department to be exercised), is to convert it, in fact, into a great consolidated government, with unlimited powers, and to divest the States, in reality, of all their rights. It is impossible to understand the force of terms, and to deny so plain a conclusion. The opposite opinion can be embraced only on hasty and imperfect views of the relation existing between the States and the General Government. But the existence of the right of judging of their powers, so clearly established from the sovereignty of States, as clearly implies a veto or control, within its limits, on the action of the General Government, on contested points of authority; and this very control is the remedy which the Constitution has provided to prevent the encroachments of the General Government on the reserved rights of the States; and by which the distribution of power, between the General and State Governments, may be preserved for ever inviolable, on the basis established by the Constitution. It is thus effectual protection is afforded to the minority, against the oppression of the majority. Nor does this important conclusion stand on the deduction of reason alone. It is sustained by the highest contemporary authority. Mr. Hamilton, in the number of the Federalist already cited, remarks that,—"in a single republic, all the power surrendered by the people is submitted to the administration of a single government; and usurpations are guarded against, by a division of the government into distinct and separate departments. In the compound republic of America, the power surrendered by the people is first divided between two distinct governments, and then the portion allotted to each subdivided among distinct and separate departments. Hence a double security arises to the rights of the people. The different governments will control each other; at the same time that each will be controlled by itself." He thus clearly affirms the control of the States over the General Government, which he traces to the division in the exercise of the sovereign powers under our political system; and by comparing this control to the veto, which the departments in most of our constitutions respectively exercise over the acts of each other, clearly indicates it as his opinion, that the control between the General and State Governments is of the same character. Mr. Madison is still more explicit. In his report, already alluded to, in speaking on this subject, he remarks;—"The resolutions, having taken this view of the Federal compact, proceed to infer that, in cases of a deliberate, palpable, and dangerous exercise of other powers, not granted by the said compact, the States, who are parties thereto, have the right, and are in duty bound to interpose to arrest the evil, and for maintaining, within their respective limits, the authorities, rights, and liberties appertaining to them. It appears to your committee to be a plain principle, founded in common sense, illustrated by common practice, and essential to the nature of compacts, that where resort can be had to no tribunal superior to the rights of the parties, the parties themselves must be the rightful judges, in the last resort, whether the bargain made has been pursued or violated. The Constitution of the United States was formed by the sanction of the States, given by each in its sovereign capacity. It adds to the stability and dignity, as well as to the authority of the Constitution, that it rests on this solid foundation. The States, then, being parties to the constitutional compact, and in their sovereign capacity, it follows of necessity that there can be no tribunal above their authority to decide, in the last resort, whether the compact made by them be violated; and, consequently, as parties to it, they must themselves decide, in the last resort, such questions as may be of sufficient magnitude to require their interposition." To these the no less explicit opinions of Mr. Jefferson may be added; who, in the Kentucky resolutions on the same subject, which have always been attributed to him, states that—"The Government, created by this compact, was not made the exclusive or final judge of the extent of the powers delegated to itself; since that would have made its discretion, and not the Constitution, the measure of its powers;—but, as in all other cases of compact between parties having no common judge, each party has an equal right to judge for itself, as well of infractions as of the mode and measure of redress."

To these authorities, which so explicitly affirm the right of the States, in their sovereign capacity, to decide, in the last resort, on the infraction of their rights and the remedy, there may be added the solemn decisions of the Legislatures of two leading States—Virginia and Kentucky—that the power in question rightfully belongs to the States,—and the implied sanction which a majority of the States gave, in the important political revolution which shortly followed, and brought Mr. Jefferson into power. It is scarcely possible to add to the weight of authority by which this fundamental principle in our system is sustained.

The committee have thus arrived, by what they deem conclusive reasoning, and the highest authority, at the constitutional and appropriate remedy against the unconstitutional oppression under which this, in common with the other staple States, labors,—and the menacing danger which now hangs over the liberty and happiness of our country;—and this brings them to the inquiry,—How is the remedy to be applied by the States? In this inquiry a question may be made,—whether a State can interpose its sovereignty through the ordinary Legislature, but which the committee do not deem it necessary to investigate. It is sufficient that plausible reasons may be assigned against this mode of action, if there be one (and there is one) free from all objections. Whatever doubts may be raised as to the question,—whether the respective Legislatures fully represent the sovereignty of the States for this high purpose, there can be none as to the fact that a Convention fully represents them for all purposes whatever. Its authority, therefore, must remove every objection as to form, and leave the question on the single point of the right of the States to interpose at all. When convened, it will belong to the Convention itself to determine, authoritatively, whether the acts of which we complain be unconstitutional; and, if so, whether they constitute a violation so deliberate, palpable, and dangerous, as to justify the interposition of the State to protect its rights. If this question be decided in the affirmative, the Convention will then determine in what manner they ought to be declared null and void within the limits of the State; which solemn declaration, based on her rights as a member of the Union, would be obligatory, not only on her own citizens, but on the General Government itself; and thus place the violated rights of the State under the shield of the Constitution.

The committee, having thus established the constitutional right of the States to interpose, in order to protect their reserved powers, it cannot be necessary to bestow much time or attention, in order to meet possible objections;—particularly as they must be raised, not against the soundness of the arguments, by which the position is sustained, and which they deem unanswerable,—but against apprehended consequences, which, even if well founded, would be an objection, not so much to the conclusions of the committee, as to the Constitution itself. They are persuaded that, whatever objection may be suggested, it will be found, on investigation, to be destitute of solidity. Under these impressions, the committee propose to discuss such as they suppose may be urged, with all possible brevity.

It may be objected, then,—in the first place, that the right of the States to interpose rests on mere inference, without any express provision in the Constitution; and that it is not to be supposed—if the Constitution contemplated the exercise of powers of such high importance—that it would have been left to inference alone. In answer, the committee would ask, whether the power of the Supreme Court to declare a law unconstitutional is not among the very highest and most important that can be exercised by any department of the Government,—and if any express provision can be found to justify its exercise? Like the power in question, it also rests on mere inference;—but an inference so clear, that no express provision could render it more certain. The simple fact, that the Judges must decide according to law, and that the Constitution is paramount to the acts of Congress, imposes a necessity on the court to declare the latter void whenever, in its opinion, they come in conflict, in any particular case, with the former. So, also, in the question under consideration. The right of the States,—even supposing it to rest on inference, stands on clearer and stronger grounds than that of the Court. In the distribution of powers between the General and State Governments, the Constitution professes to *enumerate* those assigned to the former, in whatever department they may be vested; while the powers of the latter are reserved in general terms, without attempt at enumeration. It may, therefore, constitute a presumption against the former,—that the Court has no right to declare a law unconstitutional, because the power is not enumerated among those belonging to the Judiciary;—while the omission to enumerate the power of the States to interpose in order to protect their rights,—being strictly in accord with the principles on which its framers formed the Constitution, raises not the slightest presumption against its existence. Like all other *reserved* rights, it is to be inferred from the simple fact that it is *not delegated,*—as is clearly the case in this instance.

Again—it may be objected to the power, that it is inconsistent with the necessary authority of the General Government,—and, in its consequences, must lead to feebleness, anarchy, and finally disunion.

It is impossible to propose any limitation on the authority of governments, without encountering, from the supporters of power, this very objection of feebleness and anarchy: and we accordingly find, that the history of every country which has attempted to establish free institutions. proves that, on this point, the opposing parties—the advocates of power and of freedom—have ever separated. It constituted the essence of the controversy between the Patricians and Plebeians in the Roman Republic, —the Tories and Whigs in England,—the Ultras and Liberals in France,—

and, finally, the Federalists and Republicans in our own country,—as illustrated by Mr. Madison's Report;—and if it were proposed to give to Russia or Austria a representation of the people, it would form the point of controversy between the Imperial and Popular parties. It is, in fact, not at all surprising that, to a people unacquainted with the nature of liberty, and inexperienced in its blessings, all limitations on supreme power should appear incompatible with its nature, and as tending to feebleness and anarchy. Nature has not permitted us to doubt the necessity of a paramount power in all institutions. All see and feel it; but it requires some effort of reason to perceive that, if not controlled, such power must necessarily lead to abuse;—and still higher efforts to understand that it may be checked without destroying its efficiency. With us, however, who know from our own experience, and that of other free nations, the truth of these positions, and that power can only be rendered useful and secure by being properly checked,—it is, indeed, strange that any intelligent citizen should consider limitations on the authority of government incompatible with its nature;—or should fear danger from any check properly lodged, which may be necessary to guard against usurpation or abuse, and protect the great and distinct interests of the country. That there are such interests represented by the States, and that the States are the only competent powers to protect them, has been sufficiently established; and it only remains, in order to meet the objection, to prove that, for this purpose, the States may be safely vested with the right of interposition.

If the committee do not greatly mistake, the checking or veto power never has, in any country, or under any institutions, been lodged where it was less liable to abuse. The great number, by whom it must be exercised, of the people of a State,—the solemnity of the mode,—a Convention specially called for the purpose, and representing the State in her highest capacity,—the delay,—the deliberation,—are all calculated to allay excitement,—to impress on the people a deep and solemn tone, highly favorable to calm investigation and decision. Under such circumstances, it would be impossible for a mere party to maintain itself in the State, unless the violation of its rights be palpable, deliberate, and dangerous. The attitude in which the State would be placed in relation to the other States,—the force of public opinion which would be brought to bear on her,—the deep reverence for the General Government,—the strong influence of all public men who aspire to office or distinction in the Union,—and, above all, the local parties which must ever exist in the State, and which, in this case, must ever throw the powerful influence of the minority on the side of the General Government,—constitute impediments to the exercise of this high protective right of the State, which must render it safe. So powerful, in fact, are these difficulties, that nothing but truth and a deep sense of oppression on the part of the people of the

State, will ever sustain the exercise of the power;—and if it should be attempted under other circumstances, it must speedily terminate in the expulsion of those in power, to be replaced by others who would make a merit of closing the controversy, by yielding the point in dispute.

But, in order to understand more fully what its operation really would be in practice, we must take into the estimate the effect which a recognition of the power would have on the tone of feeling, both of the General and State Governments. On the part of the former, it would necessarily produce, in the exercise of doubtful powers, the most marked moderation. In the discussion of measures involving such powers, the argument would be felt with decisive weight, that the State, also, had the right of judging of the constitutionality of the power; which would cause an abandonment of the measure,—or, at least, lead to such modifications as would make it acceptable. On the part of the State, a feeling of conscious security, depending on herself,—with the effect of moderation and kindness on the part of the General Government, would effectually put down jealousy, hatred, and animosity,—and thus give scope to the natural attachment to our institutions, to expand and grow into the full maturity of patriotism. But withhold this protective power from the State, and the reverse of all these happy consequences must follow;—which the committee will not undertake to describe, as the living example of discord, hatred, and jealousy,—threatening anarchy and dissolution, must impress on every beholder a more vivid picture than any they could possibly draw. The continuance of this unhappy state must lead to the loss of all affection;—when the Government must be sustained by *force* instead of *patriotism*. In fact, to him who will duly reflect, it must be apparent that, where there are important separate interests, there is no alternative but a veto to protect them, or the military to enforce the claims of the majority interests.

If these deductions be correct,—as can scarcely be doubted,—under that state of moderation and security, followed by mutual kindness, which must accompany the acknowledgment of the right, the necessity of exercising the veto would rarely exist, and the possibility of its abuse, on the part of the State, would be almost wholly removed. Its acknowledged existence would thus supersede its exercise. But suppose in this the committee should be mistaken,—still there exists a sufficient security. As high as this right of interposition on the part of a State may be regarded in relation to the General Government, the constitutional compact provides a remedy against its abuse. There is a higher power,—placed above all by the consent of all,—the creating and preserving power of the system,—to be exercised by three fourths of the States,—and which, under the character of the amending power, can modify the whole system at pleasure,—and to the acts of which none can object. Admit, then, the power in question to belong to the States,—and admit its liability to abuse,—and what are the utmost consequences, but to create a presumption against the constitutionality of the power exercised by the General Government,—which, if it be well founded, must compel them to abandon it;—or, if not, to remove the difficulty by obtaining the contested power in the form of an amendment to the Constitution. If, on an appeal for this purpose, the decision be favorable to the General Government, a disputed power will be converted into an expressly granted power;—but, on the other hand, if it be adverse, the refusal to grant will be tantamount to an inhibition of its exercise: and thus, in either case, the controversy will be determined. And ought not a sovereign State, as a party to the constitutional compact, and as the guardian of her citizens and her peculiar interests, to have the power in question? Without it, the amending power must become obsolete, and the Constitution, through the exercise of construction, in the end utterly subverted. Let us examine the case. The disease is, that a majority of the States, through the General Government, by construction, usurp powers not delegated, and by their exercise, increase their wealth and authority at the expense of the minority. How absurd, then, to expect the injured States to attempt a remedy by proposing an amendment to be ratified by three fourths of the States, when, by supposition, there is a majority opposed to them? Nor would it be less absurd to expect the General Government to propose amendments, unless compelled to that course by the acts of a State. The Government can have no inducement. It has a more summary mode,—the assumption of power by construction. The consequence is clear;—neither would resort to the amending power;—the one, because it would be useless,—and the other, because it could effect its purpose without it;—and thus the highest power known to the Constitution,—on the salutary influence of which, on the operations of our political institutions, so much was calculated, would become, in practice, obsolete, as stated; and in lieu of it, the will of the majority, under the agency of construction, would be substituted, with unlimited and supreme power. On the contrary, giving the right to a State to compel the General Government to abandon its pretensions to a constructive power, or to obtain a positive grant of it, by an amendment to the Constitution, would call efficiently into action, on all important disputed questions, this highest power of the system,—to whose controlling authority no one can object, and under whose operation all controversies between the States and General Government would be adjusted, and the Constitution gradually acquire all the perfection of which it is susceptible. It is thus that the *creating* becomes the *preserving* power; and we may rest assured it is no less true in politics than in theology, that the power which creates can alone preserve,—and that preservation is perpetual creation. Such will be the operation and effect of State interposition.

But it may be objected, that the exercise of the power would have the effect of placing the majority under the control of the minority. If the objection were well founded, it would be fatal. If the majority cannot be trusted, neither can the minority: and to transfer power from the former to the latter, would be but the repetition of the old error, in taking shelter under monarchy or aristocracy, against the more oppressive tyranny of an illy constructed republic. But it is not the consequence of proper checks to change places between the majority and minority. It leaves the power controlled still independent; as is exemplified in our political institutions, by the operation of acknowledged checks. The power of the Judiciary to declare an act of Congress, or of a State Legislature, unconstitutional, is, for its appropriate purpose, a most efficient check; but who that is acquainted with the nature of our Government ever supposed that it ever really vested (when confined to its proper object) a supreme power in the Court over Congress or the State Legislatures? Such was neither the intention, nor is it the effect.

The Constitution has provided another check, which will still further illustrate the nature of their operation. Among the various interests which exist under our complex system, that of large and small States is, perhaps, the most prominent, and among the most carefully guarded in the organization of our Government. To settle the relative weight of the States in the system, and to secure to each the means of maintaining its proper political consequence in its operation, formed one of the most difficult duties in framing the Constitution. No one subject occupied greater space in the proceedings of the Convention. In its final adjustment, the large States had assigned to them a preponderating influence in the House of Representatives, by having therein a weight proportioned to their numbers; but to compensate which, and to secure their political rights against this preponderance, the small States had an equality assigned them in the Senate; while, in the constitution of the Executive branch, the two were blended. To secure the consequence allotted to each, as well as to insure due deliberation in legislating, a veto is allowed to each in the passage of bills; but it would be absurd to suppose that this veto placed either above the other; or was incompatible with the portion of the sovereign power intrusted to the House, the Senate, or the President.

It is thus that our system has provided appropriate checks between the Departments,—a veto to guard the supremacy of the Constitution over the laws, and to preserve the due importance of the States, considered in reference to large and small, without creating discord or weakening the beneficent energy of the Government. And so, also, in the division of the sovereign authority between the General and State Governments,—by leaving to the States an efficient power to protect, by a veto, the minor against the major interests of the community, the framers of the Constitution acted in strict conformity with the principle which invariably prevails throughout the whole system, where separate interests exist. They were, in truth, no ordinary men. They were wise and practical statesmen, enlightened by history and their own enlarged experience, acquired in conducting our country through a most important revolution;—and understood profoundly the nature of man and of government. They saw and felt that there existed in our nature the necessity of government, and government of adequate powers;—that the selfish predominate over the social feelings; and that, without a government of such powers, universal conflict and anarchy must prevail among the component parts of society; but they also clearly saw that, our nature remaining unchanged by change of condition, unchecked power, from this very predominance of the selfish over the social feelings, which rendered government necessary, would, of necessity, lead to corruption and oppression on the part of those vested with its exercise. Thus the necessity of government and of checks originates in the same great principle of our nature; and thus the very selfishness which impels those who have power to desire more, will also, with equal force, impel those on whom power operates to resist aggression; and on the balance of these opposing tendencies, liberty and happiness must for ever depend. This great principle guided in the formation of every part of our political system. There is not one opposing interest throughout the whole that is not counterpoised. Have the rulers a separate interest from the people? To check its abuse, the relation of representative and constituent is created between them, through periodical elections, by which the fidelity of the representative to the constituent is secured. Have the States, as members of the Union, distinct political interests in reference to their magnitude? Their relative weight is carefully settled, and each has its appropriate agent, with a veto on each other, to protect its political consequence. May there be a conflict between the Constitution and the laws, whereby the rights of citizens may be affected? A remedy may be found in the power of the courts to declare the law unconstitutional in such cases as may be brought before them. Are there, among the several States, separate and peculiar geographical interests? To meet this, a particular organization is provided in the division of the sovereign powers between the State and General Governments. Is there danger, growing out of this division, that the State Legislatures may encroach on the powers of the General Government? The authority of the Supreme Court is adequate to check such encroachments. May the General Government, on the other hand, encroach on the rights reserved to the States respectively? To the States respectively—each in its sovereign capacity—is reserved the power, by its veto, or right of interposition, to arrest the encroachment. And, finally, may this power be abused by a State, so as to interfere improperly with the powers delegated to the General Government? There is provided a power, even over the Constitution itself, vested in three fourths of the

States, which Congress has the authority to invoke, and may terminate all controversies in reference to the subject, by granting or withholding the right in contest. Its authority is acknowledged by all; and to deny or resist it, would be, on the part of the State, a violation of the constitutional compact, and a dissolution of the political association, as far as it is concerned. This is the ultimate and highest power,—and the basis on which the whole system rests.

That there exists a case which would justify the interposition of this State, in order to compel the General Government to abandon an unconstitutional power, or to appeal to this high authority to confer it by express grant, the committee do not in the least doubt; and they are equally clear in the necessity of its exercise, if the General Government should continue to persist in its improper assumption of powers belonging to the States;—which brings them to the last point they propose to consider,— viz.: When would it be proper to exercise this high power?

If the committee were to judge only by the magnitude of the interests at stake, they would, without hesitation, recommend the call of a Convention without delay. But they deeply feel the obligation of respect for the other members of the confederacy, and the necessity of great moderation and forbearance in the exercise even of the most unquestionable right, between parties who stand connected by the closest and most sacred political compact. With these sentiments, they deem it advisable, after presenting the views of the Legislature in this solemn manner (if the body concur with the committee), to allow time for further consideration and reflection, in the hope that a returning sense of justice on the part of the majority, when they come to reflect on the wrongs which this and the other staple States have suffered, and are suffering, may repeal the obnoxious and unconstitutional acts,—and thereby prevent the necessity of interposing the veto of the State.

The committee are further induced, at this time, to recommend this course, under the hope that the great political revolution, which will displace from power, on the 4th of March next, those who have acquired authority by setting the will of the people at defiance,—and which will bring in an eminent citizen, distinguished for his services to his country, and his justice and patriotism, may be followed up, under his influence, with a complete restoration of the pure principles of our Government. But, in thus recommending delay, the committee wish it to be distinctly understood, that neither doubts of the rightful power of the State, nor apprehension of consequences, constitute the smallest part of their motives. They would be unworthy of the name of freemen,—of Americans,—of Carolinians, if danger, however great, could cause them to shrink from the maintenance of their constitutional rights. But they deem it preposterous to anticipate danger under a system of laws, where a sovereign party to the compact, which formed the Government, exercises a power which, after the fullest investigation, she conscientiously believes to belong to her under the guarantee of the Constitution itself,—and which is essential to the preservation of her sovereignty. The committee deem it not only the right of the State, but her duty, under the solemn sanction of an oath, to interpose, if no other remedy be applied. They interpret the oath to defend the Constitution, not simply as imposing an obligation to abstain from violation, but to prevent it on the part of others. In their opinion, he is as guilty of violating that sacred instrument, who permits an infraction, when it is in his power to prevent it, as he who actually perpetrates the violation. The one may be bolder, and the other more timid,—but the sense of duty must be weak in both.

With these views the committee are solemnly of the impression,—if the present usurpations and the professed doctrines of the existing system be persevered in,—after due forbearance on the part of the State,—that it will be her sacred duty to interpose;—a duty to herself,—to the Union,—to the present, and to future generations,—and to the cause of liberty over the world, to arrest the progress of a usurpation which, if not arrested, must, in its consequences, corrupt the public morals and destroy the liberty of the country.

27
FORT HILL ADDRESS
July 26, 1831

THE QUESTION OF THE RELATION which the States and General Government bear to each other is not one of recent origin. From the commencement of our system, it has divided public sentiment. Even in the Convention, while the Constitution was struggling into existence, there were two parties as to what this relation should be, whose different sentiments constituted no small impediment in forming that instrument. After the General Government went into operation, experience soon proved that the question had not terminated with the labors of the Convention. The great struggle that preceded the political revolution of 1801, which brought Mr. Jefferson into power, turned essentially on it, and the doctrines and arguments on both sides were embodied and ably sustained;—on the one, in the Virginia and Kentucky Resolutions, and the Report to the Virginia Legislature;—and on the other, in the replies of the Legislature of Massachusetts and some of the other States. These Resolutions and this Report, with the decision of the Supreme Court of Pennsylvania about the same time (particularly in the case of Cobbett, delivered by Chief Justice M'Kean, and concurred in by the whole bench), contain what I believe to be the true doctrine on this important subject. I refer to them in order to avoid the necessity of presenting my views, with the reasons in support of them, in detail.

As my object is simply to state my opinions, I might pause with this reference to documents that so fully and ably state all the points immediately connected with this deeply-important subject; but as there are many who may not have the opportunity or leisure to refer to them, and as it is possible, however clear they may be, that different persons may place different interpretations on their meaning, I will, in order that my sentiments may be fully known, and to avoid all ambiguity, proceed to state, summarily, the doctrines which I conceive they embrace.

The great and leading principle is, that the General Government emanated from the people of the several States, forming distinct political communities, and acting in their separate and sovereign capacity, and not from all of the people forming one aggregate political community; that the Constitution of the United States is, in fact, a compact, to which each State is a party, in the character already described; and that the several States, or parties, have a right to judge of its infractions; and in case of a deliberate, palpable, and dangerous exercise of power not delegated, they have the right, in the last resort, to use the language of the Virginia Resolutions, *"to interpose for arresting the progress of the evil, and for maintaining, within their respective limits, the authorities, rights, and liberties appertaining to them."* This right of interposition, thus solemnly asserted by the State of Virginia, be it called what it may,—State-right, veto, nullification, or by any other name,—I conceive to be the fundamental principle of our system, resting on facts historically as certain as our revolution itself, and deductions as simple and demonstrative as that of any political or moral truth whatever; and I firmly believe that on its recognition depend the stability and safety of our political institutions.

I am not ignorant that those opposed to the doctrine have always, now and formerly, regarded it in a very different light, as anarchical and revolutionary. Could I believe such, in fact, to be its tendency, to me it would be no recommendation. I yield to none, I trust, in a deep and sincere attachment to our political institutions and the union of these States. I never breathed an opposite sentiment; but, on the contrary, I have ever considered them the great instruments of preserving our liberty, and promoting the happiness of ourselves and our posterity; and next to these I have ever held them most dear. Nearly half my life has been passed in the service of the Union, and whatever public reputation I have acquired is indissolubly identified with it. To be too national has, indeed, been considered by many, even of my friends, my greatest political fault. With these strong feelings of attachment, I have examined, with the utmost care, the bearing of the doctrine in question; and, so far from anarchical or revolutionary, I solemnly believe it to be the only solid foundation of our system, and of the Union itself; and that the opposite doctrine, which denies to the States the right of protecting their reserved powers, and which would vest in the General Government (it matters not through what department) the right of determining, exclusively and finally, the powers delegated to it, is incompatible with the sovereignty of the States, and of the Constitution itself, considered as the basis of a Federal Union. As strong as this language is, it is not stronger than that used by the illustrious Jefferson, who said, to give to the General Government the final and exclusive right to judge of its powers, is to make *"its discretion,* and *not the Constitution, the measure of its powers;"* and that, *"in all cases of compact between parties having no common judge, each party has an equal right to judge for itself, as well of the infraction as of the mode and measure of redress."* Language cannot be more explicit, nor can higher authority be adduced.

That different opinions are entertained on this subject, I consider but as an additional evidence of the great diversity of the human intellect. Had not able, experienced, and patriotic individuals, for whom I have the highest respect, taken different views, I would have thought the right too clear to admit of doubt; but I am taught by this, as well as by many similar instances, to treat with deference opinions differing from my own. The error may, possibly, be with me; but if so, I can only say that, after the most mature and conscientious examination, I have not been able to detect it. But, with all proper deference, I must think that theirs is the error who deny what seems to be an essential attribute of the conceded sovereignty of the States, and who attribute to the General Government a right utterly incompatible with what all acknowledge to be its limited and restricted character: an error originating principally, as I must think, in not duly reflecting on the nature of our institutions, and on what constitutes the only rational object of all political constitutions.

It has been well said by one of the most sagacious men of antiquity, that the object of a constitution is, to *restrain the government, as that of laws* is to restrain *individuals.* The remark is correct; nor is it less true where the government is vested in a majority, than where it is in a single or a few individuals—in a republic, than a monarchy or aristocracy. No one can have a higher respect for the maxim that the majority ought to govern than I have, taken in its proper sense, subject to the restrictions imposed by the Constitution, and confined to objects in which every portion of the community have similar interests; but it is a great error to suppose, as many do, that the right of a majority to govern is a natural and not a conventional right, and therefore absolute and unlimited. By nature, every individual has the right to govern himself; and governments, whether founded on majorities or minorities, must derive their right from the assent, expressed or implied, of the governed, and be subject to such limitations as they may impose. Where the interests are the same, that is, where the laws that may benefit one will benefit all, or the reverse, it is just and proper to place them under the control of the majority; but where they are dissimilar, so that the law that may benefit one portion may be ruinous to another, it would be, on the contrary, unjust and absurd to subject them to its will; and such I conceive to be the theory on which our Constitution rests.

That such dissimilarity of interests may exist, it is impossible to doubt. They are to be found in every community, in a greater or less degree, however small or homogeneous; and they constitute every where the great difficulty of forming and preserving free institutions. To guard against the unequal action of the laws, when applied to dissimilar and opposing interests, is, in fact, what mainly renders a constitution indispensable; to overlook which, in reasoning on our Constitution, would be to omit the principal element by which to determine its character. Were there no contrariety of interests, nothing would be more simple and easy than to form and preserve free institutions. The right of suffrage alone would be a sufficient guarantee. It is the conflict of opposing interests which renders it the most difficult work of man.

Where the diversity of interests exists in separate and distinct classes of the community, as is the case in England, and was formerly the case in Sparta, Rome, and most of the free States of antiquity, the rational constitutional provision is, that each should be represented in the government, as a separate estate, with a distinct voice, and a negative on the acts of its co-estates, in order to check their encroachments. In England, the Constitution has assumed expressly this form, while in the governments of Sparta and Rome, the same thing was effected under different, but not much less efficacious forms. The perfection of their organization, in this particular, was that which gave to the constitutions of these renowned States all their celebrity, which secured their liberty for so many centuries, and raised them to so great a height of power and prosperity. Indeed, a constitutional provision giving to the great and separate interests of the community the right of self-protection, must appear, to those who will duly reflect on the subject, not less essential to the preservation of liberty than the right of suffrage itself. They, in fact, have a common object, to effect which the one is as necessary as the other to secure *responsibility;* that is, *that those who make and execute the laws should be accountable to those on whom the laws in reality operate—the only solid and durable foundation of liberty.* If, without the right of suffrage, our rulers would oppress us, so, without the right of self-protection, the major would equally oppress the minor interests of the community. The absence of the former would make the governed the slaves of the rulers; and of the latter, the feebler interests, the victim of the stronger.

Happily for us, we have no artificial and separate classes of society. We have wisely exploded all such distinctions; but we are not, on that account, exempt from all contrariety of interests, as the present distracted and dangerous condition of our country, unfortunately, but too clearly proves. With us they are almost exclusively geographical, resulting mainly from difference of climate, soil, situation, industry, and production; but are not, therefore, less necessary to be protected by an adequate constitutional provision, than where the distinct interests exist in separate classes. The necessity is, in truth, greater, as such separate and dissimilar geographical interests are more liable to come into conflict, and more dangerous, when in that state, than those of any other description; so much so, that *ours is the first instance on record where they have not formed, in an extensive territory, separate and independent* communities, *or subjected the whole to despotic sway.* That such may not be our unhappy fate also, must be the sincere prayer of every lover of his country.

So numerous and diversified are the interests of our country, that they could not be fairly represented in a single government, organized so as to give to each great and leading interest a separate and distinct voice, as in governments to which I have referred. A plan was adopted better suited to our situation, but perfectly novel in its character. The powers of government were divided, not, as heretofore, in reference to classes, but geographically. One General Government was formed for the whole, to which were delegated all the powers supposed to be necessary to regulate the interests common to all the States, leaving others subject to the separate control of the States, being, from their local and peculiar character, such that they could not be subject to the will of a majority of the whole Union, without the certain hazard of injustice and oppression. It was thus that the interests of the whole were subjected, as they ought to be, to the will of the whole, while the peculiar and local interests were left under the control of the States separately, to whose custody only they could be safely confided. This distribution of power, settled solemnly by a constitutional compact, to which all the States are parties, constitutes the peculiar character and excellence of our political system. It is truly and emphatically *American, without example or parallel.*

To realize its perfection, we must view the General Government and those of the States as a whole, each in its proper sphere independent; each perfectly adapted to its respective objects; the States acting separately, representing and protecting the local and peculiar interests; and acting jointly through one General Government, with the weight respectively assigned to each by the Constitution, representing and protecting the interest of the whole; and thus perfecting, by an admirable but simple arrangement, the great principle of representation and responsibility, without which no government can be free or just. To preserve this sacred distribution as originally settled, by coercing each to move in its prescribed orbit, is the great and difficult problem, on the solution of which the duration of our Constitution, of our Union, and, in all probability, our liberty depends. How is this to be effected?

The question is new, when applied to our peculiar political organization, where the separate and conflicting interests of society are represented by distinct but connected governments; but it is, in reality, an old question under a new form, long since perfectly solved. Whenever separate and dissimilar interests have been separately represented in any government; whenever the sovereign power has been divided in its exercise, the experience and wisdom of ages have devised but one mode by which such political organization can be preserved,—the mode adopted in England, and by all governments, ancient and modern, blessed with constitutions deserving to be called free,—to give to each co-estate the right to judge of its powers, with a negative or veto on the acts of the others, in order to protect against encroachments the interests it particularly represents: a principle which all of our constitutions recognize in the distribution of power among their respective departments, as essential to maintain the independence of each; but which, to all who will duly reflect on the subject, must appear far more essential, for the same object, in that great and fundamental distribution of powers between the General and State Governments. So essential is the principle, that, to withhold the right from either, where the sovereign power is divided, is, in fact, *to annul the division* itself, and to *consolidate,* in the one left in the exclusive possession of the right, *all* powers of government; for it is not possible to distinguish, practically, between a government having all power, and one having the right to take what powers it pleases. Nor does it in the least vary the principle, whether the distribution of power be between co-estates, as in England, or between distinctly organized but connected governments, as with us. The reason is the same in both cases, while the necessity is greater in our case, as the danger of conflict is greater where the interests of a society are divided geographically than in any other, as has already been shown.

These truths do seem to me to be incontrovertible; and I am at a loss to understand how any one, who has maturely reflected on the nature of our institutions, or who has read history or studied the principles of free government to any purpose, can call them in question. The explanation must, it appears to me, be sought in the fact that, in every free State there are those who look more to the necessity of maintaining power than guarding against its abuses. I do not intend reproach, but simply to state a fact apparently necessary to explain the contrariety of opinions among the intelligent, where the abstract consideration of the subject would seem scarcely to admit of doubt. If such be the true cause, I must think the fear of weakening the government too much, in this case, to be in a great measure unfounded, or, at least, that the danger is much less from that than the opposite side. I do not deny that a power of so high a nature may be abused by a State; but when I reflect that the States unanimously called the General Government into existence with all its powers, which they freely delegated on their part, under the conviction that their common peace, safety, and prosperity required it; that they are bound together by a common origin, and the recollection of common suffering and common triumph in the great and splendid achievement of their independence; and that the strongest feelings of our nature, and among them the love of national power and distinction, are on the side of the Union, it does seem to me that the fear which would strip the States of their sovereignty, and degrade them, in fact, to mere dependent corporations, lest they should abuse a right indispensable to the peaceable protection of those interests which they reserved under their own peculiar guardianship when they created the General Government, is unnatural and unreasonable. If those who voluntarily created the system cannot be trusted to preserve it, who can?

So far from extreme danger, I hold that there never was a free State in which this great conservative principle, indispensable to all, was ever so safely lodged. In others, when the co-estates representing the dissimilar and conflicting interests of the community came into contact, the only alternative was compromise, submission, or force. Not so in ours. Should the General Government and a State come into conflict, we have a higher remedy: the power which called the General Government into existence, which gave it all its authority, and can enlarge, contract, or abolish its powers at its pleasure, may be invoked. The States themselves may be appealed to,—three fourths of which, in fact, form a power, whose decrees are the Constitution itself, and whose voice can silence all discontent. The utmost extent, then, of the power is, that a State, acting in its sovereign capacity as one of the parties to the constitutional compact, may compel the Government, created by that compact, to submit a question touching its infraction, to the parties who created it; to avoid the supposed dangers of which, it is proposed to resort to the novel, the hazardous, and, I must add, fatal project of giving to the General Government the sole and final right of interpreting the Constitution;—thereby reversing the whole system, making that instrument the creature of its will, instead of a rule of action impressed on it at its creation, and annihilating, in fact, the authority which imposed it, and from which the Government itself derives its existence.

That such would be the result, were the right in question vested in the Legislative or Executive branch of the Government, is conceded by all. No one has been so hardy as to assert that Congress or the President ought to have the right, or deny that, if vested finally and exclusively in either, the consequences which I have stated would necessarily follow; but its advocates have been reconciled to the doctrine, on the supposition that there is one department of the General Government which, from its peculiar organization, affords an independent tribunal, through which the Government may exercise the high authority which is the subject of consideration, with perfect safety to all.

I yield, I trust, to few in my attachment to the Judiciary Department. I am fully sensible of its importance, and would maintain it, to the fullest extent, in its constitutional powers and independence; but it is impossible for me to believe it was ever intended by the Constitution that it should exercise the power in question, or that it is competent to do so; and, if it were, that it would be a safe depository of the power.

Its powers are judicial, and not political; and are expressly confined by the Constitution "to all *cases* in law and equity arising under this Constitution, the laws of the United States, and the treaties made, or which shall be made, under its authority;" and which I have high authority in asserting excludes political questions, and comprehends those only where there are parties amenable to the process of the court.* Nor is its incompetency less clear than its want of constitutional authority. There may be many, and the most dangerous infractions on the part of Congress, of which, it is conceded by all, the court, as a judicial tribunal, cannot, from its nature, take cognizance. The Tariff itself is a strong case in point; and the reason applies equally *to all others where Congress perverts a power from an object intended, to one not intended, the most insidious and dangerous of all infractions; and which may be extended to all of its powers, more especially to the taxing and appropriating.* But, supposing it competent to take cognizance of all infractions of every description, the insuperable objection still remains, that it would not be a safe tribunal to exercise the power in question.

It is a universal and fundamental political principle, that the power to

---

* I refer to the authority of Chief Justice Marshall, in the case of Jonathan Robbins. I have not been able to refer to the speech, and speak from memory.

protect can safely be confided only to those interested in protecting, or their responsible agents,—a maxim not less true in private than in public affairs. The danger in our system is, that the General Government, which represents the interests of the whole, may encroach on the States, which represent the peculiar and local interests, or that the latter may encroach on the former.

In examining this point, we ought not to forget that the Government, through all its departments, judicial as well as others, is administered by delegated and responsible agents; and that the *power which really controls, ultimately, all the movements, is not in the agents, but those who elect or appoint them.* To understand, then, its real character, and what would be the action of the system in any supposable case, we must raise our view from the mere agents to this high controlling power, which finally impels every movement of the machine. By doing so, we shall find all under the control of the will of a majority, compounded of the majority of the States, taken as political bodies, and the majority of the people of the States, estimated in federal numbers. These, united, constitute the real and final power which impels and directs the movements of the General Government. The majority of the States elect the majority of the Senate; of the people of the States, that of the House of Representatives; the two united, the President; and the President and a majority of the Senate appoint the judges: a majority of whom, and a majority of the Senate and House, with the President, really exercise all the powers of the Government, with the exception of the cases where the Constitution requires a greater number than a majority. The judges are, in fact, as truly the judicial representatives of this united majority, as the majority of Congress itself, or the President, is its legislative or executive representative; and to confide the power to the Judiciary to determine finally and conclusively what powers are delegated and what reserved, would be, in reality, to confide it to the majority, whose agents they are, and by whom they can be controlled in various ways; and, of course, to subject (against the fundamental principle of our system and all sound political reasoning) the reserved powers of the States, with all the local and peculiar interests they were intended to protect, to the will of the very majority against which the protection was intended. Nor will the tenure by which the judges hold their office, however valuable the provision in many other respects, materially vary the case. Its highest possible effect would be to *retard,* and not *finally* to *resist,* the will of a dominant majority.

But it is useless to multiply arguments. Were it possible that reason could settle a question where the passions and interests of men are concerned, this point would have been long since settled for ever by the State of Virginia. The report of her Legislature, to which I have already referred, has really, in my opinion, placed it beyond controversy. Speaking in reference to this subject, it says: "It has been objected" (to the right of a State to interpose for the protection of her reserved rights) "that the judicial authority is to be regarded as the sole expositor of the Constitution. On this objection it might be observed, first, that there may be instances of usurped powers which the forms of the Constitution could never draw within the control of the Judicial Department; secondly, that, if the decision of the judiciary be raised above the sovereign parties to the Constitution, the decisions of the other departments, not carried by the forms of the Constitution before the Judiciary, must be equally authoritative and final with the decision of that department. But the proper answer to the objection is, that the resolution of the General Assembly relates to those great and extraordinary cases, in which all the forms of the Constitution may prove ineffectual against infractions dangerous to the essential rights of the parties to it. The resolution supposes that dangerous powers, not delegated, may not only be usurped and executed by the other departments, but that the Judicial Department may also exercise or sanction dangerous powers, beyond the grant of the Constitution, and, consequently, that the ultimate right of the parties to the Constitution to judge whether the compact has been dangerously violated, must extend to violations by one delegated authority, as well as by another,—by the judiciary, as well as by the executive or legislative."

Against these conclusive arguments, as they seem to me, it is objected that, if one of the parties has the right to judge of infractions of the Constitution, so has the other; and that, consequently, in cases of contested powers between a State and the General Government, each would have a right to maintain its opinion, as is the case when sovereign powers differ in the construction of treaties or compacts; and that, of course, it would come to be a mere question of force. The error is in the assumption that the General Government is a party to the constitutional compact. The States, as has been shown, formed the compact, acting as sovereign and independent communities. The General Government is but its creature; and though, in reality, a government, with all the rights and authority which belong to any other government, within the orbit of its powers, it is, nevertheless, a government emanating from a compact between sovereigns, and partaking, in its nature and object, of the character of a joint commission, appointed to superintend and administer the interests in which all are jointly concerned; but having, beyond its proper sphere, no more power than if it did not exist. To deny this would be to deny the most incontestable facts and the clearest conclusions; while to acknowledge its truth is, to destroy utterly the objection that the appeal would be to force, in the case supposed. For, if each party has a right to judge, then, under our system of government, the final cognizance of a question of contested power would be in the States, and not in the General Government. It would be the duty of the latter, as in all similar cases of a contest between one or more of the principals and a joint commission or agency, to refer the contest to the principals themselves. Such are the plain dictates of both reason and analogy. On no sound principle can the agents have a right to final cognizance, as against the principals, much less to use force against them to maintain their construction of their powers. Such a right would be monstrous, and has never, heretofore, been claimed in similar cases.

That the doctrine is applicable to the case of a contested power between the States and the General Government, we have the authority, not only of reason and analogy, but of the distinguished statesman already referred to. Mr. Jefferson, at a late period of his life, after long experience and mature reflection, says, "With respect to our State and Federal Governments, I do not think their relations are correctly understood by foreigners. They suppose the former are subordinate to the latter. This is not the case. They are co-ordinate departments of one simple and integral whole. But you may ask, If the two departments should claim each the same subject of power, where is the umpire to decide between them? In cases of little urgency or importance, the prudence of both parties will keep them aloof from the questionable ground; but, if it can neither be avoided nor compromised, a convention of the States must be called to ascribe the doubtful power to that department which they may think best."

It is thus that our Constitution, by authorizing amendments, and by prescribing the authority and mode of making them, has, by a simple contrivance, with its characteristic wisdom, provided a power which, in the last resort, supersedes effectually the necessity, and even the pretext for force: a power to which none can fairly object; with which the interests of all are safe; which can definitively close all controversies in the only effectual mode, by freeing the compact of every defect and uncertainty, by an amendment of the instrument itself. It is impossible for human wisdom, in a system like ours, to devise another mode which shall be safe and effectual, and, at the same time, consistent with what are the relations and acknowledged powers of the two great departments of our Government. It gives a beauty and security peculiar to our system, which, if duly appreciated, will transmit its blessings to the remotest generations; but, if not, our splendid anticipations of the future will prove but an empty dream. Stripped of all its covering, the naked question is, whether ours is a federal or a consolidated government; a constitutional or absolute one; a government resting ultimately on the solid basis of the sovereignty of the States or on the unrestrained will of a majority; a form of government, as in all other unlimited ones, in which injustice, and violence, and force must finally prevail. *Let it never be forgotten that, where the majority rules without restriction, the minority is the subject;* and that, if we should absurdly attribute to the former the exclusive right of construing the Constitution, there would be, in fact, between the sovereign and subject, under such a government, no Constitution, or, at least, nothing deserving the name, or serving the legitimate object of so sacred an instrument.

How the States are to exercise this high power of interposition, which constitutes so essential a portion of their reserved rights that it *cannot be delegated without an entire surrender of their sovereignty,* and converting our system from a *federal* into a *consolidated* Government, is a question that the States only are competent to determine. The arguments which prove that they possess the power, equally prove that they are, in the language of Jefferson, *"the rightful judges of the mode and measure of redress."* But the spirit of forbearance, as well as the nature of the right itself, forbids a recourse to it, except in cases of dangerous infractions of the Constitution; and then only in the last resort, when all reasonable hope of relief from the ordinary action of the Government has failed; when, if the right to interpose did not exist, the alternative would be submission and oppression on one side, or resistance by force on the other. That our system should afford, in such extreme cases, an intermediate point between these dire alternatives, by which the Government may be brought to a pause, and thereby an interval obtained to compromise differences, or, if impracticable, be compelled to submit the question to a constitutional adjustment, through an appeal to the States themselves, is an evidence of its high wisdom: an element not, as is supposed by some, of weakness, but of strength; not of anarchy or revolution, but of peace and safety. *Its general recognition would of itself, in a great measure, if not altogether, supersede the necessity of its exercise, by impressing on the movements of the Government that moderation and justice so essential to harmony and peace, in a country of such vast extent and diversity of interests as ours;* and would, if controversy should come, turn the resentment of the aggrieved from the system to those who had abused its powers (a point all-important), and cause them to seek redress, *not in revolution or overthrow, but in reformation.* It is, in fact, properly understood, *a substitute,—where the alternative would be force,—tending to prevent, and, if that fails, to correct peaceably the aberrations to which all systems are liable, and which, if permitted to accumulate without correction, must finally end in a general catastrophe.*

I have now said what I intended in reference to the abstract question of the relation of the States to the General Government, and would here conclude, did I not believe that a mere general statement on an abstract question, without including that which may have caused its agitation, would be considered by many imperfect and unsatisfactory. Feeling that such would be justly the case, I am compelled, reluctantly, to touch on the Tariff, so far, at least, as may be necessary to illustrate the opinions which I have already advanced. Anxious, however, to intrude as little as possible on the public attention, I will be as brief as possible; and with that view will, as far as may be consistent with my object, avoid all debatable topics. . . .

As the disease will not, then, heal itself, we are brought to the question, Can a remedy be applied? and if so, what ought it to be?

To answer in the negative would be to assert that our Union has utterly failed; and that the opinion, so common before the adoption of our Constitution, that a free government could not be practically extended over a large country, was correct; and that ours had been destroyed by giving it limits so great as to comprehend, not only dissimilar, but irreconcilable interests. I am not prepared to admit a conclusion that would cast so deep a shade on the future; and that would falsify all the glorious anticipations of our ancestors, while it would so greatly lessen their high reputation for wisdom. Nothing but the clearest demonstration founded on actual experience, will ever force me to a conclusion so abhorrent to all my feelings. As strongly as I am impressed with the great dissimilarity, and, as I must add, as truth compels me to do, contrariety of interests in our country, resulting from the causes already indicated, and which are so great that they cannot be subjected to the unchecked will of a majority of the whole without defeating the great end of government, and without which it is a curse—justice—yet I see in the Union, as ordained by the Constitution, the means, if wisely used, not only of reconciling all diversities, but also the means, and the only effectual one, of securing to us justice, peace, and security, at home and abroad, and with them that national power and renown, the love of which Providence has implanted, for wise purposes, so deeply in the human heart: in all of which great objects every portion of our country, widely extended and diversified as it is, has a common and identical interest. If we have the wisdom to place a proper relative estimate on these more elevated and durable blessings, the present and every other conflict of like character may be readily terminated; but if, reversing the scale, each section should put a higher estimate on its immediate and peculiar gains, and, acting in that spirit, should push favorite measures of mere policy, without some regard to peace, harmony, or justice, our sectional conflicts would then, indeed, without some constitutional check, become interminable, except by the dissolution of the Union itself. That we have, in fact, so reversed the estimate, is too certain to be doubted, and the result is our present distempered and dangerous condition. The cure must commence in the correction of the error; and not to admit that we have erred would be the worst possible symptom. It would prove the disease to be incurable, through the regular and ordinary process of legislation; and would compel, finally, a resort to extraordinary, but I still trust, not only constitutional, but safe remedies.

No one would more sincerely rejoice than myself to see the remedy applied from the quarter where it could be most easily and regularly done. It is the only way by which those, who think that it is the only quarter from which it may constitutionally come, can possibly sustain their opinion. To omit the application by the General Government, would compel even them to admit the truth of the opposite opinion, or force them to abandon our political system in despair; while, on the other hand, all their enlightened and patriotic opponents would rejoice at such evidence of moderation and wisdom, on the part of the General Government, as would supersede a resort to what they believe to be the higher powers of our political system, as indicating a sounder state of public sentiment than has ever heretofore existed in any country; and thus affording the highest possible assurance of the perpetuation of our glorious institutions to the latest generation. For, as a people advance in knowledge, in the same degree they may dispense with mere artificial restrictions in their government; and we may imagine (but dare not expect to see) a state of intelligence so universal and high, that all the guards of liberty may be dispensed with, except an enlightened public opinion, acting through the right of suffrage; but it presupposes a state where every class and every section of the community are capable of estimating the effects of every measure, not only as it may affect itself, but every other class and section; and of fully realizing the sublime truth that the highest and wisest policy consists in maintaining justice, and promoting peace and harmony; and that, compared to these, schemes of mere gain are but trash and dross. I fear experience has already proved that we are far removed from such a state; and that we must, consequently, rely on the old and clumsy, but approved mode of checking power, in order to prevent or correct abuses; but I do trust that, though far from perfect, we are, at least, so much so as to be capable of remedying the present disorder in the ordinary way; and thus to prove that, with us, public opinion is so enlightened, and our political machine so perfect, as rarely to require for its preservation the intervention of the power that created it. How is this to be effected?

The application may be painful, but the remedy, I conceive, is certain and simple. There is but one effectual cure—an honest reduction of the duties to a fair system of revenue, adapted to the just and constitutional wants of the Government. Nothing short of this will restore the country to peace, harmony, and mutual affection. There is already a deep and growing conviction in a large section of the country, that the impost, even as a revenue system, is extremely unequal, and that it is mainly paid by those who furnish the means of paying the foreign exchanges of the country on which it is laid; and that the case would not be varied, taking into the estimate the entire action of the system, whether the producer or consumer pays in the first instance.

I do not propose to enter formally into the discussion of a point so complex and contested; but, as it has necessarily a strong practical bearing on the subject under consideration in all its relations, I cannot pass it without a few general and brief remarks.

If the producer, in reality, pays, none will doubt but the burden would mainly fall on the section it is supposed to do. The theory that the consumer pays, in the first instance, renders the proposition more complex, and will require, in order to understand where the burden, in reality, ultimately falls, on that supposition, to consider the protective, or, as its friends call it, the American System, under its threefold aspect of taxation, of protection, and of distribution,—or as performing, at the same time, the several functions of giving a revenue to the Government, of affording protection to certain branches of domestic industry, and furnishing means to Congress of distributing large sums through its appropriations: all of which are so blended in their effects, that it is impossible to understand its true operation without taking the whole into the estimate.

Admitting, then, as supposed, that he who consumes the article pays the tax in the increased price, and that the burden falls wholly on the consumers, without affecting the producers as a class (which, by the by, is far from being true, except in the single case, if there be such a one, where the producers have a monopoly of an article so indispensable to life that the quantity consumed cannot be affected by any increase of price), and that, considered in the light of a tax merely, the impost duties fall equally on every section in proportion to its population, still, when combined with its other effects, the burden it imposes as a tax may be so transferred from one section to the other as to take it from one and place it wholly on the other. Let us apply the remark first to its operation as a system of protection:

The tendency of the tax or duty on the imported article is not only to raise its price, but also, in the same proportion, that of the domestic article of the same kind, for which purpose, when intended for protection, it is, in fact, laid; and, of course, in determining where the system ultimately places the burden in reality, this effect, also, must be taken into the estimate. If one of the sections exclusively produces such domestic articles and the other purchases them from it, then it is clear that, to the amount of such increased prices, the tax or duty on the consumption of foreign articles would be transferred from the section producing the domestic articles to the one that purchased and consumed them;—unless the latter, in turn, be indemnified by the increased price of the objects of its industry, which none will venture to assert to be the case with the great staples of the country, which form the basis of our exports, the price of which is regulated by the foreign, and not the domestic market. To those who grow them, the increased price of the foreign and domestic articles both, in consequence of the duty on the former, is in reality, and in the strictest sense, a tax, while it is clear that the increased price of the latter acts as a bounty to the section producing them; and that, as the amount of such increased prices on what it sells to the other section is greater or less than the duty it pays on the imported articles, the system will, in fact, operate as a bounty or tax: if greater, the difference would be a bounty; if less, a tax.

Again, the operation may be equal in every other respect, and yet the pressure of the system, relatively, on the two sections, be rendered very unequal by the appropriations or distribution. If each section receives back what it paid into the treasury, the equality, if it previously existed, will continue; but if one receives back less, and the other proportionably more than is paid, then the difference in relation to the sections will be to the former a loss, and to the latter a gain; and the system, in this aspect, would operate to the amount of the difference, as a contribution from the one receiving less than it paid to the other that receives more. Such would be incontestably its general effects, taken in all its different aspects, even on the theory supposed to be most favorable to prove the equal action of the system, that the consumer pays, in the first instance, the whole amount of the tax.

To show how, on this supposition, the burden and advantages of the system would actually distribute themselves between the sections, would carry me too far into details; but I feel assured, after full and careful examination, that they are such as to explain, what otherwise would seem inexplicable, that one section should consider its repeal a calamity, and the other a blessing; and that such opposite views should be taken by them as to place them in a state of determined conflict in relation to the great fiscal and commercial interest of the country. Indeed, were there no satisfactory explanation, the opposite views that prevail in the two sections, as to the effects of the system, ought to satisfy all of its unequal action. There can be no safer, or more certain rule, than to suppose each portion of the country equally capable of understanding their respective interests, and that each is a much better judge of the effects of any system or measures on its peculiar interests than the other can possibly be.

But, whether the opinion of its unequal action be correct or erroneous, nothing can be more certain than that the impression is widely extending itself, that the system, under all its modifications, is essentially unequal; and if to this be added a conviction still deeper and more universal, that every duty imposed *for the purpose of protection is not only unequal, but also unconstitutional,* it would be a fatal error to suppose that any remedy, short of that which I have stated, can heal our political disorders.

In order to understand more fully the difficulty of adjusting this unhappy contest on any other ground, it may not be improper to present a general view of the constitutional objection, that it may be clearly seen how hopeless it is to expect that it can be yielded by those who have embraced it.

They believe that all the powers vested by the Constitution in Congress are, not only restricted by the limitations expressly imposed, but also by the nature and object of the powers themselves. Thus, though the power to impose duties on imports be granted in general terms, without any other express limitations but that they shall be equal, and no preference shall be given to the ports of one State over those of another, yet, as being a portion of the taxing power given with the view of raising revenue, it is, from its nature, restricted to that object, as much so as if the Convention had expressly so limited it; and that to use it to effect any other purpose not specified in the Constitution, is an infraction of the instrument in its most dangerous form—an infraction by perversion, more easily made, and more difficult to resist, than any other. The same view is believed to be applicable to the power of regulating commerce, as well as all the other powers. To surrender this important principle, it is conceived, would be to surrender all power, and to render the Government unlimited and despotic; and to yield it up, in relation to the particular power in question, would be, in fact, to surrender the control of the whole industry and capital of the country to the General Government, and would end in placing the weaker section in a colonial relation towards the stronger. For nothing are more dissimilar in their nature, or may be more unequally affected by the same laws, than different descriptions of labor and property; and if taxes, by increasing the amount and changing the intent only, may be perverted, in fact, into a system of penalties and rewards, it would give all the power that could be desired to subject the labor and property of the minority to the will of the majority, to be regulated without regarding the interest of the former in subserviency to the will of the latter. Thus thinking, it would seem unreasonable to expect, that any adjustment, based on the recognition of the correctness of a construction of the Constitution which would admit the exercise of such a power, would satisfy the weaker of two sections, particularly with its peculiar industry and property, which experience has shown may be so injuriously affected by its exercise. Thus much for one side.

The just claim of the other ought to be equally respected. Whatever excitement the system has justly caused in certain portions of our country, I hope and believe all will conceive that the change should be made with the least possible detriment to the interests of those who may be liable to be affected by it; consistently, with what is justly due to others, and the principles of the Constitution. To effect this will require the kindest spirit of conciliation and the utmost skill; but, even with these, it will be impossible to make the transition without a shock, greater or less, though I trust, if judiciously effected, it will not be without many compensating advantages. That there will be some such cannot be doubted. It will, at least, be followed by greater stability, and will tend to harmonize the manufacturing with all the other great interests of the country, and bind the whole in mutual affection. But these are not all. Another advantage of essential importance to the ultimate prosperity of our manufacturing industry will follow. *It will cheapen production;* and, in that view, the loss of any one branch will be nothing like in proportion to the reduction of duty on that particular branch. Every reduction will, in fact, operate as a bounty to every other branch except the one reduced; and thus the effect of a general reduction will be to cheapen, universally, the price of production, by cheapening living, wages, and material, so as to give, if not equal profits after the reduction—profits by no means reduced proportionally to the duties—an effect which, as it regards the foreign markets, is of the utmost importance. It must be apparent, on reflection, that the means adopted to secure the home market for our manufactures are precisely the opposite of those necessary to obtain the foreign. In the former, the increased expense of production, in consequence of a system of protection, may be more than compensated by the increased price at home of the article protected; but in the latter, this advantage is lost; and, as there is no other corresponding compensation, the increased cost of production must be a dead loss in the foreign market. But whether these advantages, and many others that might be mentioned, will ultimately compensate to the full extent or not the loss to the manufacturers, on the reduction of the duties, certain it is, that we have approached a point at which a great change cannot be much longer delayed; and that the more promptly it may be met, the less excitement there will be, and the greater leisure and calmness for a cautious and skilful operation in making the transition; and which it becomes those more immediately interested duly to consider. Nor ought they to overlook, in considering the question, the different character of the claims of the two sides. The one asks from Government no advantage, but simply to be let alone in the undisturbed possession of their natural advantages, and to secure which, as far as was consistent with the other objects of the Constitution, was one of their leading motives in entering into the Union; while the other side claims, for the advancement of their prosperity, the positive interference of the Government. In such cases, on every principle of fairness and justice, such interference ought to be restrained within limits strictly compatible with the natural advantages of the other. He who looks to all the causes in operation—the near approach of the final payment of the public debt—the growing disaffection and resistance to the system in so large a section of the country—the deeper principles on which opposition to it is gradually turning—must be, indeed, infatuated not to see a great change is unavoidable; and that the attempt to elude or much longer delay it must, finally, but increase the shock and disastrous consequences which may follow.

In forming the opinions I have expressed, I have not been actuated by an unkind feeling towards our manufacturing interest. I now am, and ever have been, decidedly friendly to them, though I cannot concur in all of the measures which have been adopted to advance them. I believe considerations higher than any question of mere pecuniary interest forbade their use. But subordinate to these higher views of policy, I regard the advancement of mechanical and chemical improvements in the arts with feelings little short of enthusiasm; not only as the prolific source of national and individual wealth, but as the great means of enlarging the domain of man over the material world, and thereby of laying the solid foundation of a highly-improved condition of society, morally and politically. I fear not that we shall extend our power too far over the great agents of nature; but, on the contrary, I consider such enlargement of our power as tending more certainly and powerfully to better the condition of our race, than any one of the many powerful causes now operating to that result. With these impressions, I not only rejoice at the general progress of the arts in the world, but in their advancement in our own country; and as far as protection may be incidentally afforded, in the fair and honest exercise of our constitutional powers, I think now, as I have always thought, that sound policy, connected with the security, independence, and peace of the country, requires it should be done; but that we cannot go a single step beyond without jeopardizing our peace, our harmony and our liberty— considerations of infinitely more importance to us than any measure of mere policy can possibly be. . . .

V

ABRAHAM LINCOLN
(1809–65)

ABRAHAM LINCOLN, the 16th President of the United States, presided over the nation during its most serious internal conflict, one which had been developing rapidly since the passage of the Kansas-Nebraska Act of 1854. At that time Lincoln, who had retired from active politics in 1849, reappeared on the political scene to take a stand on the slavery controversy. The principles which characterize Lincoln's stand are contained in some of his more important speeches of the 1854–60 period—"The Repeal of the Missouri Compromise," (1854); "A House Divided," (1858); and the "Address at Cooper Institute," (1860).

Lincoln's speech on the repeal of the Missouri Compromise, given in answer to a speech by Stephen A. Douglas at Peoria, Illinois, in 1854, was also his answer to Senator Douglas's Kansas-Nebraska bill, the passage of which brought about one of the greatest crises in American history. The act provided for the application of popular sovereignty to the Nebraska Territory, which was part of the Louisiana Territory north of the 36th parallel, where slavery had been banned forever in accordance with the Missouri Compromise of 1820. Under the terms of the 1854 act, the status of slavery in the territories of Kansas and Nebraska would be decided by popular sovereignty (by the legislatures of the territories), and when they adopted constitutions with the intention of applying for admission as states, the territories could decide the question of slavery for the new states.

According to Lincoln, the restoration of the Missouri Compromise restriction on slavery was a supreme necessity of national policy. He viewed that restriction not only as a barrier to slavery in Kansas but a barrier to slavery as such. Lincoln believed that passage of the Kansas-Nebraska Act had brought on a national crisis, in the resolution of which it would be decided either that slavery is sectional and freedom national or that freedom is sectional and slavery national. When the Kansas-Nebraska Act allowed slavery anywhere in the territories where the people wanted it, this meant for Lincoln that slavery was in the process of becoming national. He had not previously opposed slavery in public, except indirectly, and would have been willing to allow the question of its immorality to remain dormant if others had done so, and if events were moving in the direction of freedom. But now that the slavery question had been brought to the fore by the repeal of the Missouri Compromise and by aggressive efforts to open new lands to slavery, Lincoln was determined that it not be subordinated to any other question.

Lincoln's national reputation was made as a result of his debates with Senator Stephen A. Douglas of Illinois, in the course of which, in his "House Divided" speech at Springfield, Illinois, in 1858, he accepted the nomination of the Republican State Convention for the Senate. His theme in that speech was that political events had been building up in such a way as to destroy the cause of human freedom forever, unless they were reversed. Lincoln believed the political machinery built for the extension of slavery through the Kansas-Nebraska Act and the *Dred Scott* decision (19 How. 393 [1857]) would work into the "don't care" policy of Douglas's doctrine of popular sovereignty to guarantee the extension of slavery into the territories. The *Dred Scott* decision held that a territory might not forbid slavery even if it wanted to, because the Constitution affirmed the right of property in slaves and forbade either Congress or a territorial legislature from interfering with that right. Under the guise of establishing national unity, Lincoln argued, the Democratic Party had continuously pushed slavery into the new territories and had blocked all efforts to control or ultimately destroy that evil. A crisis had been reached: either national politics would have to control slavery, or slavery would control national politics.

Lincoln was defeated in the contest with Douglas for the Senate in 1858. The state legislature chose to reappoint Douglas. But Lincoln's increased stature, due to the debates with Douglas, brought him an invitation to speak before the Young Men's Republican Union at Cooper Institute in New York City in 1860. His Cooper Institute speech is well known for its exposition of the attitude toward slavery taken by the Founding Fathers, who had tolerated it as a necessary evil. Lincoln argued that their policy was to so place the institution in the public mind that it would rest in the belief that slavery was in the course of ultimate extinction. The Founding Fathers, moreover, understood the equality provision of the Declaration of Independence as a promise that all men everywhere might some day possess and enjoy their inalienable rights. Douglas's policy of "care not whether slavery be voted *down* or voted *up,*" he maintained, reversed the policy of the Founding Fathers. Although he pointed out that the Republican Party had no abolitionist aims, he indicated that there could be no compromise on its conviction of the immorality of slavery.

28
SPEECH ON REPEAL OF THE MISSOURI COMPROMISE
October 16, 1854

T HE REPEAL OF the Missouri Compromise, and the propriety of its restoration, constitute the subject of what I am about to say.

As I desire to present my own connected view of this subject, my remarks will not be, specifically, an answer to Judge Douglas; yet, as I proceed, the main points he has presented will arise, and will receive such respectful attention as I may be able to give them.

I wish further to say, that I do not propose to question the patriotism, or to assail the motives of any man, or class of men; but rather to strictly confine myself to the naked merits of the question.

I also wish to be no less than National in all the positions I may take; and whenever I take ground which others have thought, or may think, narrow, sectional and dangerous to the Union, I hope to give a reason, which will appear sufficient, at least to some, why I think differently.

And, as this subject is no other, than part and parcel of the larger general question of domestic-slavery, I wish to MAKE and to KEEP the distinction between the EXISTING institution, and the EXTENSION of it, so broad, and so clear, that no honest man can misunderstand me, and no dishonest one, successfully misrepresent me.

In order to get a clear understanding of what the Missouri Compromise is, a short history of the preceding kindred subjects will perhaps be proper. When we established our independence, we did not own, or claim, the country to which this compromise applies. Indeed, strictly speaking, the confederacy then owned no country at all; the States respectively owned the country within their limits; and some of them owned territory beyond their strict State limits. Virginia thus owned the North-Western territory—the country out of which the principal part of Ohio, all Indiana, all Illinois, all Michigan and all Wisconsin, have since been formed. She also owned (perhaps within her then limits) what has since been formed into the State of Kentucky. North Carolina thus owned what is now the State of Tennessee; and South Carolina and Georgia, in separate parts, owned what are now Mississippi and Alabama. Connecticut, I think, owned the little remaining part of Ohio—being the same where they now send Giddings to Congress, and beat all creation at making cheese. These territories, together with the States themselves, constituted all the country over which the confederacy then claimed any sort of jurisdiction. We were then living under the Articles of Confederation, which were superceded by the Constitution several years afterwards. The question of ceding these territories to the general government was set on foot. Mr. Jefferson, the author of the Declaration of Independence, and otherwise a chief actor in the revolution; then a delegate in Congress; afterwards twice President; who was, is, and perhaps will continue to be, the most distinguished politician of our history; a Virginian by birth and continued residence, and withal, a slaveholder; conceived the idea of taking that occasion, to prevent slavery ever going into the north-western territory. He prevailed on the Virginia Legislature to adopt his views, and to cede the territory, making the prohibition of slavery therein, a condition of the deed. Congress accepted the cession, with the condition; and in the first Ordinance (which the acts of Congress were then called) for the government of the territory, provided that slavery should never be permitted therein. This is the famed ordinance of '87 so often spoken of. Thenceforward, for sixty-one years, and until in 1848, the last scrap of this territory came into the Union as the State of Wisconsin, all parties acted in quiet obedience to this ordinance. It is now what Jefferson foresaw and intended—the happy home of teeming millions of free, white, prosperous people, and no slave amongst them.

Thus, with the author of the declaration of Independence, the policy of prohibiting slavery in new territory originated. Thus, away back of the constitution, in the pure fresh, free breath of the revolution, the State of Virginia, and the National congress put that policy in practice. Thus through sixty odd of the best years of the republic did that policy steadily work to its great and beneficent end. And thus, in those five states, and five millions of free, enterprising people, we have before us the rich fruits of this policy. But *now* new light breaks upon us. Now congress declares this ought never to have been; and the like of it, must never be again. The sacred right of self government is grossly violated by it! We even find some men, who drew their first breath, and every other breath of their lives, under this very restriction, now live in dread of absolute suffocation, if they should be restricted in the "sacred right" of taking slaves to Nebraska. That *perfect* liberty they sigh for—the liberty of making slaves of other people—Jefferson never thought of; their own father never thought of; they never thought of themselves, a year ago. How fortunate for them, they did not sooner become sensible of their great misery! Oh, how difficult it is to treat with respect, such assaults upon all we have ever really held sacred.

But to return to history. In 1803 we purchased what was then called Louisiana, of France. It included the now states of Louisiana, Arkansas, Missouri, and Iowa; also the territory of Minnesota, and the present bone of contention, Kansas and Nebraska. Slavery already existed among the French at New Orleans; and, to some extent, at St. Louis. In 1812 Louisiana came into the Union as a slave state, without controversy. In 1818 or '19, Missouri showed signs of a wish to come in with slavery. This was resisted by northern members of Congress; and thus began the first great slavery agitation in the nation. This controversy lasted several months, and became very angry and exciting; the House of Representatives voting steadily for the prohibition of slavery in Missouri, and the Senate voting as steadily against it. Threats of breaking up the Union were freely made; and the ablest public men of the day became seriously alarmed. At length a compromise was made, in which, like all compromises, both sides yielded something. It was a law passed on the 6th day of March, 1820, providing that Missouri might come into the Union *with* slavery, but that in all the remaining part of the territory purchased of France, which lies north of 36 degrees and 30 minutes north latitude, slavery should never be permitted. This provision of law, *is the Missouri Compromise.* In excluding slavery North of the line, the same language is employed as in the Ordinance of '87. It directly applied to Iowa, Minnesota, and to the present bone of contention, Kansas and Nebraska. Whether there should or should not, be slavery south of that line, nothing was said in the law; but Arkansas constituted the principal remaining part, south of the line; and it has since been admitted as a slave state without serious controversy. More recently, Iowa, north of the line, came in as a free state without controversy. Still later, Minnesota, north of the line, had a territorial organization without controversy. Texas principally south of the line, and West of Arkansas; though originally within the purchase from France, had, in 1819, been traded off to Spain, in our treaty for the acquisition of Florida. It had thus become a part of Mexico. Mexico revolutionized and became independent of Spain. American citizens began settling rapidly, with their slaves in the southern part of Texas. Soon they revolutionized against Mexico, and established an independent government of their own, adopting a constitution, with slavery, strongly resembling the constitutions of our slave states. By still another rapid move, Texas, claiming a boundary much further West, than when we parted with her in 1819, was brought back to the United States, and admitted into the Union as a slave state. There then was little or no settlement in the northern part of Texas, a considerable portion of which lay north of the Missouri line; and in the resolutions admitting her into the Union, the Missouri restriction was expressly extended westward across her territory. This was in 1845, only nine years ago.

Thus originated the Missouri Compromise; and thus has it been respected down to 1845. And even four years later, in 1849, our distinguished Senator, in a public address, held the following language in relation to it:

"The Missouri Compromise had been in practical operation for about a quarter of a century, and had received the sanction and approbation of men of all parties in every section of the Union. It had allayed all sectional jealousies and irritations growing out of this vexed question, and harmonized and tranquilized the whole country. It had given to Henry Clay, as its prominent champion, the proud sobriquet of the *"Great Pacificator"* and by that title and for that service, his political friends had repeatedly appealed to the people to rally under his standard, as a presidential candidate, as the man who had exhibited the patriotism and the power to suppress, an unholy and treasonable agitation, and preserve the Union. He was not aware that any man or any party from any section of the Union, had ever urged as an objection to Mr. Clay, that he was the great champion of the Missouri Compromise. On the contrary, the effort was made by the opponents of Mr. Clay, to prove that he was not entitled to the exclusive merit of that great patriotic measure, and that the honor was equally due to others as well as to him, for securing its adoption—that it had its origin in the hearts of all patriotic men, who desired to preserve and perpetuate the blessings of our glorious Union—an origin akin that of the constitution of the United States, conceived in the same spirit of fraternal affection, and calculated to remove forever, the only danger, which seemed to threaten, at some distant day, to sever the social bond of union. All the evidences of public opinion at that day, seemed to indicate that this Compromise had been canonized in the hearts of the American people, as a sacred thing which no ruthless hand would ever be reckless enough to disturb."

I do not read this extract to involve Judge Douglas in an inconsistency. If he afterwards thought he had been wrong, it was right for him to change. I bring this forward merely to show the high estimate placed on the Missouri Compromise by all parties up to so late as the year 1849.

But, going back a little, in point of time, our war with Mexico broke out in 1846. When Congress was about adjourning that session, President Polk asked them to place two millions of dollars under his control, to be used by him in the recess, if found practicable and expedient, in negotiating a treaty of peace with Mexico, and acquiring some part of her territory. A bill was duly got up, for the purpose, and was progressing swimmingly, in the House of Representatives, when a member by the name of David Wilmot, a democrat from Pennsylvania, moved as an amendment "Provided that in any territory thus acquired, there shall never be slavery."

This is the origin of the far-famed "Wilmot Proviso." It created a great flutter; but it stuck like wax, was voted into the bill, and the bill passed with it through the House. The Senate, however, adjourned without final action on it and so both appropriation and proviso were lost, for the time. The war continued, and at the next session, the president renewed his request for the appropriation, enlarging the amount, I think, to three million. Again came the proviso; and defeated the measure. Congress adjourned again, and the war went on. In Dec., 1847, the new congress assembled. I was in the lower House that term. The "Wilmot Proviso" or the principle of it, was constantly coming up in some shape or other, and I think I may venture to say I voted for it at least forty times; during the short term I was there. The Senate, however, held it in check, and it never became law. In the spring of 1848 a treaty of peace was made with Mexico; by which we obtained that portion of her country which now constitutes the territories of New Mexico and Utah, and the now state of California. By this treaty the Wilmot Proviso was defeated, as so far as it was intended to be, a condition of the acquisition of territory. Its friends however, were still determined to find some way to restrain slavery from getting into the new country. This new acquisition lay directly West of our old purchase from France, and extended west to the Pacific ocean—and was so situated that if the Missouri line should be extended straight West, the new country would be divided by such extended line, leaving some North and some South of it. On Judge Douglas' motion a bill, or provision of a bill, passed the Senate to so extend the Missouri line. The Proviso men in the House, including myself, voted it down, because by implication, it gave up the Southern part to slavery, while we were bent on having it *all* free.

In the fall of 1848 the gold mines were discovered in California. This attracted people to it with unprecedented rapidity, so that on, or soon after, the meeting of the new congress in Dec., 1849, she already had a population of nearly a hundred thousand, had called a convention, formed a state constitution, excluding slavery, and was knocking for admission into the Union. The Proviso men, of course were for letting her in, but the Senate, always true to the other side would not consent to her admission. And there California stood, kept *out* of the Union, because she would not let slavery *into* her borders. Under all the circumstances perhaps this was not wrong. There were other points of dispute, connected with the general question of slavery, which equally needed adjustment. The South clamored for a more efficient fugitive slave law. The North clamored for the abolition of a peculiar species of slave trade in the District of Columbia, in connection with which, in view from the windows of the capitol, a sort of negro-livery stable, where droves of negroes were collected, temporarily kept, and finally taken to Southern markets, precisely like droves of horses, had been openly maintained for fifty years. Utah and New Mexico needed territorial governments; and whether slavery should or should not be prohibited within them, was another question. The indefinite Western boundary of Texas was to be settled. She was received a slave state; and consequently the farther West the slavery men could push her boundary, the more slave country they secured. And the farther East the slavery opponents could thrust the boundary back, the less slave ground was secured. Thus this was just as clearly a slavery question as any of the others.

These points all needed adjustment; and they were all held up, perhaps wisely to make them help to adjust one another. The Union, now, as in 1820, was thought to be in danger; and devotion to the Union rightfully inclined men to yield somewhat, in points where nothing else could have so inclined them. A compromise was finally effected. The south got their new fugitive-slave law; and the North got California, (the far best part of our acquisition from Mexico,) as a free State. The south got a provision that New Mexico and Utah, *when admitted as States,* may come in *with* or *without* slavery as they may then choose; and the north got the slave-trade abolished in the District of Columbia. The north got the western boundary of Texas, thence further back eastward than the south desired; but, in turn, they gave Texas ten millions of dollars, with which to pay her old debts. This is the Compromise of 1850.

Preceding the Presidential election of 1852, each of the great political parties, democrats and whigs, met in convention, and adopted resolutions endorsing the compromise of '50; as a "finality," a final settlement, so far as these parties could make it so, of all slavery agitation. Previous to this, in 1851, the Illinois Legislature had indorsed it.

During this long period of time Nebraska had remained, substantially an uninhabited country, but now emigration to, and settlement within it began to take place. It is about one third as large as the present United States, and its importance so long overlooked, begins to come into view. The restriction of slavery by the Missouri Compromise directly applied to it; in fact, was first made, and has since been maintained, expressly for it. In 1853, a bill to give it a territorial government passed the House of Representatives, and, in the hands of Judge Douglas, failed of passing the Senate only for want of time. This bill contained no repeal of the Missouri Compromise. Indeed, when it was assailed because it did not contain such repeal, Judge Douglas defended it in its existing form. On January 4th, 1854, Judge Douglas introduces a new bill to give Nebraska territorial government. He accompanies this bill with a report, in which last, he expressly recommends that the Missouri Compromise shall neither be affirmed nor repealed.

Before long the bill is so modified as to make two territories instead of one; calling the Southern one Kansas.

Also, about a month after the introduction of the bill, on the judge's own motion, it is so amended as to declare the Missouri Compromise inoperative and void; and, substantially, that the People who go and settle there may establish slavery, or exclude it, as they may see fit. In this shape the bill passed both branches of congress, and became a law.

This is the *repeal* of the Missouri Compromise. The foregoing history may not be precisely accurate in every particular; but I am sure it is sufficiently so, for all the uses I shall attempt to make of it, and in it, we have before us, the chief material enabling us to correctly judge whether the repeal of the Missouri Compromise is right or wrong.

I think, and shall try to show, that it is wrong; wrong in its direct effect, letting slavery into Kansas and Nebraska—and wrong in its prospective principle, allowing it to spread to every other part of the wide world, where men can be found inclined to take it.

This *declared* indifference, but as I must think, covert *real* zeal for the spread of slavery, I can not but hate. I hate it because of the monstrous injustice of slavery itself. I hate it because it deprives our republican example of its just influence in the world—enables the enemies of free institutions, with plausibility, to taunt us as hypocrites—causes the real friends of freedom to doubt our sincerity, and especially because it forces so many really good men amongst ourselves into an open war with the very fundamental principles of civil liberty—criticising the Declaration of Independence, and insisting that there is no right principle of action but *self-interest*.

Before proceeding, let me say I think I have no prejudice against the

Southern people. They are just what we would be in their situation. If slavery did not now exist amongst them, they would not introduce it. If it did now exist amongst us, we should not instantly give it up. This I believe of the masses north and south. Doubtless there are individuals, on both sides, who would not hold slaves under any circumstances; and others who would gladly introduce slavery anew, if it were out of existence. We know that some southern men do free their slaves, go north, and become tip-top abolitionists; while some northern ones go south, and become most cruel slave-masters.

When southern people tell us they are no more responsible for the origin of slavery, than we; I acknowledge the fact. When it is said that the institution exists; and that it is very difficult to get rid of it, in any satisfactory way, I can understand and appreciate the saying. I surely will not blame them for not doing what I should not know how to do myself. If all earthly power were given me, I should not know what to do, as to the existing institution. My first impulse would be to free all the slaves, and send them to Liberia,—to their own native land. But a moment's reflection would convince me, that whatever of high hope, (as I think there is) there may be in this, in the long run, its sudden execution is impossible. If they were all landed there in a day, they would all perish in the next ten days; and there are not surplus shipping and surplus money enough in the world to carry them there in many times ten days. What then? Free them all, and keep them among us as underlings? Is it quite certain that this betters their condition? I think I would not hold one in slavery, at any rate; yet the point is not clear enough for me to denounce people upon. What next? Free them, and make them politically and socially, our equals? My own feelings will not admit of this; and if mine would, we well know that those of the great mass of white people will not. Whether this feeling accords with justice and sound judgment, is not the sole question, if indeed, it is any part of it. A universal feeling, whether well or ill-founded, can not be safely disregarded. We can not, then, make them equals. It does seem to me that systems of gradual emancipation might be adopted; but for their tardiness in this, I will not undertake to judge our brethren of the south.

When they remind us of their constitutional rights, I acknowledge them, not grudgingly, but fully, and fairly; and I would give them any legislation for the reclaiming of their fugitives, which should not, in its stringency, be more likely to carry a free man into slavery, than our ordinary criminal laws are to hang an innocent one.

But all this; to my judgment, furnishes no more excuse for permitting slavery to go into our own free territory, than it would for reviving the African slave trade by law. The law which forbids the bringing of slaves *from* Africa; and that which has so long forbid the taking them *to*

Nebraska, can hardly be distinguished on any moral principle; and the repeal of the former could find quite as plausible excuses as that of the latter.

The arguments by which the repeal of the Missouri Compromise is sought to be justified, are these:

First, that the Nebraska country needed a territorial government.

Second, that in various ways, the public had repudiated it, and demanded the repeal; and therefore should not now complain of it.

And lastly, that the repeal establishes a principle, which is intrinsically right.

I will attempt an answer to each of them in its turn.

First, then, if that country was in need of a territorial organization, could it not have had it as well without as with the repeal? Iowa and Minnesota, to both of which the Missouri restriction applied, had, without its repeal, each in succession, territorial organizations. And even, the year before, a bill for Nebraska itself, was within an ace of passing, without the repealing clause; and this in the hands of the same men who are now the champions of repeal. Why no necessity then for the repeal? But still later, when this very bill was first brought in, it contained no repeal. But, say they, because the public had demanded, or rather commanded the repeal, the repeal was to accompany the organization, whenever that should occur.

Now I deny that the public ever demanded any such thing—ever repudiated the Missouri Compromise—ever commanded its repeal. I deny it, and call for the proof. It is not contended, I believe, that any such command has ever been given in express terms. It is only said that it was done *in principle*. The support of the Wilmot Proviso, is the first fact mentioned, to prove that the Missouri restriction was repudiated in *principle,* and the second is, the refusal to extend the Missouri line over the country acquired from Mexico. These are near enough alike to be treated together. The one was to exclude the chances of slavery from the *whole* new acquisition by the lump; and the other was to reject a division of it, by which one *half* was to be given up to those chances. Now whether this was a repudiation of the Missouri line, in *principle,* depends upon whether the Missouri law contained any *principle* requiring the line to be extended over the country acquired from Mexico. I contend it did not. I insist that it contained no general principle, but that it was, in every sense, specific. That its terms limit it to the country purchased from France, is undenied and undeniable. It could have no principle beyond the intention of those who made it. They did not intend to extend the line to country which they did not own. If they intended to extend it, in the event of acquiring additional territory, why did they not say so? It was just as easy to say, that "in all the country west of the Mississippi, which we now own, *or may hereafter acquire* there shall never be slavery," as to say, what they did say; and they would have said it if they had meant it. An intention to extend the law is not only not mentioned in the law, but is not mentioned in any contemporaneous history. Both the law itself, and the history of the times are a blank as to any *principle* of extension; and by neither the known rules for construing statutes and contracts, nor by common sense, can any such *principle* be inferred.

Another fact showing the *specific* character of the Missouri law—showing that it intended no more than it expressed—showing that the line was not intended as a universal dividing line between free and slave territory, present and prospective—north of which slavery could never go—is the fact that by that very law, Missouri came in as a slave state, *north* of the line. If that law contained any prospective *principle,* the whole law must be looked to in order to ascertain what the *principle* was. And by this rule, the south could fairly contend that inasmuch as they got one slave state north of the line at the inception of the law, they have the right to have another given them *north* of it occasionally—now and then in the indefinite westward extension of the line. This demonstrates the absurdity of attempting to deduce a prospective *principle* from the Missouri Compromise line.

When we voted for the Wilmot Proviso, we were voting to keep slavery *out* of the whole Missouri acquisition; and little did we think we were thereby voting, to let it *into* Nebraska, laying several hundred miles distant. When we voted against extending the Missouri line, little did we think we were voting to destroy the old line, then of near thirty years standing. To argue that we thus repudiated the Missouri Compromise is no less absurd than it would be to argue that because we have, so far, forborne to acquire Cuba, we have thereby, *in principle,* repudiated our former acquisitions, and determined to throw them out of the Union! No less absurd than it would be to say that because I may have refused to build an addition to my house, I thereby have decided to destroy the existing house! And if I catch you setting fire to my house, you will turn upon me and say I INSTRUCTED you to do it! The most conclusive argument, however, that, while voting for the Wilmot Proviso, and while voting against the EXTENSION of the Missouri line, we never thought of disturbing the original Missouri Compromise, is found in the facts, that there was then, and still is, an unorganized tract of fine country, nearly as large as the state of Missouri, lying immediately west of Arkansas, and south of the Missouri Compromise line; and that we never attempted to prohibit slavery as to it. I wish particular attention to this. It adjoins the original Missouri Compromise line, by its northern boundary; and consequently is part of the country, into which, by implication, slavery was permitted to go, by that compromise. There it has lain open ever since, and there it still lies. And yet no effort has been made at any time to wrest it from the south. In all our struggles to prohibit slavery within our Mexican acquisitions, we never so much as lifted a finger to prohibit it, as to this tract. Is not this entirely conclusive that at all times, we have held the Missouri Compromise as a sacred thing; even when against ourselves, as well as when for us?

Senator Douglas sometimes says the Missouri line itself was, *in principle,* only an extension of the line of the ordinance of '87—that is to say, an extension of the Ohio river. I think this is weak enough on its face. I will remark, however that, as a glance at the map will show, the Missouri line is a long way farther South than the Ohio; and that if our Senator, in proposing his extension, had stuck to the *principle* of jogging southward, perhaps it might not have been voted down so readily.

But next it is said that the compromises of '50 and the ratification of them by both political parties, in '52, established a *new principle,* which required the repeal of the Missouri Compromise. This again I deny. I deny it, and demand the proof. I have already stated fully what the compromises of '50 are. The particular part of those measures, for which the virtual repeal of the Missouri compromise is sought to be inferred (for it is admitted they contain nothing about it, in express terms) is the provision in the Utah and New Mexico laws, which permits them when they seek admission into the Union as States, to come in with or without slavery as they shall then see fit. Now I insist this provision was made for Utah and New Mexico, and for no other place whatever. It had no more direct reference to Nebraska than it had to the territories of the moon. But, say they, it had reference to Nebraska, *in principle.* Let us see. The North consented to this provision, not because they considered it right in itself; but because they were compensated—paid for it. They, at the same time, got California into the Union as a free State. This was far the best part of all they had struggled for by the Wilmot Proviso. They also got the area of slavery somewhat narrowed in the settlement of the boundary of Texas. Also, they got the slave trade abolished in the District of Columbia. For all these desirable objects the North could afford to yield something; and they did yield to the South the Utah and New Mexico provision. I do not mean that the whole North, or even a majority, yielded, when the law passed; but enough yielded, when added to the vote of the South, to carry the measure. Now can it be pretended that the *principle* of this arrangement requires us to permit the same provision to be applied to Nebraska, *without any equivalent at all?* Give us another free State; press the boundary of Texas still further back, give us another step toward the destruction of slavery in the District, and you present us a similar case. But ask us not to repeat, for nothing, what you paid for in the first instance. If you wish the thing again, pay again. That is the *principle* of the compromises of '50, if indeed they had any principles beyond their specific terms—it was the system of equivalents.

Again, if Congress, at that time, intended that all future territories should, when admitted as States, come in with or without slavery, at their own option, why did it not say so? With such an universal provision, all know the bills could not have passed. Did they, then—could they—establish a *principle* contrary to their own intention? Still further, if they intended to establish the principle that wherever Congress had control, it should be left to the people to do as they thought fit with slavery why did they not authorize the people of the District of Columbia at their adoption to abolish slavery within these limits? I personally know that this has not been left undone, because it was unthought of. It was frequently spoken of by members of Congress and by citizens of Washington six years ago; and I heard no one express a doubt that a system of gradual emancipation, with compensation to owners, would meet the approbation of a large majority of the white people of the District. But without the action of Congress they could say nothing; and Congress said "no." In the measures of 1850 Congress had the subject of slavery in the District expressly in hand. If they were then establishing the *principle* of allowing the people to do as they please with slavery, why did they not apply the *principle* to that people?

Again, it is claimed that by the Resolutions of the Illinois Legislature, passed in 1851, the repeal of the Missouri compromise was demanded. This I deny also. Whatever may be worked out by a criticism of the language of those resolutions, the people have never understood them as being any more than an endorsement of the compromises of 1850; and a release of our Senators from voting for the Wilmot Proviso. The whole people are living witnesses, that this only, was their view. Finally, it is asked "If we did not mean to apply the Utah and New Mexico provision, to all future territories, what did we mean, when we, in 1852, endorsed the compromises of '50?"

For myself, I can answer this question most easily. I meant not to ask a repeal, or modification of the fugitive slave law. I meant not to ask for the abolition of slavery in the District of Columbia. I meant not to resist the admission of Utah and New Mexico, even should they ask to come in as slave States. I meant nothing about additional territories, because, as I understood, we then had no territory whose character as to slavery was not already settled. As to Nebraska, I regarded its character as being fixed, by the Missouri compromise, for thirty years—as unalterably fixed as that of my own home in Illinois. As to new acquisitions I said "sufficient unto the day is the evil thereof." When we make new acquaintances, we will, as heretofore, try to manage them some how. That is my answer. That is what I meant and said; and I appeal to the people to say, each for himself, whether that was not also the universal meaning of the free States.

And now, in turn, let me ask a few questions. If by any, or all these matters, the repeal of the Missouri Compromise was commanded, why was not the command sooner obeyed? Why was the repeal omitted in the Nebraska bill of 1853? Why was it omitted in the original bill of 1854? Why, in the accompanying report, was such a repeal characterized as a *departure* from the course pursued in 1850? and its continued omission recommended?

I am aware Judge Douglas now argues that the subsequent express repeal is no substantial alteration of the bill. This argument seems wonderful to me. It is as if one should argue that white and black are not different. He admits, however, that there is a literal change in the bill; and that he made the change in deference to other Senators, who would not support the bill without. This proves that those other Senators thought the change a substantial one; and that the Judge thought their opinions worth deferring to. His own opinions, therefore, seem not to rest on a very firm basis even in his own mind—and I suppose the world believes, and will continue to believe, that precisely on the substance of that change this whole agitation has arisen.

I conclude then, that the public never demanded the repeal of the Missouri compromise.

I now come to consider whether the repeal, with its avowed principle, is intrinsically right. I insist that it is not. Take the particular case. A controversy had arisen between the advocates and opponents of slavery, in relation to its establishment within the country we had purchased of France. The southern, and then best part of the purchase, was already in as a slave State. The controversy was settled by also letting Missouri in as a slave State; but with the agreement that within all the remaining part of the purchase, North of a certain line, there should never be slavery. As to what was to be done with the remaining part south of the line, nothing was said; but perhaps the fair implication was, that it should come in with slavery if it should so choose. The southern part, except a portion heretofore mentioned, afterwards did come in with slavery, as the State of Arkansas. All these many years since 1820, the Northern part had remained a wilderness. At length settlements began in it also. In due course, Iowa, came in as a free State, and Minnesota was given a territorial government, without removing the slavery restriction. Finally the sole remaining part, North of the line, Kansas and Nebraska, was to be organized; and it is proposed, and carried, to blot out the old dividing line of thirty-four years standing, and to open the whole of that country to the introduction of slavery. Now, this, to my mind, is manifestly unjust. After an angry and dangerous controversy, the parties made friends by dividing the bone of contention. The one party first appropriates her own share, beyond all power to be disturbed in the possession of it; and then seizes the share of the other party. It is as if two starving men had divided their only loaf; the one had hastily swallowed his half, and then grabbed the other half just as he was putting it to his mouth!

Let me here drop the main argument, to notice what I consider rather an inferior matter. It is argued that slavery will not go to Kansas and Nebraska, *in any event*. This is a *palliation*—a *lullaby*. I have some hope that it will not; but let us not be too confident. As to climate, a glance at the map shows that there are five slave States—Delaware, Maryland, Virginia, Kentucky, and Missouri—and also the District of Columbia, all north of the Missouri compromise line. The census returns of 1850 show that, within these, there are 867,276 slaves—being more than one-fourth of all the slaves in the nation.

It is not climate, then, that will keep slavery out of these territories. Is there any thing in the peculiar nature of the country? Missouri adjoins these territories, by her entire western boundary, and slavery is already within every one of her western counties. I have even heard it said that there are more slaves, in proportion to whites, in the north western county of Missouri, than within any county of the State. Slavery pressed entirely up to the old western boundary of the State, and when, rather recently, a part of that boundary, at the north-west was moved out a little farther west, slavery followed on quite up to the new line. Now, when the restriction is removed, what is to prevent it from going still further? Climate will not. No peculiarity of the country will—nothing in *nature* will. Will the disposition of the people prevent it? Those nearest the scene, are all in favor of the extension. The yankees, who are opposed to it may be more numerous; but in military phrase, the battle-field is too far from *their* base of operations.

But it is said, there now is *no* law in Nebraska on the subject of slavery; and that, in such case, taking a slave there, operates his freedom. That *is* good book-law; but is not the rule of actual practice. Wherever slavery is, it has been first introduced without law. The oldest laws we find concerning it, are not laws introducing it; but *regulating* it, as an already existing thing. A white man takes his slave to Nebraska now; who will inform the negro that he is free? Who will take him before court to test the question of his freedom? In ignorance of his legal emancipation, he is kept chopping, splitting and plowing. Others are brought, and move on in the same track. At last, if ever the time for voting comes, on the question of slavery, the institution already in fact exists in the country, and cannot well be removed. The facts of its presence, and the difficulty of its removal will carry the vote in its favor. Keep it out until a vote is taken, and a vote in favor of it, can not be got in any population of forty thousand, on earth, who have been drawn together by the ordinary motives of emigration and settlement. To get slaves into the country simultaneously with the whites, in the incipient stages of settlement, is the precise stake played for, and won in this Nebraska measure.

The question is asked us, "If slaves will go in, notwithstanding the general principle of law liberates them, why would they not equally go in against positive statute law?—go in, even if the Missouri restriction were maintained?" I answer, because it takes a much bolder man to venture in, with his property, in the latter case, than in the former—because the positive congressional enactment is known to, and respected by all, or nearly all; whereas the negative principle that *no* law is free law, is not much known except among lawyers. We have some experience of this practical difference. In spite of the Ordinance of '87, a few negroes were brought into Illinois, and held in a state of quasi slavery; not enough, however to carry a vote of the people in favor of the institution when they came to form a constitution. But in the adjoining Missouri country, where there was no ordinance of '87—was no restriction—they were carried ten times, nay a hundred times, as fast, and actually made a slave State. This is fact—naked fact.

Another LULLABY argument is, that taking slaves to new countries does not increase their number—does not make any one slave who otherwise would be free. There is some truth in this, and I am glad of it, but it is not WHOLLY true. The African slave trade is not yet effectually suppressed; and if we make a reasonable deduction for the white people amongst us, who are foreigners, and the descendants of foreigners, arriving here since 1808, we shall find the increase of the black population out-running that of the white, to an extent unaccountable, except by supposing that some of them too, have been coming from Africa. If this be so, the opening of new countries to the institution, increases the demand for, and augments the price of slaves, and so does, in fact, make slaves of freemen by causing them to be brought from Africa, and sold into bondage.

But, however this may be, we know the opening of new countries to slavery, tends to the perpetuation of the institution, and so does KEEP men in slavery who otherwise would be free. This result we do not FEEL like favoring, and we are under no legal obligation to suppress our feelings in this respect.

Equal justice to the south, it is said, requires us to consent to the extending of slavery to new countries. That is to say, inasmuch as you do not object to my taking my hog to Nebraska, therefore I must not object to you taking your slave. Now, I admit this is perfectly logical, if there is no difference between hogs and negroes. But while you thus require me to deny the humanity of the negro, I wish to ask whether you of the south yourselves, have ever been willing to do as much? It is kindly provided that of all those who come into the world, only a small percentage are natural tyrants. That percentage is no larger in the slave States than in the free. The great majority, south as well as north, have human sympathies, of which they can no more divest themselves than they can of their sensibility to physical pain. These sympathies in the bosoms of the southern people, manifest in many ways, their sense of the wrong of slavery, and their consciousness that, after all, there is humanity in the negro. If they deny this, let me address them a few plain questions. In 1820 you joined the north, almost unanimously, in declaring the African slave trade piracy, and in annexing to it the punishment of death. Why did you do this? If you did not feel that it was wrong, why did you join in providing that men should be hung for it? The practice was no more than bringing wild negroes from Africa, to sell to such as would buy them. But you never thought of hanging men for catching and selling wild horses, wild buffaloes or wild bears.

Again, you have amongst you, a sneaking individual, of the class of native tyrants, known as the "SLAVE-DEALER." He watches your necessities, and crawls up to buy your slave, at a speculating price. If you cannot help it, you sell to him; but if you can help it, you drive him from your door. You despise him utterly. You do not recognize him as a friend, or even as an honest man. Your children must not play with his; they may rollick freely with the little negroes, but not with the "slave-dealers" children. If you are obliged to deal with him, you try to get through the job without so much as touching him. It is common with you to join hands with the men you meet; but with the slave dealer you avoid the ceremony—instinctively shrinking from the snaky contact. If he grows rich and retires from business, you still remember him, and still keep up the ban of non-intercourse upon him and his family. Now why is this? You do not so treat the man who deals in corn, cattle or tobacco.

And yet again; there are in the United States and territories, including the District of Columbia, 433,643 free blacks. At $500 per head they are worth over two hundred millions of dollars. How comes this vast amount of property to be running about without owners? We do not see free horses or free cattle running at large. How is this? All these free blacks are the descendants of slaves, or have been slaves themselves, and they would be slaves now, but for SOMETHING which has operated on their white owners, inducing them, at vast pecuniary sacrifices, to liberate them. What is that SOMETHING? Is there any mistaking it? In all these cases it is your sense of justice, and human sympathy, continually telling you, that the poor negro has some natural right to himself—that those who deny it, and make mere merchandise of him, deserve kickings, contempt and death.

And now, why will you ask us to deny the humanity of the slave? and estimate him only as the equal of the hog? Why ask us to do what you will not do yourselves? Why ask us to do for *nothing,* what two hundred million of dollars could not induce you to do?

But one great argument in the support of the repeal of the Missouri Compromise, is still to come. That argument is "the sacred right of self government." It seems our distinguished Senator has found great difficulty in getting his antagonists, even in the Senate to meet him fairly on this argument—some poet has said

"Fools rush in where angels fear to tread."

At the hazzard of being thought one of the fools of this quotation, I meet that argument—I rush in, I take that bull by the horns.

I trust I understand, and truly estimate the right of self-government. My faith in the proposition that each man should do precisely as he pleases with all which is exclusively his own, lies at the foundation of the sense of justice there is in me. I extend the principles to communities of men, as well as to individuals. I so extend it, because it is politically wise, as well as naturally just: politically wise, in saving us from broils about matters which do not concern us. Here, or at Washington, I would not trouble myself with the oyster laws of Virginia, or the cranberry laws of Indiana.

The doctrine of self government is right—absolutely and eternally right— but it has no just application, as here attempted. Or perhaps I should rather say that whether it has such just application depends upon whether a negro is *not* or *is* a man. If he is *not* a man, why in that case, he who *is* a man may, as a matter of self-government, do just as he pleases with him. But if the negro *is* a man, is it not to that extent, a total destruction of self-government, to say that he too shall not govern *himself?* When the white man governs himself that is self-government; but when he governs himself, and also governs *another* man, that is *more* than self-government—that is despotism. If the negro is a *man,* why then my ancient faith teaches me that "all men are created equal;" and that there can be no moral right in connection with one man's making a slave of another.

Judge Douglas frequently, with bitter irony and sarcasm, paraphrases our argument by saying "The white people of Nebraska are good enough to govern themselves, *but they are not good enough to govern a few miserable negroes!!"*

Well I doubt not that the people of Nebraska are, and will continue to be as good as the average of people elsewhere. I do not say the contrary. What I do say is, that no man is good enough to govern another man, *without that other's consent.* I say this is the leading principle—the sheet anchor of American republicanism. Our Declaration of Independence says:

"We hold these truths to be self evident: that all men are created equal; that they are endowed by their Creator with certain inalienable rights; that among these are life, liberty and the pursuit of happiness. That to secure these rights, governments are instituted among men, DERIVING THEIR JUST POWERS FROM THE CONSENT OF THE GOVERNED."

I have quoted so much at this time merely to show that according to our ancient faith, the just powers of governments are derived from the consent of the governed. Now the relation of masters and slaves is, PRO TANTO, a total violation of this principle. The master not only governs the slave without his consent; but he governs him by a set of rules altogether different from those which he prescribes for himself. Allow ALL the governed an equal voice in the government, and that, and that only is self government.

Let it not be said I am contending for the establishment of political and social equality between the whites and blacks. I have already said the contrary. I am not now combating the argument of NECESSITY, arising from the fact that the blacks are already amongst us; but I am combating what is set up as MORAL argument for allowing them to be taken where they have never yet been—arguing against the EXTENSION of a bad thing, which where it already exists, we must of necessity, manage as we best can.

In support of his application of the doctrine of self-government, Senator Douglas has sought to bring to his aid the opinions and examples of our revolutionary fathers. I am glad he has done this. I love the sentiments of those old-time men; and shall be most happy to abide by their opinions. He shows us that when it was in contemplation for the colonies to break off from Great Britain, and set up a new government for themselves, several of the states instructed their delegates to go for the measure PROVIDED EACH STATE SHOULD BE ALLOWED TO REGULATE ITS DOMESTIC CONCERNS IN ITS OWN WAY. I do not quote; but this in substance. This was right. I see nothing objectionable in it. I also think it probable that it had some reference to the existence of slavery amongst them. I will not deny that it had. But had it, in any reference to the carrying of slavery into NEW COUNTRIES? That is the question; and we will let the fathers themselves answer it.

This same generation of men, and mostly the same individuals of the generation, who declared this principle—who declared independence—who fought the war of the revolution through—who afterwards made the constitution under which we still live—these same men passed the ordinance of '87, declaring that slavery should never go to the north-west territory. I have no doubt Judge Douglas thinks they were very inconsistent in this. It is a question of discrimination between them and him. But there is not an inch of ground left for his claiming that their opinions—their example—their authority—are on his side in this controversy.

Again, is not Nebraska, while a territory, a part of us? Do we not own the country? And if we surrender the control of it, do we not surrender the right of self-government? It is part of ourselves. If you say we shall not control it because it is ONLY part, the same is true of every other part; and when all the parts are gone, what has become of the whole? What is then left of us? What use for the general government, when there is nothing left for it to govern?

But you say this question should be left to the people of Nebraska, because they are more particularly interested. If this be the rule, you must leave it to each individual to say for himself whether he will have slaves. What better moral right have thirty-one citizens of Nebraska to say, that the thirty-second shall not hold slaves, than the people of the thirty-one States have to say that slavery shall not go into the thirty-second State at all?

But if it is a sacred right for the people of Nebraska to take and hold slaves there, it is equally their sacred right to buy them where they can buy them cheapest; and that undoubtedly will be on the coast of Africa; provided you will consent to not hang them for going there to buy them. You must remove this restriction too, from the sacred right of self-government. I am aware you say that taking slaves from the States to Nebraska, does not make slaves of freemen; but the African slave-trader can say just as much. He does not catch free negroes and bring them here. He finds them already slaves in the hands of their black captors, and he honestly buys them at the rate of about a red cotton handkerchief a head. This is very cheap, and it is a great abridgement of the sacred right of self-government to hang men for engaging in this profitable trade!

Another important objection to this application of the right of self-government, is that it enables the first FEW, to deprive the succeeding MANY, of a free exercise of the right of self-government. The first few may get slavery IN, and the subsequent many cannot easily get it OUT. How common is the remark now in the slave States—"If we were only clear of our slaves, how much better it would be for us." They are actually deprived of the privilege of governing themselves as they would, by the action of a very few, in the beginning. The same thing was true of the whole nation at the time our constitution was formed.

Whether slavery shall go into Nebraska, or other new territories, is not a matter of exclusive concern to the people who may go there. The whole nation is interested that the best use shall be made of these territories. We want them for the homes of free white people. This they cannot be, to any considerable extent, if slavery shall be planted within them. Slave States are places for poor white people to remove FROM; not to remove TO. New free States are the places for poor people to go to and better their condition. For this use, the nation needs these territories.

Still further; there are constitutional relations between the slave and free States, which are degrading to the latter. We are under legal obligations to catch and return their runaway slaves to them—a sort of dirty, disagreeable job, which I believe, as a general rule the slave-holders will not perform for one another. Then again, in the control of the government—the management of the partnership affairs—they have greatly the advantage of us. By the constitution, each State has two Senators—each has a number of Representatives; in proportion to the number of its people—and each has a number of presidential electors, equal to the whole number of its Senators and Representatives together. But in ascertaining the number of people, for this purpose, five slaves are counted as being equal to three whites. The slaves do not vote; they are only counted and so used, as to swell the influence of the white people's votes. The practical effect of this is more aptly shown by a comparison of the States of South Carolina and Maine. South Carolina has six representatives, and so has Maine; South Carolina has eight presidential electors, and so has Maine. This is precise equality so far; and, of course they are equal in Senators, each having two. Thus in the control of the government, the two States are equals precisely. But how are they in the number of their white people? Maine has 581,813 —while South Carolina has 274,567. Maine has twice as many as South Carolina, and 32,679 over. Thus each white man in South Carolina is more than the double of any man in Maine. This is all because South Carolina, besides her free people, has 384,984 slaves. The South Carolinian has precisely the same advantage over the white man in every other free State, as well as in Maine. He is more than the double of any one of us in this crowd. The same advantage, but not to the same extent, is held by all the citizens of the slave States, over those of the free; and it is an absolute truth, without an exception, that there is no voter in any slave State, but who has more legal power in the government, than any voter in any free State. There is no instance of exact equality; and the disadvantage is against us the whole chapter through. This principle, in the aggregate, gives the slave States, in the present Congress, twenty additional representatives—being seven more than the whole majority by which they passed the Nebraska bill.

Now all this is manifestly unfair; yet I do not mention it to complain of it, in so far as it is already settled. It is in the constitution; and I do not, for that cause, or any other cause, propose to destroy, or alter, or disregard the constitution. I stand to it, fairly, fully, and firmly.

But when I am told I must leave it altogether to OTHER PEOPLE to say whether new partners are to be bred up and brought into the firm, on the same degrading terms against me, I respectfully demur. I insist, that whether I shall be a whole man, or only, the half of one, in comparison with others, is a question in which I am somewhat concerned; and one which no other man can have a sacred right of deciding for me. If I am wrong in this—if it really be a sacred right of self-government, in the man who shall go to Nebraska, to decide whether he will be the EQUAL of me or the DOUBLE of me, then after he shall have exercised that right, and thereby shall have reduced me to a still smaller fraction of a man than I already am, I should like for some gentleman deeply skilled in the mysteries of sacred rights, to provide himself with a microscope, and peep about, and find out, if he can, what has become of my sacred rights! They will surely be too small for detection with the naked eye.

Finally, I insist, that if there is ANYTHING which it is the duty of the

WHOLE PEOPLE to never entrust to any hands but their own, that thing is the preservation and perpetuity, of their own liberties, and institutions. And if they shall think, as I do, that the extension of slavery endangers them, more than any, or all other causes, how recreant to themselves, if they submit the question, and with it, the fate of their country, to a mere hand-full of men, bent only on temporary self-interest. If this question of slavery extension were an insignificant one—one having no power to do harm—it might be shuffled aside in this way. But being, as it is, the great Behemoth of danger, shall the strong gripe of the nation be loosened upon him, to entrust him to the hands of such feeble keepers?

I have done with this mighty argument, of self-government. Go, sacred thing! Go in peace.

But Nebraska is urged as a great Union-saving measure. Well I too, go for saving the Union. Much as I hate slavery, I would consent to the extension of it rather than see the Union dissolved, just as I would consent to any GREAT evil, to avoid a GREATER one. But when I go to Union saving, I must believe, at least, that the means I employ has some adaptation to the end. To my mind, Nebraska has no such adaptation.

"It hath no relish of salvation in it."

It is an aggravation, rather, of the only one thing which ever endangers the Union. When it came upon us, all was peace and quiet. The nation was looking to the forming of new bonds of Union; and a long course of peace and prosperity seemed to lie before us. In the whole range of possibility, there scarcely appears to me to have been any thing, out of which the slavery agitation could have been revived, except the very project of repealing the Missouri compromise. Every inch of territory we owned, already had a definite settlement of the slavery question, and by which, all parties were pledged to abide. Indeed, there was no uninhabited country on the continent, which we could acquire; if we except some extreme northern regions, which are wholly out of the question. In this state of case, the genius of Discord himself, could scarcely have invented a way of again getting us by the ears, but by turning back and destroying the peace measures of the past. The councils of that genius seem to have prevailed, the Missouri compromise was repealed; and here we are, in the midst of a new slavery agitation, such, I think, as we have never seen before. Who is responsible for this? Is it those who resist the measure; or those who, causelessly, brought it forward, and pressed it through, having reason to know, and, in fact, knowing it must and would be so resisted? It could not but be expected by its author, that it would be looked upon as a measure for the extension of slavery, aggravated by a gross breach of faith. Argue as you will, and long as you will, this is the naked FRONT and ASPECT, of the measure. And in this aspect, it could not but produce agitation. Slavery is founded in the selfishness of man's nature—opposition to it, is in his love of justice. These principles are an eternal antagonism and when brought into collision so fiercely, as slavery extension brings them, shocks, and throes, and convulsions must ceaselessly follow. Repeal the Missouri compromise—repeal all compromises—repeal the declaration of independence—repeal all past history, you still can not repeal human nature. It still will be the abundance of man's heart, that slavery extension is wrong; and out of the abundance of his heart, his mouth will continue to speak.

The structure, too, of the Nebraska bill is very peculiar. The people are to decide the question of slavery for themselves; but WHEN they are to decide; or HOW they are to decide; or whether, when the question is once decided, it is to remain so, or is it to be subject to an indefinite succession of new trials, the law does not say, Is it to be decided by the first dozen settlers who arrive there? or is it to await the arrival of a hundred? Is it to be decided by a vote of the people? or a vote of the legislature? or, indeed by a vote of any sort? To these questions, the law gives no answer. There is a mystery about this; for when a member proposed to give the legislature express authority to exclude slavery, it was hooted down by the friends of the bill. This fact is worth remembering. Some yankees, in the east, are sending emigrants to Nebraska, to exclude slavery from it; and, so far as I can judge, they expect the question to be decided by voting, in some way or other. But the Missourians are awake too. They are within a stone's throw of the contested ground. They hold meetings, and pass resolutions, in which not the slightest allusion to voting is made. They resolve that slavery already exists in the territory; that more shall go there; that they, remaining in Missouri will protect it; and that abolitionists shall be hung, or driven away. Through all this, bowie-knives and six-shooters are seen plainly enough; but never a glimpse of the ballot-box. And, really, what is to be the result of this? Each party WITHIN, having numerous and determined backers WITHOUT, is it not probable that the contest will come to blows, and bloodshed? Could there be a more apt invention to bring about collision and violence, on the slavery question, than this Nebraska project is? I do not charge, or believe, that such was intended by Congress; but if they had literally formed a ring, and placed champions within it to fight out the controversy, the fight could be no more likely to come off, than it is. And if this fight should begin, is it likely to take a very peaceful, Union-saving turn? Will not the first drop of blood so shed, be the real knell of the Union?

The Missouri Compromise ought to be restored. For the sake of the Union, it ought to be restored. We ought to elect a House of Representatives which will vote its restoration. If by any means, we omit to do this, what follows? Slavery may or may not be established in Nebraska. But whether it be or not, we shall have repudiated—discarded from the councils of the Nation—the SPIRIT of COMPROMISE; for who after this will ever trust in a national compromise? The spirit of mutual concession—that spirit which first gave us the constitution, and which has thrice saved the Union—we shall have strangled and cast from us forever. And what shall we have in lieu of it? The South flushed with triumph and tempted to excesses; the North, betrayed, as they believe, brooding on wrong and burning for revenge. One side will provoke; the other resent. The one will taunt, the other defy; one agrees, the other retaliates. Already a few in the North, defy all constitutional restraints, resist the execution of the fugitive slave law, and even menace the institution of slavery in the states where it exists.

Already a few in the South, claim the constitutional right to take to and hold slaves in the free states—demand the revival of the slave trade; and demand a treaty with Great Britain by which fugitive slaves may be reclaimed from Canada. As yet they are but few on either side. It is a grave question for the lovers of the Union, whether the final destruction of the Missouri Compromise, and with it the spirit of all compromise will or will not embolden and embitter each of these, and fatally increase the numbers of both.

But restore the compromise, and what then? We thereby restore the national faith, the national confidence, the national feeling of brotherhood. We thereby reinstate the spirit of concession and compromise—that spirit which has never failed us in past perils, and which may be safely trusted for all the future. The south ought to join in doing this. The peace of the nation is as dear to them as to us. In memories of the past and hopes of the future, they share as largely as we. It would be on their part, a great act—great in its spirit, and great in its effect. It would be worth to the nation a hundred years' purchase of peace and prosperity. And what of sacrifice would they make? They only surrender to us, what they gave us for a consideration long, long ago; what they have not now, asked for, struggled or cared for; what has been thrust upon them, not less to their own astonishment than to ours.

But it is said we cannot restore it; that though we elect every member of the lower house, the Senate is still against us. It is quite true, that of the Senators who passed the Nebraska bill, a majority of the whole Senate will retain their seats in spite of the elections of this and the next year. But if at these elections, their several constituencies shall clearly express their will against Nebraska, will these senators disregard their will? Will they neither obey, nor make room for those who will?

But even if we fail to technically restore the compromise, it is still a great point to carry a popular vote in favor of the restoration. The moral weight of such a vote can not be estimated too highly. The authors of Nebraska are not at all satisfied with the destruction of the compromise—an endorse-ment of this PRINCIPLE, they proclaim to be the great object. With them, Nebraska alone is a small matter—to establish a principle, for FUTURE USE, is what they particularly desire.

That future use is to be the planting of slavery wherever in the wide world, local and unorganized opposition can not prevent it. Now if you wish to give them this endorsement—if you wish to establish this prin-ciple—do so. I shall regret it; but it is your right. On the contrary if you are opposed to the principle—intend to give it no such endorsement—let no wheedling, no sophistry, divert you from throwing a direct vote against it.

Some men, mostly whigs, who condemn the repeal of the Missouri Compromise, nevertheless hesitate to go for its restoration, lest they be thrown in company with the abolitionist. Will they allow me as an old whig to tell them good humoredly, that I think this is very silly? Stand with anybody that stands RIGHT. Stand with him while he is right and PART with him when he goes wrong. Stand WITH the abolitionist in restoring the Missouri Compromise; and stand AGAINST him when he attempts to repeal the fugitive slave law. In the latter case you stand with the southern dis-unionist. What of that? you are still right. In both cases you are right. In both cases you oppose the dangerous extremes. In both you stand on mid-dle ground and hold the ship level and steady. In both you are national and nothing less than national. This is good old whig ground. To desert such ground, because of any company, is to be less than a whig—less than a man—less than an American.

I particularly object to the NEW position which the avowed principle of this Nebraska law gives to slavery in the body politic. I object to it because it assumes that there CAN be MORAL RIGHT in the enslaving of one man by another. I object to it as a dangerous dalliance for a few [free?] people—a sad evidence that, feeling prosperity we forget right—that liberty, as a principle, we have ceased to revere. I object to it because the fathers of the republic eschewed, and rejected it. The argument of "Necessity" was the only argument they ever admitted in favor of slavery; and so far, and so far only as it carried them, did they ever go. They found the institu-tion existing among us, which they could not help; and they cast blame upon the British King for having permitted its introduction. BEFORE the constitution, they prohibited its introduction into the north-western Terri-tory—the only country we owned, then free from it. AT the framing and adoption of the constitution, they forbore to so much as mention the word "slave" or "slavery" in the whole instrument. In the provision for the recovery of fugitives, the slave is spoken of as a "PERSON HELD TO SERVICE OR LABOR." In that prohibiting the abolition of the African slave trade for twenty years, that trade is spoken of as "The migration or impor-tation of such persons as any of the States NOW EXISTING, shall think proper to admit," &c. These are the only provisions alluding to slavery. Thus, the thing is hid away, in the constitution, just as an afflicted man hides away a wen or a cancer, which he dares not cut out at once, lest he bleed to death; with the promise, nevertheless, that the cutting may begin at the end of a given time. Less than this our fathers COULD not do; and NOW they WOULD not do. Necessity drove them so far, and farther, they would not go. But this is not all. The earliest Congress, under the constitution, took the same view of slavery. They hedged and hemmed it in to the narrowest limits of necessity.

In 1794, they prohibited an out-going slave-trade—that is, the taking of slaves FROM the United States to sell.

In 1798, they prohibited the bringing of slaves from Africa, INTO the Mississippi Territory—this territory then comprising what are now the States of Mississippi and Alabama. This was TEN YEARS before they had the authority to do the same thing as to the States existing at the adoption of the constitution.

In 1800 they prohibited AMERICAN CITIZENS from trading in slaves between foreign countries—as, for instance, from Africa to Brazil.

In 1803 they passed a law in aid of one or two State laws, in restraint of the internal slave trade.

In 1807, in apparent hot haste, they passed the law, nearly a year in advance, to take effect the first day of 1808—the very first day the constitution would permit—prohibiting the African slave trade by heavy pecuniary and corporal penalties.

In 1820, finding these provisions ineffectual, they declared the trade piracy, and annexed to it, the extreme penalty of death. While all this was passing in the general government, five or six of the original slave States had adopted systems of gradual emancipation; and by which the institution was rapidly becoming extinct within these limits.

Thus we see, the plain unmistakable spirit of that age, towards slavery, was hostility to the PRINCIPLE, and toleration, ONLY BY NECESSITY.

But NOW it is to be transformed into a "sacred right." Nebraska brings it forth, places it on the high road to extension and perpetuity; and, with a pat on its back, says to it, "Go, and God speed you." Henceforth it is to be the chief jewel of the nation—the very figure-head of the ship of State. Little by little, but steadily as man's march to the grave, we have been giving up the OLD for the NEW faith. Near eighty years ago we began by declaring that all men are created equal; but now from that beginning we have run down to the other declaration, that for SOME men to enslave OTHERS is a "sacred right of self-government." These principles can not stand together. They are as opposite as God and mammon; and whoever holds to the one, must despise the other. When Pettit, in connection with his support of the Nebraska bill, called the Declaration of Independence "a self-evident lie" he only did what consistency and candor require all other Nebraska men to do. Of the forty odd Nebraska Senators who sat present and heard him, no one rebuked him. Nor am I apprized that any Nebraska newspaper, or any Nebraska orator, in the whole nation, has ever yet rebuked him. If this had been said among Marion's men, Southerners though they were, what would have become of the man who said it? If this had been said to the men who captured André, the man who said it, would probably have been hung sooner than André was. If it had been said in old Independence Hall, seventy-eight years ago, the very door-keeper would have throttled the man, and thrust him into the street.

Let no one be deceived. The spirit of seventy-six and the spirit of Nebraska, are utter antagonisms; and the former is being rapidly displaced by the latter.

Fellow countrymen—Americans south, as well as north, shall we make no effort to arrest this? Already the liberal party throughout the world, express the apprehension "that the one retrograde institution in America, is undermining the principles of progress, and fatally violating the noblest political system the world ever saw." This is not the taunt of enemies, but the warning of friends. Is it quite safe to disregard it—to despise it? Is there no danger to liberty itself, in discarding the earliest practice, and first precept of our ancient faith? In our greedy chase to make profit of the negro, let us beware, lest we "cancel and tear to pieces" even the white man's charter of freedom.

Our republican robe is soiled, and trailed in the dust. Let us repurify it. Let us turn and wash it white, in the spirit, if not the blood, of the Revolution. Let us turn slavery from its claims of "moral right," back upon its existing legal rights, and its arguments of "necessity." Let us return it to the position our fathers gave it; and there let it rest in peace. Let us re-adopt the Declaration of Independence, and with it, the practices, and policy, which harmonize with it. Let north and south—let all Americans—let all lovers of liberty everywhere—join in the great and good work. If we do this, we shall not only have saved the Union; but we shall have so saved it, as to make, and to keep it, forever worthy of the saving. We shall have so saved it, that the succeeding millions of free happy people, the world over, shall rise up, and call us blessed, to the latest generations.

At Springfield, twelve days ago, where I had spoken substantially as I have here, Judge Douglas replied to me—and as he is to reply to me here, I shall attempt to anticipate him, by noticing some of the points he made there.

He commenced by stating I had assumed all the way through, that the principle of the Nebraska bill, would have the effect of extending slavery. He denied that this was INTENDED, or that this EFFECT would follow.

I will not re-open the argument upon this point. That such was the intention, the world believed at the start, and will continue to believe. This was the COUNTENANCE of the thing; and, both friends and enemies, instantly recognized it as such. That countenance can not now be changed by argument. You can as easily argue the color out of the negroes' skin. Like the "bloody hand" you may wash it, and wash it, the red witness of guilt still sticks, and stares horribly at you.

Next he says, congressional intervention never prevented slavery, any where—that it did not prevent it in the north west territory, now in Illinois—that in fact, Illinois came into the Union as a slave State—that the principle of the Nebraska bill expelled it from Illinois, from several old States, from every where.

Now this is mere quibbling all the way through. If the ordinance of '87 did not keep slavery out of the north west territory, how happens it that the north west shore of the Ohio river is entirely free from it; while the south east shore, less than a mile distant, along nearly the whole length of the river, is entirely covered with it?

If that ordinance did not keep it out of Illinois, what was it that made the difference between Illinois and Missouri? They lie side by side, the Mississippi river only dividing them; while their early settlements were within the same latitude. Between 1810 and 1820 the number of slaves in Missouri INCREASED 7,211; while in Illinois, in the same ten years, they DECREASED 51. This appears by the census returns. During nearly all of that ten years, both were territories—not States. During this time, the ordinance forbid slavery to go into Illinois; and NOTHING forbid it to go into Missouri. It DID go into Missouri, and did NOT go into Illinois. That is the fact. Can any one doubt as to the reason of it?

But, he says, Illinois came into the Union as a slave State. Silence, perhaps, would be the best answer to this flat contradiction of the known history of the country. What are the facts upon which this bold assertion is based? When we first acquired the country, as far back as 1787, there were some slaves within it, held by the French inhabitants at Kaskaskia. The territorial legislation, admitted a few negroes, from the slave states, as indentured servants. One year after the adoption of the first State constitution the whole number of them was—what do you think? just 117— while the aggregate free population was 55,094—about 470 to one. Upon this state of facts, the people framed their constitution prohibiting the further introduction of slavery, with a sort of guaranty to the owners of the few indentured servants, giving freedom to their children to be born thereafter, and making no mention whatever, of any supposed slave for life. Out of this small matter, the Judge manufactures his argument that Illinois came into the Union as a slave State. Let the facts be the answer to the argument.

The principles of the Nebraska bill, he says, expelled slavery from Illinois? The principle of that bill first planted it here—that is, it first came, because there was no law to prevent it—first came before we owned the country; and finding it here, and having the ordinance of '87 to prevent its increasing, our people struggled along, and finally got rid of it as best they could.

But the principle of the Nebraska bill abolished slavery in several of the old States. Well, it is true that several of the old States, in the last quarter of the last century, did adopt systems of gradual emancipation, by which the institution has finally become extinct within their limits; but it MAY or MAY NOT be true that the principle of the Nebraska bill was the cause that led to the adoption of these measures. It is now more than fifty years, since the last of these States adopted its system of emancipation. If Nebraska bill is the real author of these benevolent works, it is rather deplorable, that he has, for so long a time, ceased working all together. Is there not some reason to suspect that it was the principle of the REVOLUTION, and not the principle of Nebraska bill, that led to emancipation in these old States? Leave it to the people of those old emancipating States, and I am quite sure they will decide, that neither that, nor any other good thing, ever did, or ever will come of Nebraska bill.

In the course of my main argument, Judge Douglas interrupted me to say, that the principle [of] the Nebraska bill was very old; that it originated when God made man and placed good and evil before him, allowing him to choose for himself, being responsible for the choice he should make. At the time I thought this was merely playful; and I answered it accordingly. But in his reply to me he renewed it, as a serious argument. In seriousness then, the facts of this proposition are not true as stated. God did not place good and evil before man, telling him to make his choice. On the contrary, he did tell him there was one tree, of the fruit of which, he should not eat, upon pain of certain death. I should scarcely wish so strong a prohibition against slavery in Nebraska.

But this argument strikes me as not a little remarkable in another particular—in its strong resemblance to the old argument for the "Divine right of Kings." By the latter, the King is to do just as he pleases with his white subjects, being responsible to God alone. By the former the white man is to do just as he pleases with his black slaves, being responsible to God alone. The two things are precisely alike; and it is but natural that they should find similar arguments to sustain them.

I had argued, that the application of the principle of self-government, as contended for, would require the revival of the African slave trade—that no argument could be made in favor of a man's right to take slaves to Nebraska, which could not be equally well made in favor of his right to bring them from the coast of Africa. The Judge replied, that the constitution requires the suppression of the foreign slave trade; but does not require the prohibition of slavery in the territories. That is a mistake, in point of fact. The constitution does NOT require the action of Congress in either case; and it does AUTHORIZE it in both. And so, there is still no difference between the cases.

In regard to what I had said, the advantage the slave States have over the free, in the matter of representation, the Judge replied that we, in the free States, count five free negroes as five white people, while in the slave States, they count five slaves as three whites only; and that the advantage, at last, was on the side of the free States.

Now, in the slave States, they count free negroes just as we do; and it so happens that besides their slaves, they have as many free negroes as we have, and thirty-three thousand over. Thus their free negroes more than balance ours; and their advantage over us, in consequence of their slaves, still remains as I stated it.

In reply to my argument, that the compromise measures of 1850, were a system of equivalents; and that the provisions of no one of them could fairly be carried to other subjects, without its corresponding equivalent being carried with it, the Judge denied out-right, that these measures had any connection with, or dependence upon, each other. This is mere desperation. If they have no connection, why are they always spoken of in connection? Why has he so spoken of them, a thousand times? Why has he constantly called them a SERIES of measures? Why does everybody call them a compromise? Why was California kept out of the Union, six or seven months, if it was not because of its connection with the other measures? Webster's leading definition of the verb "to compromise" is "to adjust and settle a difference, by mutual agreement with concessions of claims by the parties." This conveys precisely the popular understanding of the word compromise. We knew, before the Judge told us, that these measures passed separately, and in distinct bills; and that no two of them were passed by the votes of precisely the same members. But we also know, and so does he know, that no one of them could have passed both branches of Congress but for the understanding that the others were to pass also. Upon this understanding each got votes, which it could have got in no other way. It is this fact, that gives to the measures their true character; and it is the universal knowledge of this fact, that has given them the name of compromise so expressive of that true character.

I had asked "If in carrying the provisions of the Utah and New Mexico laws to Nebraska, you could clear away other objection, how can you leave Nebraska "perfectly free" to introduce slavery BEFORE she forms a constitution—during her territorial government?—while the Utah and New Mexico laws only authorize it WHEN they form constitutions, and are admitted into the Union?" To this Judge Douglas answered that the Utah and New Mexico laws, also authorized it BEFORE; and to prove this, he read from one of their laws, as follows: "That the legislative power of said territory shall extend to all rightful subjects of legislation consistent with the constitution of the United States and the provisions of this act."

Now it is perceived from the reading of this, that there is nothing express upon the subject; but that the authority is sought to be implied merely, for the general provision of "all rightful subjects of legislation." In reply to this, I insist, as a legal rule of construction, as well as the plain popular view of the matter, that the EXPRESS provision for Utah and New Mexico coming in with slavery if they choose, when they shall form constitutions, is an EXCLUSION of all implied authority on the same subject—that Congress, having the subject distinctly in their minds, when they made the express provision, they therein expressed their WHOLE meaning on that subject.

The Judge rather insinuated that I had found it convenient to forget the Washington territorial law passed in 1853. This was a division of Oregon, organizing the northern part, as the territory of Washington. He asserted that, by this act, the ordinance of '87 theretofore existing in Oregon, was repealed; that nearly all the members of Congress voted for it, beginning in the H.R., with Charles Allen of Massachusetts, and ending with Richard Yates, of Illinois; and that he could not understand how those who now oppose the Nebraska bill, so voted then, unless it was because it was then too soon after both the great political parties had ratified the compromises of 1850, and the ratification therefore too fresh, to be then repudiated.

Now I had seen the Washington act before; and I have carefully examined it since; and I aver that there is no repeal of the ordinance of '87, or of any prohibition of slavery, in it. In express terms, there is absolutely nothing in the whole law upon the subject—in fact, nothing to lead a reader to THINK of the subject. To my judgment, it is equally free from every thing from which such repeal can be legally implied; but however this may be, are men now to be entrapped by a legal implication, extracted from covert language, introduced perhaps, for the very purpose of entrapping them? I sincerely wish every man could read this law quite through, carefully watching every sentence, and every line, for a repeal of the ordinance of '87 or any thing equivalent to it.

Another point on the Washington act. If it was intended to be modelled after the Utah and New Mexico acts, as Judge Douglas, insists, why was it not inserted in it, as in them, that Washington was to come in with or without slavery as she may choose at the adoption of her constitution? It has no such provision in it; and I defy the ingenuity of man to give a reason for the omission, other than that it was not intended to follow the Utah and New Mexico laws in regard to the question of slavery.

The Washington act not only differs vitally from the Utah and New Mexico acts; but the Nebraska act differs vitally from both. By the latter act the people are left "perfectly free" to regulate their own domestic concerns, &c.; but in all the former, all their laws are to be submitted to Congress, and if disapproved are to be null. The Washington act goes even further; it absolutely prohibits the territorial legislation, by very strong and guarded language, from establishing banks, or borrowing money on the faith of the territory. Is this the sacred right of self-government we hear vaunted so much? No sir, the Nebraska bill finds no model in the acts of '50 or the Washington act. It finds no model in any law from Adam till today. As Phillips says of Napoleon, the Nebraska act is grand, gloomy, and peculiar; wrapped in the solitude of its own originality; without a model, and without a shadow upon the earth.

In the course of his reply, Senator Douglas remarked, in substance, that he had always considered this government was made for the white people and not for the negroes. Why, in point of mere fact, I think so too. But in this remark of the Judge, there is a significance, which I think is the key to the great mistake (if there is any such mistake) which he has made in this Nebraska measure. It shows that the Judge has no very vivid impression that the negro is a human; and consequently has no idea that there can be any moral question in legislating about him. In his view, the question of whether a new country shall be slave or free, is a matter of as utter indifference, as it is whether his neighbor shall plant his farm with tobacco, or stock it with horned cattle. Now, whether this view is right or wrong, it is very certain that the great mass of mankind take a totally different view. They consider slavery a great moral wrong; and their feelings against it, is not evanescent, but eternal. It lies at the very foundation of their sense of justice; and it cannot be trifled with. It is a great and durable element of popular action, and, I think, no statesman can safely disregard it.

Our Senator also objects that those who oppose him in this measure do not entirely agree with one another. He reminds me that in my firm adherence to the constitutional rights of the slave States, I differ widely from others who are co-operating with me in opposing the Nebraska bill; and he says it is not quite fair to oppose him in this variety of ways. He should remember that he took us by surprise—astounded us—by this measure. We were thunderstruck and stunned; and we reeled and fell in utter confusion. But we rose each fighting, grasping whatever he could first reach—a scythe—a pitchfork—a chopping axe, or a butcher's cleaver. We struck in the direction of the sound; and we are rapidly closing in upon him. He must not think to divert us from our purpose, by showing us that our drill, our dress, and our weapons, are not entirely perfect and uniform. When the storm shall be past, he shall find us still Americans; no less devoted to the continued Union and prosperity of the country than heretofore.

Finally, the Judge invokes against me, the memory of Clay and of Webster. They were great men; and men of great deeds. But where have I assailed them? For what is it, that their life-long enemy, shall now make profit, by assuming to defend them against me, their life-long friend? I go against the repeal of the Missouri compromise; did they ever go for it? They went for the compromise of 1850; did I ever go against them? They were greatly devoted to the Union; to the small measure of my ability, was I ever less so? Clay and Webster were dead before this question arose; by what authority shall our Senator say they would espouse his side of it, if alive? Mr. Clay was the leading spirit in making the Missouri compromise; is it very credible that if now alive, he would take the lead in the breaking of it? The truth is that some support from whigs is now a necessity with the Judge, and for thus it is, that the names of Clay and Webster are now invoked. His old friends have deserted him in such numbers as to leave too few to live by. He came to his own, and his own received him not, and Lo! he turns unto the Gentiles.

A word now as to the Judge's desperate assumption that the compromises of '50 had no connection with one another; that Illinois came into the Union as a slave state, and some other similar ones. This is no other than a bold denial of the history of the country. If we do not know that the Compromises of '50 were dependent on each other; if we do not know that Illinois came into the Union as a free state—we do not know any thing. If we do not know these things, we do not know that we ever had a revolutionary war, or such a chief as Washington. To deny these things is to deny our national axioms, or dogmas, at least; and it puts an end to all argument. If a man will stand up and assert, and repeat, and re-assert, that two and two do not make four, I know nothing in the power of argument that can stop him. I think I can answer the Judge so long as he sticks to the premises; but when he flies from them, I can not work an argument into the consistency of a maternal gag, and actually close his mouth with it. In such a case I can only commend him to the seventy thousand answers just in from Pennsylvania, Ohio and Indiana.

29

A HOUSE DIVIDED
June 16, 1858

I f WE COULD FIRST KNOW *where* we are, and *whither* we are tending, we could then better judge *what* to do, and *how* to do it.

We are now far into the *fifth* year, since a policy was initiated, with the *avowed* object, and *confident* promise, of putting an end to slavery agitation.

Under the operation of that policy, that agitation has not only, *not ceased,* but has *constantly augmented.*

In *my* opinion, it *will* not cease, until a *crisis* shall have been reached, and passed.

"A house divided against itself cannot stand."

I believe this government cannot endure, permanently half *slave* and half *free.*

I do not expect the Union to be *dissolved*—I do not expect the house to *fall*—but I *do* expect it will cease to be divided.

It will become *all* one thing, or *all* the other.

Either the *opponents* of slavery, will arrest the further spread of it, and place it where the public mind shall rest in the belief that it is in course of ultimate extinction; or its *advocates* will push it forward, till it shall become alike lawful in *all* the States, *old* as well as *new*—*North* as well as *South.*

Have we no *tendency* to the latter condition?

Let any one who doubts, carefully contemplate that now almost complete legal combination—piece of *machinery* so to speak—compounded of the Nebraska doctrine, and the Dred Scott decision. Let him consider not only *what work* the machinery is adapted to do, and *how well* adapted; but also, let him study the *history* of its construction, and trace, if he can, or rather *fail,* if he can, to trace the evidences of design, and concert of action, among its chief bosses, from the beginning.

But, so far, *Congress* only, had acted; and an *indorsement* by the people, *real* or apparent, was indispensable, to *save* the point already gained, and give chance for more.

The new year of 1854 found slavery excluded from more than half the States by State Constitutions, and from most of the national territory by Congressional prohibition.

Four days later, commenced the struggle, which ended in repealing that Congressional prohibition.

This opened all the national territory to slavery; and was the first point gained.

This necessity had not been overlooked; but had been provided for, as well as might be, in the notable argument of *"squatter sovereignty,"* otherwise called *"sacred right of self government,"* which latter phrase, though expressive of the only rightful basis of any government, was so perverted in this attempted use of it as to amount to just this: That if any *one* man, choose to enslave *another,* no *third* man shall be allowed to object.

That argument was incorporated into the Nebraska bill itself, in the language which follows: *"It being the true intent and meaning of this act not to legislate slavery into any Territory or state, not exclude it therefrom; but to leave the people thereof perfectly free to form and regulate their domestic institutions in their own way, subject only to the Constitution of the United States."*

Then opened the roar of loose declamation in favor of "Squatter Sovereignty," and "Sacred right of self government."

"But," said opposition members, "let us be more *specific*—let us *amend* the bill so as to expressly declare that the people of the territory *may* exclude slavery." "Not we," said the friends of the measure; and down they voted the amendment.

While the Nebraska bill was passing through congress, a *law case,* involving the question of a negroe's freedom, by reason of his owner having voluntarily taken him first into a free state and then a territory covered by the congressional prohibition, and held him as a slave, for a long time in each, was passing through the U.S. Circuit Court for the District of Missouri; and both Nebraska bill and law suit were brought to a decision in the same month of May, 1854. The negroe's name was "Dred Scott," which name now designates the decision finally made in the case.

Before the *then* next Presidential election, the law case came *to,* and was argued *in* the Supreme Court of the United States; but the *decision* of it was deferred until *after* the election. Still, *before* the election, Senator Trumbull, on the floor of the Senate, requests the leading advocate of the Nebraska bill to state *his opinion* whether the people of a territory can constitutionally exclude slavery from their limits; and the latter answers, "That is a question for the Supreme Court."

The election came. Mr. Buchanan was elected, and the *indorsement,* such as it was, secured. That was the *second* point gained. The indorsement, however, fell short of a clear popular majority by nearly four hundred thousand votes, and so, perhaps, was not overwhelmingly reliable and satisfactory.

The *outgoing* President, in his last annual message, as impressively as possible *echoed back* upon the people the *weight* and *authority* of the indorsement.

The Supreme Court met again; *did not* announce their decision, but ordered a re-argument.

The Presidential inauguration came, and still no decision of the court; but the *incoming* President, in his inaugural address, fervently exhorted the people to abide by the forthcoming decision, *whatever it might be.*

Then, in a few days, came the decision.

The reputed author of the Nebraska bill finds an early occasion to make a speech at this capitol indorsing the Dred Scott Decision, and vehemently denouncing all opposition to it.

The new President, too, seizes the early occasion of the Silliman letter to *indorse* and strongly *construe* that decision, and to express his *astonishment* that any different view had ever been entertained.

At length a squabble springs up between the President and the author of the Nebraska bill, on the *mere* question of *fact,* whether the Lecompton constitution was or was not, in any just sense, made by the people of Kansas; and in that squabble the latter declares that all he wants is a fair vote for the people, and that he *cares* not whether slavery be voted *down* or voted *up.* I do not understand his declaration that he cares not whether slavery be voted down or voted up, to be intended by him other than as an *apt definition* of the *policy* he would impress upon the public mind— the *principle* for which he declares he has suffered much, and is ready to suffer to the end.

And well may he cling to that principle. If he has any parental feeling, well may he cling to it. That principle, is the only *shred* left of his original Nebraska doctrine. Under the Dred Scott decision, "squatter sovereignty" squatted out of existence, tumbled down like temporary scaffolding—like the mould at the foundry served through one blast and fell back into loose sand—helped to carry an election, and then was kicked to the winds. His late *joint* struggle with the Republicans, against the Lecompton Constitution, involves nothing of the original Nebraska doctrine. That struggle was made on a point, the right of a people to make their own constitution, upon which he and the Republicans have never differed.

The several points of the Dred Scott decision, in connection with Senator Douglas' "care not" policy, constitute the piece of machinery, in its *present* state of advancement. This was the third point gained.

The *working* points of that machinery are:

First, that no negro slave, imported as such from Africa, and no descendant of such slave can ever be a *citizen* of any State, in the sense of that term as used in the Constitution of the United States.

This point is made in order to deprive the negro, in every possible event, of the benefit of this provision of the United States Constitution, which declares that—

"The citizens of each State shall be entitled to all privileges and immunities of citizens in the several States."

Secondly, that "subject to the Constitution of the United States," neither *Congress* nor a *Territorial Legislature* can exclude slavery from any United States territory.

This point is made in order that individual men may *fill up* the territories with slaves, without danger of losing them as property, and thus to enhance the chances of *permanency* to the institution through all the future.

Thirdly, that whether the holding a negro in actual slavery in a free State, makes him free, as against the holder, the United States courts will not decide, but will leave to be decided by the courts of any slave State the negro may be forced into by the master.

This point is made, not to be pressed *immediately;* but, if acquiesced in for a while, and apparently *indorsed* by the people at an election, *then* to sustain the logical conclusion that what Dred Scott's master might lawfully do with Dred Scott, in the free State of Illinois, every other master may lawfully do with any other *one,* or one *thousand* slaves, in Illinois, or in any other free State.

Auxiliary to all this, and working hand in hand with it, the Nebraska doctrine, or what is left of it, is to *educate* and *mould* public opinion, at least *Northern* public opinion, to not *care* whether slavery is voted *down* or voted *up.*

This shows exactly where we now *are;* and *partially* also, whither we are tending.

It will throw additional light on the latter, to go back, and run the mind over the string of historical facts already stated. Several things will *now* appear less *dark* and *mysterious* than they did *when* they were transpiring. The people were to be left "perfectly free" "subject only to the Constitution." What the *Constitution* had to do with it, outsiders could not *then* see. Plainly enough *now,* it was an exactly fitted *niche,* for the Dred Scott decision to afterwards come in, and declare the *perfect freedom* of the people, to be just no freedom at all.

Why was the amendment, expressly declaring the right of the people to exclude slavery, voted down? Plainly enough *now,* the adoption of it, would have spoiled the niche for the Dred Scott decision.

Why was the court decision held up? Why, even a Senator's individual opinion withheld, till *after* the Presidential election? Plainly enough *now,* the speaking out *then* would have damaged the *"perfectly free"* argument upon which the election was to be carried.

Why the *outgoing* President's felicitation on the indorsement? Why the delay of a reargument? Why the incoming President's *advance* exhortation in favor of the decision?

These things *look* like the cautious *patting* and *petting* a spirited horse, preparatory to mounting him, when it is dreaded that he may give the rider a fall.

And why the hasty after indorsements of the decision by the President and others?

We can not absolutely *know* that all these exact adaptations are the result of preconcert. But when we see a lot of framed timbers, different portions of which we know have been gotten out at different times and places and by different workmen—Stephen, Franklin, Roger and James, for instance—and when we see these timbers joined together, and see they exactly make the frame of a house or a mill, or the tenons and mortices exactly fitting, and all the lengths and proportions of the different pieces exactly adapted to their respective places, and not a piece too many or too few—not omitting even scaffolding—or, if a single piece be lacking, we can see the place in the frame exactly fitted and prepared to yet bring such piece in—in *such* a case, we find it impossible to not *believe* that Stephen and Franklin and Roger and James all understood one another from the beginning, and all worked upon a common *plan* or *draft* drawn up before the first lick was struck.

It should not be overlooked that, by the Nebraska bill, the people of a *State* as well as *Territory,* were to be left *"perfectly free"* *"subject only to the Constitution."*

Why mention a *State?* They were legislating for *territories,* and not *for* or *about* States. Certainly the people of a State *are* and *ought to be* subject to the Constitution of the United States; but why is mention of this *lugged* into this merely *territorial* law? Why are the people of a *territory* and the people of a *state* therein *lumped* together, and their relation to the Constitution therein treated as being *precisely* the same?

While the opinion of *the Court,* by Chief Justice Taney, in the Dred Scott case, and the separate opinions of all the concurring Judges, expressly declare that the Constitution of the United States neither permits Congress nor a Territorial legislature to exclude slavery from any United States territory, they all *omit* to declare whether or not the same Constitution permits a *state,* or the people of a State, to exclude it.

Possibly, this was a mere *omission;* but who can be *quite* sure, if McLean or Curtis had sought to get into the opinion a declaration of unlimited power in the people of a *state* to exclude slavery from their limits, just as Chase and Macy sought to get such declaration, in behalf of the people of a territory, into the Nebraska bill—I ask, who can be quite *sure* that it would not have been voted down, in the one case, as it had been in the other.

The nearest approach to the point of declaring the power of a State over slavery, is made by Judge Nelson. He approaches it more than once, using the precise idea, and *almost* the language too, of the Nebraska act. On one occasion his exact language is, "except in cases where the power is restrained by the Constitution of the United States, the law of the State is supreme over the subject of slavery within its jurisdiction."

In what *cases* the power of the *states is* so restrained by the U.S. Constitution, is left an *open* question, precisely as the same question, as to the restraint on the power of the *territories* was left open in the Nebraska act. Put *that* and *that* together, and we have another nice little niche, which we may, ere long, see filled with another Supreme Court decision, declaring that the Constitution of the United States does not permit a *state* to exclude slavery from its limits.

And this may especially be expected if the doctrine of "care not whether slavery be voted *down* or voted *up*," shall gain upon the public mind sufficiently to give promise that such a decision can be maintained when made.

Such a decision is all that slavery now lacks of being alike lawful in all the States.

Welcome or unwelcome, such decision *is* probably coming, and will soon be upon us, unless the power of the present political dynasty shall be met and overthrown.

We shall *lie down* pleasantly dreaming that the people of *Missouri* are on the verge of making their State *free;* and we shall *awake* to the *reality,* instead, that the *Supreme* Court has made *Illinois* a *slave* State.

To meet and overthrow the power of that dynasty, is the work now before all those who would prevent that consummation.

That is *what* we have to do.

But *how* can we best do it?

There are those who denounce us *openly* to their *own* friends, and yet whisper *us softly,* that *Senator Douglas* is the *aptest* instrument there is, with which to effect that object. *They* do *not* tell us, nor has *he* told us, that he *wishes* any such object to be effected. They wish us to *infer* all, from the facts, that he now has a little quarrel with the present head of the dynasty; and that he has regularly voted with us, on a single point, upon which, he and we, have never differed.

They remind us that *he* is a very *great man,* and that the largest of *us* are very small ones. Let this be granted. But "a *living dog* is better than a *dead lion.*" Judge Douglas, if not a *dead* lion *for this work,* is at least a *caged* and *toothless* one. How can he oppose the advances of slavery? He don't *care* anything about it. His avowed *mission is impressing* the "public heart" to *care* nothing about it.

A leading Douglas Democratic newspaper thinks Douglas' superior talent will be needed to resist the revival of the African slave trade.

Does Douglas believe an effort to revive that trade is approaching? He has not said so. Does he *really* think so? But if it is, how can he resist it? For years he has labored to prove it a *sacred right* of white men to take negro slaves into the new territories. Can he possibly show that it is *less* a sacred right to *buy* them where they can be bought cheapest? And, unquestionably they can be bought *cheaper in Africa* than in *Virginia.*

He has done all in his power to reduce the whole question of slavery to one of a mere *right of property;* and as such, how can *he* oppose the foreign slave trade—how can he refuse that trade in that "property" shall be "perfectly free"—unless he does it as a *protection* to the home production? And as the home *producers* will probably not *ask* the protection, he will be wholly without a ground of opposition.

Senator Douglas holds, we know, that a man may rightfully be *wiser to-day* than he was *yesterday*—that he may rightfully *change* when he finds himself wrong.

But, can we for that reason, run ahead, and *infer* that he *will* make any particular change, of which he, himself, has given no intimation? Can we *safely* base *our* action upon any such *vague* inference?

Now, as ever, I wish to not *misrepresent* Judge Douglas' *position,* question his *motives,* or do ought that can be personally offensive to him.

Whenever, *if ever,* he and we can come together on *principle* so that *our great cause* may have assistance from *his great ability,* I hope to have interposed no adventitious obstacle.

But clearly, he is not *now* with us—he does not *pretend* to be—he does not *promise* to *ever* be.

Our cause, then, must be intrusted to, and conducted by its own undoubted friends—those whose hands are free, whose hearts are in the work—who *do care* for the result.

Two years ago the Republicans of the nation mustered over thirteen hundred thousand strong.

We did this under the single impulse of resistance to a common danger, with every external circumstance against us.

Of *strange, discordant,* and even, *hostile* elements, we gathered from the four winds, and *formed* and fought the battle through, under the constant hot fire of a disciplined, proud, and pampered enemy.

Did we brave all *then,* to *falter* now?—*now*—when that same enemy is *wavering,* dissevered and belligerent?

The result is not doubtful. We shall not fail—if we stand firm, we shall not fail.

Wise councils may *accelerate* or *mistakes delay it,* but, sooner or later the victory is *sure* to come.

30

ADDRESS AT COOPER INSTITUTE
February 27, 1860

T HE FACTS WITH WHICH I SHALL DEAL this evening are mainly old and familiar; nor is there anything new in the general use I shall make of them. If there shall be any novelty, it will be in the mode of presenting the facts, and the inferences and observations following that presentation.

In his speech last autumn, at Columbus, Ohio, as reported in "The New-York Times," Senator Douglas said:

"Our fathers, when they framed the Government under which we live, understood this question just as well, and even better, than we do now."

I fully indorse this, and I adopt it as a text for this discourse. I so adopt it because it furnishes a precise and an agreed starting point for a discussion between Republicans and that wing of the Democracy headed by Senator Douglas. It simply leaves the inquiry: *"What was the understanding those fathers had of the question mentioned?"*

What is the frame of Government under which we live?

The answer must be: "The Constitution of the United States." That Constitution consists of the original, framed in 1787, (and under which the present government first went into operation,) and twelve subsequently framed amendments, the first ten of which were framed in 1789.

Who were our fathers that framed the Constitution? I suppose the "thirty-nine" who signed the original instrument may be fairly called our fathers who framed that part of the present Government. It is almost exactly true to say they framed it, and it is altogether true to say they fairly represented the opinion and sentiment of the whole nation at that time. Their names, being familiar to nearly all, and accessible to quite all, need not now be repeated.

I take these "thirty-nine" for the present, as being "our fathers who framed the Government under which we live."

What is the question which, according to the text, those fathers understood "just as well, and even better than we do now?"

It is this: Does the proper division of local from federal authority, or anything in the Constitution, forbid *our Federal Government* to control as to slavery in *our Federal Territories?*

Upon this, Senator Douglas holds the affirmative, and Republicans the negative. This affirmation and denial form an issue; and this issue—this question—is precisely what the text declares our fathers understood "better than we."

Let us now inquire whether the "thirty-nine," or any of them, ever acted upon this question; and if they did, how they acted upon it—how they expressed that better understanding?

In 1784, three years before the Constitution—the United States then owning the Northwestern Territory, and no other, the Congress of the Confederation had before them the question of prohibiting slavery in that Territory; and four of the "thirty-nine," who afterward framed the Constitution, were in that Congress, and voted on that question. Of these, Roger Sherman, Thomas Mifflin, and Hugh Williamson voted for the prohibition, thus showing that, in their understanding, no line dividing local from federal authority, nor anything else, properly forbade the Federal Government to control as to slavery in federal territory. The other of the four—James M'Henry—voted against the prohibition, showing that, for some cause, he thought it improper to vote for it.

In 1787, still before the Constitution, but while the Convention was in session framing it, and while the Northwestern Territory still was the only territory owned by the United States, the same question of prohibiting slavery in the territory again came before the Congress of the Confederation; and two more of the "thirty-nine" who afterward signed the Constitution, were in that Congress, and voted on the question. They were William Blount and William Few; and they both voted for the prohibition—thus showing that, in their understanding, no line dividing local from federal authority, nor anything else, properly forbade the Federal Government to control as to slavery in federal territory. This time the prohibition became a law, being part of what is now well known as the Ordinance of '87.

The question of federal control of slavery in the territories, seems not to have been directly before the Convention which framed the original Constitution; and hence it is not recorded that the "thirty-nine," or any of them, while engaged on that instrument, expressed any opinion of that precise question.

In 1789, by the first Congress which sat under the Constitution, an act was passed to enforce the Ordinance of '87, including the prohibition of slavery in the Northwestern Territory. The bill for this act was reported by one of the "thirty-nine," Thomas Fitzsimmons, then a member of the House of Representatives from Pennsylvania. It went through all its stages without a word of opposition, and finally passed both branches without yeas and nays, which is equivalent to an unanimous passage. In this Congress there were sixteen of the thirty-nine fathers who framed the original Constitution. They were John Langdon, Nicholas Gilman, Wm. S. Johnson, Roger Sherman, Robert Morris, Thos. Fitzsimmons, William Few, Abraham Baldwin, Rufus King, William Paterson, George Clymer, Richard Bassett, George Read, Pierce Butler, Daniel Carroll, James Madison.

This shows that, in their understanding, no line dividing local from federal authority, nor anything in the Constitution, properly forbade Congress to prohibit slavery in the federal territory; else both their fidelity to correct principle, and their oath to support the Constitution, would have constrained them to oppose the prohibition.

Again, George Washington, another of the "thirty-nine," was then President of the United States, and, as such, approved and signed the bill; thus completing its validity as a law, and thus showing that, in his understanding, no line dividing local from federal authority, nor anything in the Constitution, forbade the Federal Government, to control as to slavery in federal territory.

No great while after the adoption of the original Constitution, North Carolina ceded to the Federal Government the country now constituting the State of Tennessee; and a few years later Georgia ceded that which now constitutes the States of Mississippi and Alabama. In both deeds of cession it was made a condition by the ceding States that the Federal Government should not prohibit slavery in the ceded country. Besides this, slavery was then actually in the ceded country. Under these circumstances, Congress, on taking charge of these countries, did not absolutely prohibit slavery within them. But they did interfere with it—take control of it—even there, to a certain extent. In 1798, Congress organized the Territory of Mississippi. In the act of organization, they prohibited the bringing of slaves into the Territory, from any place without the United States, by fine, and giving freedom to slaves so brought. This act passed both branches of Congress without yeas and nays. In that Congress were three of the "thirty-nine" who framed the original Constitution. They were John Langdon, George Read and Abraham Baldwin. They all, probably, voted for it. Certainly they would have placed their opposition to it upon record, if, in their understanding, any line dividing local from federal authority, or anything in the Constitution, properly forbade the Federal Government to control as to slavery in federal territory.

In 1803, the Federal Government purchased the Louisiana country. Our former territorial acquisitions came from certain of our own States; but this Louisiana country was acquired from a foreign nation. In 1804, Congress gave a territorial organization to that part of it which now constitutes the State of Louisiana. New Orleans, lying within that part, was an old and comparatively large city. There were other considerable towns and settlements, and slavery was extensively and thoroughly intermingled with the people. Congress did not, in the Territorial Act, prohibit slavery; but they did interfere with it—take control of it—in a more marked and extensive way than they did in the case of Mississippi. The substance of the provision therein made, in relation to slaves, was:

First. That no slave should be imported into the territory from foreign parts.

Second. That no slave should be carried into it who had been imported into the United States since the first day of May, 1798.

Third. That no slave should be carried into it, except by the owner, and for his own use as a settler; the penalty in all the cases being a fine upon the violator of the law, and freedom to the slave.

This act also was passed without yeas and nays. In the Congress which passed it, there were two of the "thirty-nine." They were Abraham Baldwin and Jonathan Dayton. As stated in the case of Mississippi, it is probable they both voted for it. They would not have allowed it to pass without recording their opposition to it, if, in their understanding, it violated either the line properly dividing local from federal authority, or any provision of the Constitution.

In 1819–20, came and passed the Missouri question. Many votes were taken, by yeas and nays, in both branches of Congress, upon the various phases of the general question. Two of the "thirty-nine"—Rufus King and Charles Pinckney—were members of that Congress. Mr. King steadily voted for slavery prohibition and against all compromises, while Mr. Pinckney as steadily voted against slavery prohibition and against all compromises. By this, Mr. King showed that, in his understanding, no line dividing local from federal authority, nor anything in the Constitution, was violated by Congress prohibiting slavery in federal territory; while Mr. Pinckney, by his votes, showed that, in his understanding, there was some sufficient reason for opposing such prohibition in that case.

The cases I have mentioned are the only acts of the "thirty-nine," or of any of them, upon the direct issue, which I have been able to discover.

To enumerate the persons who thus acted, as being four in 1784, two in 1787, seventeen in 1789, three in 1798, two in 1804, and two in 1819–20—there would be thirty of them. But this would be counting John Langdon, Roger Sherman, William Few, Rufus King, and George Read, each twice, and Abraham Baldwin, three times. The true number of those of the "thirty-nine" whom I have shown to have acted upon the question, which, by the text, they understood better than we, is twenty-three, leaving sixteen not shown to have acted upon it in any way.

Here, then, we have twenty-three out of our thirty-nine fathers "who framed the Government under which we live," who have, upon their official responsibility and their corporal oaths, acted upon the very question which the text affirms they "understood just as well, and even better than we do now;" and twenty-one of them—a clear majority of the whole "thirty-nine"—so acting upon it as to make them guilty of gross political impropriety and wilful perjury, if, in their understanding, any proper division between local and federal authority, or anything in the Constitution they had made themselves, and sworn to support, forbade the Federal Government to control as to slavery in the federal territories. Thus the twenty-one acted; and, as actions speak louder than words, so actions, under such responsibility, speak still louder.

Two of the twenty-three voted against Congressional prohibition of slavery in the federal territories, in the instances in which they acted upon the question. But for what reasons they so voted is not known. They may have done so because they thought a proper division of local from federal authority, or some provision or principle of the Constitution, stood in the way; or they may, without any such question, have voted against the prohibition, on what appeared to them to be sufficient grounds of expediency. No one who has sworn to support the Constitution, can conscientiously vote for what he understands to be an unconstitutional measure, however expedient he may think it; but one may and ought to vote against a measure which he deems constitutional, if, at the same time, he deems it inexpedient. It, therefore, would be unsafe to set down even the two who voted against the prohibition, as having done so because, in their understanding, any proper division of local from federal authority, or anything in the Constitution, forbade the Federal Government to control as to slavery in federal territory.

The remaining sixteen of the "thirty-nine," so far as I have discovered, have left no record of their understanding upon the direct question of federal control of slavery in the federal territories. But there is much reason to believe that their understanding upon that question would not have appeared different from that of their twenty-three compeers, had it been manifested at all.

For the purpose of adhering rigidly to the text, I have purposely omitted whatever understanding may have been manifested by any person, however distinguished, other than the thirty-nine fathers who framed the original Constitution; and, for the same reason, I have also omitted whatever understanding may have been manifested by any of the "thirty-nine" even, on any other phase of the general question of slavery. If we should look into their acts and declarations on those other phases, as the foreign slave trade, and the morality and policy of slavery generally, it would appear to us that on the direct question of federal control of slavery in federal territories, the sixteen, if they had acted at all, would probably have acted just as the twenty-three did. Among that sixteen were several of the most noted anti-slavery men of those times—as Dr. Franklin, Alexander Hamilton and Gouverneur Morris—while there was not one now known to have been otherwise, unless it may be John Rutledge, of South Carolina.

The sum of the whole is, that of our thirty-nine fathers who framed the original Constitution, twenty-one—a clear majority of the whole—certainly understood that no proper division of local from federal authority, nor any part of the Constitution, forbade the Federal Government to control slavery in the federal territories; while all the rest probably had the same understanding. Such, unquestionably, was the understanding of our fathers who framed the original Constitution; and the text affirms that they understood the question "better than we."

But, so far, I have been considering the understanding of the question manifested by the framers of the original Constitution. In and by the original instrument, a mode was provided for amending it; and, as I have already stated, the present frame of "the Government under which we live" consists of that original, and twelve amendatory articles framed and adopted since. Those who now insist that federal control of slavery in federal territories violates the Constitution, point us to the provisions which they suppose it thus violates; and, as I understand, they all fix upon provisions in these amendatory articles, and not in the original instrument. The Supreme Court, in the Dred Scott case, plant themselves upon the fifth amendment, which provides that no person shall be deprived of "life, liberty or property without due process of law;" while Senator Douglas and his peculiar adherents plant themselves upon the tenth amendment, providing that "the powers not delegated to the United States by the Constitution," "are reserved to the States respectively, or to the people."

Now, it so happens that these amendments were framed by the first Congress which sat under the Constitution—the identical Congress which passed the act already mentioned, enforcing the prohibition of slavery in the Northwestern Territory. Not only was it the same Congress, but they were the identical, same individual men who, at the same session, and at the same time within the session, had under consideration, and in progress toward maturity, these Constitutional amendments, and this act prohibiting slavery in all the territory the nation then owned. The Constitutional amendments were introduced before, and passed after the act enforcing the Ordinance of '87; so that, during the whole pendency of the act to enforce the Ordinance, the Constitutional amendments were also pending.

The seventy-six members of that Congress, including sixteen of the framers of the original Constitution, as before stated, were preeminently our fathers who framed that part of "the Government under which we live," which is now claimed as forbidding the Federal Government to control slavery in the federal territories.

Is it not a little presumptuous in any one at this day to affirm that the two things which that Congress deliberately framed, and carried to maturity at the same time, are absolutely inconsistent with each other? And does not such affirmation become impudently absurd when coupled with the other affirmation from the same mouth, that those who did the two things, alleged to be inconsistent, understood whether they really were inconsistent better than we—better than he who affirms that they are inconsistent?

It is surely safe to assume that the thirty-nine framers of the original Constitution, and the seventy-six members of the Congress which framed the amendments thereto, taken together, do certainly include those who may be fairly called "our fathers who framed the Government under which we live." And so assuming, I defy any man to show that any one of them ever, in his whole life, declared that, in his understanding, any proper division of local from federal authority, or any part of the Constitution, forbade the Federal Government to control as to slavery in the federal territories. I go a step further. I defy any one to show that any living man in the whole world ever did, prior to the beginning of the present century, (and I might almost say prior to the beginning of the last half of the present century), declare that, in his understanding, any proper division of local from federal authority, or any part of the Constitution, forbade the Federal Government to control as to slavery in the federal territories. To those who now so declare, I give, not only "our fathers who framed the Government under which we live," but with them all other living men within the century in which it was framed, among whom to search, and they shall not be able to find the evidence of a single man agreeing with them.

Now, and here, let me guard a little against being misunderstood. I do not mean to say we are bound to follow implicitly in whatever our fathers did. To do so, would be to discard all the lights of current experience—to reject all progress—all improvement. What I do say is, that if we would supplant the opinions and policy of our fathers in any case, we should do so upon evidence so conclusive, and argument so clear, that even their great authority, fairly considered and weighed, cannot stand; and most surely not in a case whereof we ourselves declare they understood the question better than we.

If any man at this day sincerely believes that a proper division of local from federal authority, or any part of the Constitution, forbids the Federal Government to control as to slavery in the federal territories, he is right to say so, and to enforce his position by all truthful evidence and fair argument which he can. But he has no right to mislead others, who have less access to history, and less leisure to study it, into the false belief that "our fathers, who framed the Government under which we live," were of the same opinion—thus substituting falsehood and deception for truthful evidence and fair argument. If any man at this day sincerely believes "our fathers who framed the Government under which we live," used and applied principles, in other cases, which ought to have led them to understand that a proper division of local from federal authority or some part of the Constitution, forbids the Federal Government to control as to slavery in the federal territories, he is right to say so. But he should, at the same time, brave the responsibility of declaring that, in his opinion, he understands their principles better than they did themselves; and especially should he not shirk that responsibility by asserting that they "understood the question just as well, and even better, than we do now."

But enough! *Let all who believe that "our fathers, who framed the Government under which we live, understood this question just as well, and even better, than we do now," speak as they spoke, and act as they acted upon it. This is all Republicans ask—all Republicans desire—in relation to slavery. As those fathers marked it, so let it be again marked, as an evil not to be extended, but to be tolerated and protected only because of and so far as its actual presence among us makes that toleration and protection a necessity. Let all the guaranties those fathers gave it, be, not grudgingly, but fully and fairly maintained.* For this Republicans contend, and with this, so far as I know or believe, they will be content.

And now, if they would listen—as I suppose they will not—I would address a few words to the Southern people.

I would say to them:—You consider yourselves a reasonable and a just people; and I consider that in the general qualities of reason and justice you are not inferior to any other people. Still, when you speak of us Republicans, you do so only to denounce us as reptiles, or, at the best, as no better than outlaws. You will grant a hearing to pirates or murderers, but nothing like it to "Black Republicans." In all your contentions with one another, each of you deems an unconditional condemnation of "Black Republicanism" as the first thing to be attended to. Indeed, such condemnation of us seems to be an indispensable prerequisite—license, so to speak—among you to be admitted or permitted to speak at all. Now, can you, or not, be prevailed upon to pause and to consider whether this is quite just to us, or even to yourselves? Bring forward your charges and specifications, and then be patient long enough to hear us deny or justify.

You say we are sectional. We deny it. That makes an issue; and the burden of proof is upon you. You produce your proof; and what is it? Why, that our party has no existence in your section—gets no votes in your section. The fact is substantially true; but does it prove the issue? If it does, then in case we should, without change of principle, begin to get votes in your section, we should thereby cease to be sectional. You cannot escape this conclusion; and yet, are you willing to abide by it? If you are, you will probably soon find that we have ceased to be sectional, for we shall get votes in your section this very year. You will then begin to discover, as the truth plainly is, that your proof does not touch the issue. The fact that we get no votes in your section, is a fact of your making, and not of ours.

And if there be fault in that fact, that fault is primarily yours, and remains so until you show that we repel you by some wrong principle or practice. If we do repel you by any wrong principle or practice, the fault is ours; but this brings you to where you ought to have started—to a discussion of the right or wrong of our principle. If our principle, put in practice, would wrong your section for the benefit of ours, or for any other object, then our principle, and we with it, are sectional, and are justly opposed and denounced as such. Meet us, then, on the question of whether our principle, put in practice, would wrong your section; and so meet us as if it were possible that something may be said on our side. Do you accept the challenge? No! Then you really believe that the principle which "our fathers who framed the Government under which we live" thought so clearly right as to adopt it, and indorse it again and again, upon their official oaths, is in fact so clearly wrong as to demand your condemnation without a moment's consideration.

Some of you delight to flaunt in our faces the warning against sectional parties given by Washington in his Farewell Address. Less than eight years before Washington gave that warning, he had, as President of the United States, approved and signed an act of Congress, enforcing the prohibition of slavery in the Northwestern Territory, which act embodied the policy of the Government upon that subject up to and at the very moment he penned that warning; and about one year after he penned it, he wrote La Fayette that he considered that prohibition a wise measure, expressing in the same connection his hope that we should at some time have a confederacy of free States.

Bearing this in mind, and seeing that sectionalism has since arisen upon this same subject, is that warning a weapon in your hands against us, or in our hands against you? Could Washington himself speak, would he cast the blame of that sectionalism upon us, who sustain his policy, or upon you who repudiate it? We respect that warning of Washington, and we commend it to you, together with his example pointing to the right application of it.

But you say you are conservative—eminently conservative—while we are revolutionary, destructive, or something of the sort. What is conservatism? Is it not adherence to the old and tried, against the new and untried? We stick to, contend for, the identical old policy on the point in controversy which was adopted by "our fathers who framed the Government under which we live;" while you with one accord reject, and scout, and spit upon that old policy, and insist upon substituting something new. True, you disagree among yourselves as to what that substitute shall be. You are divided on new propositions and plans, but you are unanimous in rejecting and denouncing the old policy of the fathers. Some of you are for reviving the foreign slave trade; some for a Congressional Slave-Code for the Territories; some for Congress forbidding the Territories to prohibit Slavery within their limits; some for maintaining Slavery in the Territories through the judiciary; some for the "gur-reat pur-rinciple" that "if one man would enslave another, no third man should object," fantastically called "Popular Sovereignty;" but never a man among you in favor of federal prohibition of slavery in federal territories, according to the practice of "our fathers who framed the Government under which we live." Not one of all your various plans can show a precedent or an advocate in the century within which our Government originated. Consider, then, whether your claim of conservatism for yourselves, and your charge of destructiveness against us, are based on the most clear and stable foundations.

Again, you say we have made the slavery question more prominent than it formerly was. We deny it. We admit that it is more prominent, but we deny that we made it so. It was not we, but you, who discarded the old policy of the fathers. We resisted, and still resist, your innovation; and thence comes the greater prominence of the question. Would you have that question reduced to its former proportions? Go back to that old policy. What has been will be again, under the same conditions. If you would have the peace of the old times, readopt the precepts and policy of the old times.

You charge that we stir up insurrections among your slaves. We deny it; and what is your proof? Harper's Ferry! John Brown!! John Brown was no Republican; and you have failed to implicate a single Republican in his Harper's Ferry enterprise. If any member of our party is guilty in that matter, you know it or you do not know it. If you do know it, you are inexcusable for not designating the man and proving the fact. If you do not know it, you are inexcusable for asserting it, and especially for persisting in the assertion after you have tried and failed to make the proof. You need not be told that persisting in a charge which one does not know to be true, is simply malicious slander.

Some of you admit that no Republican designedly aided or encouraged the Harper's Ferry affair; but still insist that our doctrines and declarations necessarily lead to such results. We do not believe it. We know we hold to no doctrine, and make no declaration, which were not held to and made by "our fathers who framed the Government under which we live." You never dealt fairly by us in relation to this affair. When it occurred, some important State elections were near at hand, and you were in evident glee with the belief that, by charging the blame upon us, you could get an advantage of us in those elections. The elections came, and your expectations were not quite fulfilled. Every Republican man knew that, as to himself at least, your charge was a slander, and he was not much inclined by it to cast his vote in your favor. Republican doctrines and declarations are accompanied with a continual protest against any interference whatever with your slaves, or with you about your slaves. Surely, this does not encourage them to revolt. True, we do, in common with "our fathers, who framed the Government under which we live," declare our belief that slavery is wrong; but the slaves do not hear us declare even this. For anything we say or do, the slaves would scarcely know there is a Republican party. I believe they would not, in fact, generally know it but for your misrepresentations of us, in their hearing. In your political contests among yourselves, each faction charges the other with sympathy with Black Republicanism; and then, to give point to the charge, defines Black Republicanism to simply be insurrection, blood and thunder among the slaves.

Slave insurrections are no more common now than they were before the Republican party was organized. What induced the Southampton insurrection, twenty-eight years ago, in which, at least, three times as many lives were lost as at Harper's Ferry? You can scarcely stretch your very elastic fancy to the conclusion that Southampton was "got up by Black Republicanism." In the present state of things in the United States, I do not think a general, or even a very extensive slave insurrection, is possible. The indispensable concert of action cannot be attained. The slaves have no means of rapid communication; nor can incendiary freemen, black or white, supply it. The explosive materials are everywhere in parcels; but there neither are, nor can be supplied, the indispensable connecting trains.

Much is said by Southern people about the affection of slaves for their masters and mistresses; and a part of it, at least, is true. A plot for an uprising could scarcely be devised and communicated to twenty individuals before some one of them, to save the life of a favorite master or mistress, would divulge it. This is the rule; and the slave revolution in Hayti was not an exception to it, but a case occurring under peculiar circumstances. The gunpowder plot of British history, though not connected with slaves, was more in point. In that case, only about twenty were admitted to the secret; and yet one of them, in his anxiety to save a friend, betrayed the plot to that friend, and, by consequence, averted the calamity. Occasional poisonings from the kitchen, and open or stealthy assassinations in the field, and local revolts extending to a score or so, will continue to occur as the natural results of slavery; but no general insurrection of slaves, as I think, can happen in this country for a long time. Whoever much fears, or much hopes for such an event, will be alike disappointed.

In the language of Mr. Jefferson, uttered many years ago, "It is still in our power to direct the process of emancipation, and deportation, peaceably, and in such slow degrees, as that the evil will wear off insensibly; and their places be, *pari passu,* filled up by free white laborers. If, on the contrary, it is left to force itself on, human nature must shudder at the prospect held up."

Mr. Jefferson did not mean to say, nor do I, that the power of emancipation is in the Federal Government. He spoke of Virginia; and, as to the power of emancipation, I speak of the slaveholding States only. The Federal Government, however, as we insist, has the power of restraining the extension of the institution—the power to insure that a slave insurrection shall never occur on any American soil which is now free from slavery.

John Brown's effort was peculiar. It was not a slave insurrection. It was an attempt by white men to get up a revolt among slaves, in which the slaves refused to participate. In fact, it was so absurd that the slaves, with all their ignorance, saw plainly enough it could not succeed. That affair, in its philosophy, corresponds with the many attempts, related in history, at the assassination of kings and emperors. An enthusiast broods over the oppression of a people till he fancies himself commissioned by Heaven to liberate them. He ventures the attempt, which ends in little else than his own execution. Orsini's attempt on Louis Napoleon, and John Brown's attempt at Harper's Ferry were, in their philosophy, precisely the same. The eagerness to cast blame on old England in the one case, and on New England in the other, does not disprove the sameness of the two things.

And how much would it avail you, if you could, by the use of John Brown, Helper's Book, and the like, break up the Republican organization? Human action can be modified to some extent, but human nature cannot be changed. There is a judgment and a feeling against slavery in this nation, which cast at least a million and a half of votes. You cannot destroy that judgment and feeling—that sentiment—by breaking up the political organization which rallies around it. You can scarcely scatter and disperse an army which has been formed into order in the face of your heaviest fire; but if you could, how much would you gain by forcing the sentiment which created it out of the peaceful channel of the ballot-box, into some other channel? What would that other channel probably be? Would the number of John Browns be lessened or enlarged by the operation?

But you will break up the Union rather than submit to a denial of your Constitutional rights.

That has a somewhat reckless sound; but it would be palliated, if not fully justified, were we proposing, by the mere force of numbers, to deprive you of some right, plainly written down in the Constitution. But we are proposing no such thing.

When you make these declarations, you have a specific and well-understood allusion to an assumed Constitutional right of yours, to take slaves into the federal territories, and to hold them there as property. But no such right is specifically written in the Constitution. That instrument is literally silent about any such right. We, on the contrary, deny that such a right has any existence in the Constitution, even by implication.

Your purpose, then, plainly stated, is, that you will destroy the Government, unless you be allowed to construe and enforce the Constitution as you please, on all points in dispute between you and us. You will rule or ruin in all events.

This, plainly stated, is your language. Perhaps you will say the Supreme Court has decided the disputed Constitutional question in your favor. Not quite so. But waiving the lawyer's distinction between dictum and decision, the Court have decided the question for you in a sort of way. The Court have substantially said, it is your Constitutional right to take slaves into the federal territories, and to hold them there as property. When I say the decision was made in a sort of way, I mean it was made in a divided Court, by a bare majority of the Judges, and they not quite agreeing with one another in the reasons for making it, that it is so made as that its avowed supporters disagree with one another about its meaning, and that it was mainly based upon a mistaken statement of fact—the statement in the opinion that "the right of property in a slave is distinctly and expressly affirmed in the Constitution."

An inspection of the Constitution will show that the right of property in a slave is not "*distinctly* and *expressly* affirmed" in it. Bear in mind, the Judges do not pledge their judicial opinion that such right is *impliedly* affirmed in the Constitution; but they pledge their veracity that it is "*distinctly* and *expressly*" affirmed there—"distinctly," that is, not mingled with anything else—"expressly," that is, in words meaning just that, without the aid of any inference, and susceptible of no other meaning.

If they had only pledged their judicial opinion that such right is affirmed in the instrument by implication, it would be open to others to show that neither the word "slave" nor "slavery" is to be found in the Constitution, nor the word "property" even, in any connection with language alluding to the things slave, or slavery, and that wherever in that instrument the slave is alluded to, he is called a "person;"—and wherever his master's legal right in relation to him is alluded to, it is spoken of as "service or labor which may be due,"—as a debt payable in service or labor. Also, it would be open to show, by contemporaneous history, that this mode of alluding to slaves and slavery, instead of speaking of them, was employed on purpose to exclude from the Constitution the idea that there could be property in man.

To show all this, is easy and certain.

When this obvious mistake of the Judges shall be brought to their notice, is it not reasonable to expect that they will withdraw the mistaken statement, and reconsider the conclusion based upon it?

And then it is to be remembered that "our fathers, who framed the Government under which we live"—the men who made the Constitution—decided this same Constitutional question in our favor, long ago—decided it without division among themselves, when making the decision; without division among themselves about the meaning of it after it was made, and, so far as any evidence is left, without basing it upon any mistaken statement of facts.

Under all these circumstances, do you really feel yourselves justified to break up this Government, unless such a court decision as yours is, shall be at once submitted to as a conclusive and final rule of political action? But you will not abide the election of a Republican President! In that supposed event, you say, you will destroy the Union; and then, you say, the great crime of having destroyed it will be upon us! That is cool. A highwayman holds a pistol to my ear, and mutters through his teeth, "Stand and deliver, or I shall kill you, and then you will be a murderer!"

To be sure, what the robber demanded of me—my money—was my own; and I had a clear right to keep it; but it was no more my own than my vote is my own; and the threat of death to me, to extort my money, and the threat of destruction to the Union, to extort my vote, can scarcely be distinguished in principle.

A few words now to Republicans. *It is exceedingly desirable that all parts of this great Confederacy shall be at peace, and in harmony, one with another. Let us Republicans do our part to have it so. Even though much provoked, let us do nothing through passion and ill temper. Even though the southern people will not so much as listen to us, let us calmly consider their demands, and yield to them if, in our deliberate view of our duty, we possibly can.* Judging by all they say and do, and by the subject and nature of their controversy with us, let us determine, if we can, what will satisfy them.

Will they be satisfied if the Territories be unconditionally surrendered to them? We know they will not. In all their present complaints against us, the Territories are scarcely mentioned. Invasions and insurrections are the rage now. Will it satisfy them, if, in the future, we have nothing to do with invasions and insurrections? We know it will not. We so know, because we know we never had anything to do with invasions and insurrections; and yet this total abstaining does not exempt us from the charge and the denunciation.

The question recurs, what will satisfy them? Simply this: We must not only let them alone, but we must, somehow, convince them that we do let them alone. This, we know by experience, is no easy task. We have been so trying to convince them from the very beginning of our organization, but with no success. In all our platforms and speeches we have constantly protested our purpose to let them alone; but this has had no tendency to convince them. Alike unavailing to convince them, is the fact that they have never detected a man of us in any attempt to disturb them.

These natural, and apparently adequate means all failing, what will convince them? This, and this only: cease to call slavery *wrong,* and join them in calling it *right.* And this must be done thoroughly—done in *acts* as well as in *words*. Silence will not be tolerated—we must place ourselves avowedly with them. Senator Douglas's new sedition law must be enacted and enforced, suppressing all declarations that slavery is wrong, whether made in politics, in presses, in pulpits, or in private. We must arrest and return their fugitive slaves with greedy pleasure. We must pull down our Free State constitutions. The whole atmosphere must be disinfected from all taint of opposition to slavery, before they will cease to believe that all their troubles proceed from us.

I am quite aware they do not state their case precisely in this way. Most of them would probably say to us, "Let us alone, *do* nothing to us, and *say* what you please about slavery." But we do let them alone—have never disturbed them—so that, after all, it is what we say, which dissatisfies them. They will continue to accuse us of doing, until we cease saying.

I am also aware they have not, as yet, in terms, demanded the overthrow of our Free-State Constitutions. Yet those Constitutions declare the wrong of slavery, with more solemn emphasis, than do all other sayings against it; and when all these other sayings shall have been silenced, the overthrow of these Constitutions will be demanded, and nothing be left to resist the demand. It is nothing to the contrary, that they do not demand the whole of this just now. Demanding what they do, and for the reason they do, they can voluntarily stop nowhere short of this consummation. Holding, as they do, that slavery is morally right, and socially elevating, they cannot cease to demand a full national recognition of it, as a legal right, and a social blessing.

Nor can we justifiably withhold this, on any ground save our conviction that slavery is wrong. If slavery is right, all words, acts, laws, and constitutions against it, are themselves wrong, and should be silenced, and swept away. If it is right, we cannot justly object to its nationality—its universality; if it is wrong, they cannot justly insist upon its extension—its enlargement. All they ask, we could readily grant, if we thought slavery right; all we ask, they could as readily grant, if they thought it wrong. Their thinking it right, and our thinking it wrong, is the precise fact upon which depends the whole controversy. Thinking it right, as they do, they are not to blame for desiring its full recognition, as being right; but, thinking it wrong, as we do, can we yield to them? Can we cast our votes with their view, and against our own? In view of our moral, social, and political responsibilities, can we do this?

Wrong as we think slavery is, we can yet afford to let it alone where it is, because that much is due to the necessity arising from its actual presence in the nation; but can we, while our votes will prevent it, allow it to spread into the National Territories, and to overrun us here in these Free States? If our sense of duty forbids this, then let us stand by our duty, fearlessly and effectively. Let us be diverted by none of those sophistical contrivances wherewith we are so industriously plied and belabored—contrivances such as groping for some middle ground between the right and the wrong, vain as the search for a man who should be neither a living man nor a dead man—such as a policy of "don't care" on a question about which all true men do care—such as Union appeals beseeching true Union men to yield to Disunionists, reversing the divine rule, and calling, not the sinners, but the righteous to repentance—such as invocations to Washington, imploring men to unsay what Washington said, and undo what Washington did.

Neither let us be slandered from our duty by false accusations against us, nor frightened from it by menaces of destruction to the Government nor of dungeons to ourselves. LET US HAVE FAITH THAT RIGHT MAKES MIGHT, AND IN THAT FAITH, LET US, TO THE END, DARE TO DO OUR DUTY AS WE UNDERSTAND IT.

VI

FREDERICK DOUGLASS
(1817–95)

FREDERICK DOUGLASS, one of the greatest black American statesmen the United States has produced, was an escaped slave, an abolitionist writer and agitator, and a teacher of politics. He was aggressive in his assertion of the rights of black Americans and relentless in his resistance to racial segregation and prejudice. His public career began when, as an agent of the Massachusetts Anti-Slavery Society, he was invited to tell of his experiences as a slave. He founded the *North Star,* an abolitionist newspaper in Rochester, New York, in 1847 and edited it until 1860. He served as U.S. Marshal for the District of Columbia from 1877 to 1881, Recorder of Deeds for the District from 1881 to 1886, and U.S. Minister to Haiti from 1889 to 1891. The circumstances of the black American during the 19th century, both under slavery and after the Civil War, taught Douglass a fundamental lesson: The cause of justice can only be served through politics.

In his "Lecture on Slavery No. 1," delivered in Rochester, New York, in December 1850, Douglass maintained a hard, uncompromising abolitionist stand. Originally a disciple of William Lloyd Garrison, he accepted the argument that the Constitution was a proslavery document, finding that slavery "has become interwoven with all American institutions, and has anchored itself in the very soil of the American Constitution." But in 1851 Douglass broke with the Garrisonians, essentially over their interpretation of the Constitution as sanctioning slavery. Douglass believed that while it made necessary provision for the existing institution of slavery, the Constitution contained no principle which could be construed to sanction slavery itself.

In 1856, Douglass argued in "What Is My Duty as an Anti-Slavery Voter?" that "the purity of the cause is the success of the cause" and that the first duty of a social reformer is to be right. Therefore he preferred the loss of Kansas to the loss of his antislavery integrity. But four months later, in "Fremont and Dayton," an article in his paper, he announced his support of the Republicans in that controversy, acknowledging that the purity of the cause was subordinate to a higher morality. Douglass continued to believe that the abolition of slavery depended upon a moral regeneration of the American people, expressing the opinion that the Garrisonians were incapable of dealing with the problem because they were politically and morally defective. They needed to learn morality in the politics of a free, though imperfect, republic. Right antislavery action, he maintained, is "that which deals the severest deadliest blow upon slavery that can be given at that particular time."

In an article, "The Future of the Colored Race," which appeared in the *North American Review* for May 1866, Douglass looked at the black American as politically and socially related to the white American and measured the forces arrayed against blacks. He believed their greatest struggle was to become part of the American political community, and before they could do this, color prejudice had to be eradicated. Douglass prophesied that the black American would not be expatriated or annihilated, but absorbed and assimilated. While he did not advocate intermarriage between the races, neither did he deprecate it. If the blacks were to stay in the United States, he said, the blending of the two races was the only condition in which they could ultimately survive and flourish.

In a letter to the *Evening Star* in December 1872, Douglass argued that unwillingness to serve decent people in a public place, regardless of color, is a matter of simple justice and not a measure of social equality. In this, he was more concerned with the effect of such practices on the character of the polity than on the objects of discrimination. Douglass was determined to make America live up to her promises. The fundamental problem, he believed, was to hold the country to her basic principles so that blacks could share in them.

Douglass's oration on the occasion of the unveiling of the freedman's monument at Washington, D.C., in memory of Abraham Lincoln reveals the understanding that a Frederick Douglass could have of an Abraham Lincoln. Recognizing that the blacks were stepchildren of Abraham Lincoln as well as of the United States, Douglass saw the monument as standing not only for their praise of Lincoln, but for their right to praise him. In considering the relation between the black American and the polity, he acknowledged the basic decency of American society and accepted its fundamental justice. He taught that the black American must himself walk the road of opportunity, for his title to being an American lay in making good use of those opportunities that presented themselves.

31
LECTURE ON SLAVERY NO. 1
December 1, 1850

I COME BEFORE YOU this evening to deliver the first lecture of a course which I purpose to give in this city, during the present winter, on the subject of American Slavery.

I make this announcement with no feelings of self-sufficiency. If I do not mistake my own emotions, they are such as result from a profound sense of my incompetency to do justice to the task which I have just announced, and have now entered upon.

If any, then, demand of me why I speak, I plead as my apology, the fact that abler and more eloquent men have failed to speak, or what, perhaps, is more true, and therefore more strong, such men have spoken only on the wrong side of the question, and have thus thrown their influence against the cause of liberty, humanity and benevolence.

There are times in the experience of almost every community, when even the humblest member thereof may properly presume to teach—when the wise and great ones, the appointed leaders of the people, exert their powers of mind to complicate, mystify, entangle and obscure the simple truth—when they exert the noblest gifts which heaven has vouchsafed to man to mislead the popular mind, and to corrupt the public heart,—*then* the humblest may stand forth and be excused for opposing even his weakness to the torrent of evil.

That such a state of things exists in this community, I have abundant evidence. I learn it from the Rochester press, from the Rochester pulpit, and in my intercourse with the people of Rochester. Not a day passes over me that I do not meet with apparently good men, who utter sentiments in respect to this subject which would do discredit to savages. They speak of the enslavement of their fellow-men with an indifference and coldness which might be looked for only in men hardened by the most atrocious and villainous crimes.

The fact is, we are in the midst of a great struggle. The public mind is widely and deeply agitated; and bubbling up from its perturbed waters, are many and great impurities, whose poisonous miasma demands a constant antidote.

Whether the contemplated lectures will in any degree contribute towards answering this demand, time will determine.

Of one thing, however, I can assure my hearers—that I come up to this work at the call of duty, and with an honest desire to promote the happiness and well-being of every member of this community, as well as to advance the emancipation of every slave.

The audience will pardon me if I say one word more by way of introduction. It is my purpose to give this subject a calm, candid and faithful discussion. I shall not aim to shock nor to startle my hearers; but to convince their judgment and to secure their sympathies for the enslaved. I shall aim to be as stringent as truth, and as severe as justice; and if at any time I shall fail of this, and do injustice in any respect, I shall be most happy to be set right by any gentleman who shall hear me, subject, of course, to order and decorum. I shall deal, during these lectures, alike with individuals and institutions—men shall no more escape me than things. I shall have occasion, at times, to be even personal, and to rebuke sin in high places. I shall not hesitate to arraign either priests or politicians, church or state, and to measure all by the standard of justice, and in the light of truth. I shall not forget to deal with the unrighteous spirit of *caste* which prevails in this community; and I shall give particular attention to the recently enacted fugitive slave bill. I shall keep my eye upon the Congress which is to commence to-morrow, and fully inform myself as to its proceedings. In a word, the whole subject of slavery, in all its bearings, shall have a full and impartial discussion.

A very slight acquaintance with the history of American slavery is sufficient to show that it is an evil of which it will be difficult to rid this country. It is not the creature of a moment, which to-day is, and to-morrow is not; it is not a pigmy, which a slight blow may demolish; it is no youthful upstart, whose impertinent pratings may be silenced by a dignified contempt. No: it is an evil of gigantic proportions, and of long standing.

Its origin in this country dates back to the landing of the pilgrims on Plymouth rock.—It was here more than two centuries ago. The first spot poisoned by its leprous presence, was a small plantation in Virginia. The slaves, at that time, numbered only twenty. They have now increased to the frightful number of three millions; and from that narrow plantation, they are now spread over by far the largest half of the American Union. Indeed, slavery forms an important part of the entire history of the American people. Its presence may be seen in all American affairs. It has become interwoven with all American institutions, and has anchored itself in the very soil of the American Constitution. It has thrown its paralysing arm over freedom of speech, and the liberty of the press; and has created for itself morals and manners favorable to its own continuance. It has seduced the church, corrupted the pulpit, and brought the powers of both into degrading bondage; and now, in the pride of its power, it even threatens to bring down that grand political edifice, the American Union, unless every member of this republic shall so far disregard his conscience and his God as to yield to its infernal behests.

That must be a powerful influence which can truly be said to govern a nation; and that slavery governs the American people, is indisputably true. If there were any doubt on this point, a few plain questions (it seems to me) could not fail to remove it. *What* power has given this nation its Presidents for more than fifty years? *Slavery.* What power is that to which the present aspirants to presidential honors are bowing? *Slavery.* We may call it "Union," "Constitution," "Harmony," or "American institutions," that to which such men as Cass, Dickinson, Webster, Clay and other distinguished men of this country, are devoting their energies, is nothing more nor less than American slavery. It is for this that they are writing letters, making speeches, and promoting the holding of great mass meetings, professedly in favor of *"the Union."* These men know the service most pleasing to their master, and that which is most likely to be richly rewarded. Men may "serve God for nought," as did Job; but he who serves the devil has an eye to his reward. "Patriotism," "obedience to the law," "prosperity to the country," have come to mean, in the mouths of these distinguished statesmen, a mean and servile acquiescence in the most flagitious and profligate legislation in favor of slavery. I might enlarge here on this picture of the slave power, and tell of its influence upon the press in the free States, and upon the condition and rights of the free colored people of the North; but I forbear for the present.—Enough has been said, I trust, to convince all that the abolition of this evil will require time, energy, zeal, perseverance and patience; that it will require fidelity, a martyr-like spirit of self-sacrifice, and a firm reliance on Him who has declared Himself to be *"the God of the oppressed."* Having said thus much upon the power and prevalence of slavery, allow me to speak of the nature of slavery itself; and here I can speak, in part, from experience—I can speak with the authority of positive knowledge. . . .

First of all, I will state, as well as I can, the legal and social relation of master and slave. A master is one (to speak in the vocabulary of the Southern States) who claims and exercises a right of property in the person of a fellow man. This he does with the force of the law and the sanction of Southern religion. The law gives the master absolute power over the slave. He may work him, flog him, hire him out, sell him, and, in certain contingencies, *kill* him, with perfect impunity. The slave is a human being, divested of all rights—reduced to the level of a brute—a mere "chattel" in the eye of the law—placed beyond the circle of human brotherhood— cut off from his kind—his name, which the "recording angel" may have enrolled in heaven, among the blest, is impiously inserted in a *master's ledger,* with horses, sheep and swine. In law, the slave has no wife, no children, no country, and no home. He can own nothing, possess nothing, acquire nothing, but what must belong to another. To eat the fruit of his own toil, to clothe his person with the work of his own hands, is considered stealing. He toils that another may reap the fruit; he is industrious that another may live in idleness; he eats unbolted meal, that another may eat the bread of fine flour; he labors in chains at home, under a burning sun and a biting lash, that another may ride in ease and splendor abroad; he lives in ignorance, that another may be educated; he is abused, that another may be exalted; he rests his toil-worn limbs on the cold, damp ground, that another may repose on the softest pillow; he is clad in coarse and tattered raiment, that another may be arrayed in purple and fine linen; he is sheltered only by the wretched hovel, that a master may dwell in a magnificent mansion; and to this condition he is bound down as by an arm of iron.

From this monstrous relation, there springs an unceasing stream of most revolting cruelties. The very accompaniments of the slave system, stamp it as the offspring of hell itself. To ensure good behavior, the slaveholder relies on *the whip;* to induce proper humility, he relies on *the whip;* to rebuke what he is pleased to term insolence, he relies on *the whip;* to supply the place of wages, as an incentive to toil, he relies on *the whip;* to bind down the spirit of the slave, to imbrute and to destroy his manhood, he relies on *the whip,* the chain, the gag, the thumb-screw, the pillory, the bowie-knife, the pistol, and the blood-hound. These are the necessary and unvarying accompaniments of the system. . . .

Nor is slavery more adverse to the conscience than it is to the mind.

This is shown by the fact that in every State of the American Union, where slavery exists, except the State of Kentucky, there are laws, *absolutely* prohibitory of education among the slaves. The crime of teaching a slave to read is punishable with severe fines and imprisonment, and, in some instances, with *death itself*.

Nor are the laws respecting this matter, a dead letter. Cases may occur in which they are disregarded, and a few instances may be found where slaves may have learned to read; but such are isolated cases, and only prove the rule. The great mass of slaveholders look upon education among the slaves as utterly subversive of the slave system. I *well* remember when my mistress first announced to my master that she had discovered that I could read. His face colored at once, with surprise and chagrin. He said that "I was ruined, and my value as a slave destroyed; that a slave should know nothing but to obey his master; that to give a Negro an inch would lead him to take an ell; that having learned how to read, I would soon want to know how to write; and that, bye and bye, I would be running away." I think my audience will bear witness to the correctness of this philosophy, and to the literal fulfilment of this prophecy.

It is perfectly well understood at the South that to educate a slave is to make him discontented with slavery, and to invest him with a power which shall open to him the treasures of freedom; and since the object of the slaveholder is to maintain complete authority over his slave, his constant vigilance is exercised to prevent everything which militates against, or endangers the stability of his authority. Education being among the menacing influences, and, perhaps, the most dangerous, is, therefore, the most cautiously guarded against.

It is true that we do not often hear of the enforcement of the law, punishing as crime the teaching of slaves to read, but this is not because of a want of disposition to enforce it. The true reason, or explanation of the matter is this, there is the greatest unanimity of opinion among the white population of the South, in favor of the policy of keeping the slave in ignorance. There is, perhaps, another reason why the law against education is so seldom violated. The slave is *too* poor to be able to offer a temptation sufficiently strong to induce a white man to violate it; and it is not to be supposed that in a community where the moral and religious sentiment is in favor of slavery, many martyrs will be found sacrificing their liberty and lives by violating those prohibitory enactments.

As a general rule, then, darkness reigns over the abodes of the enslaved, and "how great is that darkness!"

We are sometimes told of the contentment of the slaves, and are entertained with vivid pictures of their happiness. We are told that they often dance and sing; that their masters frequently give them wherewith to make merry; in fine, that that they have little of which to complain. I admit that the slave *does* sometimes sing, dance, and appear to be merry. But what does this prove? It only proves to my mind, that though slavery is armed with a thousand stings, it is not able entirely to kill the elastic spirit of the bondman. That spirit will rise and walk abroad, despite of whips and chains, and extract from the cup of nature, occasional drops of joy and gladness. No thanks to the slaveholder, nor to slavery, that the vivacious captive may sometimes dance in his chains, his very mirth in such circumstances, stands before God, as an accusing angel against his enslaver.

But *who* tells us of the extraordinary contentment and happiness of the slave? What traveller has explored the balmy regions of our Southern country and brought back "these glad tidings of joy"? Bring him on the platform, and bid him answer a few plain questions, we shall then be able to determine the weight and importance that attach to his testimony. Is he a minister? Yes. Were you ever in a slave State, sir? Yes. May I inquire the object of your mission South? To preach the gospel, sir. Of what denomination are you? A Presbyterian, sir. To whom were you introduced? To the Rev. Dr. Plummer. Is he a slaveholder, sir? Yes, sir. Has slaves about his house? Yes, sir. Were you then the guest of Dr. Plummer? Yes, sir. Waited on by slaves while there? Yes, sir. Did you preach for Dr. Plummer? Yes, sir. Did you spend your nights at the great house, or at the quarter among the slaves? At the great house. You had, then, no social intercourse with the slaves? No, sir. You fraternized, then, wholly with the *white* portion of the population while there? Yes, sir. This is sufficient, sir; you can leave the platform.

Nothing is more natural than that those who go into slave States, and enjoy the hospitality of slaveholders, should bring back favorable reports of the condition of the slave. If that ultra republican, the Hon. Lewis Cass could not return from the Court of France, without paying a compliment to royalty simply because King Louis Phillippe patted him on the shoulder, called him "friend," and invited him to dinner, it is not to be expected that those hungry shadows of men in the shape of ministers, that go South, can escape a contamination even more beguiling and insidious. Alas! for the weakness of poor human nature! "Pleased with a rattle, tickled with a straw!"

Why is it that all the reports of contentment and happiness among the slaves at the South come to us upon the authority of slaveholders, or (what is equally significant,) of slaveholder's friends? *Why* is it that we do not hear from the slaves direct? The answer to this question furnishes the darkest features in the American slave system.

It is often said, by the opponents of the anti-slavery cause, that the condition of the people of Ireland is more deplorable than that of the American slaves. *Far* be it from me to underrate the sufferings of the Irish people. They have been long oppressed; and the same heart that prompts me to plead the cause of the American bondman, makes it impossible for me *not* to sympathize with the oppressed of all lands. Yet I must say that there is no analogy between the two cases. The Irishman is poor, but he is *not* a slave. He *may* be in rags, but he is *not* a slave. He is still the master of his own body, and can say with the poet, "The hand of Douglass is his own." "The world is all before him, where to choose," and poor as may be my opinion of the British Parliament, I cannot believe that it will ever sink to such a depth of infamy as to pass a law for the recapture of Fugitive Irishmen! The shame and scandal of kidnapping will long remain wholly monopolized by the American Congress! The Irishman has not only the liberty to emigrate from his country, but he has liberty at home. He can write, and speak, and co-operate for the attainment of his rights and the redress of his wrongs.

The multitude can assemble upon all the green hills, and fertile plains of the Emerald Isle—they can pour out their grievances, and proclaim their wants without molestation; and the press, that "swift-winged messenger," can bear the tidings of their doings to the extreme bounds of the civilized world. They have their "Conciliation Hall" on the banks of the Liffey, their reform Clubs, and their newspapers; they pass resolutions, send forth addresses, and enjoy the right of petition. But how is it with the American slave? *Where* may he assemble? *Where* is his Conciliation Hall? Where are his newspapers? Where is his right of petition? Where is his freedom of speech? his liberty of the press? and his right of locomotion? He is said to be happy; happy men can speak. But ask the slave—*what* is his condition?—*what* his state of mind?—*what* he thinks of his enslavement? and you had as well address your inquiries to the *silent dead*. There comes no *voice* from the enslaved, we are left to gather his feelings by imagining what ours would be, were our souls in his soul's stead.

If there were no other fact descriptive of slavery, than that the slave is dumb, this alone would be sufficient to mark the slave system as a grand aggregation of human horrors.

Most who are present will have observed that leading men, in this country, have been putting forth their skill to secure quiet to the nation. A system of measures to promote this object was adopted a few months ago in Congress.

The result of those measures is known. Instead of quiet, they have produced alarm; instead of peace, they have brought us war, and so must ever be.

While this nation is guilty of the enslavement of three millions of innocent men and women, it is as idle to think of having a sound and lasting peace, as it is to think there is no God, to take cognizance of the affairs of men. There can be no peace to the wicked while slavery continues in the land, it will be condemned, and while it is condemned there will be agitation; Nature must cease to be nature; Men must become monsters; Humanity must be transformed; Christianity must be exterminated; all ideas of justice, and the laws of eternal goodness must be utterly blotted out from the human soul, ere a system so foul and infernal can escape condemnation, or this guilty Republic can have a sound and enduring Peace.

32

WHAT IS MY DUTY AS
AN ANTI-SLAVERY VOTER?
April 25, 1856

THERE ARE AND HAVE BEEN, for the last dozen years, a band of conscientious men in this country, who have insisted upon casting their votes at
the Ballot-Box in a manner fully to indicate their earnest desire for the
abolition of Slavery. To these, the old Liberty Party of eight years ago,
furnished the required platform, and the natural channels of political cooperation. Under the Banner of this party, with many, or with few, they felt
at home, and ready to fall or flourish. It was a noble party, and was ani-
mated by a noble spirit. That party, as such, has almost vanished. Its
members are scattered, and its old armor has been borne off to a party
with another name, and of another spirit. Led by the Barnburners of New
York, it supported Martin Van Buren for the Presidency in 1848. Since
then, it has been in the wilderness, wandering in darkness. Active, to be
sure, but making little progress towards the great end which combined its
original elements. A portion of those who have filled the ranks of this wandering army, are beginning to raise the enquiry which heads this article.

The aggressive front of Slavery, openly declaring for the entire mastery
of the country—the ready enrollment of the Democratic and Know Nothing parties in the boldest enterprises of Slavery—the shocking outrages
perpetrated in Kansas—and the evident determination of the Slave Power
to make slaveholding and slave-buying and selling, the law of the whole
land—have suggested the propriety of giving up the more radical and
comprehensive measures of Abolitionists at the Ballot-Box, and the adoption of some one measure, upon which a large and important party can be
united and organized to meet the Slave Power.

It is against this suggestion that we propose to offer a few remarks—
remarks which, though coming from an humble source, may yet be deemed
entitled to consideration by some sincere enquirer for the right way.

1. The ultimate success of the Anti-Slavery movement depends upon
nothing, under God, more than upon the soundness of its principles, the

earnestness, stringency and faithfulness with which they are enforced, and the integrity, consistency and disinterestedness of those who stand forth as its advocates. The purity of the cause is the success of the cause. There can be very little necessity for sustaining this proposition by argument. We rely upon honesty, and not dishonesty, to uproot injustice and wrong. This element of power can be rallied and enlisted by its like—and only by its like.—"Men will not serve God if the Devil bid them"—and hence the necessity for purity and consistency in all who seek to leave the world better than they found it. The first duty of the Reformer is to be right. If right, he may go forward; but if wrong, or partly wrong, he is as an house divided against itself, and will fall. He will move, if he moves at all, like a man in fetters, and to no valuable purpose. To succeed against Slavery, the public must be brought to respect Anti-Slavery; and it cannot be respected unless consistent with itself, and its advocates are conscientiously consistent with it. The country must be made to feel the pulsation of an enlightened conscience, animating, supporting and directing that cause, before they will own it and bless it as a cause entitled to triumph.

2. That the National Republican party, around whose standard Abolitionists are now called upon to rally, does *not* occupy this high Anti-Slavery ground, (and what is worse, does not mean to occupy it,) is most painfully evident. From the hour that the old Liberty Party was swallowed up by the Van Buren Free Soil party in '48, the work of deterioration began and has been continued until now. Instead of going upward, the political Anti-Slavery sentiment has been going downward. The Buffalo platform in '48 was lower than that of the Liberty Party; and the Pittsburgh platform of '56, is lower than that of '52. But not only is this deterioration shown in the platform of the Pittsburgh Convention, recently adopted. It is painfully manifest in the spirit of the Convention itself. There was a spirit of cold calculation, of deliberate contriving, so to pair off the edge of Anti-Slavery truth, and so to arrange and dispose of Anti-Slavery principles, as to draw into the Republican ranks men of all parties and sentiments, except the men of the Administration party. No man could have been found in the Republican Convention, held in Pittsburgh four years ago, bold enough to have proposed a slaveholder—an actual man-stealer—to preside over that Convention of Anti-Slavery men. Such a proposition would have been scouted as an insult to the Anti-Slavery sentiment of the North. Then the tone of the speeches made on the occasion was lower and weaker than on any former occasion. The Anti-Slavery creed, after the filtration of this Convention, came out simply a measure to restore the restriction against Slavery to Kansas and Nebraska. Nothing said of the Fugitive Slave Bill—nothing said of Slavery in the District of Columbia—nothing said of the slave trade between States—nothing said of giving the dignity of the nation to Liberty—nothing said of securing the rights of citizens, from the

Northern States, in the constitutional right to enter and transact business in the slave States. There is not a single warm and living position, taken by the Republican party, except freedom for Kansas. We need not ask Radical Anti-Slavery men if this is the natural and desirable tendency of the political Anti-Slavery sentiment of the country. They instinctively recoil from it, as destructive of the great purpose of the Anti-Slavery movement of the country. They can only be induced to follow after the Republican movement under the teachings of a plausible and sinuous political philosophy, which is the grand corrupter of all reforms. The substance of this philosophy is, that the one thing needful, the thing to precede all else, is a large party; and in order to do this, we are at liberty to abandon almost everything but a name. Parties of this kind serve certain leading ones who get into office by them; but they seldom advance the cause that gave them birth.

3. We hold that the true mode to prevent this falling away from Anti-Slavery truth and duty, and to save the Anti-Slavery movement from utter destruction, is to support candidates for the Presidency and Vice Presidency, of tried Anti-Slavery character, and of decided Anti-Slavery principles. This is the true path of Anti-Slavery duty. The Anti-Slavery voters of the country must not allow themselves to be transferred from one political demagogue to another, until all vitality shall have departed from them. Nothing can be more certain, than that the habitual accommodation of Anti-Slavery men to the men opposed to them, has weakened the self-respect of the Anti-Slavery men to the men opposed to them, has weakened the self-respect of the Anti-Slavery party, and awakened the contempt of their opponents. The slaveholders themselves, seeing how ready we are to chase shadows, and to fight men of straw, are perpetually leading us away from the main issue by these trifles.—We must show the slaveholders, and the country, that we are in earnest, and cannot be drawn away from our legitimate work. For this reason, we shall look to Syracuse, rather than to Philadelphia, for the candidates to be supported in the next Presidential election. With the party at Syracuse, principles are more precious than numbers—and hence our cause is more safe there than elsewhere.

4. But it is said that by casting our votes for a man who duly represents our Radical Anti-Slavery sentiments, in the coming Presidential election, we shall probably give the Government into the hands of the Democratic Party, and thereby establish Slavery in Kansas, thus depriving the North of a Free State, and adding its power to the Slave States—the better enabling the latter to perpetuate Slavery.—This is very evidently a grave argument, and cannot be lightly disposed of. It is meet that it should be duly considered. Suppose, then, that by voting as above, the result, which is possible, should occur—Slavery should be established in Kansas, and

Kansas added to the Slave States. It then becomes us to estimate the loss which freedom would sustain, not as against the saving of Kansas to freedom, but as against the evils which would arise from the policy, which it is relied on, will save Kansas to freedom. This is the only consistent and certain method by which to arrive at the path of Duty in the premise. Looking at the matter from this point then, we hold, that great as would be the misfortune to liberty should Kansas be given to Slavery, tenfold greater would be the misfortune, should Kansas be saved by means which must certainly demoralize the Anti-Slavery sentiment of the North, and render it weak and inefficient for the greater work of saving the entire country to Liberty. Keep in mind the fact that our aim is the entire abolition of Slavery; that our work is not done till this is done; and that the real importance of establishing freedom in Kansas, is to be found in its effect to establish freedom in the country at large. We deliberately prefer the loss of Kansas to the loss of our Anti-Slavery integrity. With Kansas saved, and our Anti-Slavery integrity gone, our cause is ruined. With Kansas lost, and our Anti-Slavery integrity saved, we have, at least, means left us with which to continue the war upon Slavery, and of final victory.

5. But this is arguing at great disadvantage, far greater than our position requires. We have granted more than there is any absolute necessity for granting. It is by no means certain that Kansas can be saved by the Republican Party, even with the votes of Abolitionists. Freedom in Kansas depends, less upon politics, than upon the Anti-Slavery sentiment of the North, and the Anti-Slavery integrity of those who settle that Territory from the North.—Dark indeed would be the prospect of freedom in Kansas, if it depended entirely upon the election of a Republican President for the next four years. If that is to decide the question, Slavery has very little to fear and everything to hope. Republican enthusiasm may predict the election of a Republican President, but the calmer reason of that party must pronounce it strongly improbable. With the South united, and the North divided, it is easy to see which side will be victorious at the Polls. Republicans will have an enemy to contend with at the North, which will require all its strength, flinging the South out of the question. Again we might claim that a strong vote for Radical Abolitionists would far more certainly help freedom in Kansas than a much stronger vote for the Republicans would do.

The whole Slave population of this country whether in States, Territories, dock yards, or on the high seas, must be emancipated. For this the true friends of the Slave must toil and hope, and for nothing less than this. It is short-sighted, as a matter of policy, to aim lower than this, and it is cruel to those bleeding millions to do so. Our God, our country and the slave, alike have called us to this great work, and we cannot come down from it to mingle in a less comprehensive or a less commanding struggle.

Slavery is a sin now, a sin at all times, and a sin everywhere; and as we hold all human enactments designed to sustain it as of no binding authority, and utterly contrary to the Constitution of the United States, the coast is clear for an open, and direct war upon Slavery everywhere in the United States.—But should we not do one thing at a time?—Yes, one thing at a time; but let that thing be the abolition of Slavery. It is not doing one thing at a time, in any important sense, to limit the domain of Slavery, and to leave its continuance unlimited. It is not doing one thing at a time to establish Freedom for the white citizen in Kansas, and to hunt the black citizen from it, like a wolf; and if it is doing one thing at a time to do this, we hold that a strong vote for the Radical Abolition candidate is the best way to accomplish that one thing at a time.—"Freedom for all, or chains for all."

33
FREMONT AND DAYTON
August 15, 1856

THE READERS OF OUR JOURNAL will observe that the honored names which, for some time, stood at the head of our columns, as its candidates for the president and vice-president of the United States, have been withdrawn and although no other names have been or shall be placed at the head of our columns, we deem it proper frankly to announce our purpose to support, with whatever influence we possess, little or much, John C. Fremont and William L. Dayton, the candidates of the Republican Party for the presidency and vice-presidency of the United States, in the present political canvass.

To a part of our readers, this announcement, considering our previous position, will be an unwelcome surprise. We have, hitherto, advocated to the best of our ability, a course of political action inconsistent with our present course. It is, therefore, eminently fit that we should accompany the foregoing announcement with something like a statement of reasons for our newly adopted policy.

1. A step so important as to lead to a separation in action, at least,

between ourselves and of loved, honored, and tried friends, should not be hastily or inconsiderately taken. In full view of this truth, we have with much care examined and re-examined the subject of our political relations and duties regarding Slavery and the colored people of the United States. Our position, as well as the suggestion of wisdom just referred to, very naturally cause hesitation. The name of Gerrit Smith has long been synonymous with us as genuine, unadulterated Abolitionism. Of all men beneath the sky, we would rather see this just man made President. Our heart and judgment cling and twine around this man and his counsels as the ivy to the oak. To differ from him, and the beloved friends who may still intend to vote for him at the approaching election, is the result only of stern and irresistible conviction, the voice of which we cannot feel ourselves at liberty to disregard.

2. The time has passed for an honest man to attempt any defence of a right to change his opinion as to political methods of opposing Slavery. Anti-Slavery consistency itself, in our view, requires of the Anti-Slavery voter that disposition of his vote and his influence, which, in all the circumstances and likelihoods of the case tend most to the triumph of Free Principles in the Councils and Government of the nation. It is not to be consistent to pursue a course politically this year, merely because that course seemed the best last year, or at any previous time. Right Anti-Slavery action is that which deals the severest deadliest blow upon Slavery that can be given at that particular time. Such action is always consistent, however different may be the forms through which it expresses itself.

3. Again, in supporting Fremont and Dayton, we are in no wise required to abandon a single Anti-Slavery Truth or Principle which we have hitherto cherished, and publicly advocated. The difference between our paper this week and last week is a difference of Policy, not of Principle. Hereafter, as hitherto, we shall contend for every principle, and maintain [mutilated] the platform of the Radical Abolitionists. The unconstitutionality of Slavery, the illegality of Slavery, the Right of the Federal Government to abolish Slavery in every part of the Republic, whether in States or Territories, will be as firmly held, and as sternly insisted upon, as hitherto. Nor do we wish, by supporting the Republican Candidate in the approaching election, to be understood as merging our individuality, body and soul, into that Party, nor as separating ourselves from our Radical Abolition friends in their present endeavors to enforce the great Principles of Justice and Liberty, upon which the Radical Abolition movement is based. Furthermore, we here concede, that upon Radical Abolition grounds, the final battle against Slavery in this country must be fought out—Slavery must be seen and felt to be a huge crime, a system of lawless violence, before it can be abolished. In our Paper, upon the Platform, at home and abroad, we shall endeavor to bring Slavery before the People in this hateful light; and by so doing, shall

really be upholding the Radical Abolition Platform in the very ranks of the Republican Party.

4. Beyond all controversy, the commanding and vital issue with Slavery at the approaching Presidential election, is the extension or the limitation of Slavery. The malign purpose of extending, strengthening, and perpetuating Slavery, is the conclusion of the great mass of the slaveholders. The execution of this purpose upon Kansas, is plainly enough the business set down for the present by the friends of Slavery, North and South. And it cannot be denied that the election either of Buchanan or Fillmore would be the success of this malign purpose of the Slave Power. Other elements enter into the issue, such, for instance, as Northern or Southern ascendency of the Slave power in the Councils of the Nation, the continued humiliation of the Northern People, the reign of Terror at Washington, the crippling of the Anti-Slavery movement, and the security and preservation of Slavery from inward decay or outside destroying influences. The fact that Slaveholders had taken a united stand in favor of this measure, is, at least, an argument why Anti-Slavery men should take a stand to defeat them. The greatest triumphs of Slavery have been secured by the division of its enemies, one party insisting on attacking one point, and another class equally in earnest bending their energies in another direction. Were it in our power, the order of battle between Liberty and Slavery would be arranged differently. Anti-Slavery in our hands, at the ballot box, should be the aggressor; but it is not within our power, or within that of any other man, to control the order of events, or the circumstances which shape our course, and determine our conduct at particular times. All men will agree, that, generally speaking, the point attacked, is the point to be defended. The South has tendered to us the issue of Slavery Extension; and to meet the Slave Power here, is to rouse its most devilish animosity. It is to strike hardest, where the Slaveholders feel most keenly. The most powerful blow that could be given at that point would in our judgment, be the election to the Presidency and Vice Presidency of the Republic the Candidates of the Republican Party.

5. Briefly, then, we shall support Fremont and Dayton in the present crisis of the Anti-Slavery movement, because they are, by position, and from the very nature of the organization which supports them, the admitted and recognized antagonists of the Slave Power, of gag-law, and of all the hellish designs of the Slave Power to extend and fortify the accursed slave system. We shall support them because they are the most numerous Anti-Slavery Party, and, therefore, the most powerful to inflict a blow upon, and the most likely to achieve a valuable victory over, the Slave Oligarchy. There is not a trafficker in the bodies and souls of men, from Baltimore to New Orleans, that would not crack his bloody slave whip with fiendish delight over the defeat of Fremont and Dayton. Whereas, on the other hand, the

moral effect of the Radical Abolition vote, separated as it must be from the great Anti-Slavery body of the North, must, from the nature of the case, be very limited for good, and only powerful for mischief, where its effect would be to weaken the Republican Party. We shall support Fremont and Dayton, because there is no chance whatever in the present contest of electing better men than they. And we are the more reconciled to accepting them, by the fact that they are surrounded by a Party of progressive men. Take them, therefore, not merely for what they are, but for what we have good reason to believe they will become when they have lived for a time in the element of Anti-Slavery discussion. We shall support them by pen, by speech, by vote, because it is by no means certain that they can succeed in this State against the powerful combinations opposed to them without the support of the full and complete Abolition vote. Bitter indeed, would be the reproach, and deep and pointed would be the regret, if, through the Radical Abolitionists, victory should perch on the bloody standard of Slave Rule, as would be the case if Fremont and Dayton were defeated, and Buchanan and Breckenridge elected. For one, we are not disposed to incur this reproach, nor to experience this regret, and shall, therefore, vote for Fremont and Dayton. In supporting them, we neither dishonor our Principles nor lessen our means of securing their adoption and active application. We can reach the ears and heart of as great a number within the ranks of the Republican Party as we could possibly do by remaining outside of those ranks. We know of no law applicable to the progress and promulgation of Radical Abolition Principles which would act less favorably towards our Principles inside the Party, than outside of it.

6. Another reason for supporting the Republican Party at the ballot-box and thus supporting the Anti-Slavery vote as a unit, is, that such action conforms exactly to the facts of our existing relations as citizens. There is now, evidently, but one great question of widespread and of all-commanding national interest; and that question is Freedom or Slavery. In reality, there can be but two Parties to this question; and for ourselves, we wish it to be with the natural division for Freedom, in form, as well as in fact.

7. It seems to us both the dictate of good morals and true wisdom, that if we cannot abolish Slavery in all the States by our votes at the approaching election, we ought, if we can, keep Slavery out of Kansas by our vote. To pursue any other policy is to abandon at present, practical advantage to Freedom in an assertion of more comprehensive claims, right enough in themselves, but which reason and fact assure us can only be attained by votes in the future, when the public mind shall have been educated up to those claims. We are quite well aware that to the foregoing, objections of apparent weight may be urged by those for whose conscientious convictions we cherish the profoundest respect. And although we do not propose to anticipate objections, but intend to meet them as they shall be presented in

the progress of the canvass, we will mention and reply to one. Most plainly the greatest difficulty to be met with by a Radical Abolitionist in supporting Fremont and Dayton, is the fact that these Candidates have not declared and do not declare any purpose to abolish Slavery by legislation, in the States. They neither entertain nor declare any such purpose, and in this they are far from occupying the high Anti-Slavery position of the Radical Abolition Society. But let us not be unreasonable or impatient with the Republican Party. In considering this defect in the Anti-Slavery character and creed of the Republican Candidates, it should be borne in mind that they stand now in respect to this doctrine precisely where the Liberal Party stood ten years ago. The Right and duty of the Federal Government to abolish Slavery everywhere in the United States, is entirely true and deeply important; and yet, it must be confessed that this doctrine has been made appreciable but to a few minds, the dwellers in the mountain peaks of the moral world, who catch the first beams of morning, long before the slumberers in the valleys awake from their dreams. This new doctrine, we think, may very properly be left to take its turn in the arena of discussion. Time and argument will do more for its progress, and its final adoption by the people, than can be done for it in the present crisis, by the few votes of the isolated Radical Abolitionists. In further extenuation or apology, it may be very properly urged, that while the Republican Party has not at this point adopted the Abolition creed, it has laid down principles and promulgated doctrines, which in their application, directly tend to the Abolition of Slavery in the States. But the conclusive answer to all who object upon this ground is the indisputable Truth, that neither in Religion nor Morals, can a man be justified in refusing to assist his fellow-men to accomplish a possible good thing, simply because his fellows refuse to accomplish some other good things which they deem impossible. Most assuredly, that theory cannot be a sound one which would prevent us from voting with men for the Abolition of Slavery in Maryland simply because our companions refuse to include Virginia. In such a case, the path of duty is plainly this; go with your fellow-citizens for the Abolition of Slavery in Maryland when they are ready to go for that measure, and do all you can, meanwhile, to bring them to whatever work of righteousness may remain and which has become manifest to your clearer vision. Such, then, is the conclusion forced upon us by the philosophy of the facts of our condition as a nation. A great crime against Freedom and Civilization is about to be perpetrated. The Slave Power is resolved to plant the deadly Upas, Slavery, in the virgin soil of Kansas. This great evil may be averted, and all the likelihoods of the case, the election of John C. Fremont and William L. Dayton, will be instrumental in averting it. Their election will prevent the establishment of Slavery in Kansas, overthrow Slave Rule in the Republic, protect Liberty of Speech and of the Press, give ascendency to Northern civilization over the bludgeon and blood-hound civilization of the South, and the mark of national condemnation on Slavery, scourge doughfaces from place and from power, and inaugurate a higher and purer standard of Politics and Government. Therefore, we go for Fremont and Dayton.

34
THE FUTURE OF
THE COLORED RACE
May 1866

IT IS QUITE IMPOSSIBLE, at this early date, to say with any decided emphasis what the future of the colored people will be. Speculations of that kind, thus far, have only reflected the mental bias and education of the many who have essayed to solve the problem.

We all know what the Negro has been as a slave. In this relation we have his experience of two hundred and fifty years before us, and can easily know the character and qualities he has developed and exhibited during this long and severe ordeal. In his new relation to his environment, we see him only in the twilight of twenty years of semi-freedom; for he has scarcely been free long enough to outgrow the marks of the lash on his back and the fetters on his limbs. He stands before us, to-day, physically, a maimed and mutilated man. His mother was lashed to agony before the birth of her babe, and the bitter anguish of the mother is seen in the countenance of her offspring. Slavery has twisted his limbs, shattered his feet, deformed his body and distorted his features. He remains black, but no longer comely. Sleeping on the dirt floor of the slave cabin in infancy, cold on one side and warm on the other, a forced circulation of blood on the one side and chilled and retarded circulation on the other, it has come to pass that he has not the vertical bearing of a perfect man. His lack of symmetry, caused by no fault of his own, creates a resistance to his progress which cannot well be overestimated, and should be taken into account, when measuring his speed in the new race of life upon which he has now entered. As I have often said before, we should not measure the Negro from the heights which the white race has attained, but from the depths from which he has come. You will not find Burke, Grattan, Curran and O'Connell among the oppressed and famished poor of the famine-stricken districts of Ireland. Such men come of comfortable antecedents and sound parents.

Laying aside all prejudice in favor of or against race, looking at the Negro as politically and socially related to the American people generally, and measuring the forces arrayed against him, I do not see how he can survive and flourish in this country as a distinct and separate race, nor do I see how he can be removed from the country either by annihilation or expatriation.

Sometimes I have feared that, in some wild paroxysm of rage, the white race, forgetful of the claims of humanity and the precepts of the Christian religion, will proceed to slaughter the Negro in wholesale, as some of that race have attempted to slaughter Chinamen, and as it has been done in detail in some districts of the Southern States. The grounds of this fear, however, have in some measure decreased since the Negro has largely disappeared from the arena of Southern politics, and has betaken himself to industrial pursuits and the acquisition of wealth and education, though even here, if over-prosperous, he is likely to excite a dangerous antagonism; for the white people do not easily tolerate the presence among them of a race more prosperous than themselves. The Negro as a poor ignorant creature does not contradict the race pride of the white race. He is more a source of amusement to that race than an object of resentment. Malignant resistance is augmented as he approaches the plane occupied by the white race, and yet I think that that resistance will gradually yield to the pressure of wealth, education, and high character.

My strongest conviction as to the future of the Negro therefore is, that he will not be expatriated nor annihilated, nor will he forever remain a separate and distinct race from the people around him, but that he will be absorbed, assimilated, and will only appear finally, as the Phœnicians now appear on the shores of the Shannon, in the features of a blended race. I cannot give at length my reasons for this conclusion, and perhaps the reader may think that the wish is father to the thought, and may in his wrath denounce my conclusion as utterly impossible. To such I would say, tarry a little, and look at the facts. Two hundred years ago there were two distinct and separate streams of human life running through this country. They stood at opposite extremes of ethnological classification: all black on the one side, all white on the other. Now, between these two extremes, an intermediate race has arisen, which is neither white nor black, neither Caucasian nor Ethiopian, and this intermediate race is constantly increasing. I know it is said that marital alliance between these races is unnatural, abhorrent and impossible; but exclamations of this kind only shake the air. They prove nothing against a stubborn fact like that which confronts us daily and which is open to the observation of all. If this blending of the two races were impossible we should not have at least one-fourth of our colored population composed of persons of mixed blood, ranging all the way from a dark-brown color to the point where there is no visible admixture. Besides, it is obvious to common sense that there is no need of the passage of laws, or the adoption of other devices, to prevent what is in itself impossible.

Of course this result will not be reached by any hurried or forced process. It will not arise out of any theory of the wisdom of such blending of the two races. If it comes at all, it will come without shock or noise or violence of any kind, and only in the fullness of time, and it will be so adjusted to surrounding conditions as hardly to be observed. I would not be understood as advocating intermarriage between the two races. I am not a propagandist, but a prophet. I do not say that what I say *should* come to pass, but what I think is likely to come to pass, and what is inevitable. While I would not be understood as advocating the desirability of such a result, I would not be understood as deprecating it. Races and varieties of the human family appear and disappear, but humanity remains and will remain forever. The American people will one day be truer to this idea than now, and will say with Scotia's inspired son:

> "A man's a man for a' that."

When that day shall come, they will not pervert and sin against the verity of language as they now do by calling a man of mixed blood, a Negro; they will tell the truth. It is only prejudice against the Negro which calls everyone, however nearly connected with the white race, and however remotely connected with the Negro race, a Negro. The motive is not a desire to elevate the Negro, but to humiliate and degrade those of mixed blood; not a desire to bring the Negro up, but to cast the mulatto and the quadroon down by forcing him below an arbitrary and hated color line. Men of mixed blood in this country apply the name *"Negro"* to themselves, not because it is a correct ethnological description, but to seem especially devoted to the black side of their parentage. Hence in some cases they are more noisily opposed to the conclusion to which I have come, than either the white or the honestly black race. The opposition to amalgamation, of which we hear so much on the part of colored people, is for most part the merest affectation, and will never form an impassable barrier to the union of the two varieties.

35

THE EVENING STAR ON
SOCIAL EQUALITY
December 19, 1872

T HE FACT OF COLORED LADIES AND GENTLEMEN sitting in a public restaurant enjoying ice-cream and lemonade where white ladies and gentlemen are seated for the purpose of enjoying the above delicacies constitutes, in the profound wisdom of the *Evening Star* of this city, social equality. The occasion to which the *Star* refers as the time of the attempted forcing of social equality by colored gentlemen of this city was when a gentlemanly clerk of the Freedman's Bank entered Freund's restaurant on Pennsylvania avenue and politely asked to be served. Had the gentleman and his friends been accommodated they would have taken a table precisely as white gentlemen and ladies in company would have done, and whatever of social equality there might have been it would have been so far as this gentleman and party were concerned at their own table, and in no way that we conceive of could their decent enjoyment of refreshments called for interfere with the decent enjoyment of refreshments by others seated at different tables. There would, in all likelihood, have been no communication between the gentleman and his friends with other persons in the room if not acquainted with each other and sustaining social relations to each other. The *Star* is unjust when it charges colored persons with attempting to force social equality because they choose to eat ice-cream and go the places where it is to be found for sale. In our opinion it was the ice-cream the colored gentlemen desired and not the association with white persons, who often have no other recommendation for their toleration in respectable saloons than the whiteness of their skins. We have yet to hear of white persons of doubtful character being refused accommodation in any of our public restaurants where often the purest and best are jostled by the vile and dissipated. Will the *Star* contend that such meetings in a public restaurant constitute social equality?

The *Star* says: "Now it is well enough to say just here that this particular attempt to enforce social equality meets with very little favor from the best colored people here." The editor of the *Star* must enjoy higher social relations with colored people than we do, as we have never been able to penetrate that circle of "best colored people here" who look upon colored ladies and gentlemen receiving the treatment due respectable people with very little favor. The thrifty, industrious, educated, and thinking colored people with whom we meet are a unit in the desire to be treated exactly as all other respectable and decent people are treated, believing that color is no criterion of gentility. All that anybody has a right to demand from patrons of a restaurant is that they be decent, the color is no just excuse for refusing to serve a decent person. The trouble with the *Star* editor and those with whom he is in sympathy, is that the colored gentlemen who entered Freund's were gentlemen; had they been there in a menial capacity the noses of the white, fastidious color aristocrats would have maintained their wonted level. We firmly believe that the *Star's* definition of social equality will not stand the test of reason.

36
ORATION IN MEMORY OF
ABRAHAM LINCOLN
April 14, 1876

I WARMLY CONGRATULATE YOU upon the highly interesting object which has caused you to assemble in such numbers and spirit as you have today. This occasion is in some respects remarkable. Wise and thoughtful men of our race, who shall come after us, and study the lesson of our history in the United States; who shall survey the long and dreary spaces over which we have traveled; who shall count the links in the great chain of events by which we have reached our present position, will make a note of this occasion; they will think of it and speak of it with a sense of manly pride and complacency.

I congratulate you, also, upon the very favorable circumstances in which we meet to-day. They are high, inspiring, and uncommon. They lend grace, glory, and significance to the object for which we have met. Nowhere else in this great country, with its uncounted towns and cities, unlimited wealth, and immeasurable territory extending from sea to sea, could conditions be found more favorable to the success of this occasion than here.

We stand to-day at the national centre to perform something like a national act—an act which is to go into history; and we are here where every pulsation of the national heart can be heard, felt, and reciprocated. A thousand wires, fed with thought and winged with lightning, put us in instantaneous communication with the loyal and true men all over this country.

Few facts could better illustrate the vast and wonderful change which has taken place in our condition as a people than the fact of our assembling here for the purpose we have to-day. Harmless, beautiful, proper, and praiseworthy as this demonstration is, I cannot forget that no such demonstration would have been tolerated here twenty years ago. The spirit of slavery and barbarism, which still lingers to blight and destroy in some dark and distant parts of our country, would have made our assembling here the signal and excuse for opening upon us all the flood-gates of wrath and violence. That we are here in peace to-day is a compliment and a credit to American civilization, and a prophecy of still greater national enlightenment and progress in the future. I refer to the past not in malice, for this is no day for malice; but simply to place more distinctly in front the gratifying and glorious change which has come both to our white fellow-citizens and ourselves, and to congratulate all upon the contrast between now and then; the new dispensation of freedom with its thousand blessings to both races, and the old dispensation of slavery with its ten thousand evils to both races—white and black. In view, then, of the past, the present, and the future, with the long and dark history of our bondage behind us, and with liberty, progress, and enlightenment before us, I again congratulate you upon this auspicious day and hour.

Friends and fellow-citizens, the story of our presence here is soon and easily told. We are here in the District of Columbia, here in the city of Washington, the most luminous point of American territory; a city recently transformed and made beautiful in its body and in its spirit; we are here in the place where the ablest and best men of the country are sent to devise the policy, enact the laws, and shape the destiny of the Republic; we are here, with the stately pillars and majestic dome of the Capitol of the nation looking down upon us; we are here, with the broad earth freshly adorned with the foliage and flowers of spring for our church, and all races, colors, and conditions of men for our congregation—in a word, we are here to express, as best we may, by appropriate forms and ceremonies, our grateful sense of the vast, high, and preeminent services rendered to ourselves, to our race, to our country, and to the whole world by Abraham Lincoln.

The sentiment that brings us here to-day is one of the noblest that can stir and thrill the human heart. It has crowned and made glorious the high places of all civilized nations with the grandest and most enduring works of art, designed to illustrate the characters and perpetuate the memories of great public men. It is the sentiment which from year to year adorns with fragrant and beautiful flowers the graves of our loyal, brave, and patriotic soldiers who fell in defence of the Union and liberty. It is the sentiment of gratitude and appreciation, which often, in the presence of many who hear me, has filled yonder heights of Arlington with the eloquence of eulogy and the sublime enthusiasm of poetry and song; a sentiment which can never die while the Republic lives.

For the first time in the history of our people, and in the history of the whole American people, we join in this high worship, and march conspicuously in the line of this time-honored custom. First things are always interesting, and this is one of our first things. It is the first time that, in this form and manner, we have sought to do honor to an American great man, however deserving and illustrious. I commend the fact to notice; let it be told in every part of the Republic; let men of all parties and opinions hear it; let those who despise us, not less than those who respect us, know that now and here, in the spirit of liberty, loyalty, and gratitude, let it be known everywhere, and by everybody who takes an interest in human progress and in the amelioration of the condition of mankind, that, in the presence and with the approval of the members of the American House of Representatives, reflecting the general sentiment of the country; that in the presence of that august body, the American Senate, representing the highest intelligence and the calmest judgment of the country; in the presence of the Supreme Court and Chief-Justice of the United States, to whose decisions we all patriotically bow; in the presence and under the steady eye of the honored and trusted President of the United States, with the members of his wise and patriotic Cabinet, we, the colored people, newly emancipated and rejoicing in our blood-bought freedom, near the close of the first century in the life of this Republic, have now and here unveiled, set apart, and dedicated a monument of enduring granite and bronze, in every line, feature, and figure of which the men of this generation may read, and those of aftercoming generations may read, something of the exalted character and great works of Abraham Lincoln, the first martyr President of the United States.

Fellow-citizens, in what we have said and done to-day, and in what we may say and do hereafter, we disclaim everything like arrogance and assumption. We claim for ourselves no superior devotion to the character, history, and memory of the illustrious name whose monument we have here dedicated to-day. We fully comprehend the relation of Abraham Lincoln both to ourselves and to the white people of the United States. Truth is proper and beautiful at all times and in all places, and it is never more proper and beautiful in any case than when speaking of a great public man whose example is likely to be commended for honor and imitation long after his departure to the solemn shades, the silent continents of eternity. It must be admitted, truth compels me to admit, even here in the presence of the monument we have erected to his memory, Abraham Lincoln was not, in the fullest sense of the word, either our man or our model. In his interests, in his associations, in his habits of thought, and in his prejudices, he was a white man.

He was pre-eminently the white man's President, entirely devoted to the welfare of white men. He was ready and willing at any time during the first years of his administration to deny, postpone, and sacrifice the rights of humanity in the colored people to promote the welfare of the white people of this country. In all his education and feeling he was an American of the Americans. He came into the Presidential chair upon one principle alone, namely, opposition to the extension of slavery. His arguments in further- ance of this policy had their motive and mainspring in his patriotic devotion to the interests of his own race. To protect, defend, and perpetuate slavery in the states where it existed Abraham Lincoln was not less ready than any other President to draw the sword of the nation. He was ready to execute all the supposed guarantees of the United States Constitution in favor of the slave system anywhere inside the slave States. He was willing to pursue, recapture, and send back the fugitive slave to his master, and to suppress a slave rising for liberty, though his guilty master were already in arms against the Government. The race to which we belong were not the special objects of his consideration. Knowing this, I concede to you, my white fellow-citizens, a pre-eminence in this worship at once full and supreme. First, midst, and last, you and yours were the objects of his deepest affec- tion and his most earnest solicitude. You are the children of Abraham Lincoln. We are at best only his step-children; children by adoption, chil- dren by force of circumstances and necessity. To you it especially belongs to sound his praises, to preserve and perpetuate his memory, to multiply his statues, to hang his pictures high upon your walls, and commend his example, for to you he was a great and glorious friend and benefactor. Instead of supplanting you at his altar, we would exhort you to build high his monuments; let them be of the most costly material, of the most cun- ning workmanship; let their forms be symmetrical, beautiful, and perfect; let their bases be upon solid rocks, and their summits lean against the unchanging blue, overhanging sky, and let them endure forever! But while in the abundance of your wealth, and in the fullness of your just and patriotic devotion, you do all this, we entreat you to despise not the humble offering we this day unveil to view; for while Abraham Lincoln saved for you a country, he delivered us from a bondage, according to Jefferson, one hour of which was worse than ages of the oppression your fathers rose in rebellion to oppose.

Fellow-citizens, ours is no new-born zeal and devotion—merely a thing of this moment. The name of Abraham Lincoln was near and dear to our hearts in the darkest and most perilous hours of the Republic. We were no more ashamed of him when shrouded in clouds of darkness, of doubt, and defeat than when we saw him crowned with victory, honor, and glory. Our faith in him was often taxed and strained to the uttermost, but it never failed. When he tarried long in the mountain; when he strangely told us that we were the cause of the war; when he still more strangely told us to leave the land in which we were born; when he refused to employ our arms in defence of the Union; when, after accepting our services as colored soldiers, he refused to retaliate our murder and torture as colored prisoners; when he told us he would save the Union if he could with slavery; when he revoked the Proclamation of Emancipation of General Fremont; when he refused to remove the popular commander of the Army of the Potomac, in the days of its inaction and defeat, who was more zealous in his efforts to protect slavery than to suppress rebellion; when we saw all this, and more, we were at times grieved, stunned, and greatly bewildered; but our hearts believed while they ached and bled. Nor was this, even at that time, a blind and unreasoning superstition. Despite the mist and haze that surrounded him; despite the tumult, the hurry, and confusion of the hour, we were able to take a comprehensive view of Abraham Lincoln, and to make reasonable allowance for the circumstances of his position. We saw him, measured him, and estimated him; not by stray utterances to injudicious and tedious delegations, who often tried his patience, not by isolated facts torn from their connection; not by any partial and imperfect glimpses, caught at inopportune moments; but by a broad survey, in the light of the stern logic of great events, and in view of that divinity which shapes our ends, rough hew them how we will, we came to the conclusion that the hour and the man of our redemption had somehow met in the person of Abraham Lincoln. It mattered little to us what language he might employ on special occasions; it mattered little to us, when we fully knew him, whether he was swift or slow in his movements; it was enough for us that Abraham Lincoln was at the head of a great movement, and was in living and earnest sympathy with that movement, which, in the nature of things, must go on until slavery should be utterly and forever abolished in the United States.

When, therefore, it shall be asked what we have to do with the memory of Abraham Lincoln, or what Abraham Lincoln had to do with us, the answer is ready, full, and complete. Though he loved Caesar less than Rome, though the Union was more to him than our freedom or our future, under his wise and beneficent rule we saw ourselves gradually lifted from the depths of slavery to the heights of liberty and manhood; under his wise and beneficent rule, and by measures approved and vigorously pressed by him, we saw that the handwriting of ages, in the form of prejudice and proscription, was rapidly fading away from the face of our whole country; under his rule, and in due time, about as soon after all as the country could tolerate the strange spectacle, we saw our brave sons and brothers laying off the rags of bondage, and being clothed all over in the blue uniforms of the soldiers of the United States; under his rule we saw two hundred thousand of our dark and dusky people responding to the call of Abraham Lincoln, and with muskets on their shoulders, and eagles on their buttons, timing their high footsteps to liberty and union under the national flag; under his rule we saw the independence of the black republic of Hayti, the special object of slaveholding aversion and horror, fully recognized, and her minister, a colored gentleman, duly received here in the city of Washington; under his rule we saw the internal slave-trade, which so long disgraced the nation, abolished, and slavery abolished in the District of Columbia; under his rule we saw for the first time the law enforced against the foreign slave-trade, and the first slave-trader hanged like any other pirate or murderer; under his rule, assisted by the greatest captain of our age, and his inspiration, we saw the Confederate States, based upon the idea that our race must be slaves, and slaves forever, battered to pieces and scattered to the four winds; under his rule, and in the fullness of time, we saw Abraham Lincoln, after giving the slaveholders three months' grace in which to save their hateful slave system, penning the immortal paper, which, though special in its language, was general in its principles and effect, making slavery forever impossible in the United States. Though we waited long, we saw all this and more.

Can any colored man, or any white man friendly to the freedom of all men, ever forget the night which followed the first day of January, 1863, when the world was to see if Abraham Lincoln would prove to be as good as his word? I shall never forget that memorable night, when in a distant city I waited and watched at a public meeting, with three thousand others not less anxious than myself, for the word of deliverance which we have heard read today. Nor shall I ever forget the outburst of joy and thanksgiving that rent the air when the lightning brought to us the emancipation proclamation. In that happy hour we forgot all delay, and forgot all tardiness, forgot that the President had bribed the rebels to lay down their arms by a promise to withhold the bolt which would smite the slave-system with destruction; and we were thenceforward willing to allow the President all the latitude of time, phraseology, and every honorable device that statesmanship might require for the achievement of a great and beneficent measure of liberty and progress.

Fellow-citizens, there is little necessity on this occasion to speak at length and critically of this great and good man, and of his high mission in the world. That ground has been fully occupied and completely covered both here and elsewhere. The whole field of fact and fancy has been gleaned and garnered. Any man can say things that are true of Abraham Lincoln, but no man can say anything that is new of Abraham Lincoln. His personal traits and public acts are better known to the American people than are those of any other man of his age. He was a mystery to no man who saw him and heard him. Though high in position, the humblest could approach him and feel at home in his presence. Though deep, he was transparent; though strong, he was gentle; though decided and pronounced in his convictions, he was tolerant towards those who differed from him, and patient under reproaches. Even those who only knew him through his public utterances obtained a tolerably clear idea of his character and his personality. The image of the man went out with his words, and those who read them, knew him.

I have said that President Lincoln was a white man, and shared the prejudices common to his countrymen towards the colored race. Looking back to his times and to the condition of his country, we are compelled to admit that this unfriendly feeling on his part may be safely set down as one element of his wonderful success in organizing the loyal American people for the tremendous conflict before them, and bringing them safely through the conflict. His great mission was to accomplish two things: first, to save his country from dismemberment and ruin; and, second, to free his country from the great crime of slavery. To do one or the other, or both, he must have the earnest sympathy and the powerful co-operation of his loyal fellow-countrymen. Without this primary and essential condition to success his efforts must have been vain and utterly fruitless. Had he put the abolition of slavery before the salvation of the Union, he would have inevitably driven from him a powerful class of the American people and rendered resistance to rebellion impossible. Viewed from the genuine abolition ground, Mr. Lincoln seemed tardy, cold, dull, and indifferent; but measuring him by the sentiment of his country, a sentiment he was bound as a statesman to consult, he was swift, zealous, radical, and determined.

Though Mr. Lincoln shared the prejudices of his white fellow-countrymen against the negro, it is hardly necessary to say that in his heart of hearts he loathed and hated slavery. The man who could say, "Fondly do we hope, fervently do we pray, that this mighty scourge of war shall soon pass away, yet if God wills it continue till all the wealth piled by two hundred years of bondage shall have been wasted, and each drop of blood drawn by the lash shall have been paid for by one drawn by the sword, the judgments of the Lord are true and righteous altogether," gives all needed proof of his feeling on the subject of slavery. He was willing, while the South was loyal, that it should have its pound of flesh, because he thought that it was so nominated in the bond; but farther than this no earthly power could make him go.

Fellow-citizens, whatever else in this world may be partial, unjust, and uncertain, time, time! is impartial, just, and certain in its action. In the realm of mind, as well as in the realm of matter, it is a great worker, and often works wonders. The honest and comprehensive statesman, clearly discerning the needs of his country, and earnestly endeavoring to do his whole duty, though covered and blistered with reproaches, may safely leave his course to the silent judgment of time. Few great public men have ever been the victims of fiercer denunciation than Abraham Lincoln was during his administration. He was often wounded in the house of his friends. Reproaches came thick and fast upon him from within and from without, and from opposite quarters. He was assailed by Abolitionists; he was assailed by slaveholders; he was assailed by the men who were for peace at any price; he was assailed by those who were for a more vigorous prosecution of the war; he was assailed for not making the war an abolition war; and he was bitterly assailed for making the war an abolition war.

But now behold the change: the judgment of the present hour is, that taking him for all in all, measuring the tremendous magnitude of the work before him, considering the necessary means to ends, and surveying the end from the beginning, infinite wisdom has seldom sent any man into the world better fitted for his mission than Abraham Lincoln. His birth, his training, and his natural endowments, both mental and physical, were strongly in his favor. Born and reared among the lowly, a stranger to wealth and luxury, compelled to grapple single-handed with the flintiest hardships of life, from tender youth to sturdy manhood, he grew strong in the manly and heroic qualities demanded by the great mission to which he was called by the votes of his countrymen. The hard condition of his early life, which would have depressed and broken down weaker men, only gave greater life, vigor, and buoyancy to the heroic spirit of Abraham Lincoln. He was ready for any kind and any quality of work. What other young men dreaded in the shape of toil, he took hold of with the utmost cheerfulness.

> A spade, a rake, a hoe,
> A pick-axe, or a bill;
> A hook to reap, a scythe to mow,
> A flail, or what you will.

All day long he could split heavy rails in the woods, and half the night long he could study his English Grammar by the uncertain flare and glare of the light made by a pine-knot. He was at home on the land with his axe, with his maul, with gluts, and his wedges; and he was equally at home on water, with his oars, with this poles, with his planks, and with his boat-hooks. And whether in his flat-boat on the Mississippi river, or at the fireside of his frontier cabin, he was a man of work. A son of toil himself, he was linked in brotherly sympathy with the sons of toil in every loyal part of the Republic. This very fact gave him tremendous power with the American people, and materially contributed not only to selecting him to the Presidency, but in sustaining his administration of the Government.

Upon his inauguration as President of the United States, an office, even where assumed under the most favorable conditions, fitted to tax and strain the largest abilities, Abraham Lincoln was met by a tremendous crisis. He was called upon not merely to administer the Government, but to decide, in the face of terrible odds, the fate of the Republic.

A formidable rebellion rose in his path before him; the Union was already practically dissolved; his country was torn and rent asunder at the centre. Hostile armies were already organized against the Republic, armed with the munitions of war which the Republic had provided for its own defence. The tremendous question for him to decide was whether his country should survive the crisis and flourish, or be dismembered and perish. His predecessor in office had already decided the question in favor of national dismemberment, by denying to it the right of self-defence and self-preservation—a right which belongs to the meanest insect.

Happily for the country, happily for you and for me, the judgment of James Buchanan, the patrician, was not the judgment of Abraham Lincoln, the plebeian. He brought his strong common sense, sharpened in the school of adversity, to bear upon the question. He did not hesitate, he did not doubt, he did not falter; but at once resolved that at whatever peril, at whatever cost, the union of the States should be preserved. A patriot himself, his faith was strong and unwavering in the patriotism of his countrymen. Timid men said before Mr. Lincoln's inauguration, that we had seen the last President of the United States. A voice in influential quarters said, "Let the Union slide." Some said that a Union maintained by the sword was worthless. Others said a rebellion of 8,000,000 cannot be suppressed; but in the midst of all this tumult and timidity, and against all this, Abraham Lincoln was clear in his duty, and had an oath in heaven. He calmly and bravely heard the voice of doubt and fear all around him; but he had an oath in heaven, and there was not power enough on the earth to make this honest boatman, backwoodsman, and broad-handed splitter of rails evade or violate that sacred oath. He had not been schooled in the ethics of slavery; his plain life had favored his love of truth. He had not been taught that treason and perjury were the proof of honor and honesty. His moral training was against his saying one thing when he meant another. The trust which Abraham Lincoln had in himself and in the people was surprising and grand, but it was also enlightened and well founded. He knew the American people better than they knew themselves, and his truth was based upon this knowledge.

Fellow-citizens, the fourteenth day of April, 1865, of which this is the eleventh anniversary, is now and will ever remain a memorable day in the annals of this Republic. It was on the evening of this day, while a fierce and sanguinary rebellion was in the last stages of its desolating power; while its armies were broken and scattered before the invincible armies of Grant and Sherman; while a great nation, torn and rent by war, was already beginning to raise to the skies loud anthems of joy at the dawn of peace, it was startled, amazed, and overwhelmed by the crowning crime of slavery—the assassination of Abraham Lincoln. It was a new crime, a pure act of malice. No purpose of the rebellion was to be served by it. It was the simple gratification of a hell-black spirit of revenge. But it has done good after all. It has filled the country with a deeper abhorrence of slavery and a deeper love for the great liberator.

Had Abraham Lincoln died from any of the numerous ills to which flesh is heir; had he reached that good old age of which his vigorous constitution and his temperate habits gave promise; had he been permitted to see the end of his great work; had the solemn curtain of death come down but gradually—we should still have been smitten with a heavy grief, and treasured his name lovingly. But dying as he did die, by the red hand of violence, killed, assassinated, taken off without warning, not because of personal hate—for no man who knew Abraham Lincoln could hate him—but because of his fidelity to union and liberty, he is doubly dear to us, and his memory will be precious forever.

Fellow-citizens, I end, as I began, with congratulations. We have done a good work for our race to-day. In doing honor to the memory of our friend and liberator, we have been doing highest honors to ourselves and these who come after us; we have been fastening ourselves to a name and fame imperishable and immortal; we have also been defending ourselves from a blighting scandal. When now it shall be said that the colored man is soulless, that he has no appreciation of benefits or benefactors; when the foul reproach of ingratitude is hurled at us, and it is attempted to scourge us beyond the range of human brotherhood, we may calmly point to the monument we have this day erected to the memory of Abraham Lincoln.

THE TEST OF LIBERAL DEMOCRACY

You have made yourself the Trustee for those in every country who seek to mend the evils of our condition by reasoned experiment within the framework of the existing social system. If you fail, rational change will be gravely prejudiced throughout the world, leaving orthodoxy and revolution to fight it out.

An Open Letter to President Roosevelt
by John Maynard Keynes
December 31, 1933

VII

OLIVER WENDELL HOLMES, JR.
(1841–1935)

OLIVER WENDELL HOLMES, JR., was the son of Oliver Wendell Holmes, the poet and essayist. His book *The Common Law* (1881) led to his appointment in 1882 to the faculty of Harvard Law School, but he was not destined to be a professor, for later that year he was appointed to the Supreme Judicial Court of Massachusetts, on which he served from 1882 until 1902, the last three years as Chief Justice. In 1902 Theodore Roosevelt appointed him Associate Justice of the U.S. Supreme Court, in which position he served until his retirement in 1932.

The Supreme Court of the United States is notable for the long tenure of its members, as was intended by those who wrote the Constitution, and Holmes's service on it is among the longest. He sat for nearly 30 years. Of the 100 men who have been appointed to the Court, from Jay to Rehnquist, only 10 others have thus far sat so long. But his influence on the law was even greater than would have accrued from such long service. To the extent that such influence can be measured by popular acclaim, perhaps only one or two—Black, maybe Frankfurter—are his rivals. (Marshall, of course, is in a class by himself.) A great part of the praise which has been bestowed upon him is based on the assertion that he was not only a judge but a "philosopher," but the problematic character of that assertion is nowhere better seen than in the article written on him for the *Dictionary of American Biography* by his greatest admirer, and one of his possible rivals, Felix Frankfurter. In one place in that biography, Frankfurter argued that "at a time when judges boasted of a want of philosophy, Holmes realized that decisions are functions of some juristic philosophy." But a few pages later on we are told that Holmes "exhibited the judicial function at its purest," and the proof of this is that he had "reached the democratic result by the philosophic route of skepticism—by his disbelief in ultimate answers to social questions." Surely it is open to question whether or not deference to democracy deserves to be called "philosophy," whatever one may say about its constitutional or judicial virtues.

Holmes's popularity rests in large part on his judicial opinions and certain memorable phrases in them. In the first case in which the Supreme Court ruled on the scope of the First Amendment guarantee of free speech, Holmes wrote an opinion for a unanimous Court which affirmed the conviction of a man who had distributed an anticonscription circular to draftees during World War I. He said that "the character of every act depends upon the circumstances in which it is done," and, against the claim that the defendant's speech was protected by the First Amendment, that the "question in every case is whether the words used are used in such circumstances and are of such a nature as to create a clear and present danger that they will bring about the substantive evils that Congress has a right to prevent" (*Schenck* v. *United States,* 249 U.S. 47 [1919]). This reference to a "clear and present danger" was subsequently formulated as a kind of "test" or "doctrine." He relied on that "doctrine" in dissenting from the Court's affirmance of another conviction by a U.S. Court (*Abrams* v. *United States,* 250 U.S. 616 [1919]) and, by linking the First Amendment to the Fourteenth, in dissenting from an affirmance of a state court conviction. (*Gitlow* v. *New York*, 268 U.S. 652 [1925]).

When the Court reversed a New York conviction for employing someone in a bakery for more than 60 hours per week, on the basis of infringement of a claimed "liberty of contract" which was said to be a deprivation of due process of law as guaranteed by the Fourteenth Amendment, Holmes again dissented. He went so far as to say that a constitution (and, so, *the* Constitution) was "not intended to embody a particular economic theory, whether of paternalism and the organic relation of the citizen to the state or of *laissez faire*. It is made for people of fundamentally differing views . . ." (*Lochner* v. *New York,* 198 U.S. 45 [1905]). One need not join the Court majority in its support of the "liberty of contract" against all state regulatory efforts to question whether Holmes is correct in supposing that the Constitution is *utterly* without an economic dimension. While the Constitution surely tolerates differing views, does it not presuppose or demand *some* "fundamental" agreement?

In ringing words which even his most ardent supporters have been reluctant to quote since the experience of the Nazi regime in Germany, Holmes upheld the compulsory sterilization of an inmate of the Virginia State Colony for Epileptics and Feeble Minded for a nearly unanimous Court (only Mr. Justice Butler dissented, and he did so without writing an opinion). "It is better for all the world," said Holmes, "if instead of waiting to execute degenerate offspring for crime, or to let them starve for their imbecility, society can prevent those who are manifestly unfit from continuing their kind. The principle that sustains compulsory vaccination is broad enough to cover cutting the Fallopian tubes. Three generations of imbeciles are enough" (*Buck* v. *Bell,* 274 U.S. 200 [1927]).

Two public addresses and one brief article by Holmes are given here. On February 4, 1901, while Holmes presided over the Massachusetts Supreme Judicial Court, a motion was made to adjourn in honor of the 100th anniversary of the seating of John Marshall as Chief Justice of the United States. Holmes responded with remarks addressed even more to the importance of history, accident, and circumstance than to the importance of Marshall. In February of 1913, at a dinner of the Harvard Law School Association of New York, Holmes, then a Justice of the U.S. Supreme Court, presented a speech entitled "Law and the Court" in which he linked the development of law to general historical forces. His absolute disbelief in "absolutes" was demonstrated in a 1918 *Harvard Law Review* piece entitled "Natural Law," in which he raised questions about the nature and causes and the dignity of the law.

37

JOHN MARSHALL
February 4, 1901

A s we walk down Court Street in the midst of a jostling crowd, intent like us upon to-day and its affairs, our eyes are like to fall upon the small, dark building that stands at the head of State Street, and, like an ominous reef, divides the stream of business in its course to the gray cliffs that tower beyond. And, whoever we may be, we may chance to pause and forget our hurry for a moment, as we remember that the first waves that foretold the coming storm of the Revolution broke around that reef. But, if we are lawyers, our memories and our reverence grow more profound. In the Old State House, we remember, James Otis argued the case of the writs of assistance, and in that argument laid one of the foundations for American constitutional law. Just as that little building is not diminished, but rather is enhanced and glorified, by the vast structures which somehow it turns into a background, so the beginnings of our national life, whether in battle or in law, lose none of their greatness by contrast with all the mighty things of later date, beside which, by every law of number and measure, they ought to seem so small. To us who took part in the Civil War, the greatest battle of the Revolution seems little more than a reconnoissance in force, and Lexington and Concord were mere skirmishes that would not find mention in the newspapers. Yet veterans who have known battle on a modern scale, are not less aware of the spiritual significance of those little fights, I venture to say, than the enlightened children of commerce who tell us that soon war is to be no more.

If I were to think of John Marshall simply by number and measure in the abstract, I might hesitate in my superlatives, just as I should hesitate over the battle of the Brandywine if I thought of it apart from its place in the line of historic cause. But such thinking is empty in the same proportion that it is abstract. It is most idle to take a man apart from the circumstances which, in fact, were his. To be sure, it is easier in fancy to separate a person from his riches than from his character. But it is just as futile. Remove a square inch of mucous membrane, and the tenor will sing no more.

Remove a little cube from the brain, and the orator will be speechless; or another, and the brave, generous and profound spirit becomes a timid and querulous trifler. A great man represents a great ganglion in the nerves of society, or, to vary the figure, a strategic point in the campaign of history, and part of his greatness consists in his being *there*. I no more can separate John Marshall from the fortunate circumstance that the appointment of Chief Justice fell to John Adams, instead of to Jefferson a month later, and so gave it to a Federalist and loose constructionist to start the working of the Constitution, than I can separate the black line through which he sent his electric fire at Fort Wagner from Colonel Shaw. When we celebrate Marshall we celebrate at the same time and indivisibly the inevitable fact that the oneness of the nation and the supremacy of the national Constitution were declared to govern the dealings of man with man by the judgments and decrees of the most august of courts.

I do not mean, of course, that personal estimates are useless or teach us nothing. No doubt to-day there will be heard from able and competent persons such estimates of Marshall. But I will not trench upon their field of work. It would be out of place when I am called on only to express the answer to a motion addressed to the court and when many of those who are here are to listen this afternoon to the accomplished teacher who has had every occasion to make a personal study of the judge, and again this evening to a gentleman who shares by birth the traditions of the man. My own impressions are only those that I have gathered in the common course of legal education and practice. In them I am conscious, perhaps, of some little revolt from our purely local or national estimates, and of a wish to see things and people judged by more cosmopolitan standards. A man is bound to be parochial in his practice—to give his life, and if necessary his death, for the place where he has his roots. But his thinking should be cosmopolitan and detached. He should be able to criticise what he reveres and loves.

The Federalist, when I read it many years ago, seemed to me a truly original and wonderful production for the time. I do not trust even that judgment unrevised when I remember that *The Federalist* and its authors struck a distinguished English friend of mine as finite; and I should feel a greater doubt whether, after Hamilton and the Constitution itself, Marshall's work proved more than a strong intellect, a good style, personal ascendancy in his court, courage, justice and the convictions of his party. My keenest interest is excited, not by what are called great questions and great cases, but by little decisions which the common run of selectors would pass by because they did not deal with the Constitution or a telephone company, yet which have in them the germ of some wider theory, and therefore of some profound interstitial change in the very tissue of the law. The men whom I should be tempted to commemorate would be the originators of transforming thought. They often are half obscure, because what the world pays for is judgment, not the original mind.

But what I have said does not mean that I shall join in this celebration or in granting the motion before the court in any half-hearted way. Not only do I recur to what I said in the beginning, and remembering that you cannot separate a man from his place, remember also that there fell to Marshall perhaps the greatest place that ever was filled by a judge; but when I consider his might, his justice, and his wisdom, I do fully believe that if American law were to be represented by a single figure, sceptic and worshipper alike would agree without dispute that the figure could be one alone, and that one, John Marshall.

A few words more and I have done. We live by symbols, and what shall be symbolized by any image of the sight depends upon the mind of him who sees it. The setting aside of this day in honor of a great judge may stand to a Virginian for the glory of his glorious State; to a patriot for the fact that time has been on Marshall's side, and that the theory for which Hamilton argued, and he decided, and Webster spoke, and Grant fought, and Lincoln died, is now our corner-stone. To the more abstract but farther-reaching contemplation of the lawyer, it stands for the rise of a new body of jurisprudence, by which guiding principles are raised above the reach of statute and State, and judges are entrusted with a solemn and hitherto unheard-of authority and duty. To one who lives in what may seem to him a solitude of thought, this day—as it marks the triumph of a man whom some Presidents of his time bade carry out his judgments as he could—this day marks the fact that all thought is social, is on its way to action; that, to borrow the expression of a French writer, every idea tends to become first a catechism and then a code; and that according to its worth his unhelped meditation may one day mount a throne, and without armies, or even with them, may shoot across the world the electric despotism of an unresisted power. It is all a symbol, if you like, but so is the flag. The flag is but a bit of bunting to one who insists on prose. Yet, thanks to Marshall and to the men of his generation—and for this above all we celebrate him and them—its red is our lifeblood, its stars our world, its blue our heaven. It owns our land. At will it throws away our lives.

The motion of the bar is granted, and the court will now adjourn.

38

LAW AND THE COURT
February 15, 1913

V ANITY IS THE MOST PHILOSOPHICAL of those feelings that we are taught to despise. For vanity recognizes that if a man is in a minority of one we lock him up, and therefore longs for an assurance from others that one's work has not been in vain. If a man's ambition is the thirst for a power that comes not from office but from within, he never can be sure that any happiness is not a fool's paradise—he never can be sure that he sits on that other bench reserved for the masters of those who know. Then too, at least until one draws near to seventy, one is less likely to hear the trumpets than the rolling fire of the front. I have passed that age, but I still am on the firing line, and it is only in rare moments like this that there comes a pause and for half an hour one feels a trembling hope. They are the rewards of a lifetime's work.

But let me turn to more palpable realities—to that other visible Court to which for ten now accomplished years it has been my opportunity to belong. We are very quiet there, but it is the quiet of a storm centre, as we all know. Science has taught the world scepticism and has made it legitimate to put everything to the test of proof. Many beautiful and noble reverences are impaired, but in these days no one can complain if any institution, system, or belief is called on to justify its continuance in life. Of course we are not excepted and have not escaped. Doubts are expressed that go to our very being. Not only are we told that when Marshall pronounced an Act of Congress unconstitutional he usurped a power that the Constitution did not give, but we are told that we are the representatives of a class—a tool of the money power. I get letters, not always anonymous, intimating that we are corrupt. Well, gentlemen, I admit that it makes my heart ache. It is very painful, when one spends all the energies of one's soul in trying to do good work, with no thought but that of solving a problem according to the rules by which one is bound, to know that many see sinister motives and would be glad of evidence that one was consciously bad. But we must take such things philosophically and try to see what we can learn from hatred and distrust and whether behind them there may not be some germ of inarticulate truth.

The attacks upon the Court are merely an expression of the unrest that seems to wonder vaguely whether law and order pay. When the ignorant are taught to doubt they do not know what they safely may believe. And it seems to me that at this time we need education in the obvious more than investigation of the obscure. I do not see so much immediate use in committees on the high cost of living and inquiries how far it is due to the increased production of gold, how far to the narrowing of cattle ranges and the growth of population, how far to the bugaboo, as I do in bringing home to people a few social and economic truths. Most men think dramatically, not quantitatively, a fact that the rich would be wise to remember more than they do. We are apt to contrast the palace with the hovel, the dinner at Sherry's with the working man's pail, and never ask how much or realize how little is withdrawn to make the prizes of success (subordinate prizes—since the only prize much cared for by the powerful is power. The prize of the general is not a bigger tent, but command). We are apt to think of ownership as a terminus, not as a gateway, and not to realize that except the tax levied for personal consumption large ownership means investment, and investment means the direction of labor towards the production of the greatest returns—returns that so far as they are great show by that very fact that they are consumed by the many, not alone by the few. If I may ride a hobby for an instant, I should say we need to think things instead of words—to drop ownership, money, etc., and to think of the stream of products; of wheat and cloth and railway travel. When we do, it is obvious that the many consume them; that they now as truly have substantially all there is, as if the title were in the United States; that the great body of property is socially administered now, and that the function of private ownership is to divine in advance the equilibrium of social desires—which socialism equally would have to divine, but which, under the illusion of self-seeking, is more poignantly and shrewdly foreseen.

I should like to see it brought home to the public that the question of fair prices is due to the fact that none of us can have as much as we want of all the things we want; that as less will be produced than the public wants, the question is how much of each product it will have and how much go without; that thus the final competition is between the objects of desire, and therefore between the producers of those objects; that when we oppose labor and capital, labor means the group that is selling its product and capital all the other groups that are buying it. The hated capitalist is simply the mediator, the prophet, the adjuster according to his divination of the future desire. If you could get that believed, the body of the people would have no doubt as to the worth of law.

That is my outside thought on the present discontents. As to the truth embodied in them, in part it cannot be helped. It cannot be helped, it is as it should be, that the law is behind the times. I told a labor leader once that what they asked was favor, and if a decision was against them they called it wicked. The same might be said of their opponents. It means that the law is growing. As law embodies beliefs that have triumphed in the battle of ideas and then have translated themselves into action, while there still is doubt, while opposite convictions still keep a battle front against each other, the time for law has not come; the notion destined to prevail is not yet entitled to the field. It is a misfortune if a judge reads his conscious or unconscious sympathy with one side or the other prematurely into the law, and forgets that what seem to him to be first principles are believed by half his fellow men to be wrong. I think that we have suffered from this misfortune, in State courts at least, and that this is another and very important truth to be extracted from the popular discontent. When twenty years ago a vague terror went over the earth and the word socialism began to be heard, I thought and still think that fear was translated into doctrines that had no proper place in the Constitution or the common law. Judges are apt to be naif, simple-minded men, and they need something of Mephistopheles. We too need education in the obvious—to learn to transcend our own convictions and to leave room for much that we hold dear to be done away with short of revolution by the orderly change of law.

I have no belief in panaceas and almost none in sudden ruin. I believe with Montesquieu that if the chance of a battle—I may add, the passage of a law—has ruined a state, there was a general cause at work that made the state ready to perish by a single battle or a law. Hence I am not much interested one way or the other in the nostrums now so strenuously urged. I do not think the United States would come to an end if we lost our power to declare an Act of Congress void. I do think the Union would be imperiled if we could not make that declaration as to the laws of the several States. For one in my place sees how often a local policy prevails with those who are not trained to national views and how often action is taken that embodies what the Commerce Clause was meant to end. But I am not aware that there is any serious desire to limit the Court's power in this regard. For most of the things that properly can be called evils in the present state of the law I think the main remedy, as for the evils of public opinion, is for us to grow more civilized.

If I am right it will be a slow business for our people to reach rational views, assuming that we are allowed to work peaceably to that end. But as I grow older I grow calm. If I feel what are perhaps an old man's apprehensions, that competition from new races will cut deeper than working men's disputes and will test whether we can hang together and can fight; if I fear that we are running through the world's resources at a pace that we cannot keep; I do not lose my hopes. I do not pin my dreams for the future to my country or even to my race. I think it probable that civilization somehow will last as long as I care to look ahead—perhaps with smaller numbers, but perhaps also bred to greatness and splendor by science. I think it not improbable that man, like the grub that prepares a chamber for the winged thing it never has seen but is to be—that man may have cosmic destinies that he does not understand. And so beyond the vision of battling races and an impoverished earth I catch a dreaming glimpse of peace.

The other day my dream was pictured to my mind. It was evening. I was walking homeward on Pennsylvania Avenue near the Treasury, and as I looked beyond Sherman's Statue to the west the sky was aflame with scarlet and crimson from the setting sun. But, like the note of downfall in Wagner's opera, below the sky line there came from little globes the pallid discord of the electric lights. And I thought to myself the Götterdämmerung will end, and from those globes clustered like evil eggs will come the new masters of the sky. It is like the time in which we live. But then I remembered the faith that I partly have expressed, faith in a universe not measured by our fears, a universe that has thought and more than thought inside of it, and as I gazed, after the sunset and above the electric lights there shone the stars.

39
NATURAL LAW
August 1918

I T IS NOT ENOUGH for the knight of romance that you agree that his lady is a very nice girl—if you do not admit that she is the best that God ever made or will make, you must fight. There is in all men a demand for the superlative, so much so that the poor devil who has no other way of reaching it attains it by getting drunk. It seems to me that this demand is at the bottom of the philosopher's effort to prove that truth is absolute and of the jurist's search for criteria of universal validity which he collects under the head of natural law.

I used to say, when I was young, that truth was the majority vote of that nation that could lick all others. Certainly we may expect that the received opinion about the present war will depend a good deal upon which side wins (I hope with all my soul it will be mine), and I think that the statement was correct in so far as it implied that our test of truth is a reference to either a present or an imagined future majority in favor of our view. If, as I have suggested elsewhere, the truth may be defined as the system of my (intellectual) limitations, what gives it objectivity is the fact that I find my fellow man to a greater or less extent (never wholly) subject to the same *Can't Helps*. If I think that I am sitting at a table I find that the other persons present agree with me; so if I say that the sum of the angles of a triangle is equal to two right angles. If I am in a minority of one they send for a doctor or lock me up; and I am so far able to transcend the to me convincing testimony of my senses or my reason as to recognize that if I am alone probably something is wrong with my works.

Certitude is not the test of certainty. We have been cock-sure of many things that were not so. If I may quote myself again, property, friendship, and truth have a common root in time. One can not be wrenched from the rocky crevices into which one has grown for many years without feeling that one is attacked in one's life. What we most love and revere generally is determined by early associations. I love granite rocks and barberry bushes, no doubt because with them were my earliest joys that reach back through the past eternity of my life. But while one's experience thus makes certain preferences dogmatic for oneself, recognition of how they came to be so leaves one able to see that others, poor souls, may be equally dogmatic about something else. And this again means scepticism. Not that one's belief or love does not remain. Not that we would not fight and die for it if important—we all, whether we know it or not, are fighting to make the kind of a world that we should like—but that we have learned to recognize that others will fight and die to make a different world, with equal sincerity or belief. Deep-seated preferences can not be argued about—you can not argue a man into liking a glass of beer—and therefore, when differences are sufficiently far reaching, we try to kill the other man rather than let him have his way. But that is perfectly consistent with admitting that, so far as appears, his grounds are just as good as ours.

The jurists who believe in natural law seem to me to be in that naïve state of mind that accepts what has been familiar and accepted by them and their neighbors as something that must be accepted by all men everywhere. No doubt it is true that, so far as we can see ahead, some arrangements and the rudiments of familiar institutions seem to be necessary elements in any society that may spring from our own and that would seem to us to be civilized—some form of permanent association between the sexes—some residue of property individually owned—some mode of binding oneself to specified future conduct—at the bottom of all, some protection for the person. But without speculating whether a group is imaginable in which all but the last of these might disappear and the last be subject to qualifications that most of us would abhor, the question remains as to the *Ought* of natural law.

It is true that beliefs and wishes have a transcendental basis in the sense that their foundation is arbitrary. You can not help entertaining and feeling them, and there is an end of it. As an arbitrary fact people wish to live, and we say with various degrees of certainty that they can do so only on certain conditions. To do it they must eat and drink. That necessity is absolute. It is a necessity of less degree but practically general that they should live in society. If they live in society, so far as we can see, there are further conditions. Reason working on experience does tell us, no doubt, that if our wish to live continues, we can do it only on those terms. But that seems to me the whole of the matter. I see no *a priori* duty to live with others and in that way, but simply a statement of what I must do if I wish to remain alive. If I do live with others they tell me that I must do and abstain from doing various things or they will put the screws on to me. I believe that they will, and being of the same mind as to their conduct I not only accept the rules but come in time to accept them with sympathy and emotional affirmation and begin to talk about duties and rights. But for legal purposes a right is only the hypostasis of a prophecy—the imagination of a substance supporting the fact that the public force will be brought to bear upon those who do things said to contravene it—just as we talk of the force of gravitation accounting for the conduct of bodies in space. One phrase adds no more than the other to what we know without it. No doubt behind these legal rights is the fighting will of the subject to maintain them, and the spread of his emotions to the general rules by which they are maintained; but that does not seem to me the same thing as the supposed *a priori* discernment of a duty or the assertion of a preëxisting right. A dog will fight for his bone.

The most fundamental of the supposed preëxisting rights—the right to life—is sacrificed without a scruple not only in war, but whenever the interest of society, that is, of the predominant power in the community, is thought to demand it. Whether that interest is the interest of mankind in the long run no one can tell, and as, in any event, to those who do not think with Kant and Hegel it is only an interest, the sanctity disappears. I remember a very tender-hearted judge being of opinion that closing a hatch to stop a fire and the destruction of a cargo was justified even if it was known that doing so would stifle a man below. It is idle to illustrate further, because to those who agree with me I am uttering commonplaces and to those who disagree I am ignoring the necessary foundations of thought. The *a priori* men generally call the dissentients superficial. But I do agree with them in believing that one's attitude on these matters is closely connected with one's general attitude toward the universe. Proximately, as has been suggested, it is determined largely by early associations and temperament, coupled with the desire to have an absolute guide. Men to a great extent believe what they want to—although I see in that no basis for a philosophy that tells us what we should want to want.

Now when we come to our attitude toward the universe I do not see any rational ground for demanding the superlative—for being dissatisfied unless we are assured that our truth is cosmic truth, if there is such a thing—that the ultimates of a little creature on this little earth are the last word of the unimaginable whole. If a man sees no reason for believing that significance, consciousness and ideals are more than marks of the finite, that does not justify what has been familiar in French sceptics; getting upon a pedestal and professing to look with haughty scorn upon a world in ruins. The real conclusion is that the part can not swallow the whole—that our categories are not, or may not be, adequate to formulate what we cannot know. If we believe that we come out of the universe, not it out of us, we must admit that we do not know what we are talking about when we speak of brute matter. We do know that a certain complex of energies can wag its tail and another can make syllogisms. These are among the powers of the unknown, and if, as may be, it has still greater powers that we can not understand, as Fabre in his studies of instinct would have us believe, studies that gave Bergson one of the strongest strands for his philosophy and enabled Maeterlinck to make us fancy for a moment that we heard a clang from behind phenomena—if this be true, why should we not be content? Why should we employ the energy that is furnished to us by the cosmos to defy it and shake our fist at the sky? It seems to me silly.

That the universe has in it more than we understand, that the private soldiers have not been told the plan of campaign, or even that there is one, rather than some vaster unthinkable to which every predicate is an impertinence, has no bearing upon our conduct. We still shall fight—all of us because we want to live, some, at least, because we want to realize our spontaneity and prove our powers, for the joy of it, and we may leave to the unknown the supposed final valuation of that which in any event has value to us. It is enough for us that the universe has produced us and has within it, as less than it, all that we believe and love. If we think of our existence not as that of a little god outside, but as that of a ganglion within, we have the infinite behind us. It gives us our only but our adequate significance. A grain of sand has the same, but what competent person supposes that he understands a grain of sand? That is as much beyond our grasp as man. If our imagination is strong enough to accept the vision of ourselves as parts inseverable from the rest, and to extend our final interest beyond the boundary of our skins, it justifies the sacrifice even of our lives for ends outside of ourselves. The motive, to be sure, is the common wants and ideals that we find in man. Philosophy does not furnish motives, but it shows men that they are not fools for doing what they already want to do. It opens to the forlorn hopes on which we throw ourselves away, the vista of the farthest stretch of human thought, the chords of a harmony that breathes from the unknown.

VIII
WOODROW WILSON
(1856–1924)

WOODROW WILSON, 28th President of the United States, was the only political scientist to ever hold that office. He taught at Bryn Mawr College (1885–88), at Wesleyan University (1888–90), and at Princeton University (1890–1902), and published *Congressional Government* in 1885, *The Modern Democratic State* in 1885 (from which his "Address on the Nature of Democracy in the United States," presented before the Owl Club in Hartford, Connecticut, May 17, 1889, is drawn), *The State* in 1889, *Division and Reunion* in 1893, and *Constitutional Government in the United States* in 1908. After serving as president of Princeton University from 1902 to 1910, he was elected governor of New Jersey. This led to his nomination for the Presidency by the Democratic Party and his election to that office in 1912. From 1913 to 1915 Wilson and the Democratic-controlled Congress enacted what was called the "New Freedom" program, calling for tariff reduction, the establishment of the Federal Reserve System (the most important domestic achievement of his administration), the strengthening of antitrust legislation, the first federal child labor law, federal rural credits, and the eight-hour day for railroad workers. He was reelected in 1916: Although his campaign had looked to peace, an all-out German submarine campaign against American merchant shipping precipitated the entrance of the United States into World War I in April 1917.

Wilson undertook the task of articulating American peace aims as early as January 1917, even before America was drawn into the war. In an address to the Senate entitled "Peace without Victory," he posed the question: "Is the present war a struggle for a just and secure peace, or only for a new balance of power?" His answer was that instead of a new balance of power, there must be a community of power that would ensure an organized common peace. The peace aims must include: (1) a peace without victory, for victory would mean a peace forced upon the loser; (2) the equality of nations, with no difference recognized between large and small nations and powerful and weak ones; (3) the worldwide adoption of the principles of the Monroe Doctrine that held that no nation should seek to extend its sovereignty over any other nation or people, but each should be left free to determine its own way of development; (4) a radical reconsideration of many of the rules of international law in order to secure freedom of the seas; (5) limitations on naval and military armaments; and (6) the avoidance of entangling alliances which might draw nations into competitions of power. Moreover, he pledged America's willingness to participate in a postwar organization for the preservation of peace.

Wilson's "Peace without Victory" speech was meant more immediately for Europe than America. It had two closely related aims: to appeal to the masses of common people in the belligerent countries over the heads of their governments, and to lay the groundwork for actual peace negotiations. A noted Wilsonian scholar, Arthur Link, points out that it was the first time in history that an American President had made such a vigorous thrust into European affairs.

After the war ended in November 1918, Wilson went to the Paris Peace Conference to present his peace program. That program, stated most succinctly in his "Fourteen Points" address of January 1918, which was delivered to a joint session of Congress, specifically called for (1) an end to secret alliances, (2) a settlement of colonial claims, (3) restitution of Belgium, (4) return of Alsace-Lorraine to France, (5) autonomy for the subject peoples of the Austro-Hungarian and Ottoman empires, (6) nonintervention in the Russian civil war, and (7) establishment of a League of Nations, in addition to points made previously. Wilson presented three subsequent elaborations on his Fourteen Points: the Four Supplementary points of February 11, 1918, the Four Additional Points of July 4, 1918, and the Five Additional Points, presented in an address opening the Fourth Liberty Loan Campaign at New York City on September 27, 1918, which is given here.

Wilson's attempts to force Clemenceau and Lloyd George to accept his 14 points as the theoretical basis of the peace, saw only partial success in the Treaty of Versailles, but his presence at the peace conference was the main reason the treaty was not so harsh as the other Allied leaders would have liked. He managed to block most of the more extreme demands of his colleagues but made concessions on the matter of reparations in order to obtain approval of the plan for the League. He believed that the League would be the heart of a postwar peace structure and would provide the machinery through which defects in the peace settlement could gradually be remedied. He insisted that the Covenant of the League be made an integral part of the treaty and that the League be entrusted with the execution of the treaty. The United States Senate, however, on two separate occasions refused to consent to the ratification of the treaty. The treaty included the League of Nations. Thus the League, which Wilson had helped to bring into being was established in 1920 without the inclusion of the United States.

40

THE NATURE OF DEMOCRACY IN THE UNITED STATES
May 17, 1889

THERE IS ONE THOUGHT which must, I am sure, have been common to all serious minds during the past few weeks, namely, *That it is a long time since 1789,*—if time is to be measured by change. Everything apprises us of the fact that we are not the same nation now that we were then. And I suppose that in looking back to the time in which our government was formed you have gotten the same impression that has for some time been fixing itself upon my mind, and that is, that we started with sundry wrong ideas about ourselves. We thought ourselves rank democrats, whereas we were in fact only progressive Englishmen. Turn the leaves of that sage manual of constitutional interpretation and advocacy, the *Federalist,* and note the perverse tendency of its writers to refer to *Greece and Rome* for precedents,—that Greece and Rome which haunted all our earlier and even some of our more mature years. Recall, too, that familiar story of Daniel Webster which tells of his coming home exhausted from an interview with the first President-elect Harrison, whose Secretary of State he was to be, and explaining that he had been obliged in the course of the conference, which concerned the inaugural address about to be delivered, *to kill nine Roman consuls,* whom it had been the intention of the good conqueror of Tippecanoe publicly to take into office with him. The truth is that we long imagined ourselves related in some unexplained way to all ancient republicans. Strangely enough, too, we at the same time accepted the quite incompatible theory that we were related also to the French philosophical radicals. We claimed kinship with democrats everywhere—with all democrats.

We can now scarcely realize the atmosphere of those thoughts. We do not now often refer to the ancients or to the French for sanction of what we do. We have had abundant experience of our own by which to reckon.

"Hardly any fact in history," says Mr. Bagehot, writing about the middle of the century, "is so incredible as that forty and a few years ago England was ruled by Mr. Percival. It seems almost the same as being ruled by the *Record* newspaper" (Mr. Bagehot would now probably say the *Standard* newspaper). "He had the same poorness of thought, the same petty Conservatism, the same dark and narrow superstition." "The mere fact of such a premier being endured shows how deeply the whole national spirit and interest was absorbed in the contest with Napoleon, how little we understood the sort of man who should regulate its conduct,—'in the crisis of Europe,' as Sidney Smith said, 'he safely brought the *Curates' Salaries Improvement Bill* to a hearing'—and it still more shows the horror of all innovation which the recent events of French history had impressed on our wealthy and comfortable classes. They were afraid of catching revolution, as old women of catching cold. Sir Archibald Allison to this day holds that revolution is an infectious disease, beginning no one knows how, and going on no one knows where. There is but one rule of escape, explains the great historian, 'Stay still, don't move; do what you have been accustomed to do, and consult your grandmother on everything.' "

Almost equally incredible to us is the ardour of revolution that then filled the world—the fact that one of the rulers of the world's mind in that generation was *Rousseau,* the apostle of all that is fanciful, unreal, and misleading in politics. To be ruled by him was like taking an account of life from *Mr. Rider Haggard.* And yet there is still much sympathy in this timid world for the dull people who felt safe in the hands of Mr. Percival; and happily much sympathy still among those who can conceive ideals for those also who caught a generous elevation of spirit from the speculative enthusiasm of Rousseau.

Indeed, I think that you will agree with me that for us who stand in the dusty, matter-of-fact world of to-day there is even a touch of pathos in recollections of the ardour for democratic liberty that filled the air of Europe and America a century ago with such quickening influences. We may even catch ourselves regretting that the innoculations of experience have closed our systems against the infections of hopeful revolution.

> Bliss was it in that dawn to be alive,
> But to be young was very heaven!—oh times
> In which the meagre, stale, forbidding ways
> Of custom, law, and statute took at once
> The attraction of a country in romance!
> When Reason seemed the most to assert her rights,
> When most intent on making of herself
> A prime Enchantress—to assist the work
> Which then was going forward in her name!
> Not favoured spots alone, but the whole earth,
> *The beauty wore of promise,* that which sets
> (As at some moment might not be unfelt
> Among the bowers of paradise itself)
> The *budding* rose above the rose *full blown.*

Such was the inspiration which, not Wordsworth alone, but Coleridge also and many another generous spirit whom we love caught in that day of hope.

It is common to say, in explanation of our regret that that dawn and youth of democracy's day is past; that our principles are cooler now and more circumspect, with the coolness and circumspection of advanced years. It seems to some that as our sinews have hardened our enthusiasms have become tamer and more decorous: that as experience has grown idealism has declined.

But to speak thus is to speak with old self-deception as to the character of our politics. If we are suffering disappointment, it is the disappointment of an awakening: we were dreaming. For we never had any business harkening to Rousseau or consorting with Europe in revolutionary sentiment. Our Government, founded one hundred years ago, was no type of an experiment in advanced democracy, as we allowed Europe and even ourselves to suppose; it was simply an adaptation of English constitutional government. If we suffered Europe to study our institutions as instances in point touching experimentation in politics *she was the more deceived.* If we began the *first* century of our national existence under a similar impression ourselves, there is the greater reason why we should start out upon a *new* century of national life with accurate conceptions about our place in history. It is my modest purpose to-night to make such contribution as I may to this end. I shall, therefore, ask you to note:

(1) That there are certain influences astir in this century which make for democracy the world over, and that these influences owe their origin in part to the radical thought of the last century; but that it was not such forces that made us democratic, nor are we responsible for them.

(2) That, so far from owing our governments to these general influences, we began, not by carrying out any theory, but by simply carrying out a history, inventing nothing, only establishing a specialized species of English government. That we founded, not Democracy, but Constitutional government, in America.

(3) That the government which we set up thus in a quite normal manner has nevertheless *changed greatly* under our hands by reason both of growth and of the operation of the general democratic forces,—the European or rather world-wide democratic forces, of which I have spoken; and

(4) That the very *size* to which our governmental organism has attained, and more particularly this new connection of its character and destiny with the character and destiny of the common democratic forces of the age of steam and electricity have created new *problems of organization* which it behooves us to meet in such spirit and with such measures as I shall briefly indicate before closing. If you will vouchsafe me much kind patience, I will make such expedition as I may in this large undertaking.

First, then, for the forces which are bringing in democratic temper and method the world over. You familiarly know what these forces are, but it will be profitable to our thought to pass them once more in review. They are freedom of thought and the diffusion of enlightenment among the people. Steam and electricity have coöperated with systematic popular education to accomplish this diffusion. The progress of popular education and the progress of democracy have been inseparable. The publication of their great *Encyclopaedia* by Diderot and his associates in France in the last century was the sure sign of the change that was setting in. Learning was turning its face away from the studious few to the curious many. The intellectual movement of the modern time was emerging from the narrow courses of scholastic thought and beginning *to spread itself abroad* over the extended, if shallow, levels of the common mind. The serious forces of democracy will be found, upon analysis, to reside, not in the disturbing doctrines of eloquent revolutionary writers, not in the turbulent discontent of the pauperized and oppressed, but in the educational forces of the last hundred and forty years which have elevated the masses in many countries to a plane of understanding and of orderly, intelligent purpose more nearly on a level with the average man of the hitherto governing classes. The movements towards democracy which have mastered all the other political tendencies of our own day are not older than the middle of the last century: and that is just the age of the now ascendent movement towards systematic popular education.

Organized popular education is, after all, however, only *one* of the quick-ening influences which have been producing the general enlightenment which is everywhere becoming the promise of general liberty: or, rather, it is only part of a great whole vastly larger than itself. Schools are but sepa-rated seedbeds in which only the staple thoughts of the steady and stay-at-home people are prepared and nursed. Not much of the world, after all, goes to school in the school-house. But through the mighty influences of commerce and the press *the world itself has become a school.* The air is alive with the multitudinous voices of information. Steady trade-winds of intercommunication have sprung up which carry the seeds of education and enlightenment, wheresoever planted, to every quarter of the globe. No scrap of new thought can escape being borne away from its place of birth by these all-absorbing currents. No idea can be kept exclusively at home, but is taken up by the trader, the reporter, the traveller, the missionary, the explorer, and is *given to all the world,* in the newspaper, the novel, the memoir, the poem, the treatise, till every community may know, not only itself, but all the world as well for the small price of learning to read and keeping its ears open. All the world, so far as its news and its stronger thought are concerned, is fast being made every man's neighbour.

Carlyle unquestionably touched one of the greater truths concerning modern democracy when he declared it to be the result of *printing.* In the newspaper press a whole population is made critic of all human affairs: democracy is "virtually extant," and "democracy virtually extant will insist on becoming palpably extant." Looked at in the large, the newspaper press is a type of democracy, bringing all men without distinction under comment made by any man without distinction; every topic reduced to a common standard of news; everything noted and argued about by everybody. Noth-ing could give surer promise of popular power than the activity and alert-ness of thought which is made through such agencies to accompany the training of the public schools. The activity may often be misdirected or unwholesome, may sometimes be only feverish and mischievous, a grievous product of narrow information and hasty conclusion; but it is none the less a growing and potent activity. It at least marks the initial stages of effective thought. It makes men conscious of the existence and interest of affairs lying outside of the dull round of their own daily lives. It gives them nations, instead of neighborhoods, to look upon and think about. They catch glimpses of the international connexions of their trades, of the uni-versal application of law, of the endless variety of life, of diversities of race, of a world teeming with men like themselves and yet full of strange cus-toms, puzzled by dim omens, stained by crime, ringing with voices familiar and unfamiliar.

And all this a man can get nowadays without stirring from home, by merely spelling out the print that covers every piece of paper about him. If men throw themselves from any reason into the swift and easy currents of travel, they find themselves brought daily face to face with persons native of every clime, with practices suggestive of whole histories, with a thousand things which challenge curiosity to satisfy itself, with enquiries which enlarge knowledge of life and shake one imperatively loose from old preconceptions.

These are the forces which have established the drift towards democracy. When all sources of information are accessible to all men alike, when the world's thought and the world's news are scattered broadcast where the poorest may find them, the nondemocratic forms of government find life a desperate venture. Exclusive privilege needs privacy, but cannot have it. Kingship of the elder patterns needs sanctity, but can find it nowhere obtainable in a world of news items and satisfied curiosity. The many will no longer receive submissively the thought of a ruling few, but insist upon having opinions of their own. The reaches of public opinion have been infinitely extended: the number of voices that must be heeded in legislation and in executive policy has been infinitely multiplied. Modern influences have inclined every man to clear his throat for a word in the world's debates. They have popularized everything they have touched.

In the newspapers, it is true, there is but little concerted between the writers; little but piece-meal opinion is created by their comment and argument; there is no common voice amidst their counsellings. But the *aggregate* voice thunders with tremendous volume; and that aggregate voice is 'public opinion.' Popular education and cheap printing and travel vastly thicken the ranks of thinkers everywhere that their influence is felt, and by rousing the multitude to take *knowledge* of the affairs of government directly prepare the time when the multitude will, so far as possible, take *charge* of the affairs of government,—the time when, to repeat Carlyle's phrase, democracy will become palpably extant.

But, mighty as such forces are,—democratic as they are,—no one can fail to see that they are inadequate to *produce of themselves* such a government as ours. There is little in them of *constructive* efficacy. They could not of themselves build any government at all. They are critical, analytical, questioning, quizzing forces;—but not architectural, not powers that devise and build. The influences of popular education, of the press, of travel, of commerce, of the innumerable agencies which nowadays send knowledge and thought in quick pulsations through every part and member of society, do not necessarily mould men for effective endeavour. They may only confuse and paralyze the mind with their myriad stinging lashes of excitement. They may only strengthen the impression that 'the world's a stage' and that no one need do more than sit and look on through his ready glass, the newspaper. They overwhelm one with impressions, but do they give stalwartness to his manhood; do they make his hand any steadier on the plow, or his purpose any clearer with reference to the duties of the moment? They stream light about him, it may be, but do they clear his vision? Is he better able to see because they give him countless things to look at? Is he better able to judge because they fill him with a delusive sense of knowing everything? Activity of mind is not necessarily strength of mind. It may manifest itself in mere dumb show; it may run into jigs as well as into strenuous work at noble tasks. A man's farm does not yield its fruit the more abundantly in its season because he reads the world's news in the papers. A merchant's shipments do not multiply because he studies history. Banking is none the less hazardous to the banker's capital or taxing to his powers because the best writing of the best essayists is to be bought cheap.

Having thus expanded my first point by exhibiting the general forces of that democracy which we recognize as belonging to the age and to the world at large, rather than exclusively or even characteristically to ourselves, I now ask you to turn to view by contrast our origins in politics.

How different were the forces back of us! Nothing establishes the republican state save trained capacity for self-government, practical aptitude for public affairs, habitual soberness and temperateness of united action. When we look back to the moderate sagacity and steadfast, self-contained habit in self-government of the men to whom we owe the establishment of our institutions in the United States we are at once made aware that there is no communion between their democracy and the radical thought and restless spirit called by that name in Europe. There is almost nothing in common between popular outbreaks such as took place in France at her great Revolution and the establishment of a government like our own. Our memories of the year 1789 are as far as possible removed from the memories which Europe retains of that pregnant year. We *manifested* one hundred years ago what Europe *lost,* namely self-command, self-possession. Democracy in Europe, outside of closeted Switzerland, has acted always *in rebellion* as a *destructive* force: it can scarcely be said to have had, even yet, any period of organic development. It has built such temporary governments as it has had opportunity to erect on the old foundations and out of the discredited materials of centralized rule, elevating the people's representatives for a season to the throne, but securing almost as little as ever of that every-day local self-government which lies so near to the heart of liberty. Democracy in America, on the other hand, and in the English colonies, has had, almost from the first, a truly organic growth. There was nothing revolutionary in its movements: it had not to overthrow other polities; it had only to organize itself. It had, not to create, but only to expand self-government. It did not need to spread propaganda: it needed nothing but to methodize its ways of living.

In brief, we were doing nothing essentially new a century ago. Our politics and our character were derived from a

land that freemen till,
That sober-suited Freedom chose.

The land, where girt with friends or foes
A man may speak the thing he will;

A land of settled government,
A land of just and old renown,
Where freedom broadens slowly down
From precedent to precedent:

Where faction seldom gathers head,
But by degrees to fulness wrought,
The strength of some diffusive thought
Hath time and space to work and spread.

Our strength and our facility alike inhered in our traditions; those traditions made our character and shaped our institutions. Liberty is not something that can be created by a document; neither is it something which, when created, can be laid away in a document, a completed work. It is an *organic* principle, a principle of *life,* renewing and being renewed. Democratic institutions are never done; they are like living tissue, always a-making. It is a strenuous thing, this of living the life of a free people; and our success in it depends upon training, not upon clever invention.

Our democracy, plainly, was not a body of doctrine: it was a stage of development. Our democratic state was not a piece of developed theory, but a piece of developed habit. It was not created by mere aspirations or by new faith; it was built up by slow custom. Its process was experience, its basis old wont, its meaning national organic oneness and effective life. It came, like manhood, as the fruit of youth. An immature people could not have had it, and the maturity to which it was vouchsafed was the maturity of freedom and self-control. Such government as ours is a form of conduct, and its only stable foundation is character. A particular form of government may no more be *adopted* than a particular type of character may be adopted: both institutions and character must be developed by conscious effort and through transmitted aptitudes.

Governments such as ours are founded upon discussion and government by discussion comes as late in political as scientific thought in intellectual development. It is a habit of state life created by long-established circumstance, and possible for a nation only in the adult age of its political life. The people which successfully maintains it must have gone through a period of political training which shall have prepared it by gradual steps of acquired privilege for assuming the entire control of its affairs. Long and slowly widening experience in local self-direction must have prepared them for national self-direction. They must have acquired adult self-reliance, self-knowledge, and self-control, adult soberness and deliberateness of judgment, adult sagacity in self-government, adult vigilance of thought and quickness of insight. When practiced, not by small communities, but by wide nations, democracy, far from being a crude form of government, is possible only amongst peoples of the highest and steadiest political habit. It is the heritage of races purged alike of hasty barbaric passions and of patient servility to rulers, and schooled in temperate common counsel. It is an institution of political noon-day, not of the half light of political dawn. It can never be made to sit easily or safely on *first generations,* but strengthens through long heredity. It is poison to the infant, but tonic to the man. Monarchies may be made, but democracies must grow.

It is a deeply significant fact, . . . , again and again to be called to mind, that only in the United States, in a few other governments begotten of the English race and in Switzerland where old Teutonic habit has had the same persistency as in England, have examples yet been furnished of successful democracy of the modern type. England herself is close upon democracy. Her backwardness in entering upon its full practice is no less instructive as to the conditions prerequisite to democracy than is the forwardness of her offspring. She sent out to all her colonies which escaped the luckless beginning of being made penal settlements comparatively small, homogeneous populations of pioneers with strong instincts of self-government and with no social materials out of which to build government otherwise than democratically. She herself, meanwhile, retained masses of population never habituated to participation in government, untaught in political principle either by the teachers of the hustings or of the school house. She has had to approach democracy, therefore, by slow and cautious extensions of the franchise to those prepared for it: while her better colonies, born into democracy, have had to receive all comers into its pale. She has been paring down exclusive privileges and levelling classes; they have from the first been asylums of civil equality. They have assimilated new, she has prepared old, populations.

Erroneous as it is to represent government as only a commonplace sort of business, little elevated in method above merchandizing, and to be regulated by counting-house principles, the favour easily won for such views among our own people is very significant. It means self-reliance in government. It gives voice to the eminently modern democratic feeling that government is no hidden cult to be left to a few specially prepared individuals, but a common everyday concern of life, even if the biggest such concern. It is this self-confidence, in many cases mistaken, which is gradually spreading among other peoples, less justified in it than are ours.

One cannot help marvelling that facts so obvious as these should have escaped the perception of some of the sagest thinkers and most thorough historical scholars of our day. And yet so it is. Sir Henry Maine even, the great interpreter to Englishmen of the historical forces operative in law and social institutions, has utterly failed, in his plausible work on Popular Government to distinguish the democracy, or rather the popular government, of the English race, which is bred by slow circumstance and founded upon habit, from the democracy of other peoples, which is bred by discontent and founded upon revolution. He has missed that most obvious teaching of events, that successful democracy differs from unsuccessful in being a product of history, a product of forces not suddenly become operative, but slowly working upon whole peoples for generations together. The level of democracy is the level of everyday habit, the level of common national experiences, and lies far below the elevations of ecstasy to which the revolutionist climbs.

So much for my second main point, as to the origins of our institutions in constitutional precedents rather than in democratic precepts. It is my object to consider, in the third place, the changes which have been or may be wrought in our institutions by means of the influences of the age, of our own growth as a political organism, and of our adulterated populations.

While there can be no doubt about the derivation of our government from habit rather than from doctrine, from English experience rather than from European thought; while there can be no doubt that our institutions were originally but products of a long, unbroken, unperverted constitutional history; and while there can be no doubt that we shall preserve our institutions in their integrity and efficiency only so long as we keep true in our practice to the traditions from which our strength is derived; there is as little doubt that the forces peculiar to the new civilization of our day, and not only these but also the restless forces of European democratic thought and anarchic turbulence brought to us in such alarming masses by immigration, have deeply affected and may deeply modify the forms and habits of our politics.

All *vital* governments,—and by vital governments I mean those which have life *in their outlying members,* as well as life in their heads,—all systems in which self-government indeed *lives* and retains its self-possession must be governments *by neighbours,* by peoples homogeneous not only but characterized within by the existence of easy neighbourly knowledge of each other among their members. Not foreseeing steam and electricity or the diffusions of news and knowledge which we have witnessed, our fathers were right in thinking it impossible for the government which they had founded to spread without strain or break over the whole of the continent. Were not California now as near neighbour to the Atlantic states as Massachusetts once was to New York, national self-government on our present scale would assuredly hardly be possible or conceivable even. Modern science, scarcely less than our pliancy and steadiness in political habit, may be said to have created the United States of to-day.

Upon some aspects of this growth it is very pleasant to dwell, and very profitable. It is significant of a strength which it is even inspiring to contemplate. The advantages of bigness accompanied by abounding life are many and invaluable. It is impossible among us to hatch in a corner any plot which will *affect* more than a corner. With life everywhere throughout the continent it is impossible to seize illicit power over the whole people by seizing any central offices. To hold Washington would be as useless to a usurper as to hold Duluth. *Self-government cannot be usurped.*

It has been said by a French writer that the autocratic ascendency of Andrew Jackson illustrated anew the long credited tendency of democracies to give themselves over to one hero. The country is older now than it was when Andrew Jackson delighted in his power, and few can believe that it would again approve or applaud childish arrogance and ignorant arbitrariness like his: but even in his case, singular and ominous as it was, it must not be overlooked that he was suffered only to strain the Constitution, not to break it. He held his office by orderly election; he exercised its functions within the letter of the law; he could silence not one word of hostile criticism; and, his second term expired, he passed into private life as harmlessly as did James Monroe. A nation that can quietly reabsorb a vast victorious army is no more safely free and healthy than is a nation that could reabsorb such a President as Andrew Jackson, sending him into seclusion at the Hermitage to live without power and die almost forgotten.

A huge stalwart organism like our own nation, with quick life in every individual limb and sinew, is apt, too, to have the strength of variety of judgment. Thoughts which in one quarter kindle enthusiasm may in another meet coolness or arouse antagonism. Events which are fuel to the *passions* of one section may be but as a passing wind to the minds of another section. No single *moment* of indiscretion, surely, can easily betray the whole country at once. There will be entire populations still cool, self-reliant, unaffected. Revolutions have to take such nations as ours in detail. Generous emotions sometimes sweep whole peoples, but evil passions, happily, sinister views, base purposes do not and cannot. Sedition cannot surge through the hearts of a wakeful nation as patriotism can. In such organisms poisons diffuse themselves slowly, only healthful life has unbroken course. The sweep of agitations set afoot for purposes unfamiliar or uncongenial to the customary popular thought is broken by a thousand obstacles. It may be easy to re-awaken old enthusiasms, but it must be infinitely hard to create new ones, and impossible to surprise the people into unpremeditated action.

I wish to give full weight to these great advantages of our big and strenuous and yet familiar way of conducting affairs; but I wish at the same time to make very plain the influences which are pointing towards threatening changes in our politics—changes which threaten loss of organic wholeness and soundness in carrying on an efficient and honest government. The union of strength with bigness depends upon the maintenance of *character,* and it is just the character of the nation which is being most deeply affected and modified by the enormous immigration which year after year pours into the country from Europe: our own temperate blood, schooled to self-possession and to the measured conduct of self-government is receiving a constant infusion and yearly experiencing a partial corruption of foreign blood: our own equable habits have been crossed with the feverish habits of the restless old world. We are unquestionably facing an ever-increasing difficulty of self-command with ever-deteriorating materials, possibly with degenerating fibre. We have so far succeeded in remaining

> A nation yet, the rulers and the ruled—
> Some sense of duty, something of a faith,
> Some reverence for the laws ourselves have made,
> Some patient force to change them when we will,
> Some civic manhood firm against the crowd.

But we must reckon our power to continue to do so with a people made up of minds cast in every mould of race, minds inheriting every bias of environment, warped by the diverse histories of a score of different nations, warmed or chilled, closed or expanded by almost every climate in the globe.

What was true of our early circumstances is not true of our present. We are not now simply carrying out under normal conditions the principles and habits of English constitutional history. Our tasks of construction are not done: we have, not simply to conduct but also to preserve and freshly adjust our government. Europe has sent her habits to us; and she has sent also her political philosophy,—that philosophy which has never been purged by the cold bath of practical politics. The communion which we did not have at first with her heated and mistaken ambitions, with her radical speculative habit in politics, with her readiness to experiment in forms of government, we may possibly have to suffer now that we are receiving her populations. Not only printing and steam and electricity have gotten hold of us to expand our English civilization, but also those general, and yet to us alien, forces of democracy of which I have spoken; and these are apt to tell disastrously upon our Saxon habits in government.

It is thus that I am brought to my fourth and last point. I have endeavored (1) to show you the general forces of democracy which have been sapping old forms of government in all parts of the world; (2) to remind you of the error of supposing ourselves indebted to those forces for the creation of our government, or in any way connected with them in our origins; and (3) to point out the effect they have nevertheless had upon us as parts of the general influences of the age as well as by reason of our vast immigation from Europe,—an immigration which brings to us European ideas and European habits. I am now to speak of the *new problems* which have been prepared for our solution by reason of our growth and of the effects of immigration, and which may require as much political capacity for their proper solution as any that faced the architects of our government.

These problems are chiefly problems of organization and leadership. Were the nation homogeneous, were it composed simply of later generations of the same stock by which our institutions were planted, few adjustments of the old machinery of our politics would, perhaps, be necessary to meet the exigencies of growth. But every added element of variety, particularly every added element of foreign variety, complicates even the simpler questions of politics. The dangers attending that variety which is heterogeneity in so vast an organism as ours are of course the dangers of *disintegration,* nothing less: and it is unwise to think these dangers remote and merely contingent because they are not as yet pressing. We are conscious of oneness as a nation, of vitality, of strength, of progress; but are we often conscious of common thought in the concrete things of national policy? Does not our legislation, rather, wear the features of a vast conglomerate? Are we conscious of any national leadership: are we not, rather, dimly conscious of being pulled in a score of directions by a score of crossing influences and contending forces?

This vast and miscellaneous democracy of ours must be led: its giant faculties must be schooled and directed. Leadership cannot belong to the multitude: masses of men cannot be self-directed. Neither can groups of communities. We speak of the sovereignty of the people, but that sovereignty, we know very well, is of a peculiar sort, quite unlike the sovereignty of a king or of a small easily concerting group of confident men. It is judicial merely, not creative. It passes judgment or gives sanction, but it cannot direct or suggest. It furnishes standards, not policies. Questions of government are infinitely complex questions, and no multitude can of themselves form clear-cut, comprehensive, consistent conclusions touching them. And yet without such conclusions, without single and prompt purposes, government cannot be carried on. Neither legislation nor administration can be done at the ballot-box. The people can only accept the governing act of representatives. But the size of the modern democracy necessitates the exercise of persuasive power by dominant minds in the shaping of popular judgments in a very different way from that in which it was exercised in former times. "It is said by eminent censors of the press," said Mr. Bright on one occasion in the House of Commons, "that this debate will yield about thirty hours of talk, and will end in no result. I have observed that all great questions in this country require thirty hours of talk many times repeated before they are settled. There is much shower and much sunshine between the sowing of the seed and the reaping of the harvest, but the harvest is generally reaped after all." And so it must be in all self-governing nations of to-day. They are not a single audience within sound of an orator's voice; but a thousand audiences. Their actions do not spring from a single thrill of feeling, but from slow conclusions following upon much talk.

The talk must slowly percolate through the whole mass. It cannot be sent through them straight like the pulse which is stirred by the call of a trumpet. A score of platforms in every neighbourhood must ring with the insistent voice of controversy; and for a few hundreds who hear what is said by the public speakers, many thousands must read of the matter in the newspapers, discuss it interjectionally at the breakfast table, desultorily in the street-cars, laconically on the streets, dogmatically at dinner. And all this with a certain advantage, of course. Through so many stages of consideration passion cannot possibly hold out. *It gets chilled by over-exposure.* It finds the modern popular state organized for giving and hearing counsel in such a way that those who give it must be careful that it is such counsel as will *wear well,* and those who hear it handle and examine it enough to *test* its wearing qualities to the utmost.

All this, however, when looked at from another point of view, but illustrates an infinite difficulty of achieving *energy and organization.* There is a certain peril almost of disintegration attending such phenomena.

Everyone now knows familiarly enough how we accomplished the wide aggregations of self-government characteristic of the modern time, how we have articulated governments as vast and yet as whole as continents like our own. The instrumentality has been *representation,* of which the ancient world knew nothing, and lacking which it always lacked national integration. Because of representation and the railroads to carry representatives to distant capitals, we have been able to rear colossal structures like the government of the United States as easily as the ancients gave political organization to a city, and our great building is as stout as their little one.

But not until recently have we been able to see the full effects of thus sending men to legislate for us at capitals distant the breadth of a continent. It makes the leaders of our politics many of them mere names to our consciousness instead of real persons, whom we have seen and heard, and whom we know. We have to accept rumours concerning them, we have to know them through the variously coloured accounts of others: we can seldom test our impressions of their sincerity by standing with them face to face. Here certainly the ancient pocket republics had much the advantage of us: in them citizens and leaders were always neighbours; they stood constantly in each other's presence. Every Athenian knew Themistocles' manner and gait and address, and had felt directly the just influence of Aristides. No Athenian of a later period needed to be told of the vanities and fopperies of Alcibiades, any more than the elder generation needed to have described to them the personality of Pericles.

Our separation from our leaders is the greater peril because democratic government more than any other needs organization in order to escape disintegration, and it can have organization only by full knowledge of its leaders and full confidence in them. Just because it is a vast body to be persuaded it must know its persuaders: in order to be effective it must always have choice of men who are *impersonated policies.* Just because none but the finest mental batteries, with pure metals and unadulterated acids, can send a current through so huge and yet so rare a medium as democratic opinion, it is the more necessary to look to the excellence of these instrumentalities. There is no permanent place in democratic leadership except for him who 'hath clean hands and a pure heart.' If other men come temporarily into power among us, it is because we cut our leadership up into so many little parts and do not subject any one man to the purifying influences of centred responsibility. Never before was consistent leadership so necessary; never before was it necessary to concert measures over so vast areas, to adjust laws to so many interests, to make a compact and intelligible unit out of so many fractions, to maintain a central and dominant force where there are so many forces.

It is a noteworthy fact that the admiration for our institutions which has during the past few years so suddenly grown to large proportions among publicists abroad is almost all of it directed to the *restraints* we have effected upon the action of government. Sir Henry Maine thought our federal Constitution an admirable *reservoir* in which the mighty waters of democracy are held at rest, kept back from free destructive course. Lord Rosebery has wondering praise for the *security of our Senate* against usurpation of its functions by the House of Representatives. Mr. Goldwin Smith supposes the saving act of organization for a democracy to be the drafting and adoption of a *written constitution.* Thus it is always the *statical,* never the *dynamic* forces of our government which are praised. The greater part of our foreign admirers find our success to consist in the achievement of stable safeguards against hasty or retrogressive action: we are asked to believe that we have succeeded because we have taken Sir Archibald Allison's advice and have resisted the infection of revolution by staying quite still.

But, after all, progress is motion, government is action. The waters of democracy are useless in their reservoirs unless they may be used to drive the wheels of policy and administration. Though we be the most law-abiding and law-directed nation in the world, law has not yet attained to such efficacy among us as to frame or adjust or administer *itself.* It may restrain but it cannot lead us: and I believe that unless we concentrate legislative leadership, leadership, i.e., in progressive policy, unless we give leave to our nationality and practice to it *by* such concentration, we shall sooner or later suffer something like national paralysis in the face of emergencies. We have no one in Congress who stands for the nation. Each man stands but for his part of the nation,—and so management and combination, which may be effected in the dark, are given the place that should be held by centred and responsible leadership, which would of necessity work in the focus of the national gaze.

What is the valuable element in *monarchy* which causes men constantly to turn to it as to an ideal form of government, could it but be kept pure and wise? It is its *cohesion,* its readiness and power to act, its abounding loyalty to certain concrete things, to certain visible persons, its concerted organization, its perfect model of progressive order. Democracy abounds with vitality; but how shall it combine with its other elements of life and strength this power of the governments that know their own minds and their own aims? We have not yet reached the age when government may be made impersonal.

I believe that the only way in which we can preserve our nationality in its integrity and its old-time originative force in the face of growth and imported change is by *concentrating* it, by putting leaders forward vested with abundant authority in the conception and execution of policy. There is plenty of the old vitality in our national character to tell, if you will but give it leave. Give it leave and it will the more impress and mould those who come to us from abroad. I believe that we have not made enough of leadership.

> A people is but the attempt of many
> To rise to the completer life of one;
> And those who live as models for the mass
> Are singly of more value than they all.

We shall not again have a true national life until we compact it by such legislative leadership as other nations have. But, once thus compacted and embodied, our nationality is safe. An acute English historical scholar has said that "the Americans of the United States are a nation because they once obeyed a king": we shall remain a nation only by obeying leaders.

> Keep but the model safe
> New men will rise to study it.

41

PEACE WITHOUT VICTORY
January 22, 1917

O<small>N THE EIGHTEENTH OF</small> D<small>ECEMBER</small> last I addressed an identic note to the governments of the nations now at war requesting them to state, more definitely than they had yet been stated by either group of belligerents, the terms upon which they would deem it possible to make peace. I spoke on behalf of humanity and of the rights of all neutral nations like our own, many of whose most vital interests the war puts in constant jeopardy. The Central Powers united in a reply which stated merely that they were ready to meet their antagonists in conference to discuss terms of peace. The Entente Powers have replied much more definitely and have stated, in general terms, indeed, but with sufficient definiteness to imply details, the arrangements, guarantees, and acts of reparation which they deem to be the indispensable conditions of a satisfactory settlement. We are that much nearer a definite discussion of the peace which shall end the present war. We are that much nearer the discussion of the international concert which must thereafter hold the world at peace. In every discussion of the peace that must end this war it is taken for granted that that peace must be followed by some definite concert of power which will make it virtually impossible that any such catastrophe should ever overwhelm us again. Every lover of mankind, every sane and thoughtful man must take that for granted.

I have sought this opportunity to address you because I thought that I owed it to you, as the counsel associated with me in the final determination of our international obligations, to disclose to you without reserve the thought and purpose that have been taking form in my mind in regard to the duty of our Government in the days to come when it will be necessary to lay afresh and upon a new plan the foundations of peace among the nations.

It is inconceivable that the people of the United States should play no part in that great enterprise. To take part in such a service will be the opportunity for which they have sought to prepare themselves by the very principles and purposes of their policy and the approved practices of their

Government ever since the days when they set up a new nation in the high and honorable hope that it might in all that it was and did show mankind the way to liberty. They cannot in honor withhold the service to which they are now about to be challenged. They do not wish to withhold it. But they owe it to themselves and to the other nations of the world to state the conditions under which they will feel free to render it.

That service is nothing less than this, to add their authority and their power to the authority and force of other nations to guarantee peace and justice throughout the world. Such a settlement cannot now be long postponed. It is right that before it comes this Government should frankly formulate the conditions upon which it would feel justified in asking our people to approve its formal and solemn adherence to a League for Peace. I am here to attempt to state those conditions.

The present war must first be ended; but we owe it to candor and to a just regard for the opinion of mankind to say that, so far as our participation in guarantees of future peace is concerned, it makes a great deal of difference in what way and upon what terms it is ended. The treaties and agreements which bring it to an end must embody terms which will create a peace that is worth guaranteeing and preserving, a peace that will win the approval of mankind, not merely a peace that will serve the several interests and immediate aims of the nations engaged. We shall have no voice in determining what those terms shall be, but we shall, I feel sure, have a voice in determining whether they shall be made lasting or not by the guarantees of a universal covenant, and our judgment upon what is fundamental and essential as a condition precedent to permanency should be spoken now, not afterwards when it may be too late.

No covenant of cooperative peace that does not include the peoples of the New World can suffice to keep the future safe against war; and yet there is only one sort of peace that the peoples of America could join in guaranteeing. The elements of that peace must be elements that engage the confidence and satisfy the principles of the American governments, elements consistent with their political faith and with the practical convictions which the peoples of America have once for all embraced and undertaken to defend.

I do not mean to say that any American government would throw any obstacle in the way of any terms of peace the governments now at war might agree upon, or seek to upset them when made, whatever they might be. I only take it for granted that mere terms of peace between the belligerents will not satisfy even the belligerents themselves. Mere agreements may not make peace secure. It will be absolutely necessary that a force be created as a guarantor of the permanency of the settlement so much greater than the force of any nation now engaged or any alliance hitherto formed or projected that no nation, no probable combination of nations, could face or withstand it. If the peace presently to be made is to endure, it must be a peace made secure by the organized major force of mankind.

The terms of the immediate peace agreed upon will determine whether it is a peace for which such a guarantee can be secured. The question upon which the whole future peace and policy of the world depends is this: Is the present war a struggle for a just and secure peace, or only for a new balance of power? If it be only a struggle for a new balance of power, who will guarantee, who can guarantee, the stable equilibrium of the new arrangement? Only a tranquil Europe can be a stable Europe. There must be, not a balance of power, but a community of power; not organized rivalries, but an organized common peace.

Fortunately we have received very explicit assurances on this point. The statesmen of both of the groups of nations now arrayed against one another have said, in terms that could not be misinterpreted, that it was no part of the purpose they had in mind to crush their antagonists. But the implications of these assurances may not be equally clear to all—may not be the same on both sides of the water. I think it will be serviceable if I attempt to set forth what we understand them to be.

They imply, first of all, that it must be a peace without victory. It is not pleasant to say this. I beg that I may be permitted to put my own interpretation upon it and that it may be understood that no other interpretation was in my thought. I am seeking only to face realities and to face them without soft concealments. Victory would mean peace forced upon the loser, a victor's terms imposed upon the vanquished. It would be accepted in humiliation, under duress, at an intolerable sacrifice, and would leave a sting, a resentment, a bitter memory upon which terms of peace would rest, not permanently, but only as upon quicksand. Only a peace between equals can last. Only a peace the very principle of which is equality and a common participation in a common benefit. The right state of mind, the right feeling between nations, is as necessary for a lasting peace as is the just settlement of vexed questions of territory or of racial and national allegiance.

The equality of nations upon which peace must be founded if it is to last must be an equality of rights; the guarantees exchanged must neither recognize nor imply a difference between big nations and small, between those that are powerful and those that are weak. Right must be based upon the common strength, not upon the individual strength, of the nations upon whose concert peace will depend. Equality of territory or of resources there of course cannot be; nor any other sort of equality not gained in the ordinary peaceful and legitimate development of the peoples themselves. But no one asks or expects anything more than an equality of rights. Mankind is looking now for freedom of life, not for equipoises of power.

And there is a deeper thing involved than even equality of rights among organized nations. No peace can last, or ought to last, which does not recognize and accept the principle that governments derive all their just powers from the consent of the governed, and that no right anywhere exists to hand peoples about from sovereignty to sovereignty as if they were property. I take it for granted, for instance, if I may venture upon a single example, that statesmen everywhere are agreed that there should be a united, independent, and autonomous Poland, and that henceforth inviolable security of life, of worship, and of industrial and social development should be guaranteed to all peoples who have lived hitherto under the power of governments devoted to a faith and purpose hostile to their own.

I speak of this, not because of any desire to exalt an abstract political principle which has always been held very dear by those who have sought to build up liberty in America, but for the same reason that I have spoken of the other conditions of peace which seem to me clearly indispensable— because I wish frankly to uncover realities. Any peace which does not recognize and accept this principle will inevitably be upset. It will not rest upon the affections or the convictions of mankind. The ferment of spirit of whole populations will fight subtly and constantly against it, and all the world will sympathize. The world can be at peace only if its life is stable, and there can be no stability where the will is in rebellion, where there is not tranquillity of spirit and a sense of justice, of freedom, and of right.

So far as practicable, moreover, every great people now struggling towards a full development of its resources and of its powers should be assured a direct outlet to the great highways of the sea. Where this cannot be done by the cession of territory, it can no doubt be done by the neutralization of direct rights of way under the general guarantee which will assure the peace itself. With a right comity of arrangement no nation need be shut away from free access to the open paths of the world's commerce.

And the paths of the sea must alike in law and in fact be free. The freedom of the seas is the *sine qua non* of peace, equality, and cooperation. No doubt a somewhat radical reconsideration of many of the rules of international practice hitherto thought to be established may be necessary in order to make the seas indeed free and common in practically all circumstances for the use of mankind, but the motive for such changes is convincing and compelling. There can be no trust or intimacy between the peoples of the world without them. The free, constant, unthreatened intercourse of nations is an essential part of the process of peace and of development. It need not be difficult either to define or to secure the freedom of the seas if the governments of the world sincerely desire to come to an agreement concerning it.

It is a problem closely connected with the limitation of naval armaments and the cooperation of the navies of the world in keeping the seas at once free and safe. And the question of limiting naval armaments opens the wider and perhaps more difficult question of the limitation of armies and of all programs of military preparations. Difficult and delicate as these questions are, they must be faced with the utmost candor and decided in a spirit of real accommodation if peace is to come with healing in its wings, and come to stay. Peace cannot be had without concession and sacrifice. There can be no sense of safety and equality among the nations if great preponderating armaments are henceforth to continue here and there to be built up and maintained. The statesmen of the world must plan for peace and nations must adjust and accommodate their policy to it as they have planned for war and made ready for pitiless contest and rivalry. The question of armaments, whether on land or sea, is the most immediately and intensely practical question connected with the future fortunes of nations and of mankind.

I have spoken upon these great matters without reserve and with the utmost explicitness because it has seemed to me to be necessary if the world's yearning desire for peace was anywhere to find free voice and utterance. Perhaps I am the only person in high authority amongst all the peoples of the world who is at liberty to speak and hold nothing back. I am speaking as an individual, and yet I am speaking also, of course, as the responsible head of a great government, and I feel confident that I have said what the people of the United States would wish me to say. May I not add that I hope and believe that I am in effect speaking for liberals and friends of humanity in every nation and of every program of liberty? I would fain believe that I am speaking for the silent mass of mankind everywhere who have as yet had no place or opportunity to speak their real hearts out concerning the death and ruin they see to have come already upon the persons and the homes they hold most dear.

And in holding out the expectation that the people and Government of the United States will join the other civilized nations of the world in guaranteeing the permanence of peace upon such terms as I have named, I speak with the greater boldness and confidence because it is clear to every man who can think that there is in this promise no breach in either our traditions or our policy as a nation, but a fulfillment, rather, of all that we have professed or striven for.

I am proposing, as it were, that the nations should with one accord adopt the doctrine of President Monroe as the doctrine of the world: that no nation should seek to extend its polity over any other nation or people, but that every people should be left free to determine its own polity, its own way of development, unhindered, unthreatened, unafraid, the little along with the great and powerful.

I am proposing that all nations henceforth avoid entangling alliances which would draw them into competitions of power; catch them in a net of intrigue and selfish rivalry, and disturb their own affairs with influences intruded from without. There is no entangling alliance in a concert of power. When all unite to act in the same sense and with the same purpose all act in the common interest and are free to live their own lives under a common protection.

I am proposing government by the consent of the governed; that freedom of the seas which in international conference after conference representatives of the United States have urged with the eloquence of those who are the convinced disciples of liberty; and that moderation of armaments which makes of armies and navies a power for order merely, not an instrument of aggression or of selfish violence.

These are American principles, American policies. We could stand for no others. And they are also the principles and policies of forward looking men and women everywhere, of every modern nation, of every enlightened community. They are the principles of mankind and must prevail.

42
THE FOURTEEN POINTS SPEECH
January 8, 1918

IT WILL BE OUR WISH AND PURPOSE that the processes of peace, when they are begun, shall be absolutely open and that they shall involve and permit henceforth no secret understandings of any kind. The day of conquest and aggrandizement is gone by; so is also the day of secret covenants entered into in the interest of particular governments and likely at some unlooked-for moment to upset the peace of the world. It is this happy fact, now clear to the view of every public man whose thoughts do not still linger in an age that is dead and gone, which makes it possible for every nation whose purposes are consistent with justice and the peace of the world to avow now or at any other time the objects it has in view.

We entered this war because violations of right had occurred which touched us to the quick and made the life of our own people impossible unless they were corrected and the world secured once for all against their recurrence. What we demand in this war, therefore, is nothing peculiar to ourselves. It is that the world be made fit and safe to live in; and particularly that it be made safe for every peace-loving nation which, like our own, wishes to live its own life, determine its own institutions, be assured of justice and fair dealing by the other peoples of the world as against force and selfish aggression. All the peoples of the world are in effect partners in this interest, and for our own part we see very clearly that unless justice be done to others it will not be done to us. The program of the world's peace, therefore, is our program; and that program, the only possible program, as we see it, is this:

I. Open covenants of peace, openly arrived at, after which there shall be no private international understandings of any kind but diplomacy shall proceed always frankly and in the public view.

II. Absolute freedom of navigation upon the seas, outside territorial waters, alike in peace and in war, except as the seas may be closed in whole or in part by international action for the enforcement of international covenants.

III. The removal, so far as possible, of all economic barriers and the establishment of an equality of trade conditions among all the nations consenting to the peace and associating themselves for its maintenance.

IV. Adequate guarantees given and taken that national armaments will be reduced to the lowest point consistent with domestic safety.

V. A free, open-minded, and absolutely impartial adjustment of all colonial claims, based upon a strict observance of the principle that in determining all such questions of sovereignty the interests of the populations concerned must have equal weight with the equitable claims of the government whose title is to be determined.

VI. The evacuation of all Russian territory and such a settlement of all questions affecting Russia as will secure the best and freest coöperation of the other nations of the world in obtaining for her an unhampered and unembarrassed opportunity for the independent determination of her own political development and national policy and assure her of a sincere welcome into the society of free nations under institutions of her own choosing; and, more than a welcome, assistance also of every kind that she may need and may herself desire. The treatment accorded Russia by her sister nations in the months to come will be the acid test of their good will, of their comprehension of her needs as distinguished from their own interests, and of their intelligent and unselfish sympathy.

VII. Belgium, the whole world will agree, must be evacuated and restored, without any attempt to limit the sovereignty which she enjoys in common with all other free nations. No other single act will serve as this will serve to restore confidence among the nations in the laws which they have themselves set and determined for the government of their relations with one another. Without this healing act the whole structure and validity of international law is forever impaired.

VIII. All French territory should be freed and the invaded portions restored, and the wrong done to France by Prussia in 1871 in the matter of Alsace-Lorraine, which has unsettled the peace of the world for nearly fifty years, should be righted, in order that peace may once more be made secure in the interest of all.

IX. A readjustment of the frontiers of Italy should be effected along clearly recognizable lines of nationality.

X. The peoples of Austria-Hungary, whose place among the nations we wish to see safeguarded and assured, should be accorded the freest opportunity of autonomous development.

XI. Rumania, Serbia, and Montenegro should be evacuated; occupied territories restored; Serbia accorded free and secure access to the sea; and the relations of the several Balkan states to one another determined by friendly counsel along historically established lines of allegiance and nationality; and international guarantees of the political and economic independence and territorial integrity of the several Balkan states should be entered into.

XII. The Turkish portions of the present Ottoman Empire should be assured a secure sovereignty, but the other nationalities which are now under Turkish rule should be assured an undoubted security of life and an absolutely unmolested opportunity of autonomous development, and the Dardanelles should be permanently opened as a free passage to the ships and commerce of all nations under international guarantees.

XIII. An independent Polish state should be erected which should include the territories inhabited by indisputably Polish populations, which should be assured a free and secure access to the sea, and whose political and economic independence and territorial integrity should be guaranteed by international covenant.

XIV. A general association of nations must be formed under specific covenants for the purpose of affording mutual guarantees of political independence and territorial integrity to great and small states alike.

In regard to these essential rectifications of wrong and assertions of right we feel ourselves to be intimate partners of all the governments and peoples associated together against the Imperialists. We cannot be separated in interest or divided in purpose. We stand together until the end.

For such arrangements and covenants we are willing to fight and to continue to fight until they are achieved; but only because we wish the right to prevail and desire a just and stable peace such as can be secured only by removing the chief provocations to war, which this program does remove. We have no jealousy of German greatness, and there is nothing in this program that impairs it. We grudge her no achievement or distinction of learning or of pacific enterprise such as have made her record very bright and very enviable. We do not wish to injure her or to block in any way her legitimate influence or power. We do not wish to fight her either with arms or with hostile arrangements of trade if she is willing to associate herself with us and the other peace-loving nations of the world in covenants of justice and law and fair dealing. We wish her only to accept a place of equality among the peoples of the world,—the new world in which we now live,—instead of a place of mastery.

Neither do we presume to suggest to her any alteration or modification of her institutions. But it is necessary, we must frankly say, and necessary as a preliminary to any intelligent dealings with her on our part, that we should know whom her spokesmen speak for when they speak to us, whether for the Reichstag majority or for the military party and the men whose creed is imperial domination.

We have spoken now, surely, in terms too concrete to admit of any further doubt or question. An evident principle runs through the whole program I have outlined. It is the principle of justice to all peoples and nationalities, and their right to live on equal terms of liberty and safety with one another, whether they be strong or weak. Unless this principle be made its foundation no part of the structure of international justice can stand. The people of the United States could act upon no other principle; and to the vindication of this principle they are ready to devote their lives, their honor, and everything that they possess. The moral climax of this the culminating and final war for human liberty has come, and they are ready to put their own strength, their own highest purpose, their own integrity and devotion to the test.

43

SPEECH OPENING CAMPAIGN
FOR FOURTH LIBERTY LOAN
September 27, 1918

I AM NOT HERE TO PROMOTE the loan. That will be done,—ably and enthusiastically done,—by the hundreds of thousands of loyal and tireless men and women who have undertaken to present it to you and to our fellow citizens throughout the country; and I have not the least doubt of their complete success; for I know their spirit and the spirit of the country. My confidence is confirmed, too, by the thoughtful and experienced coöperation of the bankers here and everywhere, who are lending their invaluable aid and guidance. I have come, rather, to seek an opportunity to present to you some thoughts which I trust will serve to give you, in perhaps fuller measure than before, a vivid sense of the great issues involved, in order that you may appreciate and accept with added enthusiasm the grave significance of the duty of supporting the Government by your men and your means to the utmost point of sacrifice and self-denial. No man or woman who has really taken in what this war means can hesitate to give to the very limit of what he or she has; and it is my mission here to-night to try to make it clear once more what the war really means. You will need no other stimulation or reminder of your duty.

At every turn of the war we gain a fresh consciousness of what we mean to accomplish by it. When our hope and expectation are most excited we think more definitely than before of the issues that hang upon it and of the purposes which must be realized by means of it. For it has positive and well-defined purposes which we did not determine and which we cannot alter. No statesman or assembly created them; no statesman or assembly can alter them. They have arisen out of the very nature and circumstances of the war. The most that statesmen or assemblies can do is to carry them out or be false to them. They were perhaps not clear at the outset; but they are clear now. The war has lasted more than four years and the whole world has been drawn into it. The common will of mankind has been substituted for the particular purposes of individual states. Individual statesmen may have started the conflict, but neither they nor their opponents can stop it as they please. It has become a people's war, and peoples of all sorts and races, of every degree of power and variety of fortune, are involved in its sweeping processes of change and settlement. We came into it when its character had become fully defined and it was plain that no nation could stand apart or be indifferent to its outcome. Its challenge drove to the heart of everything we cared for and lived for. The voice of the war had become clear and gripped our hearts. Our brothers from many lands, as well as our own murdered dead under the sea, were calling to us, and we responded, fiercely and of course.

The air was clear about us. We saw things in their full, convincing proportions as they were; and we have seen them with steady eyes and unchanging comprehension ever since. We accepted the issues of the war as facts, not as any group of men either here or elsewhere had defined them, and we can accept no outcome which does not squarely meet and settle them. Those issues are these:

Shall the military power of any nation or group of nations be suffered to determine the fortunes of peoples over whom they have no right to rule except the right of force?

Shall strong nations be free to wrong weak nations and make them subject to their purpose and interest?

Shall peoples be ruled and dominated, even in their own internal affairs, by arbitrary and irresponsible force or by their own will and choice?

Shall there be a common standard of right and privilege for all peoples and nations or shall the strong do as they will and the weak suffer without redress?

Shall the assertion of right be haphazard and by casual alliance or shall there be a common concert to oblige the observance of common rights?

No man, no group of men, chose these to be the issues of the struggle. They *are* the issues of it; and they must be settled,—by no arrangement or compromise or adjustment of interests, but definitely and once for all and with a full and unequivocal acceptance of the principle that the interest of the weakest is as sacred as the interest of the strongest.

This is what we mean when we speak of a permanent peace, if we speak sincerely, intelligently, and with a real knowledge and comprehension of the matter we deal with.

We are all agreed that there can be no peace obtained by any kind of bargain or compromise with the governments of the Central Empires, because we have dealt with them already and have seen them deal with other governments that were parties to this struggle, at Brest-Litovsk and Bucharest. They have convinced us that they are without honor and do not intend justice. They observe no covenants, accept no principle but force and their own interest. We cannot "come to terms" with them. They have made it impossible. The German people must by this time be fully aware that we cannot accept the word of those who forced this war upon us. We do not think the same thoughts or speak the same language of agreement.

It is of capital importance that we should also be explicitly agreed that no peace shall be obtained by any kind of compromise or abatement of the principles we have avowed as the principles for which we are fighting. There should exist no doubt about that. I am, therefore, going to take the liberty of speaking with the utmost frankness about the practical implications that are involved in it.

If it be in deed and in truth the common object of the Governments associated against Germany and of the nations whom they govern, as I believe it to be, to achieve by the coming settlements a secure and lasting peace, it will be necessary that all who sit down at the peace table shall come ready and willing to pay the price, the only price, that will procure it; and ready and willing, also, to create in some virile fashion the only instrumentality by which it can be made certain that the agreements of the peace will be honored and fulfilled.

That price is impartial justice in every item of the settlement, no matter whose interest is crossed; and not only impartial justice, but also the satisfaction of the several peoples whose fortunes are dealt with. That indispensable instrumentality is a League of Nations formed under covenants that will be efficacious. Without such an instrumentality, by which the peace of the world can be guaranteed, peace will rest in part upon the word of outlaws and only upon that word. For Germany will have to redeem her character, not by what happens at the peace table, but by what follows.

And, as I see it, the constitution of that League of Nations and the clear definition of its objects must be a part, is in a sense the most essential part, of the peace settlement itself. It cannot be formed now. If formed now, it would be merely a new alliance confined to the nations associated against a common enemy. It is not likely that it could be formed after the settlement. It is necessary to guarantee the peace; and the peace cannot be guaranteed as an afterthought. The reason, to speak in plain terms again, why it must be guaranteed is that there will be parties to the peace whose promises have proved untrustworthy, and means must be found in connection with the peace settlement itself to remove that source of insecurity. It would be folly to leave the guarantee to the subsequent voluntary action of the Governments we have seen destroy Russia and deceive Rumania.

But these general terms do not disclose the whole matter. Some details are needed to make them sound less like a thesis and more like a practical program. These, then, are some of the particulars, and I state them with the greater confidence because I can state them authoritatively as representing this Government's interpretation of its own duty with regard to peace:

First, the impartial justice meted out must involve no discrimination between those to whom we wish to be just and those to whom we do not wish to be just. It must be a justice that plays no favorites and knows no standard but the equal rights of the several peoples concerned;

Second, no special or separate interest of any single nation or any group of nations can be made the basis of any part of the settlement which is not consistent with the common interest of all;

Third, there can be no leagues or alliances or special covenants and understandings within the general and common family of the League of Nations.

Fourth, and more specifically, there can be no special, selfish economic combinations within the League and no employment of any form of economic boycott or exclusion except as the power of economic penalty by exclusion from the markets of the world may be vested in the League of Nations itself as a means of discipline and control.

Fifth, all international agreements and treaties of every kind must be made known in their entirety to the rest of the world.

Special alliances and economic rivalries and hostilities have been the prolific source in the modern world of the plans and passions that produce war. It would be an insincere as well as insecure peace that did not exclude them in definite and binding terms.

The confidence with which I venture to speak for our people in these matters does not spring from our traditions merely and the well-known principles of international action which we have always professed and followed. In the same sentence in which I say that the United States will enter into no special arrangements or understandings with particular nations let me say also that the United States is prepared to assume its full share of responsibility for the maintenance of the common covenants and understandings upon which peace must henceforth rest. We still read Washington's immortal warning against "entangling alliances" with full comprehension and an answering purpose. But only special and limited alliances entangle; and we recognize and accept the duty of a new day in which we are permitted to hope for a general alliance which will avoid entanglements and clear the air of the world for common understandings and the maintenance of common rights.

I have made this analysis of the international situation which the war has created, not, of course, because I doubted whether the leaders of the great nations and peoples with whom we are associated were of the same mind and entertained a like purpose, but because the air every now and again gets darkened by mists and groundless doubtings and mischievous perversions of counsel and it is necessary once and again to sweep all the irresponsible talk about peace intrigues and weakening morale and doubtful purpose on the part of those in authority utterly, and if need be unceremoniously, aside and say things in the plainest words that can be found, even when it is only to say over again what has been said before, quite as plainly if in less unvarnished terms.

As I have said, neither I nor any other man in governmental authority created or gave form to the issues of this war. I have simply responded to them with such vision as I could command. But I have responded gladly and with a resolution that has grown warmer and more confident as the issues have grown clearer and clearer. It is now plain that they are issues which no man can pervert unless it be willfully. I am bound to fight for them, and happy to fight for them as time and circumstance have revealed them to me as to all the world. Our enthusiasm for them grows more and more irresistible as they stand out in more and more vivid and unmistakable outline.

And the forces that fight for them draw into closer and closer array, organize their millions into more and more unconquerable might, as they become more and more distinct to the thought and purpose of the peoples engaged. It is the peculiarity of this great war that while statesmen have seemed to cast about for definitions of their purpose and have sometimes seemed to shift their ground and their point of view, the thought of the mass of men, whom statesmen are supposed to instruct and lead, has grown more and more unclouded; more and more certain of what it is that they are fighting for. National purposes have fallen more and more into the background and the common purpose of enlightened mankind has taken their place. The counsels of plain men have become on all hands more simple and straightforward and more unified than the counsels of sophisticated men of affairs, who still retain the impression that they are playing a game of power and playing for high stakes. That is why I have said that this is a peoples' war, not a statesmen's. Statesmen must follow the clarified common thought or be broken.

I take that to be the significance of the fact that assemblies and associations of many kinds made up of plain workaday people have demanded, almost every time they came together, and are still demanding, that the leaders of their Governments declare to them plainly what it is, exactly what it is, that they were seeking in this war, and what they think the items of the final settlement should be. They are not yet satisfied with what they have been told. They still seem to fear that they are getting what they ask for only in statesmen's terms,—only in the terms of territorial arrangements and divisions of power, and not in terms of broad-visioned justice and mercy and peace and the satisfaction of those deep-seated longings of oppressed and distracted men and women and enslaved peoples that seem to them the only things worth fighting a war for that engulfs the world. Perhaps statesmen have not always recognized this changed aspect of the whole world of policy and action. Perhaps they have not always spoken in direct reply to the questions asked because they did not know how searching those questions were and what sort of answers they demanded.

But I, for one, am glad to attempt the answer again and again, in the hope that I may make it clearer and clearer that my one thought is to satisfy those who struggle in the ranks and are, perhaps above all others, entitled to a reply whose meaning no one can have any excuse for misunderstanding, if he understands the language in which it is spoken or can get some one to translate it correctly into his own. And I believe that the leaders of the governments with which we are associated will speak, as they have occasion, as plainly as I have tried to speak. I hope that they will feel free to say whether they think that I am in any degree mistaken in my interpretation of the issues involved or in my purpose with regard to the means by which a satisfactory settlement of those issues may be obtained. Unity of purpose and of counsel are as imperatively necessary in this war as was unity of command in the battlefield; and with perfect unity of purpose and counsel will come assurance of complete victory. It can be had in no other way. "Peace drives" can be effectively neutralized and silenced only by showing that every victory of the nations associated against Germany brings the nations nearer the sort of peace which will bring security and reassurance to all peoples and make the recurrence of another such struggle of pitiless force and bloodshed forever impossible, and that nothing else can. Germany is constantly intimating the "terms" she will accept; and always finds that the world does not want terms. It wishes the final triumph of justice and fair dealing.

IX

FRANKLIN D. ROOSEVELT
(1882–1945)

FRANKLIN D. ROOSEVELT, as 32nd President of the United States, inaugurated and carried out a "New Deal" domestic program and led the country during World War II. He died just before the war ended and just after starting his fourth term as President, having served longer than any other man in that office—from 1933 to 1945.

One result of the climactic experience of the Great Depression (and the manner in which that depression was understood) was a challenge to the established ideals of liberalism. Roosevelt made clear his break with the earlier liberalism in his address to the Young Democratic Clubs of America in. August 1935, in which he showed the consequences of unrestrained devotion to the principles of individual enterprise. Because the President was deeply concerned about the dangers to freedom in America posed by economic inequality, he saw freedom as a problem that went beyond the earlier liberal understanding of the term. Roosevelt believed freedom must be construed as consisting not only in security of political rights, but also in guarantees safeguarding the economically weak from the actions of the economically strong. Roosevelt believed that in a highly centralized industrial society, the limited freedom which can be generally enjoyed is most likely to be secured by a regime that restrains inequalities as well as concerns itself with the virtues of individual enterprise.

The struggle between Roosevelt and the Supreme Court in 1937 represented a severe breakdown in cooperation between the executive and judicial branches of government. The Court's action in striking down many major pieces of New Deal legislation in 1935 and 1936 theatened the virtual extinction of the program. After having won an overwhelming second-term victory, Roosevelt sent a proposal for reform of the judiciary to the Congress in early February of 1937, focussing on the inefficiency of the Courts, injustices caused by delays, and the inability of the aged justices to understand present-day issues. In his "Fireside Chat on Reorganization of the Judiciary" in March 1937, Roosevelt revealed the underlying intent of the proposal: an attempt to change the balance of power between those Supreme Court justices who took a narrow view of the constitutional power of the national government in economic matters and those who took a broader view. The Congress, however, was not willing to go along with the President, and the proposal was dead by midsummer.

In his next important speech, on the celebration of the 150th anniversary of the Constitution in September 1937, Roosevelt used the occasion to explain what he thought the Constitution was. The speech, delivered at Washington, D.C., is a revealing and important document in the controversy between Roosevelt and the Supreme Court led by Chief Justice Charles Evans Hughes from 1930 to 1941. The theme was that an adequate understanding of the meaning of the Constitution requires more than a mere understanding of its words, for behind the words are the working principles and goals of democratic government. The Constitution is a layman's document, not a lawyer's contract. He emphasized, moreover, that different constructions ought to be given to different clauses in the Constitution. Some call for interpretation within narrow limits, whereas others are clearly general. Where a power is expressly granted in general terms, as in the commerce clause, the exact limits of the powers of the general government may not always be capable of being defined or ascertained. The broad and general language of the Constitution, he indicated, was intended to allow variations in detail which changing circumstances might require. Specific limitations on government, on the other hand, ought to be enforced strictly.

The President's relations with his own party were never more strained than in 1938, when he attempted to "purge" it of some of its more dissident elements. FDR's influence over some elements within the party was already deteriorating in 1937, following defeat of the court-packing plan, the wages and hours bill, and the administrative reorganization bill. The President's move against the dissident Democrats came in the 1938 party primaries, when administration candidates were selected to oppose them and Roosevelt charged that certain elements in the party who claimed they were progressive-minded nevertheless obstructed all measures intended to carry out liberal objectives. In a "Fireside Chat on Party Primaries" in June 1938, Roosevelt criticized Democrats who were willing to run on a liberal party platform with him in 1936 and then voted against the very pledges on which they had been elected. He also took this opportunity to elaborate the differences between liberals and conservatives within the Democratic Party, proclaiming it the liberal party. But, with the exception of Representative John J. O'Connor of New York, all the dissidents he opposed, most of whom were from southern constituencies, were returned to office.

Roosevelt attempted to state the principles upon which the New Deal stood in an Address at the University of Pennsylvania in September 1940, after having been nominated for a third time by the Democratic party. He explained that there was an emphasis in the New Deal on the positive function of government that had been insufficiently acknowledged by the earlier liberalism. The objective of the New Deal was the welfare state, which called for the emergence of a higher plane of thought in regard to American ends than that which had informed the Progressive movement. The vigorous view of active government which the Founding Fathers themselves had had was to be restored, as was the proper relation between the purposes of the Preamble and the instrumental clauses in the body of the Constitution. The central errors of the earlier liberalism, Roosevelt believed, were its unrestricted individualism, its policy of encouraging smallness and discouraging economic concentration (that is, its antitrust approach of breaking down and destroying concentrated economic power), and its narrow and inflexible view of the functions of government. The Great Depression had thrust upon the government the responsibility for the general performance of the economy. Rejecting the notion that an economic system such as that of the United States could regulate itself automatically by the uncontrolled competition of private enterprise, FDR's New Deal imposed regulations and controls on the economy as a whole. Welfare or economic well-being was seen as a vital function of government.

44

ADDRESS TO YOUNG DEMOCRATIC
CLUBS OF AMERICA
August 24, 1935

YOU DOUBTLESS KNOW EVERYTHING that I am going to say to you, because starting as early as last Monday certain special writers of a few papers have given you a complete outline of my remarks. I have been interested and somewhat amused by these clairvoyants who put on the front page many days ago this speech, which, because of pressure of time, I could only think out and dictate this very morning.

Whatever his party affiliations may be, the President of the United States, in addressing the youth of the country—even when speaking to the younger citizens of his own party—should speak as President of the whole people. It is true that the Presidency carries with it, for the time being, the leadership of a political party as well. But the Presidency carries with it a far higher obligation than this—the duty of analyzing and setting forth national needs and ideals which transcend and cut across all lines of party affiliation. Therefore, what I am about to say to you, members of the Young Democratic Clubs, is precisely—word for word—what I would say were I addressing a convention of the youth of the Republican Party.

A man of my generation comes to the councils of the younger warriors in a very different spirit from that in which the older men addressed the youth of my time. Party or professional leaders who talked to us twenty-five or thirty years ago almost inevitably spoke in a mood of achievement and of exultation. They addressed us with the air of those who had won the secret of success for themselves and of permanence of achievement for their country for all generations to come. They assumed that there was a guarantee of final accomplishment for the people of this country and that the grim specter of insecurity and want among the great masses would never haunt this land of plenty as it had widely visited other portions of the world. And so the elders of that day used to tell us, in effect, that the job of youth was merely to copy them and thereby to preserve the great things they had won for us.

I have no desire to underestimate the achievements of the past. We have no right to speak slightingly of the heritage, spiritual and material, that comes down to us. There are lessons that it teaches that we abandon only at our own peril. "Hold fast to that which is permanently true" is still a counsel of wisdom.

While my elders were talking to me about the perfection of America, I did not know then of the lack of opportunity, the lack of education, the lack of many of the essential needs of civilization which existed among millions of our people who lived not alone in the slums of the great cities and in the forgotten corners of rural America but even under the very noses of those who had the advantages and the power of Government of those days.

I say from my heart that no man of my generation has any business to address youth unless he comes to that task not in a spirit of exultation, but in a spirit of humility. I cannot expect you of a newer generation to believe me, of an older generation, if I do not frankly acknowledge that had the generation that brought you into the world been wiser and more provident and more unselfish, you would have been saved from needless difficult problems and needless pain and suffering. We may not have failed you in good intentions but we have certainly not been adequate in results. Your task, therefore, is not only to maintain the best in your heritage, but to labor to lift from the shoulders of the American people some of the burdens that the mistakes of a past generation have placed there.

There was a time when the formula for success was the simple admonition to have a stout heart and willing hands. A great, new country lay open. When life became hard in one place it was necessary only to move on to another. But circumstances have changed all that. Today we can no longer escape into virgin territory: we must master our environment. The youth of this generation finds that the old frontier is occupied, but that science and invention and economic evolution have opened up a new frontier—one not based on geography but on the resourcefulness of men and women applied to the old frontier.

The cruel suffering of the recent depression has taught us unforgettable lessons. We have been compelled by stark necessity to unlearn the too comfortable superstition that the American soil was mystically blessed with every kind of immunity to grave economic maladjustments, and that the American spirit of individualism—all alone and unhelped by the cooperative efforts of Government—could withstand and repel every form of economic disarrangement or crisis. The severity of the recent depression, toward which we had been heading for a whole generation, has taught us that no economic or social class in the community is so richly endowed and so independent of the general community that it can safeguard its own security, let alone assure security for the general community.

The very objectives of young people have changed. In the older days a great financial fortune was too often the goal. To rule through wealth, or through the power of wealth, fired our imagination. This was the dream of the golden ladder—each individual for himself.

It is my firm belief that the newer generation of America has a different dream. You place emphasis on sufficiency of life, rather than on a plethora of riches. You think of the security for yourself and your family that will give you good health, good food, good education, good working conditions, and the opportunity for normal recreation and occasional travel. Your advancement, you hope, is along a broad highway on which thousands of your fellow men and women are advancing with you.

You and I know that this modern economic world of ours is governed by rules and regulations vastly more complex than those laid down in the days of Adam Smith or John Stuart Mill. They faced simpler mechanical processes and social needs. It is worth remembering, for example, that the business corporation, as we know it, did not exist in the days of Washington and Hamilton and Jefferson. Private businesses then were conducted solely by individuals or by partnerships in which every member was immediately and wholly responsible for success or failure. Facts are relentless. We must adjust our ideas to the facts of today.

Our concepts of the regulation of money and credit and industrial competition, of the relation of employer and employee, created for the old civilization, are being modified to save our economic structure from confusion, destruction and paralysis. The rules that governed the relationship between an employer and employee in the blacksmith's shop in the days of Washington cannot, of necessity, govern the relationship between the fifty thousand employees of a great corporation and the infinitely complex and diffused ownership of that corporation. If fifty thousand employees spoke with fifty thousand voices, there would be a modern Tower of Babel. That is why we insist on their right to choose their representatives to bargain collectively in their behalf with their employer. In the case of the employees, every individual employee will know in his daily work whether he is adequately represented or not. In the case of the hundreds of thousands of stockholders in the present-day ownership of great corporations, however, their knowledge of the success of the management is based too often solely on a financial balance sheet. Things may go wrong in the management without their being aware of it for a year, or for many years to come. Without their day-to-day knowledge they may be exploited and their investments jeopardized. Therefore, we have come to the recognition of the need of simple but adequate public protection for the rights of the investing public.

A rudimentary concept of credit control appropriate for financing the economic life of a Nation of 3,000,000 people can hardly be urged as a means of directing and protecting the welfare of our twentieth-century industrialism. The simple banking rules of Hamilton's day, when all the transactions of a fairsized bank could be kept in the neat penmanship of a clerk in one large ledger, fail to protect the millions of individual depositors of a great modern banking institution. And so it goes through all the range of economic life. Aggressive enterprise and shrewd invention have been at work on our economic machine. Our rules of conduct for the operation of that machine must be subjected to the same constant development.

And so in our social life. Forty years ago, slum conditions in our great cities were much worse than today. Living conditions on farms and working conditions in mines and factories were primitive. But they were taken for granted. Few people considered that the Government had responsibility for sanitation, for safety devices, for preventing child labor and night work for women. In 1911, twenty-four years ago, when I was first a member of the New York State Legislature, a number of the younger members of the Legislature worked against these old conditions and called for laws governing factory inspection, for workmen's compensation and for the limitation of work for women and children to fifty-four hours, with one day's rest in seven. Those of us who joined in this movement in the Legislature were called reformers, socialists, and wild men. We were opposed by many of the same organizations and the same individuals who are now crying aloud about the socialism involved in social security legislation, in bank deposit insurance, in farm credit, in the saving of homes, in the protection of investors and the regulation of public utilities. The reforms, however, for which we were condemned twenty-four years ago are taken today as a matter of course. And so, I believe, will be regarded the reforms that now cause such concern to the reactionaries of 1935. We come to an understanding of these new ways of protecting people because our knowledge enlarges and our capacity for organized action increases. People have learned that they can carry their burdens effectively only by cooperation. We have found out how to conquer the ravages of diseases that years ago were regarded as unavoidable and inevitable. We must learn that many other social ills can be cured.

Let me emphasize that serious as have been the errors of unrestrained individualism, I do not believe in abandoning the system of individual enterprise. The freedom and opportunity that have characterized American development in the past can be maintained if we recognize the fact that the individual system of our day calls for the collaboration of all of us to provide, at the least, security for all of us. Those words "freedom" and "opportunity" do not mean a license to climb upwards by pushing other people down.

Any paternalistic system which tries to provide for security for everyone from above only calls for an impossible task and a regimentation utterly uncongenial to the spirit of our people. But Government cooperation to help make the system of free enterprise work, to provide that minimum security without which the competitive system cannot function, to restrain the kind of individual action which in the past has been harmful to the community—that kind of governmental cooperation is entirely consistent with the best tradition of America.

Just as the evolution of economic and social life has shown the need for new methods and practices, so has the new political life developed the need for new political practices and methods. Government now demands the best trained brains of every business and profession. Government today requires higher and higher standards of those who would serve it. It must bring to its service greater and greater competence. The conditions of public work must be improved and protected. Mere party membership and loyalty can no longer be the exclusive test. We must be loyal not merely to persons or parties, but we must be loyal also to the higher conceptions of ability and devotion that modern Government requires. . . .

I, for one, am willing to place my trust in the youth of America. If they demand action as well as preachments, I should be ashamed to chill their enthusiasm with the dire prophecy that to change is to destroy. I am unwilling to sneer at the vision of youth merely because vision is sometimes mistaken. But vision does not belong only to the young.

There are millions of older people who have vision, just as there are some younger men and women who are ready to put a weary, selfish or greedy hand upon the clock of progress and turn it back.

We who seek to go forward must ever guard ourselves against a danger which history teaches. More than ever, we cherish the elective form of democratic government, but progress under it can easily be retarded by disagreements that relate to method and to detail rather than to the broad objectives upon which we are agreed. It is as if all of us were united in the pursuit of a common goal, but that each and every one of us were marching along a separate road of our own. If we insist on choosing different roads, most of us will not reach our common destination. The reason that the forces of reaction so often defeat the forces of progress is that the Tories of the world are agreed and united in standing still on the same old spot and, therefore, never run the danger of getting lost on divergent trails. One might remark in passing that one form of standing still on the same spot consists in agreeing to condemn all progress and letting it go at that.

Therefore, to the American youth of all parties I submit a message of confidence—Unite and Challenge! Rules are not necessarily sacred; principles are. The methods of the old order are not, as some would have you believe, above the challenge of youth.

Let us carry on the good that the past gave us. The best of that good is the spirit of America. And the spirit of America is the spirit of inquiry, of readjustment, of improvement, above all a spirit in which youth can find the fulfillment of its ideals. It is for the new generation to participate in the decisions and to give strength and spirit and continuity to our Government and to our national life.

45

FIRESIDE CHAT ON
REORGANIZATION OF JUDICIARY
March 9, 1937

Tonight, sitting at my desk in the White House, I make my first radio report to the people in my second term of office.

I am reminded of that evening in March, four years ago, when I made my first radio report to you. We were then in the midst of the great banking crisis.

Soon after, with the authority of the Congress, we asked the Nation to turn over all of its privately held gold, dollar for dollar, to the Government of the United States.

Today's recovery proves how right that policy was.

But when, almost two years later, it came before the Supreme Court its constitutionality was upheld only by a five-to-four vote. The change of one vote would have thrown all the affairs of this great Nation back into hopeless chaos. In effect, four Justices ruled that the right under a private contract to exact a pound of flesh was more sacred than the main objectives of the Constitution to establish an enduring Nation.

In 1933 you and I knew that we must never let our economic system get completely out of joint again—that we could not afford to take the risk of another great depression.

We also became convinced that the only way to avoid a repetition of those dark days was to have a government with power to prevent and to cure the abuses and the inequalities which had thrown that system out of joint.

We then began a program of remedying those abuses and inequalities— to give balance and stability to our economic system—to make it bomb-proof against the causes of 1929.

Today we are only part-way through that program—and recovery is speeding up to a point where the dangers of 1929 are again becoming possible, not this week or month perhaps, but within a year or two.

National laws are needed to complete that program. Individual or local or state effort alone cannot protect us in 1937 any better than ten years ago.

It will take time—and plenty of time—to work out our remedies administratively even after legislation is passed. To complete our program of protection in time, therefore, we cannot delay one moment in making certain that our National Government has power to carry through.

Four years ago action did not come until the eleventh hour. It was almost too late.

If we learned anything from the depression we will not allow ourselves to run around in new circles of futile discussion and debate, always postponing the day of decision.

The American people have learned from the depression. For in the last three national elections an overwhelming majority of them voted a mandate that the Congress and the President begin the task of providing that protection—not after long years of debate, but now.

The Courts, however, have cast doubts on the ability of the elected Congress to protect us against catastrophe by meeting squarely our modern social and economic conditions.

We are at a crisis in our ability to proceed with that protection. It is a quiet crisis. There are no lines of depositors outside closed banks. But to the far-sighted it is far-reaching in its possibilities of injury to America.

I want to talk with you very simply about the need for present action in this crisis—the need to meet the unanswered challenge of one-third of a Nation ill-nourished, ill-clad, ill-housed.

Last Thursday I described the American form of Government as a three horse team provided by the Constitution to the American people so that their field might be plowed. The three horses are, of course, the three branches of government—the Congress, the Executive and the Courts. Two of the horses are pulling in unison today; the third is not. Those who have intimated that the President of the United States is trying to drive that team, overlook the simple fact that the President, as Chief Executive, is himself one of the three horses.

It is the American people themselves who are in the driver's seat.

It is the American people themselves who want the furrow plowed.

It is the American people themselves who expect the third horse to pull in unison with the other two.

I hope that you have re-read the Constitution of the United States in these past few weeks. Like the Bible, it ought to be read again and again.

It is an easy document to understand when you remember that it was called into being because the Articles of Confederation under which the original thirteen States tried to operate after the Revolution showed the need of a National Government with power enough to handle national problems. In its Preamble, the Constitution states that it was intended to form a more perfect Union and promote the general welfare; and the powers given to the Congress to carry out those purposes can be best described by saying that they were all the powers needed to meet each and every problem which then had a national character and which could not be met by merely local action.

But the framers went further. Having in mind that in succeeding generations many other problems then undreamed of would become national problems, they gave to the Congress the ample broad powers "to levy taxes . . . and provide for the common defense and general welfare of the United States."

That, my friends, is what I honestly believe to have been the clear and underlying purpose of the patriots who wrote a Federal Constitution to create a National Government with national power, intended as they said, "to form a more perfect union . . . for ourselves and our posterity."

For nearly twenty years there was no conflict between the Congress and the Court. Then Congress passed a statute which, in 1803, the Court said violated an express provision of the Constitution. The Court claimed the power to declare it unconstitutional and did so declare it. But a little later the Court itself admitted that it was an extraordinary power to exercise and through Mr. Justice Washington laid down this limitation upon it: "It is but a decent respect due to the wisdom, the integrity and the patriotism of the legislative body, by which any law is passed, to presume in favor of its validity until its violation of the Constitution is proved beyond all reasonable doubt."

But since the rise of the modern movement for social and economic progress through legislation, the Court has more and more often and more and more boldly asserted a power to veto laws passed by the Congress and State Legislatures in complete disregard of this original limitation.

In the last four years the sound rule of giving statutes the benefit of all reasonable doubt has been cast aside. The Court has been acting not as a judicial body, but as a policy-making body.

When the Congress has sought to stabilize national agriculture, to improve the conditions of labor, to safeguard business against unfair competition, to protect our national resources, and in many other ways, to serve our clearly national needs, the majority of the Court has been assuming the power to pass on the wisdom of these Acts of the Congress—and to approve or disapprove the public policy written into these laws.

That is not only my accusation. It is the accusation of most distinguished Justices of the present Supreme Court. I have not the time to quote to you all the language used by dissenting Justices in many of these cases. But in the case holding the Railroad Retirement Act unconstitutional, for instance, Chief Justice Hughes said in a dissenting opinion that the majority opinion was "a departure from sound principles," and placed "an unwarranted limitation upon the commerce clause." And three other Justices agreed with him.

In the case holding the A.A.A. unconstitutional, Justice Stone said of the majority opinion that it was a "tortured construction of the Constitution." And two other Justices agreed with him.

In the case holding the New York Minimum Wage Law unconstitutional, Justice Stone said that the majority were actually reading into the Constitution their own "personal economic predilections," and that if the legislative power is not left free to choose the methods of solving the problems of poverty, subsistence and health of large numbers in the community, then "government is to be rendered impotent." And two other Justices agreed with him.

In the face of these dissenting opinions, there is no basis for the claim made by some members of the Court that something in the Constitution has compelled them regretfully to thwart the will of the people.

In the face of such dissenting opinions, it is perfectly clear, that as Chief Justice Hughes has said: "We are under a Constitution, but the Constitution is what the Judges say it is."

The Court in addition to the proper use of its judicial functions has improperly set itself up as a third House of the Congress—a super-legislature, as one of the justices has called it—reading into the Constitution words and implications which are not there, and which were never intended to be there.

We have, therefore, reached the point as a Nation where we must take action to save the Constitution from the Court and the Court from itself. We must find a way to take an appeal from the Supreme Court to the Constitution itself. We want a Supreme Court which will do justice under the Constitution—not over it. In our Courts we want a government of laws and not of men.

I want—as all Americans want—an independent judiciary as proposed by the framers of the Constitution. That means a Supreme Court that will enforce the Constitution as written—that will refuse to amend the Constitution by the arbitrary exercise of judicial power—amendment by judicial say-so. It does not mean a judiciary so independent that it can deny the existence of facts universally recognized.

How then could we proceed to perform the mandate given us? It was said in last year's Democratic platform, "If these problems cannot be effectively solved within the Constitution, we shall seek such clarifying amendment as will assure the power to enact those laws, adequately to regulate commerce, protect public health and safety, and safeguard economic security." In other words, we said we would seek an amendment only if every other possible means by legislation were to fail.

When I commenced to review the situation with the problem squarely before me, I came by a process of elimination to the conclusion that, short of amendments, the only method which was clearly constitutional, and would at the same time carry out other much needed reforms, was to infuse new blood into all our Courts. We must have men worthy and equipped to carry out impartial justice. But, at the same time, we must have Judges who will bring to the Courts a present-day sense of the Constitution—Judges who will retain in the Courts the judicial functions of a court, and reject the legislative powers which the courts have today assumed.

In forty-five out of the forty-eight States of the Union, Judges are chosen not for life but for a period of years. In many States Judges must retire at the age of seventy. Congress has provided financial security by offering life pensions at full pay for Federal Judges on all Courts who are willing to retire at seventy. In the case of Supreme Court Justices, that pension is $20,000 a year. But all Federal Judges, once appointed, can, if they choose, hold office for life, no matter how old they may get to be.

What is my proposal? It is simply this: whenever a Judge or Justice of any Federal Court has reached the age of seventy and does not avail himself of the opportunity to retire on a pension, a new member shall be appointed by the President then in office, with the approval, as required by the Constitution, of the Senate of the United States.

The plan has two chief purposes. By bringing into the judicial system a steady and continuing stream of new and younger blood, I hope, first, to make the administration of all Federal justice speedier and, therefore, less costly; secondly, to bring to the decision of social and economic problems younger men who have had personal experience and contact with modern facts and circumstances under which average men have to live and work. This plan will save our national Constitution from hardening of the judicial arteries.

The number of Judges to be appointed would depend wholly on the decision of present Judges now over seventy, or those who would subsequently reach the age of seventy.

If, for instance, any one of the six Justices of the Supreme Court now over the age of seventy should retire as provided under the plan, no additional place would be created. Consequently, although there never can be more than fifteen, there may be only fourteen, or thirteen, or twelve. And there may be only nine.

There is nothing novel or radical about this idea. It seeks to maintain the Federal bench in full vigor. It has been discussed and approved by many persons of high authority ever since a similar proposal passed the House of Representatives in 1869.

Why was the age fixed at seventy? Because the laws of many States, the practice of the Civil Service, the regulations of the Army and Navy, and the rules of many of our Universities and of almost every great private business enterprise, commonly fix the retirement age at seventy years or less.

The statute would apply to all the courts in the Federal system. There is general approval so far as the lower Federal courts are concerned. The plan has met opposition only so far as the Supreme Court of the United States itself is concerned. If such a plan is good for the lower courts it certainly ought to be equally good for the highest Court from which there is no appeal.

Those opposing this plan have sought to arouse prejudice and fear by crying that I am seeking to "pack" the Supreme Court and that a baneful precedent will be established.

What do they mean by the words "packing the Court"?

Let me answer this question with a bluntness that will end all *honest* misunderstanding of my purposes.

If by that phrase "packing the Court" it is charged that I wish to place on the bench spineless puppets who would disregard the law and would decide specific cases as I wished them to be decided, I make this answer: that no President fit for his office would appoint, and no Senate of honorable men fit for their office would confirm, that kind of appointees to the Supreme Court.

But if by that phrase the charge is made that I would appoint and the Senate would confirm Justices worthy to sit beside present members of the Court who understand those modern conditions, that I will appoint Justices who will not undertake to override the judgment of the Congress on legislative policy, that I will appoint Justices who will act as Justices and not as legislators—if the appointment of such Justices can be called "packing the Courts," then I say that I and with me the vast majority of the American people favor doing just that thing—now.

Is it a dangerous precedent for the Congress to change the number of the Justices? The Congress has always had, and will have, that power. The number of Justices has been changed several times before, in the Administrations of John Adams and Thomas Jefferson—both signers of the Declaration of Independence—Andrew Jackson, Abraham Lincoln and Ulysses S. Grant.

I suggest only the addition of Justices to the bench in accordance with a clearly defined principle relating to a clearly defined age limit. Fundamentally, if in the future, America cannot trust the Congress it elects to refrain from abuse of our Constitutional usages, democracy will have failed far beyond the importance to it of any kind of precedent concerning the Judiciary.

We think it so much in the public interest to maintain a vigorous judiciary that we encourage the retirement of elderly Judges by offering them a life pension at full salary. Why then should we leave the fulfillment of this public policy to chance or make it dependent upon the desire or prejudice of any individual Justice?

It is the clear intention of our public policy to provide for a constant flow of new and younger blood into the Judiciary. Normally every President appoints a large number of District and Circuit Judges and a few members of the Supreme Court. Until my first term practically every President of the United States had appointed at least one member of the Supreme Court. President Taft appointed five members and named a Chief Justice; President Wilson, three; President Harding, four, including a Chief Justice; President Coolidge, one; President Hoover, three, including a Chief Justice.

Such a succession of appointments should have provided a Court well-balanced as to age. But chance and the disinclination of individuals to leave the Supreme bench have now given us a Court in which five Justices will be over seventy-five years of age before next June and one over seventy. Thus a sound public policy has been defeated.

I now propose that we establish by law an assurance against any such ill-balanced Court in the future. I propose that hereafter, when a Judge reaches the age of seventy, a new and younger Judge shall be added to the Court automatically. In this way I propose to enforce a sound public policy by law instead of leaving the composition of our Federal Courts, including the highest, to be determined by chance or the personal decision of individuals.

If such a law as I propose is regarded as establishing a new precedent, is it not a most desirable precedent?

Like all lawyers, like all Americans, I regret the necessity of this controversy. But the welfare of the United States, and indeed of the Constitution itself, is what we all must think about first. Our difficulty with the Court today rises not from the Court as an institution but from human beings within it. But we cannot yield our constitutional destiny to the personal judgment of a few men who, being fearful of the future, would deny us the necessary means of dealing with the present.

This plan of mine is no attack on the Court; it seeks to restore the Court to its rightful and historic place in our system of Constitutional Government and to have it resume its high task of building anew on the Constitution "a system of living law." The Court itself can best undo what the Court has done.

I have thus explained to you the reasons that lie behind our efforts to secure results by legislation within the Constitution. I hope that thereby the difficult process of constitutional amendment may be rendered unnecessary. But let us examine that process.

There are many types of amendment proposed. Each one is radically different from the other. There is no substantial group within the Congress or outside it who are agreed on any single amendment.

It would take months or years to get substantial agreement upon the type and language of an amendment. It would take months and years thereafter to get a two-thirds majority in favor of that amendment in *both* Houses of the Congress.

Then would come the long course of ratification by three-fourths of all the States. No amendment which any powerful economic interests or the leaders of any powerful political party have had reason to oppose has ever been ratified within anything like a reasonable time. And thirteen States which contain only five percent of the voting population can block ratification even though the thirty-five States with ninety-five percent of the population are in favor of it.

A very large percentage of newspaper publishers, Chambers of Commerce, Bar Associations, Manufacturers' Associations, who are trying to give the impression that they really do want a constitutional amendment would be the first to exclaim as soon as an amendment was proposed, "Oh! I was for an amendment all right, but this amendment that you have proposed is not the kind of an amendment that I was thinking about. I am, therefore, going to spend my time, my efforts and my money to block that amendment, although I would be awfully glad to help get some other kind of amendment ratified."

Two groups oppose my plan on the ground that they favor a constitutional amendment. The first includes those who fundamentally object to social and economic legislation along modern lines. This is the same group who during the campaign last Fall tried to block the mandate of the people.

Now they are making a last stand. And the strategy of that last stand is to suggest the time-consuming process of amendment in order to kill off by delay the legislation demanded by the mandate.

To them I say: I do not think you will be able long to fool the American people as to your purposes.

The other group is composed of those who honestly believe the amendment process is the best and who would be willing to support a reasonable amendment if they could agree on one.

To them I say: we cannot rely on an amendment as the immediate or only answer to our present difficulties. When the time comes for action, you will find that many of those who pretend to support you will sabotage any constructive amendment which is proposed. Look at these strange bed-fellows of yours. When before have you found them really at your side in your fights for progress?

And remember one thing more. Even if an amendment were passed, and even if in the years to come it were to be ratified, its meaning would depend upon the kind of Justices who would be sitting on the Supreme Court bench. An amendment, like the rest of the Constitution, is what the Justices say it is rather than what its framers or you might hope it is.

This proposal of mine will not infringe in the slightest upon the civil or religious liberties so dear to every American.

My record as Governor and as President proves my devotion to those liberties. You who know me can have no fear that I would tolerate the destruction by any branch of government of any part of our heritage of freedom.

The present attempt by those opposed to progress to play upon the fears of danger to personal liberty brings again to mind that crude and cruel strategy tried by the same opposition to frighten the workers of America in a pay-envelope propaganda against the Social Security Law. The workers were not fooled by that propaganda then. The people of America will not be fooled by such propaganda now.

I am in favor of action through legislation:

First, because I believe that it can be passed at this session of the Congress.

Second, because it will provide a reinvigorated, liberal-minded Judiciary necessary to furnish quicker and cheaper justice from bottom to top.

Third, because it will provide a series of Federal Courts willing to enforce the Constitution as written, and unwilling to assert legislative powers by writing into it their own political and economic policies.

During the past half century the balance of power between the three great branches of the Federal Government, has been tipped out of balance by the Courts in direct contradiction of the high purposes of the framers of the Constitution. It is my purpose to restore that balance. You who know me will accept my solemn assurance that in a world in which democracy is under attack, I seek to make American democracy succeed. You and I will do our part.

46
ADDRESS ON CONSTITUTION DAY
September 17, 1937

ONE HUNDRED FIFTY YEARS AGO TONIGHT, thirty-eight weary delegates to a Convention in Philadelphia signed the Constitution. Four handwritten sheets of parchment were enough to state the terms on which thirteen independent weak little republics agreed to try to survive together as one strong nation.

A third of the original delegates had given up and gone home. The moral force of Washington and Franklin had kept the rest together. Those remained who cared the most; and caring most, dared most.

The world of 1787 provided a perfect opportunity for the organization of a new form of government thousands of miles removed from influences hostile to it. How we then governed ourselves did not greatly concern Europe. And what occurred in Europe did not immediately affect us.

Today the picture is different.

Now what we do has enormous immediate effect not only among the nations of Europe but also among those of the Americas and the Far East, and what in any part of the world they do as surely and quickly affects us.

In such an atmosphere our generation has watched democracies replace monarchies which had failed their people, and dictatorships displace democracies which had failed to function. And of late we have heard a clear challenge to the democratic idea of representative government.

We do not deny that the methods of the challengers—whether they be called "communistic" or "dictatorial" or "military"—have obtained for many who live under them material things they did not obtain under democracies which they had failed to make function. Unemployment has been lessened, even though the cause is a mad manufacturing of armaments. Order prevails, even though maintained by fear, at the expense of liberty and individual rights.

So their leaders laugh at all constitutions, predict the copying of their own methods, and prophesy the early end of democracy throughout the world.

Both that attitude and that prediction are denied by those of us who still believe in democracy—that is, by the overwhelming majority of the nations of the world and by the overwhelming majority of the people of the world.

And the denial is based on two reasons eternally right.

The first reason is that modern men and women will not tamely commit to one man or one group the permanent conduct of their government. Eventually they will insist not only on the right to choose who shall govern them, but also upon the periodic reconsideration of that choice by the free exercise of the ballot.

And the second reason is that the state of world affairs brought about by those new forms of government threatens civilization. Armaments and deficits pile up together. Trade barriers multiply and merchant ships are threatened on the high seas. Fear spreads throughout the world, fear of aggression, fear of invasion, fear of revolution, fear of death.

The people of America are rightly determined to keep that growing menace from our shores.

The known and measurable danger of becoming involved in war we face confidently. As to that, your government knows your mind, and you know your government's mind.

But it takes even more foresight, intelligence and patience to meet the subtle attack which spreading dictatorship makes upon the morale of a democracy.

In our generation, a new idea has come to dominate thought about government, the idea that the resources of the nation can be made to produce a far higher standard of living for the masses of the people if only government is intelligent and energetic in giving the right direction to economic life.

That idea—or more properly that ideal—is wholly justified by the facts. It cannot be thrust aside by those who want to go back to the conditions of ten years ago or even preserve the conditions of today. It puts all forms of government to their proof.

That ideal makes understandable the demands of labor for shorter hours and higher wages, the demands of farmers for a more stable income, the demands of the great majority of business men for relief from disruptive trade practices, the demands of all for the end of that kind of license, often mistermed "Liberty," which permits a handful of the population to take far more than its tolerable share from the rest of the people.

And as other forms of government in other lands parade their pseudo-science of economic organization, even some of our own people may wonder whether democracy can match dictatorship in giving this generation the things it wants from government.

We have those who really fear the majority rule of democracy, who want old forms of economic and social control to remain in a few hands. They say in their hearts: "If constitutional democracy continues to threaten our control why should we be against a *plutocratic* dictatorship if that would perpetuate our control?"

And we have those who are in too much of a hurry, who are impatient at the processes of constitutional democracies, who want Utopia overnight and are not sure that some vague form of *proletarian* dictatorship is not the quickest road to it.

Both types are equally dangerous. One represents cold-blooded resolve to hold power. We have engaged in a definite, and so far successful, contest against that. The other represents a reckless resolve to seize power. Equally we are against that.

And the overwhelming majority of the American people fully understand and completely approve that course as the course of the present government of the United States.

To hold to that course our constitutional democratic form of government must meet the insistence of the great mass of our people that economic and social security and the standard of American living be raised from what they are to levels which the people know our resources justify.

Only by succeeding in *that* can we ensure against internal doubt as to the worthwhileness of our democracy and dissipate the illusion that the necessary price of efficiency is dictatorship with its attendant spirit of aggression.

That is why I have been saying for months that there is a crisis in American affairs which demands action now, a crisis particularly dangerous because its external and internal difficulties reenforce each other.

Purposely I paint a broad picture. For only if the problem is seen in perspective can we see its solution in perspective.

I am not a pessimist. I believe that democratic government in this country can do all the things which common-sense people, seeing that picture as a whole, have the right to expect. I believe that these things can be done under the Constitution, without the surrender of a single one of the civil and religious liberties it was intended to safeguard.

And I am determined that under the Constitution these things *shall* be done.

The men who wrote the Constitution were the men who fought the Revolution. They had watched a weak emergency government almost lose the war, and continue economic distress among thirteen little republics, at peace but without effective national government.

So when these men planned a new government, they drew the kind of agreement which men make when they really want to work together under it for a very long time.

For the youngest of nations they drew what is today the oldest written instrument under which men have continuously lived together as a nation.

The Constitution of the United States was a layman's document, not a lawyer's contract. *That* cannot be stressed too often. Madison, most responsible for it, was not a lawyer; nor was Washington or Franklin, whose sense of the give-and-take of life had kept the Convention together.

This great layman's document was a charter of general principles, completely different from the "whereases" and the "parties of the first part" and the fine print which lawyers put into leases and insurance policies and installment agreements.

When the Framers were dealing with what they rightly considered eternal verities, unchangeable by time and circumstance, they used specific language. In no uncertain terms, for instance, they forbade titles of nobility, the suspension of habeas corpus and the withdrawal of money from the Treasury except after appropriation by law. With almost equal definiteness they detailed the Bill of Rights.

But when they considered the fundamental powers of the new national government they used generality, implication and statement of mere objectives, as intentional phrases which flexible statesmanship of the future, within the Constitution, could adapt to time and circumstance. For instance, the framers used broad and general language capable of meeting evolution and change when they referred to commerce between the States, the taxing power and the general welfare.

Even the Supreme Court was treated with that purposeful lack of specification. Contrary to the belief of many Americans, the Constitution says nothing about any power of the Court to declare legislation unconstitutional; nor does it mention the number of judges for the Court. Again and again the Convention voted down proposals to give Justices of the Court a veto over legislation. Clearly a majority of the delegates believed that the relation of the Court to the Congress and the Executive, like the other subjects treated in general terms, would work itself out by evolution and change over the years.

But for one hundred and fifty years we have had an unending struggle between those who would preserve this original broad concept of the Constitution as a layman's instrument of government and those who would shrivel the Constitution into a lawyer's contract.

Those of us who really believe in the enduring wisdom of the Constitution hold no rancor against those who professionally or politically talk and think in purely legalistic phrases. We cannot seriously be alarmed when they cry "unconstitutional" at every effort to better the condition of our people.

Such cries have always been with us; and, ultimately, they have always been overruled.

Lawyers distinguished in 1787 insisted that the Constitution itself was unconstitutional under the Articles of Confederation. But the ratifying conventions overruled them.

Lawyers distinguished in their day warned Washington and Hamilton that the protective tariff was unconstitutional, warned Jefferson that the Louisiana Purchase was unconstitutional, warned Monroe that to open up roads across the Alleghenies was unconstitutional. But the Executive and the Congress overruled them.

Lawyers distinguished in their day persuaded a divided Supreme Court that the Congress had no power to govern slavery in the territories, that the long-standing Missouri Compromise was unconstitutional. But a War Between the States overruled them.

Lawyers distinguished in their day persuaded the Odd Man on the Supreme Court that the methods of financing the Civil War were unconstitutional. But a new Odd Man overruled them.

That great Senatorial constitutional authority of his day, Senator Evarts, issued a solemn warning that the proposed Interstate Commerce Act and the Federal regulation of railway rates which the farmers demanded would be unconstitutional. But both the Senate and the Supreme Court overruled him.

Less than two years ago fifty-eight of the highest priced lawyers in the land gave the Nation (without cost to the Nation) a solemn and formal opinion that the Wagner Labor Relations Act was unconstitutional. And in a few months, first a national election and later the Supreme Court overruled them.

For twenty years the Odd Man on the Supreme Court refused to admit that State minimum wage laws for women were constitutional. A few months ago, after my message to the Congress on the rejuvenation of the Judiciary, the Odd Man admitted that the Court had been wrong—for all those twenty years—and overruled himself.

In this constant struggle the lawyers of no political party, mine or any other, have had a consistent or unblemished record. But the lay rank and file of political parties *has* had a consistent record.

Unlike some lawyers, they have respected as sacred *all* branches of their government. They have seen nothing *more* sacred about one branch than about either of the others. They have considered as *most* sacred the concrete welfare of the generation of the day. And with laymen's common sense of what government is for, they have demanded that all three branches be efficient, that all three be interdependent as well as independent, and that all three work together to meet the living generation's expectations of government.

That lay rank and file can take cheer from the historic fact that every effort to construe the Constitution as a lawyer's contract rather than a lay-man's charter has ultimately failed. Whenever legalistic interpretation has clashed with contemporary sense on great questions of broad national policy, ultimately the people and the Congress have had their way.

But that word "ultimately" covers a terrible cost.

It cost a Civil War to gain recognition of the constitutional power of the Congress to legislate for the territories.

It cost twenty years of taxation on those *least* able to pay to recognize the constitutional power of the Congress to levy taxes on those *most* able to pay.

It cost twenty years of exploitation of women's labor to recognize the constitutional power of the States to pass minimum wage laws for their protection.

It has cost twenty years already—and no one knows how many more are to come—to obtain a constitutional interpretation that will let the Nation regulate the shipment in national commerce of goods sweated from the labor of little children.

We know it takes time to adjust government to the needs of society. But modern history proves that reforms too long delayed or denied have jeopardized peace, undermined democracy and swept away civil and religious liberties.

Yes, time more than ever before is vital in statesmanship and in government, in all three branches of it.

We will no longer be permitted to sacrifice each generation in turn while the law catches up with life.

We can no longer afford the luxury of twenty-year lags.

You will find no justification in any of the language of the Constitution for delay in the reforms which the mass of the American people now demand.

Yet nearly every attempt to meet those demands for social and economic betterment has been jeopardized or actually forbidden by those who have sought to *read* into the Constitution language which the framers refused to *write* into the Constitution.

No one cherishes more deeply than I the civil and religious liberties achieved by so much blood and anguish through the many centuries of Anglo-American history. But the Constitution guarantees liberty, not license masquerading as liberty.

Let me put the real situation in the simplest terms. The present government of the United States has never taken away and never will take away any liberty from any minority, unless it be a minority which so abuses its liberty as to do positive and definite harm to its neighbors constituting the majority. But the government of the United States refuses to forget that the Bill of Rights was put into the Constitution not only to protect minorities against intolerance of majorities, but to protect majorities against the enthronement of minorities.

Nothing would so surely destroy the substance of what the Bill of Rights protects than its perversion to prevent social progress. The surest protection of the individual and of minorities is that fundamental tolerance and feeling for fair play which the Bill of Rights assumes. But tolerance and fair play would disappear here as it has in some other lands if the great mass of people were denied confidence in their justice, their security and their self-respect. Desperate people in other lands surrendered their liberties when freedom came merely to mean humiliation and starvation. The crisis of 1933 should make us understand that.

On this solemn anniversary I ask that the American people rejoice in the wisdom of their Constitution.

I ask that they guarantee the effectiveness of each of its parts by living by the Constitution as a *whole*.

I ask that they have faith in its ultimate capacity to work out the problems of democracy, but that they justify that faith by making it work now rather than twenty years from now.

I ask that they give their fealty to the Constitution *itself* and not to its misinterpreters.

I ask that they exalt the glorious simplicity of its purposes rather than a century of complicated legalism.

I ask that majorities and minorities subordinate intolerance and power alike to the common good of all.

For us the Constitution is a common bond, without bitterness, for those who see America as Lincoln saw it, "the last, best hope of earth."

So we revere it, not because it is old but because it is ever new, not in the worship of its past alone but in the faith of the living who keep it young, now and in the years to come.

47
FIRESIDE CHAT ON
PARTY PRIMARIES
June 24, 1938

OUR GOVERNMENT, happily, is a democracy. As part of the democratic process, your President is again taking an opportunity to report on the progress of national affairs to the real rulers of this country—the voting public.

The Seventy-fifth Congress, elected in November, 1936, on a platform uncompromisingly liberal, has adjourned. Barring unforeseen events, there will be no session until the new Congress, to be elected in November, assembles next January.

On the one hand, the Seventy-fifth Congress has left many things undone.

For example, it refused to provide more businesslike machinery for running the Executive Branch of the Government. The Congress also failed to meet my suggestion that it take the far-reaching steps necessary to put the railroads of the country back on their feet.

But, on the other hand, the Congress, striving to carry out the Platform on which most of its members were elected achieved more for the future good of the country than any Congress between the end of the World War and the spring of 1933.

I mention tonight only the more important of these achievements.

1. It improved still further our agricultural laws to give the farmer a fairer share of the national income, to preserve our soil, to provide an all-weather granary, to help the farm tenant toward independence, to find new uses for farm products, and to begin crop insurance.

2. After many requests on my part the Congress passed a Fair Labor Standards Act, commonly called the Wages and Hours Bill. That Act—

applying to products in interstate commerce—ends child labor, sets a floor below wages and a ceiling over hours of labor.

Except perhaps for the Social Security Act, it is the most far-reaching, far-sighted program for the benefit of workers ever adopted here or in any other country. Without question it starts us toward a better standard of living and increases purchasing power to buy the products of farm and factory.

Do not let any calamity-howling executive with an income of $1,000 a day, who has been turning his employees over to the Government relief rolls in order to preserve his company's undistributed reserves, tell you—using his stockholders' money to pay the postage for his personal opinions—that a wage of $11 a week is going to have a disastrous effect on all American industry. Fortunately for business as a whole, and therefore for the Nation, that type of executive is a rarity with whom most business executives heartily disagree.

3. The Congress has provided a fact-finding Commission to find a path through the jungle of contradictory theories about wise business practices— to find the necessary facts for any intelligent legislation on monopoly, on price-fixing and on the relationship between big business and medium-sized business and little business. Different from a great part of the world, we in America persist in our belief in individual enterprise and in the profit motive; but we realize we must continually seek improved practices to insure the continuance of reasonable profits, together with scientific progress, individual initiative, opportunities for the little fellow, fair prices, decent wages and continuing employment.

4. The Congress has coordinated the supervision of commercial aviation and air mail by establishing a new Civil Aeronautics Authority; and it has placed all postmasters under the civil service for the first time in our history.

5. The Congress set up the United States Housing Authority to help finance large-scale slum clearance and provide low rent housing for the low income groups in our cities. And by improving the Federal Housing Act, the Congress made it easier for private capital to build modest homes and low rental dwellings.

6. The Congress has properly reduced taxes on small corporate enterprises, and has made it easier for the Reconstruction Finance Corporation to make credit available to all business. I think the bankers of the country can fairly be expected to participate in loans where the Government, through the Reconstruction Finance Corporation, offers to take a fair portion of the risk.

7. The Congress has provided additional funds for the Works Progress Administration, the Public Works Administration, the Rural Electrification Administration, the Civilian Conservation Corps and other agencies, in order to take care of what we hope is a temporary additional number of unemployed and to encourage production of every kind by private enterprise.

All these things together I call our program for the national defense of our economic system. It is a program of balanced action—of moving on all fronts at once in intelligent recognition that all our economic problems, of every group, of every section, are essentially one.

8. Because of increasing armaments in other nations and an international situation which is definitely disturbing to all of us, the Congress has authorized important additions to the national armed defense of our shores and our people.

On another important subject the net result of a struggle in the Congress has been an important victory for the people of the United States—a lost battle which won a war.

You will remember that on February 5, 1937, I sent a message to the Congress dealing with the real need of Federal Court reforms of several kinds. In one way or another, during the sessions of this Congress, the ends—the real objectives—sought in that message, have been substantially attained.

The attitude of the Supreme Court toward constitutional questions is entirely changed. Its recent decisions are eloquent testimony of a willingness to collaborate with the two other branches of Government to make democracy work. The Government has been granted the right to protect its interests in litigation between private parties involving the constitutionality of Federal statutes, and to appeal directly to the Supreme Court in all cases involving the constitutionality of Federal statutes; and no single judge is any longer empowered to suspend a Federal statute on his sole judgment as to its constitutionality. Justices of the Supreme Court may now retire at the age of seventy after ten years service; a substantial number of additional judgeships have been created in order to expedite the trial of cases; and greater flexibility has been added to the Federal judicial system by allowing judges to be assigned to congested districts.

Another indirect accomplishment of this Congress has been its response to the devotion of the American people to a course of sane consistent liberalism. The Congress has understood that under modern conditions government has a continuing responsibility to meet continuing problems, and that Government cannot take a holiday of a year, a month, or even a day just because a few people are tired or frightened by the inescapable pace of this modern world in which we live.

Some of my opponents and some of my associates have considered that I have a mistakenly sentimental judgment as to the tenacity of purpose and the general level of intelligence of the American people.

I am still convinced that the American people, since 1932, continue to insist on two requisites of private enterprise, and the relationship of Government to it. The first is complete honesty at the top in looking after the use of other people's money, and in apportioning and paying individual and corporate taxes according to ability to pay. The second is sincere respect for the need of all at the bottom to get work—and through work to get a really fair share of the good things of life, and a chance to save and rise.

After the election of 1936 I was told, and the Congress was told, by an increasing number of politically—and worldly—wise people that I should coast along, enjoy an easy Presidency for four years, and not take the Democratic platform too seriously. They told me that people were getting weary of reform through political effort and would no longer oppose that small minority which, in spite of its own disastrous leadership in 1929, is always eager to resume its control over the Government of the United States.

Never in our lifetime has such a concerted campaign of defeatism been thrown at the heads of the President and Senators and Congressmen as in the case of this Seventy-fifth Congress. Never before have we had so many Copperheads—and you will remember that it was the Copperheads who, in the days of the War Between the States, tried their best to make Lincoln and his Congress give up the fight, let the Nation remain split in two and return to peace—peace at any price.

This Congress has ended on the side of the people. My faith in the American people—and their faith in themselves—have been justified. I congratulate the Congress and the leadership thereof and I congratulate the American people on their own staying power.

One word about our economic situation. It makes no difference to me whether you call it a recession or a depression. In 1932 the total national income of all the people in the country had reached the low point of thirty-eight billion dollars in that year. With each succeeding year it rose. Last year, 1937, it had risen to seventy billion dollars—despite definitely worse business and agricultural prices in the last four months of last year. This year, 1938, while it is too early to do more than give an estimate, we hope that the national income will not fall below sixty billion dollars. We remember also that banking and business and farming are not falling apart like the one-hoss shay, as they did in the terrible winter of 1932–1933.

Last year mistakes were made by the leaders of private enterprise, by the leaders of labor and by the leaders of Government—all three.

Last year the leaders of private enterprise pleaded for a sudden curtailment of public spending, and said they would take up the slack. But they made the mistake of increasing their inventories too fast and setting many of their prices too high for their goods to sell.

Some labor leaders, goaded by decades of oppression of labor, made the mistake of going too far. They were not wise in using methods which frightened many well-wishing people. They asked employers not only to bargain with them but to put up with jurisdictional disputes at the same time.

Government, too, made mistakes—mistakes of optimism in assuming that industry and labor would themselves make no mistakes—and Government made a mistake of timing, in not passing a farm bill or a wage and hour bill last year.

As a result of the lessons of all these mistakes we hope that in the future private enterprise—capital and labor alike—will operate more intelligently together, and in greater cooperation with their own Government than they have in the past. Such cooperation on the part of both of them will be very welcome to me. Certainly at this stage there should be a united stand on the part of both of them to resist wage cuts which would further reduce purchasing power.

Today a great steel company announced a reduction in prices with a view to stimulating business recovery, and I was gratified to know that this reduction involved no wage cut. Every encouragement should be given to industry which accepts a large volume of high wage policy.

If this is done, it ought to result in conditions which will replace a great part of the Government spending which the failure of cooperation made necessary this year.

From March 4, 1933, down, not a single week has passed without a cry from the opposition "to do something, to say something, to restore confidence." There is a very articulate group of people in this country, with plenty of ability to procure publicity for their views, who have consistently refused to cooperate with the mass of the people, whether things were going well or going badly, on the ground that they required more concessions to their point of view before they would admit having what they called "confidence."

These people demanded "restoration of confidence" when the banks were closed—and again when the banks were reopened.

They demanded "restoration of confidence" when hungry people were thronging the streets—and again when the hungry people were fed and put to work.

They demanded "restoration of confidence" when droughts hit the country—again now when our fields are laden with bounteous yields and excessive crops.

They demanded "restoration of confidence" last year when the automobile industry was running three shifts and turning out more cars than the country could buy—and again this year when the industry is trying to get rid of an automobile surplus and has shut down its factories as a result.

It is my belief that many of these people who have been crying aloud for "confidence" are beginning today to realize that that hand has been overplayed, and that they are now willing to talk cooperation instead. It is my belief that the mass of the American people do have confidence in themselves—have confidence in their ability, with the aid of Government, to solve their own problems.

It is because you are not satisfied, and I am not satisfied, with the progress we have made in finally solving our business and agricultural and social problems that I believe the great majority of you want your own Government to keep on trying to solve them. In simple frankness and in simple honesty, I need all the help I can get—and I see signs of getting more help in the future from many who have fought against progress with tooth and nail.

And now, following out this line of thought, I want to say a few words about the coming political primaries.

Fifty years ago party nominations were generally made in conventions—a system typified in the public imagination by a little group in a smoke-filled room who made out the party slates.

The direct primary was invented to make the nominating process a more democratic one—to give the party voters themselves a chance to pick their party candidates.

What I am going to say to you tonight does not relate to the primaries of any particular political party, but to matters of principle in all parties—Democratic, Republican, Farmer-Labor, Progressive, Socialist, or any other. Let that be clearly understood.

It is my hope that everybody affiliated with any party will vote in the primaries, and that every such voter will consider the fundamental principles for which his party is on record. That makes for a healthy choice between the candidates of the opposing parties on Election Day in November.

An election cannot give a country a firm sense of direction if it has two or more national parties which merely have different names but are as alike in their principles and aims as peas in the same pod.

In the coming primaries in all parties, there will be many clashes between two schools of thought, generally classified as liberal and conservative. Roughly speaking, the liberal school of thought recognizes that the new conditions throughout the world call for new remedies.

Those of us in America who hold to this school of thought, insist that these new remedies can be adopted and successfully maintained in this country under our present form of government if we use government as an instrument of cooperation to provide these remedies. We believe that we can solve our problems through continuing effort, through democratic processes instead of Fascism or Communism. We are opposed to the kind of moratorium on reform which, in effect, is reaction itself.

Be it clearly understood, however, that when I use the word "liberal," I mean the believer in progressive principles of democratic, representative government and not the wild man who, in effect, leans in the direction of Communism, for that is just as dangerous as Fascism.

The opposing or conservative school of thought, as a general proposition, does not recognize the need for Government itself to step in and take action to meet these new problems. It believes that individual initiative and private philanthropy will solve them—that we ought to repeal many of the things we have done and go back, for instance, to the old gold standard, or stop all this business of old age pensions and unemployment insurance, or repeal the Securities and Exchange Act, or let monopolies thrive unchecked—return, in effect, to the kind of Government we had in the twenties.

Assuming the mental capacity of all the candidates, the important question which it seems to me the primary voter must ask is this: "To which of these general schools of thought does the candidate belong?"

As President of the United States, I am not asking the voters of the country to vote for Democrats next November as opposed to Republicans or members of any other party. Nor am I, as President, taking part in Democratic primaries.

As the head of the Democratic Party, however, charged with the responsibility of carrying out the definitely liberal declaration of principles set forth in the 1936 Democratic platform, I feel that I have every right to speak in those few instances where there may be a clear issue between candidates for a Democratic nomination involving these principles, or involving a clear misuse of my own name.

Do not misunderstand me. I certainly would not indicate a preference in a State primary merely because a candidate, otherwise liberal in outlook, had conscientiously differed with me on any single issue. I should be far more concerned about the general attitude of a candidate toward present day problems and his own inward desire to get practical needs attended to in a practical way. We all know that progress may be blocked by outspoken reactionaries and also by those who say "yes" to a progressive objective, but who always find some reason to oppose any specific proposal to gain that objective. I call that type of candidate a "yes, but" fellow.

And I am concerned about the attitude of a candidate or his sponsors with respect to the rights of American citizens to assemble peaceably and to express publicly their views and opinions on important social and economic issues. There can be no constitutional democracy in any community which denies to the individual his freedom to speak and worship as he wishes. The American people will not be deceived by anyone who attempts to suppress individual liberty under the pretense of patriotism.

This being a free country with freedom of expression—especially with freedom of the press—there will be a lot of mean blows struck between now and Election Day. By "blows" I mean misrepresentation, personal attack and appeals to prejudice. It would be a lot better, of course, if campaigns everywhere could be waged with arguments instead of blows.

I hope the liberal candidates will confine themselves to argument and not resort to blows. In nine cases out of ten the speaker or writer who, seeking to influence public opinion, descends from calm argument to unfair blows hurts himself more than his opponent.

The Chinese have a story on this—a story based on three or four thousand years of civilization: Two Chinese coolies were arguing heatedly in the midst of a crowd. A stranger expressed surprise that no blows were being struck. His Chinese friend replied: "The man who strikes first admits that his ideas have given out."

I know that neither in the summer primaries nor in the November elections will the American voters fail to spot the candidate whose ideas have given out.

48
ADDRESS AT UNIVERSITY
OF PENNSYLVANIA
September 20, 1940

I AM VERY HAPPY with the present University of Pennsylvania. I cannot say that I am wholly happy that the founders of the University chose the year 1740. They might have had that great attribute which I have so long sought of looking ahead and planning. They would have founded the University in 1739, lest the two hundredth anniversary should fall in an election year. Thereby, I, at least, would have been saved much embarrassment. But what I want to say to you today I might as readily and easily have related in the autumn of 1939.

Even then we were in the midst of a strange period of relapse in the history of the civilization of the world—for in some lands it has become the custom to burn the books of scholars and to fix by Government decree the national forms of religion, morality, culture and education. It is more than a mere formality, at a time like this, to join with you in celebrating the two hundredth anniversary of this free and independent institution of scholarship. Therefore, I am doubly honored in becoming an alumnus of the University of Pennsylvania.

The very foundation of this University was concerned with freedom of religious teaching, and with free learning for the many who could not pay for higher education. As I understand my history, this was originally proposed as a place where the good and Reverend Doctor George Whitefield who, incidentally, used to go to my little County of Dutchess on the Hudson River—might preach his religion without certain difficulties which the old conservatives of Philadelphia at that time threw in his path. Indeed, it was desired to make it unnecessary for the good gentleman to preach in the sun and the rain of the open fields, when the doors of the established churches were closed against him. And it was the dream of the founders to make it a source of education to the children of the poor who otherwise might have gone untaught.

The survival and the growth of the University through these two centuries are particularly symbolic of the eternal strength that is inherent in the American concept of the freedom of human thought and action. Here is living proof of the validity and force of single-minded service to the cause of truth.

Events in this world of ours today are making the vast majority of our citizens think more and more clearly about the manner of the growth of their liberty and freedom, and how hard their people in the olden days fought and worked to win and to hold the privilege of free Government.

With the gaining of our political freedom you will remember that there came a conflict between the point of view of Alexander Hamilton, sincerely believing in the superiority of Government by a small group of public-spirited and usually wealthy citizens, and, on the other hand, the point of view of Thomas Jefferson, an advocate of Government by representatives chosen by all the people, an advocate of the universal right of free thought, free personal living, free religion, free expression of opinion and, above all, the right of free universal suffrage.

Many of the Jeffersonian school of thought were frank to admit the high motives and disinterestedness of Hamilton and his school. Many Americans of those days were willing to concede that if Government could be guaranteed to be kept always on the high level of unselfish service suggested by the Hamiltonians there would be nothing to fear. For the very basis of the Hamiltonian philosophy was that through a system of elections every four years, limited to the votes of the most highly educated and the most successful citizens, the best of those qualified to govern could always be selected.

It was, however, with rare perspicuity, as time has shown, that Jefferson pointed out that, on the doctrine of sheer human frailty, the Hamilton theory was bound to develop, in the long run, into Government by selfishness or Government for personal gain or Government by class, that would ultimately lead to the abolishment of free elections. For he recognized that it was our system of free unhampered elections which was the surest guaranty of popular Government. Just so long as the voters of the Nation, regardless of higher education or property possessions, were free to exercise their choice in the polling place without hindrance, the country would have no cause to fear the head of tyranny.

At all times in our history of nearly a century and a half since then, there have been many Americans who have sought to confine the ballot to limited groups of people. It was a quarter of a century ago that President Eliot of Harvard University summarized this view when he said to me something like this: "Roosevelt, I am convinced that even though we have multiplied our universities in every State of the Union, even though higher learning seems to have come into its own, nevertheless, if the ballot were to be confined to the holders of college degrees, the Nation would go on the rocks in a very few years." It may seem ungracious for a very new degree-holder to say this to this audience of older degree-holders, but my authority for that view is a great educator, noted for his efforts to disseminate college education throughout the country.

I must admit that I agree with him thoroughly in his estimate of the superior ability of the whole of the voters to pass upon political and social issues in free and unhampered elections, as against the exclusive ability of a smaller group of individuals at the top of the social structure.

On candidates and on election issues—and remember that I am trying to think of this year as being 1939—I would rather trust the aggregate judgment of all the people in a factory—the president, all the vice presidents, the board of directors, the managers, the foremen, plus all the laborers—rather than the judgment of the few who may have financial control at the time. On such questions the aggregate total judgment of a farm owner, of the farmer and of all the farm hands will be sounder, I think, than that of the farm owner alone. I would rather rely on the aggregate opinion, on matters affecting Government, of a railroad president and its superintendents, its engineers, foremen, brakemen, conductors, trainmen, telegraphers, porters and all the others, than on the sole opinion of the few in control of the management, or of the principal stockholders themselves.

Only too often—and we know many examples—in our political history, the few at the top have tried to advise or dictate to the many lower down how they should vote.

Even today in certain quarters there are, I regret to say, demands for a return of Government to the control of a fewer number of people, people who, because of business ability or economic omniscience are supposed to be just a touch above the average of our citizens. I took four years of economics when I was an undergraduate at Harvard, and everything I was taught is outside of all the textbooks today. The older I grow, the less omniscient I become in regard to economics, and I think most of us do. As in the days of Hamilton, we of our own generation should give those who demand government by the few all credit for pure intention and high ideals. Nevertheless, their type of political thinking could easily lead to Government by selfish seekers for power and riches and glory. For the great danger is that once the Government falls into the hands of a few élite, curtailment or even abolition of free elections might be adopted as the means of keeping them in power.

I can never forget that some well-meaning people have even recently seriously suggested that the right to vote be denied to American men and women who through no fault of their own had lost their jobs and, in order to keep the family and the home going, were working on work relief projects.

As long as periodic free elections survive, no set of people can permanently control Government. In the maintenance of free elections rests the complete and the enduring safety of our form of Government.

No dictator in history has ever dared to run the gauntlet of a really free election.

Fundamental truths like these have been stated so often that they are perhaps commonplace among Americans, but it is well constantly to keep them in mind in order to understand what has happened in other lands. A decade ago, for example, in 1930, the German people despaired of the processes of their democracy, which were based on the free use of the franchise. They were willing to lend ear to a new cult called "Nazi-ism"—a minority group which professed extraordinary patriotism, and offered bread and shelter and better Government through the rule of a handful of persons boasting of special aptitude for Government. In those days loudly professed emphasis was placed by that special group on their own purity of purpose. Nothing was ever said by them about abolishing free elections. Many people of large business affairs, influenced by several factors, and dissatisfied with the democratic system, as it was working out, formed political and economic alliances with this new small group.

You and I know the subsequent history of Germany. The right of free elections and the free choice of heads of Government were suddenly wiped out by a new regime, still professing the same purity of purpose. It is a travesty on fact to claim that there is any free choice of public officials in Germany today, or that there ever has been one since 1933.

What Jefferson prophesied might happen in this country, if the philosophy of the restricted vote and of Government by special class were adopted, did actually happen in Germany before our very eyes.

Many years ago, speaking in San Francisco, I pointed out that new conditions imposed new requirements upon Government and upon those who conducted Government. As Jefferson wrote a long time ago: "I know also that laws and institutions must go hand in hand with the progress of the human mind. . . . As new discoveries are made, new truths disclosed, and manners and opinions change with the change of circumstances, institutions must advance also, and keep pace with the times."

We must follow that rule today as readily as then, always with the condition that any change in institutions or in economic methods must remain within the same old framework of a freely elected democratic form of Government.

I have pointed out many times that western migration and the free use of unoccupied lands have ended with the advent of the industrial age; that with the changes wrought by new inventions of steam and electricity, new relationships have arisen between units of finance and industry on one side and the great mass of workers and small businessmen on the other; and that certain Government controls have become necessary to prevent a few financial and industrial groups from harming or curbing the threats of other groups that are smaller in size but much greater in number.

We have at the same time developed new beliefs in governmental responsibilities to humanity as a whole. It is a relatively new thing in American life to consider what the relationship of Government is to its starving people and to its unemployed citizens, and to take steps to fulfill its governmental duties to them.

A generation ago people had scarcely given thought to the terms "social security," "minimum wages" or "maximum hours." It is only within recent years that Government has given its attention in a serious, effective way to the insurance of bank deposits, to soil conservation, relief to farmers and to farm tenants, development of cheap electric water power, reclamation of soil by proper use of water and forests; to the prevention of fraud and deceit in the sale of securities; to the assurance of the principle of collective bargaining by workers in industry; to Government assistance to the blind and the handicapped; or to the need of taking care of elderly people without throwing them into the poorhouse.

These are some of the new instruments of social justice that America has forged to meet the new conditions of industry, agriculture, finance and labor—conditions which had been neglected too long and which were beginning to endanger our internal security. These many new instruments are the means that our own generation have adopted to overcome the threats to economic democracy in our land—threats which in other lands led quickly to political despotism.

Benjamin Franklin, to whom this University owes so much, realized too that while basic principles of natural science, of morality and of the science of society were eternal and immutable, the application of these principles necessarily changes with the patterns of living conditions from generation to generation. I am certain that he would insist, were he with us today, that it is the whole duty of the philosopher and the educator to apply the eternal ideals of truth and goodness and justice in terms of the present and not terms of the past. Growth and change are the law of all life. Yesterday's answers are inadequate for today's problems—just as the solutions of today will not fill the needs of tomorrow.

Eternal truths will be neither true nor eternal unless they have fresh meaning for every new social situation.

It is the function of education, the function of all of the great institutions of learning in the United States, to provide continuity for our national life—to transmit to youth the best of our culture that has been tested in the fire of history. It is equally the obligation of education to train the minds and the talents of our youth; to improve, through creative citizenship, our American institutions in accord with the requirements of the future.

We cannot always build the future for our youth, but we can build our youth for the future.

It is in great universities like this that the ideas which can assure our national safety and make tomorrow's history, are being forged and shaped. Civilization owes most to the men and women, known and unknown, whose free, inquiring minds and restless intellects could not be subdued by the power of tyranny.

This is no time for any man to withdraw into some ivory tower and proclaim the right to hold himself aloof from the problems and the agonies of his society. The times call for bold belief that the world can be changed by man's endeavor, and that this endeavor can lead to something new and better. No man can sever the bonds that unite him to his society simply by averting his eyes. He must ever be receptive and sensitive to the new; and have sufficient courage and skill to face novel facts and to deal with them.

If democracy is to survive, it is the task of men of thought, as well as men of action, to put aside pride and prejudice; and with courage and single-minded devotion—and above all with humility—to find the truth and teach the truth that shall keep men free.

We may find in that sense of purpose, the personal peace, not of repose, but of effort, the keen satisfaction of doing, the deep feeling of achievement for something far beyond ourselves, the knowledge that we build more gloriously than we know.

X

FELIX FRANKFURTER
(1882–1965)

FELIX FRANKFURTER, a professor at Harvard Law School, was a close personal friend and confidant of Franklin D. Roosevelt, who appointed him an Associate Justice of the United States Supreme Court in 1939. He served on that court until a stroke forced him to retire in 1962. An enormously prolific output of speeches, letters, lectures, pronouncements, articles, reports, and books flowed from his pen. In his work as a judge, he produced over 700 opinions.

Like Holmes, whom he greatly admired, Frankfurter has been regarded widely as a "philosopher" and, also like Holmes, he enjoyed a great deal of popularity. Hugo Black, who served on the Court from 1937 until 1971, and Frankfurter were seen as the great protagonists of opposing schools of jurisprudential thought, Black as the representative of what was called "judicial activism" and Frankfurter as the proponent of "judicial restraint." Without suggesting, even for the sake of argument, that Black was correct, it may nonetheless be asked of Frankfurter (as it may also be asked of Holmes) whether the particular character of his self-imposed restraint did not amount to judicial abdication. That would be the determining question in any effort to judge his jurisprudence and his statesmanship.

A large part of the contest between the views represented by Black and Frankfurter took place over the question of the extent to which the due-process clause of the Fourteenth Amendment imposed upon the states the limitations that the first eight amendments had imposed upon the United States. A related question involved the meaning of the first eight amendments, particularly the First, Fourth, Fifth, and Sixth. Black was of the view that the due-process clause simply "incorporated" the provisions of the first eight amendments and imposed them in full strength upon the states. Frankfurter maintained what had been the established view, that the due-process clause of the Fifth Amendment was separate from the other clauses of that amendment and had an "independent potency," and that the due-process clause of the Fourteenth Amendment imposed upon the states *exactly* what the due-process clause of the Fifth Amendment imposed upon the United States. Far from "incorporating" the several explicit provisions of the first eight amendments, it imposed upon the states something quite different from and independent of them, something understood as "essential fairness." Black's view was that the judicial effort to find "essential fairness" would loose the judge in the boundlessness of a "discredited" natural law doctrine. Frankfurter denied that judges were cast adrift, maintaining that they could determine "due process" without being merely "subjective." While the Court has never quite endorsed Black's view, it has surely drifted from Frankfurter's traditional view, perhaps never more so than in the instructive debate over the opposing principles in *Adamson* v. *California* (332 U.S. 46 [1947]).

The character of Frankfurter's "judicial restraint" appears in a clearer and more unalloyed form in his dissent in *West Virginia State Board of Education* v. *Barnette* (319 U.S. 624 [1943]). This opinion shows both the strongest and the most problematic aspects of his view. He had written the opinion for the Court in *Minersville School District* v. *Gobitis* (310 U.S. 586 [1940]) which had upheld the power of public schools to require a flag salute against the asserted First Amendment protection of the religious scruples of Jehovah's Witnesses. Three years later, in *Barnette,* he found himself dissenting against a reversal of the *Gobitis* ruling. "Were my purely personal attitude relevant," he said, "I should wholeheartedly associate myself with the general libertarian views in the Court's opinion . . . [but] . . . I am not justified in writing my private notions of policy into the Constitution, no matter how deeply I may cherish them or how mischievous I may deem their disregard." He asserted that it could "never be emphasized too much that one's own opinion about the wisdom or evil of a law should be excluded altogether when one is doing one's duty on the bench."

But after arguing quite persuasively that the West Virginia enact-ment being nullified was altogether permissible under the Constitu-tion, he went so far as to deny that the Constitution had *any* general character which could be effective in deciding a case.

In the past this Court has from time to time set its views of policy against that embodied in legislation by finding laws in conflict with what was called the "spirit of the Constitution." Such undefined destructive power was not conferred on this Court by the Constitution. . . . The attitude of judicial humility which these considerations enjoin is not an abdication of the judicial function. It is a due observance of its limits . . .

"The Zeitgeist and the Judiciary," an address by Frankfurter at the 25th anniversary dinner of the *Harvard Law Review* in 1912, outlines a view he held throughout his life. In an address he gave to the Ameri-can Philosophical Society in 1954, he attempts to explain "The Judi-cial Process and the Supreme Court" to a peculiarly qualified lay audience. "John Marshall and the Judicial Function" is an address Frankfurter delivered to a conference on Government under Law con-vened by Harvard Law School in commemoration of the 200th anni-versary of John Marshall's birth. He shows, subtly and tastefully, his disagreements with Marshall but also delineates the statesmanship of Marshall and the demand for statesmanship laid upon the Justices of the Supreme Court by their duties.

49

THE ZEITGEIST AND
THE JUDICIARY
1912

I AM SURE THAT NONE OF US will ever again enjoy the divine feeling of being one of the potentates of the profession that the editorship of the *Review* afforded; no, not even were we to sit on the Supreme Bench, for it was our frequent and joyous duty to reverse even that tribunal in an infallible judgment of one hundred and sixty-five words. Representing those to whom that luxury is still a green memory, I suppose I am to give expression to the ardor of youth, still untempered by responsibility, and not yet disillusioned by experience.

Last August, the American Bar Association with solemnity adopted vigorous resolutions condemning the recall of judges. I was one of those who favored the resolution, and I should vote for it again. But as I left the meeting, I had a conviction that the action was inadequate, that the American Bar Association fell short of its responsibility in not going beyond negative criticism and inquiring into the cause of the ferment that partly expresses itself in the ill-conceived proposal of the judicial recall. The fallacy of a specific remedy may be crushingly exposed, but we cannot whistle down the wind a widespread, insistent, and well-vouched feeling of dissatisfaction.

The tremendous economic and social changes of the last fifty years have inevitably reacted upon the functions of the state. More and more government is conceived as the biggest organized social effort for dealing with social problems. Our whole evolutionary thinking leads to the conclusion that economic independence lies at the very foundation of social and moral well-being. Growing democratic sympathies, justified by the social message of modern scientists, demand to be translated into legislation for economic betterment, based upon the conviction that laws can make men better by affecting the conditions of living. We are persuaded that evils are not inevitable, and that it is the business of statesmanship to tackle them step by step, tentatively, experimentally, not demanding perfection from social reforms any more than from any other human efforts.

340

This movement, this hopeful experiment, is world-wide, but in this country it encounters a unique factor—in the United States, a social legislation must pass challenge in the courts, it must have the visé of our judiciary. Having regard to things and not words, the fate of social legislation in this country rests ultimately with our judges.

The existence of this power is so elementary a feature of our constitutional system that until recently we little considered the true nature of the problems involved in the exercise of the power. Social legislation concerns itself with economic and social conditions, and aims at their conscious readjustments, for social legislation deals with the stuff of life. And, in so far as they have the last word on this legislation, our courts, of necessity, are concerned with economic and social questions, which can be rightfully solved only by a due regard to the facts which induced the legislation. For instance, in passing upon the constitutionality of an eight-hour law for bakers, just what principles of jurisprudence are to be resorted to for guidance? Questions of hygiene, of health, of the present conditions of the industry, the occasion for protecting this particular class against its employers, and the public against both employer and employee—these are the considerations, it would seem, which ought to be vitally in the minds of the judges. Is it really to be doubted that in passing upon the validity of a workmen's compensation act, a court cannot get at the heart of the question without concerning itself, whether avowedly or implicitly, with economic and social questions? It involves a consideration of the vital changes produced by modern industrialism, the bearing of such legislation to the fairer adjustments of the inevitable risks of modern industry, the promotion of harmonious relations between capital and labor and the resulting peace to the community—in a word, its promotion of the social welfare. When the Supreme Court sustained the validity of legislation restricting the hours of work for women, it invoked no legal principles, it resorted to no lawbooks for guidance, but considered the facts of life, marshaled with overwhelming force by Mr. Brandeis, drawn from medical data, industrial reports, and the experience of the world. And so, when the minimum wage bills, the first of which is now before the Massachusetts Legislature, will, without doubt, soon come up for judicial determination, will not the decisive consideration that will inevitably confront the courts be the facts of the particular industries and the right of the community to insist upon a social wage as the first condition of human welfare over against the claim of the individual unrestricted industrial enterprise? Must not of necessity facts, not general principles or well-worn phrases, be the determinants?

This, which may now have the sound of heterodoxy, will, one is warranted in hoping, before long enjoy the respectability of the commonplace. For the viewpoint here urged has, fortunately, during the last few years, received the tremendous authority of, and increasing application from, the

Supreme Court of the United States. Far in advance of any state court, our Supreme Bench recently has come to realize Time's change of emphasis, that new conditions bring new problems and press for new solutions. Social legislation, under our constitutional system, must rest upon the exercise of the police power. Only the other day the Supreme Court told us that "in a sense the police power is but another name for the power of government," and "that it extends to so dealing with the conditions which exist in the state as to bring out of them the greatest welfare of the people." But "the power of the government is a living power, constantly changing and developing to meet new conditions and accomplish new purposes." And the conception of the people's welfare varies, according to the dominant opinion, with time and place. Of necessity, therefore, the police power, as the power of government, is no more stable than the conditions which induce its exercise. If facts are changing, law cannot be static. So-called immutable principles must accommodate themselves to facts of life, for facts are stubborn and will not yield. In truth, what are now deemed immutable principles once, themselves, grew out of living conditions. Thus, the notion of unrestrained liberty of contract arose at a time when industrial conditions were shackled by restrictive legislation and the slogan of the hour was unrestricted industrial enterprise. The conditions of life have changed; the shibboleths remain. There is an increasing conviction of the need of collective responsibility and a demand of governmental intervention for fairer social adjustment. More and more we realize that there is no greater inequality than the equality of unequals. And, happily, the Supreme Court, unlike some of the state courts, realizes, in the words of Justice Holmes, that "the Fourteenth Amendment does not interfere [with legislation] by creating fictitious equality where there is a real difference." In a word, may not one venture the suggestion that constitutional law, in its relation to social legislation, is not at all a science, but applied politics, using the word in its noble sense?

It is important to recognize this not only abstractly, as an intellectual proposition, but to make it a dynamic part of our professional equipment of the legal habits of thought.

The felt necessities of the time, the prevalent moral and political theories, institutions of public policy, avowed or unconscious, even the prejudices which judges share with their fellow men, have had a good deal more to do than the syllogism in determining the rules by which men should be governed.

Thus wrote Mr. Holmes more than thirty years ago. And because he has so vitally felt this, Justice Holmes has been a powerful influence in the changed attitude of the Supreme Court. Again and again we find him yielding to the social expression of the day, with which, if one should make a guess, as an individual, he was probably not in sympathy. Speaking of the

English bench, Professor Dicey, a distinguished Conservative, says while the judges

are swayed by the prevailing beliefs of a particular time, they are also guided by professional opinions and ways of thinking which are, to a certain extent, independent of, and possibly opposed to, the general tone of public opinion. The judges are the heads of the legal profession. They have acquired the intellectual and moral tone of English lawyers. They are men advanced in life. They are for the most part persons of a conservative disposition.

It is because of this natural tendency of our profession, and because of the far-reaching power enjoyed by the bench in this country, that it is essential that a correct appreciation of the problems raised by social legislation should become a vital part of our professional thinking. It is not only a delicate but an infinitely difficult human function that our courts discharge in passing upon the limits of their own power. In so far as these questions are necessarily questions of fact, dealing with actual conditions of life and current dominant public opinion, it is essential that the stream of the Zeitgeist must be allowed to flood the sympathies and the intelligence of our judges. This is necessary, not only for the well-being of the state and the social order, but for the unimpaired continuance of our judicial system. Until social and economic legislation came before the courts, they did not touch the people at large. But dealing with such legislation, involving as they do the vital interests of life of a vast body of the community, the courts necessarily are brought in direct contact with the public needs, and their work has intimate public significance. Hence the importance of recognizing the true character of the questions that come before them. If this is done, it is safe to say that courts generally will reach the conclusion which one may gather from the recent Supreme Court decisions: namely, that which is reasonably defensible on economic or social grounds, whether or not it accords with our individual notion of economics, cannot be offensive on constitutional grounds. Otherwise, it necessarily follows that the Constitution definitively incorporated an economic theory prevalent over a hundred years ago that may well be inadequate and unsuited to modern conditions, whereas, in truth, "a constitution is not intended to embody a particular economic theory . . . it is made for people of fundamentally differing views."

One of the great leaders of the bar, and a distinguished statesman, seeking for a deeper explanation for the present widespread unrest than one generally hears, attributes it to our failure, as yet, to make through our legislation and constitutions the readjustments demanded by the new conditions incident to the extraordinary industrial development of the last half century. One ventures the suggestion that it is demonstrable, as Professor Roscoe Pound has shown, that one of the prime factors contributing to the dissatisfaction is the fact that judges have thwarted legislative efforts at such read-justments, not because of any coercion of the Constitution, but by reason of their constitutional conservatism. Therefore, as to legislation of this char-acter, the suggestion of constitutional amendments does not meet the situa-tion, for back of the constitutional amendment is the construing power of the courts. Unless our profession, from whose ranks the courts are recruited, has the right attitude of approach to these questions, human ingenuity can-not frame language specific enough, even if desirable, to meet the situation. Mere words cannot induce insight and right sympathies or appreciative interpretation. On the other hand, if our courts, generally, will have the attitude that the Supreme Court now has, it is safe to say that all social legislation which has the commanding facts of life behind it will be allowed to justify itself by experience.

The standards here suggested in dealing with the constitutionality of this class of legislation are broad, but not indefinite. The limits of the life of a people cannot be charted by easy rules of thumb. We are dealing with con-siderations as flexible and complex as the public welfare. The constitutional limitation upon the law-making power is as definite, but not more so, as a reasonably possible view of the public welfare. This leaves us still unim-paired the benefits of the reviewing power of the judiciary in our govern-mental system, for the reflex action of the *existence* of this power on the part of the courts to set aside legislation restrains unwise legislative action and induces the scientific attitude of basing legislation only upon adequately ascertained facts. On the other hand, it does not make of the Constitution a mere charter of negation upon the power of the state. The courts should be a restraining, but not a hampering, force. Doubtless, grave mistakes in legislation will thus go unchallenged through the courts, but legislation is essentially empirical, experimental, and the Constitution was not intended to limit this field of experimentation. Think of the gain of having experience demonstrate the fallacy of a law after the Supreme Court has sustained its constitutionality. For, as a wise man has truly said, to fail and learn by failure is one of the sacred rights of a democracy.

50

THE JUDICIAL PROCESS AND
THE SUPREME COURT
April 22, 1954

I F ONE IS TO TALK AT ALL before an audience as learned as this, he had best talk about that of which he is least ignorant. And so I have chosen the topic I have, circumscribed as one in my position is to talk about it. But this is not to be a technical professional paper. What I shall say derives from the assumption that I am talking about complicated and subtle problems to those who are not professionally concerned with them, nor professionally trained to their understanding, and yet feel free to make judgments, because as citizens they are deeply involved in these problems. Broadly speaking, the chief reliance of law in a democracy is the habit of popular respect for law. Especially true is it that law as promulgated by the Supreme Court ultimately depends upon confidence of the people in the Supreme Court as an institution. Indispensable, therefore, for the country's welfare is an appreciation of what the nature of the enterprise is in which that Court is engaged—an understanding of what the task is that has been committed to the succession of nine men.

I said I shall speak "circumscribed" as I am in doing so. I am circumscribed not only by the very limited freedom of speech that his position imposes on a member of the Court. I am no less circumscribed by want of those qualities that are not the normal endowment of judges, nor cultivated in them by training. Those who know tell me that the most illuminating light on painting has been furnished by painters, and that the deepest revelations on the writing of poetry have come from poets. It is not so with the business of judging. The power of searching analysis of what it is that they are doing seems rarely to be possessed by judges, either because they are lacking in the art of critical exposition or because they are inhibited from practicing it. The fact is that pitifully little of significance has been contributed by judges

From "Some Observations on the Nature of the Judicial Process of Supreme Court Litigation," by Felix Frankfurter, *Proceedings* of the American Philosophical Society, Vol. 98, No. 4 (1954): pp. 233–239.

regarding the nature of their endeavor, and, I might add, that which is written by those who are not judges is too often a confident caricature rather than a seer's vision of the judicial process of the Supreme Court. . . .

. . . I am advised by an arithmetically minded scholar that the Constitution of the United States is composed of some 6,000 words. Not every provision of that document that becomes controversial can come before the Supreme Court for adjudication. The questions that are not meet for judicial determination have elicited their own body of literature. A hint of the nature of such questions is given by their fair characterization as an exercise of judicial self-limitation. This area constitutes one very important and very troublesome aspect of the Court's functioning—its duty not to decide.

Putting to one side instances of this judicial self-restraint, De Tocqueville showed his characteristic discernment when he wrote: "Scarcely any political question arises in the United States that is not resolved sooner or later into a judicial question." (1 *Democracy in America,* (Bradley ed., 1948), p. 280.) Those provisions of the Constitution that do raise justiciable issues vary in their incidence from time to time. The construction of all of them, however, is related to the circumambient condition of our Constitution— that our nation is a federalism. The most exacting problems that in recent years have come before the Court have invoked two provisions expressed in a few undefined words—the clause giving Congress power to regulate commerce among the States and the Due Process Clauses of the Fifth and Fourteenth Amendments.

A federalism presupposes the distribution of governmental powers between national and local authority. Between these two authorities there is shared the power entirely possessed by a unitary state. In addition to the provisions of our Constitution making this distribution of authority between the two governments, there is also in the United States Constitution a withdrawal of power from both governments, or, at least, the exercise of governmental power is subject to limitations protective of the rights of the individual. Of the two types of constitutional provision calling for construction from case to case, the limitation in the interest of the individual presents the most delicate and most pervasive of all issues to come before the Court, for these cases involve no less a task than the accommodation by a court of the interest of an individual over against the interest of society.

Human society keeps changing. Needs emerge, first vaguely felt and unexpressed, imperceptibly gathering strength, steadily becoming more and more exigent, generating a force which, if left unheeded and denied response so as to satisfy the impulse behind it at least in part, may burst forth with an intensity that exacts more than reasonable satisfaction. Law as the response to these needs is not merely a system of logical deduction, though considerations of logic are far from irrelevant. Law presupposes sociological wisdom as well as logical unfolding. The nature of the interplay of the two has been admirably conveyed, if I may say so, by Professor Alfred North Whitehead:

It is the first step in sociological wisdom, to recognize that the major advances in civilization are processes which all but wreck the societies in which they occur:—like unto an arrow in the hand of a child. The art of free society consists first in the maintenance of the symbolic code; and secondly in fearlessness of revision, to secure that the code serves those purposes which satisfy an enlightened reason. Those societies which cannot combine reverence to their symbols with freedom of revision, must ultimately decay either from anarchy, or from the slow atrophy of a life stifled by useless shadows. (Whitehead, *Symbolism,* (1927), p. 88.)

The Due Process Clauses of our Constitution are the vehicles for giving response by law to this felt need by allowing accommodations or modifications in the rules and standards that govern the conduct of men. Obviously, therefore, due process as a concept is neither fixed nor finished.

The judgment of history on the inherently living and therefore changing applicability of due process was thus pronounced by Mr. Justice Sutherland, one of the most traditionally minded of judges:

Regulations, the wisdom, necessity and validity of which, as applied to existing conditions, are so apparent that they are now uniformly sustained, a century ago, or even half a century ago, probably would have been rejected as arbitrary and oppressive. (*Village of Euclid* v. *Ambler Realty Co.,* 272 U.S. 365, 387.)

A more expansive attempt at indicating the viable function of the guarantee of due process was made in a recent opinion:

The requirement of "due process" is not a fair-weather or timid assurance. It must be respected in periods of calm and in times of trouble; it protects aliens as well as citizens. But "due process," unlike some legal rules, is not a technical conception with a fixed content unrelated to time, place and circumstances. Expressing as it does in its ultimate analysis respect enforced by law for that feeling of just treatment which has been evolved through centuries of Anglo-American constitutional history and civilization, "due process" cannot be imprisoned within the treacherous limits of any formula. Representing a profound attitude of fairness between man and man, and more particularly between the individual and government, "due process" is compounded of history, reason, the past course of decisions, and stout confidence in the strength of the democratic faith which we profess. Due process is not a mechanical instrument. It is not a yardstick. It is a process. It is a delicate process of adjustment inescapably involving the exercise of judgment by those whom the Constitution entrusted with the unfolding of the process. (*Joint Anti-Fascist Refugee Committee* v. *McGrath,* 341 U.S. 123, 162–163, concurring opinion.)

This conception of due process meets resistance from what has been called our pigeonholing minds, which seek to rest uninquiringly on formulas—phrases which, as Holmes pointed out long ago, "by their very felicity delay further analysis," and often do so for a long time. This is, of course, a form of intellectual indulgence, sometimes called the law of imitation. "[T]raditions which no longer meet their original end" must be subjected to the critique of history whereby we are enabled "to make up our minds dispassionately whether the survival which we are enforcing answers any new purpose when it has ceased to answer the old." (Holmes, *Collected Legal Papers*, (1920), p. 225.)

But a merely private judgment that the time has come for a shift of opinion regarding law does not justify such a shift. Departure from an old view, particularly one that has held unquestioned sway, "must be duly mindful of the necessary demands of continuity in a civilized society. A reversal of a long current of decisions can be justified only if rooted in the Constitution itself as an historic document designed for a developing nation." (*Graves* v. *N. Y. ex. rel. O'Keefe,* 306 U.S. 466, 487–488, concurring opinion.) It makes an important difference, of course, if the validity of an old doctrine on which decisions were based was always in controversy and so did not embed deeply and widely in men's feelings justifiable reliance on the doctrine as part of the accepted outlook of society. What is most important, however, is that the Constitution of the United States, except in what might be called the skeleton or framework of our society—the anatomical as against the physiological aspects,—"was designed for a developing nation." As to those features of our Constitution which raise the most frequent perplexities for decision by the Court, they were drawn in many particulars with purposeful vagueness so as to leave room for the unfolding but undisclosed future.

At this point one wishes there were time to document these generalizations with concrete instances which would help to define the problem and illustrate generalities from which the Court starts and differences of opinion which naturally enough arise in their application. Such documentation would expose divergencies by which common starting points lead to different destinations because of differences in emphasis and valuation in the process of reasoning. They would also shed some light on the interplay between language and thought. Differences in style eventually may embody differences of content, just as a sonnet may sometimes focus thought more trenchantly than a diffuse essay.

The other major source of puzzling problems is the Commerce Clause. With us the Commerce Clause is perhaps the most fruitful and important means for asserting national authority against the particularism of state policy. The role of the Court in striking the balance between the respective spheres of federal and state power was thus adumbrated by the Court:

The interpenetrations of modern society have not wiped out state lines. It is not for us to make inroads upon our federal system either by indifference to its maintenance or excessive regard for the unifying forces of modern technology. Scholastic reasoning may prove that no activity is isolated within the boundaries of a single State, but that cannot justify absorption of legislative power by the United States over every activity. On the other hand, the old admonition never becomes stale that this Court is concerned with the bounds of legal power and not with the bounds of wisdom in its exercise by Congress. When the conduct of an enterprise affects commerce among the States is a matter of practical judgment, not to be determined by abstract notions. The exercise of this practical judgment the Constitution entrusts primarily and very largely to the Congress, subject to the latter's control by the electorate. Great power was thus given to the Congress: the power of legislation and thereby the power of passing judgment upon the needs of a complex society. Strictly confined though far-reaching power was given to this Court: that of determining whether the Congress has exceeded limits allowable in reason for the judgment which it has exercised. To hold that Congress could not deem the activities here in question to affect what men of practical affairs would call commerce, and to deem them related to such commerce merely by gossamer threads and not by solid ties, would be to disrespect the judgment that is open to men who have the constitutional power and responsibility to legislate for the Nation. (*Polish National Alliance v. Labor Board,* 322 U.S. 643, 650–651.)

The problems which the Commerce Clause raises as a result of the diffusion of power between a national government and its constituent parts are shared in variant forms by Canada, Australia, and India. While the distribution of powers between each national government and its parts varies, leading at times to different legal results, the problems faced by the United States Supreme Court under the Commerce Clause are not different in kind, as are the problems of judicial review under the Due Process Clause, from those which come before the Supreme Court of Canada and the High Court of Australia.

Judicial judgment in these two classes of the most difficult cases must take deep account, if I may paraphrase Maitland, of the day before yesterday in order that yesterday may not paralyze today, and it must take account of what it decrees for today in order that today may not paralyze tomorrow.

A judge whose preoccupation is with such matters should be compounded of the faculties that are demanded of the historian and the philosopher and the prophet. The last demand upon him—to make some forecast of the consequences of his action—is perhaps the heaviest. To pierce the curtain of the future, to give shape and visage to mysteries still in the womb of time, is the gift of imagination. It requires poetic sensibilities with which judges are rarely endowed and which their education does not normally develop.

These judges, you will infer, must have something of the creative artist in them; they must have antennae registering feeling and judgment beyond logical, let alone quantitative, proof.

The decisions in the cases that really give trouble rest on judgment, and judgment derives from the totality of a man's nature and experience. Such judgment will be exercised by two types of men, broadly speaking, but of course with varying emphasis—those who express their private views or revelations, deeming them, if not *vox dei,* at least *vox populi;* or those who feel strongly that they have no authority to promulgate law by their merely personal view and whose whole training and proved performance substantially insure that their conclusions reflect understanding of, and due regard for, law as the expression of the views and feelings that may fairly be deemed representative of the community as a continuing society.

Judges are men, not disembodied spirits. Of course a judge is not free from preferences, or, if you will, biases. But he may deprive a bias of its meretricious authority by stripping it of the uncritical assumption that it is founded on compelling reason or the coercive power of a syllogism. He will be alert to detect that though a conclusion has a logical form it in fact represents a choice of competing considerations of policy, one of which for the time has won the day.

An acute historian recently concluded that those "who have any share of political power . . . usually obtain it because they are exceptionally able to emancipate their purposes from the control of their unformulated wishes and impressions." (Richard Pares, "Human Nature in Politics—III," *The Listener,* Dec. 17, 1953, p. 1037.) For judges, it is not merely a desirable capacity "to emancipate their purposes" from their private desires; it is their duty. It is a cynical belief in too many quarters, though I believe this cult of cynicism is receding, that it is at best a self-delusion for judges to profess to pursue disinterestedness. It is asked with sophomoric brightness, does a man cease to be himself when he becomes a Justice? Does he change his character by putting on a gown? No, he does not change his character. He brings his whole experience, his training, his outlook, his social, intellectual, and moral environment with him when he takes a seat on the supreme bench. But a judge worth his salt is in the grip of his function. The intellectual habits of self-discipline which govern his mind are as much a part of him as the influence of the interest he may have represented at the bar, often much more so. For example, Mr. Justice Bradley was a "corporation lawyer" par excellence when he went on the Court. But his decisions on matters affecting corporate control in the years following the Civil War were strikingly free of bias in favor of corporate power.

To assume that a lawyer who becomes a judge takes on the bench merely his views on social or economic questions leaves out of account his rooted notions regarding the scope and limits of a judge's authority. The outlook of a lawyer fit to be a Justice regarding the role of a judge cuts across all his personal preferences for this or that social arrangement. The conviction behind what John Adams wrote in the provision of the Massachusetts Declaration of Rights regarding the place of the judiciary in our governmental scheme, and the considerations which led the framers of the Constitution to give federal judges life tenure and other safeguards for their independence, have, I believe, dominated the outlook and therefore the action of the generality of men who have sat on the Supreme Court. Let me recall the Massachusetts Declaration:

It is essential to the preservation of the rights of every individual, his life, liberty, property, and character, that there be an impartial interpretation of the laws, and administration of justice. It is the right of every citizen to be tried by judges as free, impartial, and independent as the lot of humanity will admit. . . . (Article XXIX.)

Need it be stated that true humility and its offspring, disinterestedness, are more indispensable for the work of the Supreme Court than for a judge's function on any other bench? These qualities alone will not assure another indispensable requisite. This is the capacity for self-searching. What Jacques Maritain said in another connection applies peculiarly to members of the Supreme Court. A Justice of that Court cannot adequately discharge his function "without passing through the door of the knowing, obscure as it may be, of his own subjective." (Maritain, *Creative Intuition in Art and Poetry,* (1953), p. 114.)

This is not to say that the application of this view of the judge's function—that he is there not to impose his private views upon society, that he is not to enforce personalized justice—assures unanimity of judgments. Inevitably there are bound to be fair differences of opinion. And it would be pretense to deny that in the self-righteous exercise of this role obscurantist and even unjustifiable decisions are sometimes rendered. Why should anyone be surprised at this? The very nature of the task makes some differences of view well-nigh inevitable. The answers that the Supreme Court is required to give are based on questions and on data that preclude automatic or even undoubting answers. If the materials on which judicial judgments must be based could be fed into a machine so as to produce ineluctable answers, if such were the nature of the problems that come before the Supreme Court and such were the answers expected, we would have IBM machines doing the work instead of judges.

How amazing it is that, in the midst of controversies on every conceivable subject, one should expect unanimity of opinion upon difficult legal questions! In the highest ranges of thought, in theology, philosophy and science, we find differences of view on the part of the most distinguished experts,—theologians, philosophers and scientists. The history of scholarship is a record of disagreements. And when we deal with questions relating to principles of law and their application, we do not suddenly rise into a stratosphere of icy certainty. (Address by Mr. Chief Justice Hughes, 13 American Law Institute Proceedings, (1936), pp. 61, 64.)

The core of the difficulty is that there is hardly a question of any real difficulty before the Court that does not entail more than one so-called principle. Anybody can decide a question if only a single principle is in controversy. Partisans and advocates often cast a question in that form, but the form is deceptive. In a famous passage Mr. Justice Holmes has exposed this misconception:

All rights tend to declare themselves absolute to their logical extreme. Yet all in fact are limited by the neighborhood of principles of policy which are other than those on which the particular right is founded, and which become strong enough to hold their own when a certain point is reached. . . . The boundary at which the conflicting interests balance cannot be determined by any general formula in advance, but points in the line, or helping to establish it, are fixed by decisions that this or that concrete case falls on the nearer or farther side. (*Hudson County Water Co.* v. *McCarter,* 209 U.S. 349, 355.)

This contest between conflicting principles is not limited to law. In a recent discussion of two books on the conflict between the claims of literary individualism and dogma, I came across this profound observation: "But when, in any field of human observation, two truths appear in conflict it is wiser to assume that neither is exclusive, and that their contradiction, though it may be hard to bear, is part of the mystery of things." ("Literature and Dogma," *Times Literary Supplement* [London], Jan. 22, 1954, p. 51.) But judges cannot leave such contradiction between two conflicting "truths" as "part of the mystery of things." They have to adjudicate. If the conflict cannot be resolved, the task of the Court is to arrive at an accommodation of the contending claims. This is the core of the difficulties and misunderstandings about the judicial process. This, for any conscientious judge, is the agony of his duty.

TWO HUNDRED YEARS AGO a great man was born who indisputably is the "one alone" to be chosen "if American law were to be represented by a single figure." John Marshall was the chief architect "of a new body of jurisprudence, by which guiding principles are raised above the reach of statute and State, and judges are entrusted with a solemn and hitherto unheard-of authority and duty." (Holmes, *Collected Legal Papers*, (1920), p. 270.) Such is the verdict of one whom so qualified a critic as Mr. Justice Cardozo deemed probably the greatest intellect in the history of the English-speaking judiciary.

Unlike other great pioneers in the law, Hardwicke in equity, Mansfield in commercial law, Stowell in prize law, Holmes in torts, the essential heritage of Marshall, because of the very nature of constitutional law, does not lie in specific precepts, definite rules more or less easy of application in new circumstances. Of his opinions it is peculiarly true that their "radiating potencies" go far beyond the actual holdings of the decisions. See *Hawks* v. *Hamill,* 288 U.S. 52, 58 (1933). The tendencies propelled by his opinions give him his unique place in our history; through them he belongs among the main builders of our Nation. Although he led an important diplomatic mission and was not an otiose Secretary of State, the decisive claim to John Marshall's distinction as a great statesman is as a judge. And he is the only judge who has that distinction. It derives from the happy conjunction of Marshall's qualities of mind and character, the opportunities afforded by the Court over which he was called to preside, the duration of his service, and the time in which he served—the formative period in the country's history.

When Jefferson heard that Hamilton was urging John Marshall to enter

Felix Frankfurter, "John Marshall and the Judical Function," *Harvard Law Review* (December 1955) Vol. 69, No. 2, pp. 217–238. Copyright 1955 by The Harvard Law Review Association.

Congress, he wrote to Madison, on June 29, 1792: "I am told that Marshall has expressed half a mind to come. Hence I conclude that Hamilton has plyed him well with flattery & sollicitation, and I think nothing better could be done than to make him a judge." (6 *The Writings of Thomas Jefferson,* (Ford ed., 1895), pp. 95–97.) How ironically Fate outwitted Jefferson in his desire to sidetrack Marshall to what Jefferson conceived to be the innocuous role of a judge. (I am indebted to Professor Julian P. Boyd for calling my attention to this letter as well as for its exact phrasing, based on the recipient's copy in the Madison Papers, Library of Congress.)

When Marshall came to the Supreme Court, the Constitution was still essentially a virgin document. By a few opinions—a mere handful—he gave institutional direction to the inert ideas of a paper scheme of government. Such an achievement demanded an undimmed vision of the union of States as a Nation and the determination of an uncompromising devotion to such insight. Equally indispensable was the power to formulate views expressing this outlook with the persuasiveness of compelling simplicity.

It is shallow to deny that general ideas have influence or to minimize their importance. Marshall's ideas, diffused in all sorts of ways, especially through the influence of the legal profession, have become the presuppositions of our political institutions. He released an enduring spirit, a mode of approach for generations of judges charged with the awesome duty of subjecting the conduct of government and the claims of individual rights to the touchstone of a written document, binding the Government and safeguarding such rights. He has afforded this guidance not only for his own country. In the federalisms that have evolved out of the British Empire, Marshall's outlook in constitutional adjudications has been the lodestar. Unashamedly I recall the familiar phrase in which he expressed the core of his constitutional philosophy: "It is *a constitution* we are expounding." *M'Culloch* v. *Maryland,* 4 Wheat. 316, 407 (1819). It bears repeating because it is, I believe, the single most important utterance in the literature of constitutional law—most important because most comprehensive and comprehending.

I should like to follow James Bradley Thayer in believing that the conception of the Nation which Marshall derived from the Constitution and set forth in *M'Culloch* v. *Maryland* is his greatest single judicial performance. It *is* that, both in its persuasiveness and in its effect. As good a test as I know of the significance of an opinion is to contemplate the consequences of its opposite. The courage of *Marbury* v. *Madison,* 1 Cranch 137 (1803), is not minimized by suggesting that its reasoning is not impeccable and its conclusion, however wise, not inevitable. I venture to say this though fully aware that, since Marshall's time and largely, I suspect, through the momentum of the experience which he initiated, his conclusion in *Marbury* v. *Madison* has been deemed by great English-speaking courts an indispensable, implied characteristic of a written constitution. Holmes could say, as late as 1913: "I do not think the United States would come to an end if we lost our power to declare an Act of Congress void." But he went on to say: "I do think the Union would be imperiled if we could not make that declaration as to the laws of the several States. For one in my place sees how often a local policy prevails with those who are not trained to national views and how often action is taken that embodies what the Commerce Clause was meant to end." (Holmes, *Collected Legal Papers,* (1920), pp. 295–96.) One can, I believe, say with assurance that a failure to conceive the Constitution as Marshall conceived it in *M'Culloch* v. *Maryland,* to draw from it the national powers which have since been exercised and to exact deference to such powers from the States, would have been reflected by a very different United States than history knows. Marshall surely was right when he wrote, a month after he rejected the argument for Maryland: "If the principles which have been advanced on this occasion were to prevail, the Constitution would be converted into the old Confederation."

Marshall's intrinsic achievements are too solid and his personal qualities too homespun to tolerate mythical treatment. It is important not to make untouchable dogmas of the fallible reasoning of even our greatest judge, and not to attribute godlike qualities to the builders of our Nation. Does it not border on the ludicrous that by questioning whether Marshall was an original thinker Holmes nearly barred his way to the Supreme Court? So deeply had uncritical reverence for Marshall's place in our national pantheon lodged itself in the confident judgment of President Theodore Roosevelt. (See I *Correspondence of Theodore Roosevelt and Henry Cabot Lodge,* (1925), pp. 517–19.) As though one should look among even the greatest of judges for what Holmes called "originators of transforming thought." (Holmes, *Collected Legal Papers,* (1920), p. 269.) I venture to suggest that had they the mind of such originators, the bench is not the place for its employment. Transforming thought implies too great a break with the past, implies too much discontinuity, to be imposed upon society by one who is entrusted with enforcing its law.

Marshall's creativeness has from time to time been discounted by attributing the ground he broke in his opinions to the arguments of the great lawyers who appeared before him, especially Webster. The latter was no mean appreciator of his own performance, but an examination of his argument in *Gibbons* v. *Ogden,* 9 Wheat. 1 (1824), hardly confirms his boast that Marshall's opinion "was little else than a recital of my argument." (Harvey, *Reminiscences and Anecdotes of Daniel Webster,* (1877), p. 142.) Powerful counsel no doubt have impact upon the strongest Court, and probably never in the history of the Supreme Court has such a galaxy of talent appeared before it as in Marshall's day. Not the least distinction of a great judge in his capacity to assimilate, to modify or to reject the discursive and inevitably partisan argument of even the most persuasive counsel and to transform their raw material into a judicial judgment. So it was with Marshall.

Again, it is not to be assumed that what Marshall wrote was wholly the product of his own brain, freed from infusion of his brethren's thinking. In his day there was the closest intimacy among the judges. It is inconceivable that they did not discuss their cases in their common boardinghouse. A man of Marshall's charm and power was bound to make himself deeply felt among his brethren. But the assumption that he dominated his colleagues leaves out of reckoning the strong personalities among them. Story had the deepest devotion to Marshall, but he also had views and vanity. Johnson's opinions reveal tough-mindedness, abounding intellectual energy, and a downright character. Likewise, we may be sure that Bushrod Washington was no mere echo. And so one may be confident in inferring that the novelty of the issues, the close social relations of the Justices, the ample opportunities they had for discussion among themselves, precluded Marshall's path-breaking opinions from being exclusively solo performances. Then as now, constitutional decisions are the outcome of the deliberative process, and as such, more or less, composite products. But their expression is individual. The voice of the Court cannot avoid imparting the distinction of its own accent to a Court opinion. In the leading constitutional cases Marshall spoke for the Court. But *he* spoke. The prestige of his office, the esteem which he personally aroused, the deference evoked, enabled Marshall to formulate in his own way an agreement collectively reached. Thus, in his exposition of the Commerce Clause, Marshall indulged in observations not only beyond the necessities of the cases but outside the demands of his own analysis.

To slight these phases of his opinions as dicta, though such they were on a technical view, is to disregard significant aspects of his labors and the ways in which constitutional law develops. There can be little doubt that Marshall saw and seized his opportunities to educate the country to a spacious view of the Constitution, to accustom the public mind to broad national powers, to counteract the commercial and political self-centeredness of States. He was on guard against every tendency to continue treating the new Union as though it were the old Confederation. He imparted such a momentum to his views that the Court and eventually the country were moved in his general direction, beyond his own time and into our own.

The role that Marshall played in the evolution of our Nation ought, I should think, to make it difficult for those who believe that history is reducible to laws, to fit him into their schemata. Surely the course of American history would have been markedly different if the Senate had not rejected the nomination of John Rutledge to succeed Jay as Chief Justice; if the benign Cushing, a Federalist of different composition from Marshall's, had not withdrawn after a week and had continued as Chief Justice till his death in 1810; if Ellsworth's resignation had come later; if John Adams had persuaded Jay to return as Chief Justice; or if some readily imaginable circumstance had delayed Ellsworth's replacement till John Adams was out of the White House so that the new Chief Justice would have been a Jeffersonian. (That it would have been Spencer Roane is an unsubstantiated tradition.) John Marshall is a conspicuous instance of Cleopatra's nose.

This does not make me an adherent of the hero theory of history. If I may quote Mr. Isaiah Berlin: "Historical movements exist, and we must be allowed to call them so. Collective acts do occur; societies do rise, flourish, decay, die. Patterns, 'atmospheres,' complex interrelationships of men or cultures are what they are, and cannot be analysed away into atomic constituents. Nevertheless, to take such expressions so literally that it becomes natural and normal to attribute to them causal properties, active powers, transcendent properties . . . is to be fatally deceived by myths. . . . There is no formula which guarantees a successful escape from either the Scylla of populating the world with imaginary powers and dominions, or the Charybdis of reducing everything to the verifiable behavior of identifiable men and women in precisely denotable places and times." (Berlin, *Historical Inevitability*, (1954), p. 16.) Certainly on this occasion it is appropriate to assert with emphasis that John Marshall was not the fated agency of inevitable economic and social forces to make his decisive contribution in the shaping of this country's destiny.

Temperament, experience, and association converged to his outlook in judicial action. Even more truly than Gibbon could say of himself, "the Captain of the Hampshire grenadiers . . . has not been useless to the historian of the Roman Empire" can it be claimed that Marshall's experience at Valley Forge was not without decisive influence in the work of the great Chief Justice. (*Autobiographies of Edward Gibbon*, (John Murray ed., 1896), p. 190.) Ties of friendship and effective participation in the struggle for the Constitution confirmed his national outlook. Local government had become associated in his mind with the petty bickerings of narrow ambition and dangerous indifference to rights of property and social cohesion. This revealed the need of a strong central government to whose authority the States must be obedient. Subordination of the States to the authority of the National Government within the scope of its powers was the deepest article of his faith, political and judicial. Experience of men and affairs in the Virginia House of Burgesses, in Congress, as a diplomat, and as Secretary of State, doubtless reinforced a temperament to which abstract theorizing was never congenial. He reflected the literary tradition of his time in his partiality for abstract language to support concrete results. But he had a hard-headed appreciation of the complexities of government, particularly in a federal system. His deep instinct for the practical saved him, on the whole, from rigidities to bind the changing future. Uncompromising as was his aim to promote adequate national power, he was not dogmatic in the choice of doctrine for attaining this end. And so at times, conspicuously in *Gibbons* v. *Ogden,* his views appear to reflect crosscurrents of doctrine, ambiguously expressed. In one striking instance, *Willson* v. *The Black Bird Creek Marsh Co.,* 2 Pet. 245 (1829), he did little more than decide, stating hardly any doctrine but hinting enough to foreshadow, certainly in direction, the vitally important accommodation between national and local needs formulated more than twenty years later in *Cooley* v. *Board of Wardens of the Port of Philadelphia,* 12 How. 299, 319 (1851).

There is a rather supercilious tendency to speak disparagingly of Marshall's work on the Court when dealing with lawyers' law. In contrast to Jefferson's view, which continues to have echoes, of regarding Marshall's associates as his tools in the constitutional cases, praise of his judicial statecraft is sometimes used to emphasize his inferiority in non-constitutional adjudications. Story, Bushrod Washington, William Johnson, Brockholst Livingston are counted as his superiors. Joseph Story, to be sure, carried great learning, even if not always lightly. Disregard of Bushrod Washington's judicial qualities bespeaks unfamiliarity with Judge Hopkinson's and Horace Binney's estimates of him, and Professor Donald G. Morgan's recent book on Mr. Justice Johnson ought to bring wider appreciation of one of the strongest minds in the Court's history. But none of Marshall's associates will suffer depreciation by recognizing his performance in cases that are lawyers' law. After all, this constituted nine-tenths of the Court's business during the thirty-four years of Marshall's magistracy. He was not a bookish lawyer, though he was no stranger to books. He could, as wise judges do, make them his servants. He eschewed precedents, such as were then available, in his opinions for the Court. But he showed mastery in treatment of precedents where they had been relied on for an undesirable result. By way of example, I avouch his dissent in *The Venus,* 8 Cranch 253, 288 (1814), against the strong views of Washington, J., supported by Story. Likewise, he was not overwhelmed by the parade of Story's learning in *The Nereide,* 9 Cranch 388 (1851), when such learning led to a harsh view of neutral rights. Though he respected Lord Stowell as "a very great man," he cut free from that master of prize law, deeming him to have a leaning, strong even if unconscious, in favor of captors.

As good an insight as any into the quality of Marshall's intellect is afforded by Francis Walker Gilmer, a brilliant Virginia contemporary of high promise. Marshall's mind, he wrote, "is not very richly stored with knowledge, but it is so creative, so well organized by nature, or disciplined by early education, and constant habits of systematick thinking, that he embraces every subject with the clearness and facility of one prepared by previous study to comprehend and explain it." (Gilmer, *Sketches, Essays, and Translations,* pp. 23–24, quoted in 2 Beveridge, *John Marshall,* (1916), p. 178.)

Charged as I have been with opening a conference to commemorate the two-hundredth anniversary of the birth of John Marshall, I surely have been obedient to my duty in speaking of him. But once I leave the secure footing of that well-trodden ground, what else can be pertinent to an opening address of a three-day conference on Government under Law, systematically planned with definite parts appropriately assigned to learned inquirers into the perplexities of the problems summarized by this great theme?

Insofar as I have not already exhausted my function, my further relation to the resplendent show to follow is like unto that of the Greek chorus. In view of the preoccupation of this conference, of course I want to keep strictly within the law of my assignment. Accordingly, I have briefed myself on the proper task of the Greek chorus. While in early days the destiny of the chorus was "involved in that of the principal characters," when the Attic stage was at its highest perfection the chorus was "thrown much further into the background," and appears "not as a participant in the action, but merely as a sympathetic witness." The chorus was, so my authority continues, "removed from the stress and turmoil of the action into a calmer and more remote region, though it still preserves its interest in the events upon the stage." This clearly is my cue, rather than the later still more receding role of the chorus, whereby it "begins to lose even its interest in the action" and "sings odes of a mythological character, which have only the remotest connexion with the incidents of the plot." (Haigh, *Attic Theatre,* (2d ed., 1898), pp. 320–21.)

There is little danger that in my remaining observations I shall be intruding on the fertile areas of inquiry that belong to the distinguished speakers whom we are to hear these three days. I hope I shall be equally successful in not straying outside my confining judicial curtilage. One brought up in the traditions of James Bradley Thayer, echoes of whom were still resounding in this very building in my student days, is committed to Thayer's statesmanlike conception of the limits within which the Supreme Court should move, and I shall try to be loyal to his admonition regarding the restricted freedom of members of that Court to pursue their private views.

Marshall's significance could not be more fittingly celebrated than by scrutinizing, which is the aim of this conference, the state of "government under law," more particularly under the legal system to which Marshall so heavily contributed, a hundred and twenty years after he wrote his last opinion. Could he listen to these proceedings, nothing would be bound to strike him more than the enlarged scope of law since his day. He would, of course, think of law as legally enforceable rights. For, while he occasionally referred to "natural law," it was not much more than literary garniture, even as in our own day, and not a guiding means for adjudication. He would have sympathized, as other judges have, with Sir Frederick Pollock's remark: "In the Middle Ages natural law was regarded as the senior branch of divine law and therefore had to be treated as infallible (but there was no infallible way of knowing what it was)." (I *Holmes-Pollock Letters,* (Howe ed., 1941), p. 275.) Marshall would be amazed by the interpenetration of law in government, because during his whole era he was concerned with the Constitution as an instrument predominantly regulating the machinery of government, and more particularly, distributing powers between the central government and the States. The Constitution was not thought of as the repository of the supreme law limiting all government, with a court wielding the deepest-cutting power of deciding whether there is any authority in government at all to do what is sought to be done.

Thus, the gravamen of the attack in the Virginia and Kentucky Resolutions against the Alien and Sedition Acts of 1798 was that they infringed on the rights of the states and were promotive of "a general consolidated government." It deserves to be recalled that even Jefferson attributed to the States the power which he denied to the Federal Government. "Nor does the opinion of the unconstitutionality and consequent nullity of that law [the Sedition Act]," he wrote to Abigail Adams, "remove all restraint from the overwhelming torrent of slander which is confounding all vice and virtue, all truth and falsehood in the US. The power to do that is fully possessed by the several state legislatures. . . . While we deny that Congress have a right to controul the freedom of the press, we have ever asserted the right of the states, and their exclusive right, to do so." (I am indebted for the exact text of this letter, dated September 11, 1804, to the kindness of Professor Julian P. Boyd, in one of whose forthcoming volumes of *The Papers of Thomas Jefferson* it will duly appear in its entirety.)

The only two Marshallian constitutional opinions that concern individual rights as such, *Fletcher* v. *Peck,* 6 Cranch 87 (1810), and the *Dartmouth College Case,* 4 Wheat. 518 (1819), rather than the delimitation of power between two governments, are, in the perspective of time, not of great importance. This came to pass partly because of easy legislative correction, partly because the doctrine of strict construction devised in the *Charles River Bridge Case,* 11 Pet. 420 (1837), took the sting out of the decision of the *Dartmouth College Case.* Moreover, insofar as the latter case forbade legislative transfer of the property of the college to the trustees, it is a safe assumption that the Due Process Clauses would condemn such an attempt. See Chief Justice Doe's opinion in *Dow* v. *Northern R. Co.,* 67 N.H. 1, 27–53, 36 Atl. 510, 524–37 (1887); Doe, "A New View of the Dartmouth College Case," 6 Harv. L. Rev. 161, 213 (1892); and Jeremiah Smith in 1 Proc. N.H. Bar Ass'n 287, 302 (N.S. 1901).

The vast change in the scope of law between Marshall's time and ours is at bottom a reflection of the vast change in the circumstances of society. The range of business covered by Marshall's Court, though operating under a written Constitution, was in the main not very different from the concerns of the English courts, except that the latter dealt much more with property settlements. The vast enveloping present-day role of law is not the design of a statesman nor attributable to the influence of some great thinker. It is a reflection of the great technological revolution which brought in its train what a quiet writer in *The Economist* could call "the tornado of economic and social change of the last century." Law has been an essential accompaniment of the shift from "watch-dog government"—the phrase is George Kennan's—to the service state. For government has become a service state, whatever the tint of the party in power and whatever time-honored slogans it may use to enforce and promote measures that hardly vindicate the slogans. Profound social changes continue to be in the making, due to movements of industrialization, urbanization, and permeating egalitarian ideas.

With crude accuracy I have just summarized the situation in the countries of the English-speaking world, about which alone I may speak. But when these transforming economic and social forces got under full swing in the United States, lawyers and courts found available in the Fourteenth Amendment resources for curbing legislative responses to new pressures. That Amendment was gradually invoked against the substance of legislation and not merely to support claims based on traditionally fair procedure.

I have thus reached the slippery slope of due process. But not even to take a glance at it in a reconnaissance, however sketchy, of government under law, would indeed be to play *Hamlet* without Hamlet.

It has been frequently stated that when a question arises in due course of a litigation, whether a constitutional provision has been infringed, the established courts of justice "must of necessity determine that question." See Lord Selborne in *The Queen* v. *Burah,* 3 A.C. 889, 904 (1878), quoted approvingly by Lord Wright in *James* v. *Commonwealth,* [1936] A.C. 578, 613; and see also *Swart, N.O. and Nicol, N.O.* v. *de Kock and Garner,* 1951 (3) S.A. 589, 601–02 and 611. This is only qualifiedly true regarding our Constitution. Thus, the explicit provision requiring one State to surrender to another a fugitive from justice (Art. IV, § 2, cl. 2) is "merely declaratory of a moral duty" and is not, because of the subject matter, enforceable in the courts. *Kentucky* v. *Dennison,* 24 How. 66 (1861). Likewise, the "guarantee to every state" of "a Republican Form of Government," must, because of the subject-matter, look elsewhere than to the courts for observance. *Pacific States Tel. & Tel. Co.* v. *Oregon,* 223 U.S. 118 (1912). There are not a few other instances in which judicial relief was barred because "political questions" were deemed to be involved.

It is not for me to find the common denominator of these judicial abstentions, or to give the contour and content of what questions are "political," in the sense of precluding judicial examination. But I do venture to believe that no judge charged with the duty of enforcing the Due Process Clauses of the Fifth and Fourteenth Amendments, and the Equal Protection of the Laws Clause of the Fourteenth Amendment, can free himself from the disquietude that the line is often very thin between the cases in which the Court felt compelled to abstain from adjudication because of their "political" nature, and the cases that so frequently arise in applying the concepts of "liberty" and "equality."

In his First Inaugural Jefferson spoke of the "sacred principle" that "the will of the majority is in all cases to prevail." Jefferson himself hardly meant all by "all." (See Jefferson's answers to Démeunier's first queries, reprinted in 10 *The Papers of Thomas Jefferson,* (Boyd ed., 1954), p. 18.) In any event, one need not give full adherence to his view to be deeply mindful of the fact that judicial review is a deliberate check upon democracy through an organ of government not subject to popular control. In relation to the judiciary's task in the type of cases I am now discussing, I am raising difficulties which I think must in all good conscience be faced, unless perchance the Court is expected to register a particular view and unless the profession that the judiciary is the disinterested guardian of our Constitution be pretense.

It may be that responsibility for decision dulls the capacity of discernment. The fact is that one sometimes envies the certitude of outsiders regarding the compulsions to be drawn from vague and admonitory constitutional provisions. Only for those who have not the responsibility of decision can it be easy to decide the grave and complex problems they raise, especially in controversies that excite public interest. This is so because they too often present legal issues inextricably and deeply bound up in emotional reactions to sharply conflicting economic, social, and political views. It is not the duty of judges to express their personal attitudes on such issues, deep as their individual convictions may be. The opposite is the truth; it is their duty not to act on merely personal views. But "due process," once we go beyond its strictly procedural aspect, and the "equal protection of the laws" enshrined in the Constitution, are precisely defined neither by history nor in terms. It deserves to be noted that so far as gaining light from pertinent data on the intention of Congress on specific issues in formulating the Fourteenth Amendment, the Supreme Court found that "[a]t best, they are inconclusive." *Brown* v. *Board of Education,* 347 U.S. 483, 489 (1954). This finding of darkness was reached not for want of searching inquiry by Court and counsel.

No doubt, these provisions of the Constitution were not calculated to give permanent legal sanction merely to the social arrangements and beliefs of a particular epoch. Like all legal provisions without a fixed technical meaning, they are ambulant, adaptable to the changes of time. That is their strength; that also makes dubious their appropriateness for judicial enforcement—dubious because their vagueness readily lends itself to make of the Court a third chamber with drastic veto power. This danger has been pointed out by our greatest judges too often to be dismissed as a bogey.

Holding democracy in judicial tutelage is not the most promising way to foster disciplined responsibility in a people. See *AFL* v. *American Sash & Door Co.,* 335 U.S. 538, 555–557 (1949) (concurring opinion).

It is, of course, no longer to be questioned that claims under the Fourteenth Amendment are subject to judicial judgment. This makes it all the more important to realize what is involved in the discharge of this function of the Court, particularly since this is probably the largest source of the Court's business. It is important, that is, fully to appreciate the intrinsic nature of the issues when the Court is called upon to determine whether the legislature or the executive has regulated "liberty" or "property" "without due process of law" or has denied "equal protection of the laws"; to appreciate the difficulties in making a judgment upon such issues, difficulties of a different order from those normally imposed upon jural tribunals; and, not least, to appreciate the qualifications requisite for those who exercise this extraordinary authority, demanding as it does a breadth of outlook and an invincible disinterestedness rooted in temperament and confirmed by discipline. Of course, individual judgment and feeling cannot be wholly shut out of the judicial process. But if they dominate, the judicial process becomes a dangerous sham. The conception by a judge of the scope and limits of his function may exert an intellectual and moral force as much as responsiveness to a particular audience or congenial environment.

We are dealing with constitutional provisions the nature of which can be best conveyed compendiously by Judge Learned Hand's phrase that they "represent a mood rather than a command, that sense of moderation, of fair play, of mutual forbearance, without which states become the prey of faction." *Daniel Reeves, Inc.* v. *Anderson,* 43 F. 2d 679, 682 (1930). Alert search for enduring standards by which the judiciary is to exercise its duty in enforcing those provisions of the Constitution that are expressed in what Ruskin called "chameleon words," needs the indispensable counterpoise of sturdy doubt that one has found those standards. Yesterday the active area in this field was concerned with "property." Today it is "civil liberties." Tomorrow it may again be "property." Who can say that in a society with a mixed economy, like ours, these two areas are sharply separated, and that certain freedoms in relation to property may not again be deemed, as they were in the past, aspects of individual freedom?

Let me sharpen these difficulties by concreteness. In *Plessy* v. *Ferguson,* 163 U.S. 537, 559 (1896), Mr. Justice Harlan floated an oft-quoted epigram, but in a few short years he did not apply it, proving once more that sonorous abstractions do not solve problems with intractable variables. See *Cumming* v. *Richmond County Board of Education,* 175 U.S. 528 (1899), and its influence on *Gong Lum* v. *Rice,* 275 U.S. 78, 85 (1927). Thinking of "equality" in abstract terms led Mr. Justice Harlan to be blind to the meaning of "yellow-dog contracts" as a serious curtailment of liberty in the context of antiunion strategy, *Adair* v. *United States,* 208 U.S. 161 (1908); Richard Olney, "Discrimination against Union Labor," 42 Am. L. Rev. 161 (1908), and to be equally blind to the fact that important differences between industry and agriculture may justify differentiation in legislation. See *Connolly* v. *Union Sewer Pipe Co.,* 184 U.S. 540 (1902), and compare with *Tigner* v. *Texas,* 310 U.S. 141 (1940).

Take the other side of the medal. It is too easy to attribute judicial review resulting in condemnation of restrictions on activities pertaining to property to "economic predilection" of particular judges. The Due Process Clauses extend to triune interests—life, liberty and property—and "property" cannot be deleted by judicial fiat rendering it nugatory regarding legislation touching property. Moreover, protection of property interests may, as already indicated, quite fairly be deemed, in appropriate circumstances, an aspect of liberty. Regulation of property may be struck down on assumptions of beliefs other than narrow economic views. And so we find that Justices who were the most tolerant of legislative power dealing with economic interests have found in due process a protection even against an exercise of the so-called police power. It was true of Mr. Justice Holmes in *Pennsylvania Coal Co.* v. *Mahon,* 260 U.S. 393 (1922), and of Mr. Justice Brandeis in *Thompson* v. *Consolidated Gas Utilities Corp.,* 300 U.S. 55 (1937).

Let us turn to the much-mooted "clear and present danger" doctrine. It is at least interesting that that phrase originated in one (*Schenck* v. *United States,* 249 U.S. 47, 52 (1919)) of a series of cases in which convictions for heavy sentences were sustained against defendants who had invoked the right of free speech in circumstances which led Mr. Justice Holmes to characterize them as "poor fools whom I should have been inclined to pass over if I could." (2 *Holmes-Pollock Letters,* (Howe ed., 1941), p. 11.) "Clear and present danger" thus had a compulsion for Mr. Justice Holmes against recognizing Debs's freedom to an utterance that in retrospect hardly seems horrendous. *Debs* v. *United States,* 249 U.S. 211 (1919). Would it carry equal compulsion with other judges? One can be confident, in any event, that Mr. Justice Holmes would not have deemed his doctrine a bar to the power of a State to safeguard the fair conduct of a trial for a capital offense from being thwarted by intrusion of utterances from without. See *Maryland* v. *Baltimore Radio Show Inc.,* 338 U.S. 912 (1950), denying certiorari to 193 Md. 300, 67 A. 2d 497 (1949). There is the best of reasons for believing that Mr. Justice Brandeis would not have carried his natural devotion to the place of freedom of speech in a democracy to such a doctrinaire denial of an equally indispensable need of a free society—trial in court, not outside it.

Concerned as I am with the evolution of social policy by way of judicial application of Delphic provisions of the Constitution, recession of judicial doctrine is as pertinent as its expansion. The history of the constitutional position of the right to strike affords an illuminating instance. After invalidating a law withdrawing the use of the injunction against strikes, *Truax* v. *Corrigan,* 257 U.S. 312 (1921), the Court came to conceive of the conduct of a strike as an aspect of the constitutionally protected freedom of discussion, *Thornhill* v. *Alabama,* 310 U.S. 88 (1940), but soon retreated from this position and recognized that picketing, as the weapon of strikes, is not merely a means of communication, *Giboney* v. *Empire Storage & Ice Co.,* 336 U.S. 490 (1949). No matter how often the Court insists that it is not passing on policy when determining constitutionality, the emphasis on constitutionality and its fascination for the American public seriously confound problems of constitutionality with the merits of a policy. Industrial relations are not alone in presenting problems that suffer in their solution from having public opinion too readily assume that because some measure is found to be constitutional it is wise and right, and, contrariwise, because it is found unconstitutional it is intrinsically wrong. That such miseducation of public opinion, with its effect upon action, has been an important consequence of committing to the Court the enforcement of "the mood" represented by these vague constitutional provisions, can hardly be gainsaid by any student of their history.

Much as the constitution-makers of other countries have drawn upon our experience, it is precisely because they have drawn upon it that they have, one and all, abstained from including a "due process" clause. They have rejected it in conspicuous instances after thorough consideration of our judicial history of "due process." See Wallace Mendelson, "Foreign Reactions to American Experience with 'Due Process of Law,'" 41 Va. L. Rev. 493 (1955). It is particularly noteworthy that such was the course of events in framing the constitution of India. Sir B. N. Rau, one of the most penetrating legal minds of our time, had a major share in its drafting, and for the purpose he made a deep study of the workings of the Due Process Clause during an extensive stay here.

Is it the tenor of these remarks that courts should have no concern with other than material interests, that they must be unmindful of the imponderable rights and dignities of the individual which are, I am sure I shall have your agreement in saying, the ideals which the Western world holds most high? Of course not. Recognition of them should permeate the law, and it does so effectively even in courts that do not have veto power over legislation. They constitute presuppositions where parliaments have not spoken unequivocally and courts are left with the jural task of construction in its fair sense.

Thus, while the Chief Justice of Canada could say: "We have not a Bill of Rights such as is contained in the United States Constitution and decisions on that part of the latter are of no assistance," he reached the same result in *Saumur* v. *City of Quebec,* [1953] 2 S.C.R. 299, as a matter of construction, that was reached under the Due Process Clause in *Lovell* v. *City of Griffin,* 303 U.S. 444 (1938). Again, only the other day the Supreme Court of Canada rejected the view that the mere claim of immunity by a minister of the Crown from producing in court a document relevant to its proceeding is conclusive. It deemed such a claim "not in harmony with the basic conceptions of our polity." The reason given by Mr. Justice Rand deserves to be quoted: "What is secured by attributing to the courts this preliminary determination of possible prejudice is protection against executive encroachments upon the administration of justice; and in the present trend of government little can be more essential to the maintenance of individual security. In this important matter, to relegate the courts to such a subserviency as is suggested would be to withdraw from them the confidence of independence and judicial appraisal that so far appear to have served well the organization of which we are the heirs." *Regina* v. *Snider,* [1954] S.C.R. 479, 485, 486. So, likewise, the Appellate Division of the Supreme Court of South Africa ruled that when an Act conferred autocratic powers upon a minister—it was the Suppression of Communism Act—it must, in the absence of explicit direction by Parliament, be construed with the least interference with the liberty of the subject. *R.* v. *Ngwevela,* 1954 (1) S.A. 123.

While the subjection to parliamentary criticism is the only remedy for much in Great Britain that with us becomes the stuff of lawsuits, the English executive is amenable to challenge in court for exceeding statutorily defined legal powers. In construing such authority, English courts enforce the right to a hearing as a presupposition of English law, unless Parliament has clearly enough indicated the contrary. See S. A. de Smith, "The Right to a Hearing in English Administrative Law," 68 Harv. L. Rev. 569 (1955); so, likewise in Canada, *L'Alliance des Professeurs Catholiques* v. *Labour Relations Board,* [1953] 2 S.C.R. 140; and in New Zealand, *New Zealand Dairy Board* v. *Okitu Co-operative Dairy Co.,* [1953] N.Z.L.R. 366. The English courts have also been resourceful, through the use they make of *certiorari,* in setting aside executive action when based on reasons not justifiable in law. For application of this principle in the United States see *Perkins* v. *Elg,* 307 U.S. 325 (1939), and *Securities and Exchange Commission* v. *Chenery Corp.,* 318 U.S. 80 (1943). This increasing tendency of courts to scrutinize the legal grounds given by administrative agencies for their actions may well promote greater responsibility in the agencies' exercise of authority and in their justification of that exercise.

If government under law were confined to what is judicially enforced, law in government would be very restricted, no matter how latitudinarian one's conception of what is fitting for judicial examination of governmental action. For one thing, courts have a strong tendency to abstain from constitutional controversies. *E.g., Peters* v. *Hobby,* 349 U.S. 331 (1955). Thereby, they may avoid conflict, at least prematurely if not permanently, with the other branches of the government and they may avoid also the determination of conflict between the Nation and the States. Moreover, settlement of complicated public issues, particularly on the basis of constitutional provisions conveying indeterminate standards, is subject to the inherent limitations and contingencies of the judicial process. For constitutional adjudications involve adjustment of vast and incommensurable public interests through episodic instances, upon evidence and information limited by the narrow rules of litigation, shaped and intellectually influenced by the fortuitous choice of particular counsel.

Mr. Justice Brandeis made a fair estimate in saying that by applying its restrictive canons for adjudication, the Court has in the course of its history "avoided passing upon a large part of all the constitutional questions pressed upon it for decision." *Ashwander* v. *Tennessee Valley Authority,* 297 U.S. 288, 346 (1936). This is true not only of our Supreme Court, which cannot render advisory opinions however compelling the appeal for legal guidance even at times of national emergency. (See Chief Justice Jay's reply to President Washington's inquiry, conveyed by Thomas Jefferson, in 3 *The Correspondence and Public Papers of John Jay,* (Johnston ed., 1891), pp. 486–89.) Insistence on an immediate, substantial, and threatened interest in raising such constitutional issues is a characteristic of all high courts with power to pass upon them. See the recent Australian case, *Australian Boot Trade Employees' Federation* v. *Commonwealth,* (1954) 90 C.L.R. 24; see also *Musgrove* v. *Chun Teeong Toy,* [1891] A.C. 272, 283. But even where advisory opinions are constitutionally authorized, tribunals are reluctant to pronounce in situations that are hypothetical or abstract or otherwise not conducive to judicial disposition. See Lord Haldane, in *Attorney General for British Columbia* v. *Attorney General for Canada,* [1914] A.C. 153, 162; Lord Sankey, in *In re the Regulation and Control of Aeronautics,* [1932] A.C. 54, 66. It is, I believe, not inaccurate to say that most of the occasions when the Supreme Court has come into virulent conflict with public opinion were those in which the Court disregarded its settled tradition against needlessly pronouncing on constitutional issues. (The *Dred Scott Case,* 19 How. 393 (1857), does not stand alone; see the *Income Tax Cases,* 157 U.S. 429 and 158 U.S. 601 (1895), controlling until the Sixteenth Amendment of February 25, 1913; *Adkins* v. *Children's Hospital,* 261 U.S. 525, 543 (1923), overruled by *West Coast Hotel Co.* v. *Parrish,* 300 U.S. 379 (1937).)

The confining limits within which courts thus move in expounding law is not the most important reason for a conception of government under law far transcending merely law that is enforced in the courts. The day has long gone by when Austin's notions exhaust the content of law. Law is not set above the government. It defines its orbit. But government is not law except insofar as law infuses government. This is not word-playing. Also indispensable to government is ample scope of individual insight and imaginative origination by those entrusted with the public interest. If society is not to remain stagnant, there is need of action beyond uniformities found recurring in instances which sustain a generalization and demand its application. But law is not a code of fettering restraints, a litany of prohibitions and permissions. It is an enveloping and permeating habituation of behavior, reflecting the counsels of reason on the part of those entrusted with power in reconciling the pressures of conflicting interests. Once we conceive of "the rule of law" as embracing the whole range of presuppositions on which government is conducted and not as a technical doctrine of judicial authority, the relevant question is not, has it been achieved, but, is it conscientiously and systematically pursued.

What matters most is whether the standards of reason and fair dealing are bred in the bones of people. Hyde Park represents a devotion to free speech far more dependable in its assurances, though unprotected by formal constitutional requirement, than reliance upon the litigious process for its enjoyment. Again, widespread popular intolerance of the third degree, such as manifested itself in the well-known Savidge affair, reflects a more deeply grounded rule of law than is disclosed by the painful story of our continuing judicial endeavor to root out this evil through decisions in occasional dramatic cases. (For the Savidge case, see 220 *Hans. Deb.* (Commons), cols. 5, 805 *et seq.* (July 20, 1928); Inquiry in regard to the Interrogation by the Police of Miss Savidge (1928, Cmd. 3147). As to our experience, see, *e.g.,* "Report on the Third Degree" by Chafee, Pollak and Stern in 4 *National Commission on Law Observation and Enforcement, Reports,* p. 13 (1931), and the series of well-known cases in the Supreme Court Reports.) Let me give another illustration. "Crichel Down" will, in its way, serve to summarize the duty of obedience to standards of fair dealing and avoidance even of the appearance of official arbitrariness. As such it will affect the future conduct of English government as much as some of the leading cases which have been important factors in the development of a democratic society. See Public Inquiry ordered by the Ministry of Agriculture into the disposal of land at Crichel Down (1954, Cmd. 9176); R. Douglas Brown, *The Battle of Crichel Down.* You will note that the instances I have given of manifestations of law responsive to the deep feelings of people are drawn from a nation that does not rely on a written constitution. I need not add that the distinctive historical development in Great Britain, in the context of its progressive cultural and economic homogeneity, has made possible accommodation between stability and change, defining the powers of government and the limits within which due regard for individual rights require it to be kept, without embodying it in a single legal document enforceable in courts of law.

I hope, however, that you will not deem me unduly romantic in deriving comfort from the undertaking given the other day by the Kabaka, as a condition of his return to his people in Buganda, when he promised that he "will well and truly govern Buganda according to law." (The [London] *Times,* Aug. 13, 1955, p. 6, col. 5.) I find reason for my comfort in the fascinating account by Professor Max Gluckman of Manchester University of the extent to which law permeates the lives of the Barotse tribes of Northern Rhodesia, law in the sense in which this conference is discussing it and not something religious in nature. (Gluckman, *The Judicial Process among the Barotse of Northern Rhodesia,* (1955).)

If what I have brought you, in my endeavor to give you as frankly as I may the distillation of sixteen years of reflection from within the tribunal peculiarly concerned with government under law, is charged with being an old-fashioned liberal's view of government and law, I plead guilty. For the charge implies allegiance to the humane and gradualist tradition in dealing with refractory social and political problems, recognizing them to be fractious because of their complexity and not amenable to quick and propitious solutions without resort to methods which deny law as the instrument and offspring of reason.

I have not been able to submit to you large generalizations that illumine or harmoniously assimilate discrete instances. Still less have I been able to fashion criteria for easier adjudication of the specific cases that will trouble future judges. They are bound to be troubled, whether they will be faced with variant aspects of old problems—old conflicts between liberty and authority, between the central government and its constituent members— or new problems inevitably thrown up by the everlasting flux of life.

Believing it still important to do so, I have tried to dispel the age-old illusion that the conflicts to which the energy and ambition and imagination of the restless human spirit give rise can be subdued, even if not settled, by giving the endeavors of reason we call law a mechanical or automatic or enduring configuration. Law cannot be confined within any such mold because life cannot be so confined. Man's most piercing discernment of the future cannot see very far beyond his day, even when guided by the prophet's insight and the compassionate humility of a Lincoln. And I am the last to claim that judges are apt to be endowed with these gifts. But a fair appraisal of Anglo-American judicial history ought to leave us not without encouragement that modest goals, uncompromisingly pursued, may, promote what I hope you will let me call civilized ends without the need of defining them.

In what I have been saying you have no doubt heard undertones of a judge's perplexities—particularly of a judge who has to construe, as it is called, vague and admonitory constitutional provisions. But I am very far from meaning to imply a shriveled conception of government under law.

Quite the contrary. The intention of my emphasis has been not on the limited scope of judicial enforcement of laws. My concern is an affirmation— my plea is for the pervasiveness throughout the whole range of government of the spirit of law, at least in the sense of excluding arbitrary official action. But however limited the area of adjudication may be, the standards of what is fair and just set by courts in controversies appropriate for their adjudication are perhaps the single most powerful influence in promoting the spirit of law throughout government. These standards also help shape the dominant civic habits and attitudes which ultimately determine the ethos of a society.

In exercising their technical jurisdiction, courts thus release contagious consequences. Nothing is farther from my mind than to suggest that judges should exceed the professional demands of a particular decision. If judges want to be preachers, they should dedicate themselves to the pulpit; if judges want to be primary shapers of policy, the legislature is their place. Self-willed judges are the least defensible offenders against government under law. But since the grounds of decisions and their general direction suffuse the public mind and the operations of government, judges cannot free themselves from the responsibility of the inevitable effect of their opinions in constricting or promoting the force of law throughout government. Upon no functionaries is there a greater duty to promote law.

INDEX